Taming
❦ the
Chaos

Emerson R. Marks

Taming & the Chaos

ENGLISH

POETIC

DICTION THEORY

SINCE THE

RENAISSANCE

Wayne
State
University
Press
Detroit

Library of Congress Cataloging-in-Publication Data

Marks, Emerson R.

   Taming the chaos : English poetic diction theory since
the Renaissance / Emerson R. Marks.

      p.   cm.

   Includes bibliographical references and index.

   ISBN 0-8143-2698-6 (alk. paper)

   1. English poetry—History and criticism—Theory, etc.
2. English language—Versification.   3. English
language—Diction.   4. Poetics.   I. Title.

PR508.D5M37   1998

821.009—dc21   97-35272

Book design by S. R. Tenenbaum

IN MEMORY OF RENÉ WELLEK,

BELOVED TEACHER AND FRIEND

Contents

Acknowledgments

IT IS A PLEASURE TO RECORD my gratitude to the National Endowment for the Humanities, the Widener and Houghton Libraries at Harvard, and the Margaret Clapp Library at Wellesley College, including especially the hospitable staff of its Special Collections department. For their encouragement and the stimulation of their conversations on my topic over the years, I owe much to the late Alfred Hoelzel, to Robert Spaethling, and to Heather Dubrow, friends and University of Massachusetts-Boston colleagues; to my former students Martin Bucco and Robert Eberwein; and to Catherine Brettschneider.

My greatest debt is to several distinguished scholar-critics—Ralph Nash, Philip J. Finkelpearl, Myron Simon, James Engell, and Walter Jackson Bate—all of whom read the manuscript of this book in whole or part. I have no way of proving that without their sage advice, practical suggestions, and sharp-eyed spotting of errors my project would never have reached fruition. But I believe it.

Parts of chapters IV, VI, and VII appeared earlier in *Philological Quarterly* (Winter, 1975) and in my *Coleridge on the Language of Verse* (Princeton University Press, 1981). Except where otherwise noted, the translations of quotations in foreign languages are my own.

E. R. M.
WELLESLEY HILLS

Introduction

THIS BOOK TRACES, FOR
the first time, the course of some four centuries of commentary by
writers in English on the nature of poetic language. The frequent
allusions to Continental European and classical writing on the subject serve mainly to indicate the broader cultural context in which
Anglophone conceptions arose. They are largely limited to those
foreign ideas which bear directly on what was thought and written
in the English-speaking countries. This procedure was unavoidable
in a study which aspires beyond mere reportage to evaluative exposition, since evaluation can neither evade questions of priority nor
overlook the relative accuracy of varying formulations of a single
concept, wherever made. The latter consideration, I might add, accounts for the unusual amount of direct quotation in my text.

In modern times the problem of poetic diction has been more
than a single strand among others in the fabric of poetic theory; it
has been rather a major, latterly *the* major, preoccupation of poeticians. In common with other ideas and institutions, modern speculation on poetry begins in the early Renaissance, during which
the primary concern of the literary community was whether the
modern languages could ever constitute media of poetry to compare with those so magnificently provided by Greek and Latin.
The result was a focus on the verbal medium that for added reasons has never since abated, one that markedly differentiates
modern from classical poetics. Such stylistic treatises as those of

Demetrius, Longinus, and Quintilian, dealing primarily with the prose arts of oratory and historiography, took only rudimentary steps toward distinguishing the special category of poetic eloquence. Ancient doctrine never considered that part of a poetic work labeled "diction" to require much more than the peripheral treatment it had received in Aristotle's *Poetics*. As an object of disciplined scrutiny, the verbal materiality of human utterance was thought to be more germane to rhetorical science than to poetics.

Even without my reference to evaluation, it will be obvious to readers that the mode of treatment in this book rejects the figment of judgmental neutrality. Whether or not that phantom ideal any longer has respectable adherents, it presupposes a self-discrediting naivete where it is not a cover for intellectual dishonesty. Although, as much as any other kind of historian, chroniclers of ideas must take care to avoid predilective distortion of their data, they neither can nor should eschew judgment. They cannot do so because, as is often pointed out, evaluation is entailed in the very choice of proponents and the amount of space allotted to each. These choices and decisions reflect the author's recognition of relative degrees of cogency, penetration, precision of formulation, or sheer originality—a judgmental act which need not in every case imply a corresponding degree of personal endorsement.

The facile dogma urged by some recent modish theorizers, arguing the total subjective relativity of all assessments of artistic products, must necessarily extend to judgments of the relevance and validity of the principles to which those assessments overtly or silently appeal. But that dogma, anything but novel, is largely refuted by what George Saintsbury styled the history of criticism and literary taste, which hardly supports the rule of *quot homines, tot sententiae*. The relatively small dissent among literary historians as to who were the major writers and who the most durable theorists suggests rather that the bulk of opinion is intersubjective. No one would deny—at least I can think of no one who *has* denied—that even the most informed and perceptive analyst's opinions on relative merit are colored by an irreducible infusion of both personal bias and cultural conditioning. But by the same token those distortions are minimized by the constant corrective of the divergent views he is forced to contemplate, many of them incorporating the mind- set of earlier ages. Though each historian approaches his task with certain evaluative convictions, they are seldom to any appreciable extent of his idiosyncratic devising.

Even were it possible, the aim of total neutrality is best avoided if only because the more nearly it is attained the greater the risk of encyclopedic dullness. The reader's attention is drawn to a succession of intellectual flora in which the fine trees of compelling theory inevitably tending to obscure the contours of the forest are, to compound confusion, themselves undistinguished from the undergrowth of casual or derivative conjecture. The speciousness of the relativist position has often enough been exposed. I will only add that no aspect of this intellectually fascinating problem impressed me more than the strains of conceptual harmony clearly audible above the contentious cacophony of brilliant insights, fortuitous intuitions, deductions deft or ponderous, and facile parrotings of received opinion that make up its tangled record.

Considered from the viewpoint of some current academic lore, the primary interest of this study may well center not on the inevitable disagreements during four centuries of recorded opinion on a notoriously thorny critical issue, but on the one premise to which overtly or implicitly most of the disputants subscribe: *that in poetry language is employed in a manner, and with an effect, that sets it apart from all other kinds of speech or writing.* With few and doubtful exceptions, they also agree that poems are verbal creations instinct with values superior in degree or in kind to those of normal discourse. This consensus alone undermines the pretension that fictive literature in general possesses no quality to justify placing it in an esteemed category separate from more utilitarian uses of words. One decrier of that category has complained that "the assumption of literary superiority" has persisted for too long. Long indeed—about 2,400 years in Western thought since Aristotle's *Poetics*. If this protester is right, how can we explain the firm persuasion to the contrary in the minds of so many writers, some of them celebrated for unusual acumen and sophistication? Surely it would be less plausible to assume that two millennia of devoted students of literature in several languages and national cultures have been deluded, than to suspect that unless the adherents of literary egalitarianism are led astray by some ulterior motive, they are afflicted with a rare atrophy of the imagination. They profess to detect in poems nothing to differentiate them, for interpretation and appreciation, from sermons or advertising copy. The Pauline cloud of witnesses whose testimony constitutes the subject of this book is arrayed against them. The conclusion to be drawn was put with fitting finality by John Stuart Mill when he considered the issue in 1833: "Where everyone feels a difference, a difference there must be."

In a rough and uneven way, ideas of poetic language tend through succeeding generations to develop from cruder to more refined conceptions, as do most other aspects of literary doctrine. Any expectation of a tidier and more comprehensive ameliorative evolution, however, is disappointed by the record. The one exception, to be sure a major one, occurs with the advent of Romanticism. The historical evidence gives clear warrant for the widespread assumption that the organic view of poetic structure first formulated in Germany and England during the 1790s nurtured a poetics notably sounder than the systems it was ultimately to supplant. Poetic diction theory was perhaps the main beneficiary of that change, most fruitfully in the altered understanding of meter that emerged from visualizing the structure of a poem as a union of elements held together in polar tension. It would of course be rash to assume that future scholarship will not overturn our persuasion that the organicist account of poetic expression is a fundamental improvement over what had gone before. That caveat aside, the present estimate of the Romantic contribution is strenuously ratified in modernist Anglo-American criticism, especially by the fact recently reaffirmed in Lubomír Doležel's *Occidental Poetics* (1990) that "modern theory of poetic language has its origins in romantic poetics." Still true of Slavic and most Anglophone linguistic formalism, his generalization is invalidated only with the eruption of poststructuralism in the late 1960s.

The efficacy of poetic language has long been regarded as nothing short of mysterious, as impenetrable today as ever. Some writers darkened counsel by assigning to the words of a literary work a function purely analogous to those of the sculptor's marble, bronze, or clay, a parallel since ably discredited by Leo Spitzer in a 1957 essay on the medium of poetry, but still occasionally revived in casual commentary. For in fact the baffling nature of the poetic medium arises from its inherent disparity with those of every other art. Poor in the palpable materiality of the plastic substances, pigments, and tones which sculptors, painters, and musicians readily exploit to immediate sensuous effect, words are also by nature aesthetically recalcitrant. Inseparable ingredients of human mental and emotional life, they come to the artist's hand so charged with meanings that their effect is preponderantly referential or symbolic, and therefore mediate rather than immediate. Since, however, that unique and troublesome distinction enables

poets who can overcome it to enrich their creations with a range
and precision of thought unattainable in either graphic or musical
art, some writers have therefore assigned poetry a superior status
among the arts. Others have on different grounds taken the opposite view. To them the immediately striking fact is that compared
to pigments, tones, or plastic substances, the poet's words are a
singularly unpromising medium. Yet, though they ought not to
work, unaccountably they do. The anomaly was perhaps never
more starkly underscored than by A. W. Schlegel in 1795: "The
most beautiful poem consists only of verses, the verses of words,
the words of syllables, the syllables of individual sounds." Considering the creative process, Jacques Maritain was moved to wonder
and despair when he reflected that a poem is an object made of
words, which, intrinsically poor in color and variety, and worn out
by social use, he judged to be "the most ungrateful and treacher-
ous material." Alone among artists, Maritain concluded, the poet
must perform the impossible.

No one has outdone the poets themselves in deploring the
stuff of their craft for its inherently poor quality. Envying the musician the purity of his tones, Paul Valéry reverted often and bit-
terly to the poet's constant battle against messy material. Now and
then a poet has made this familiar lament the burden of his song.
Eliot's complaint in *Four Quartets* about his own never ending—
and never fully rewarded—struggle with words, each attempt at
composition "a raid on the inarticulate / With shabby equipment," has distinguished precedents. Often these take the form of
protests against the disparity between conception and the means
of conveying it. Readers of Chaucer will recall his confession of an
incapacity to articulate the amorous delights of his lovers in
Troilus and Criseyde. I suppose the *locus classicus* of the *topos* is
Dante's ejaculation of creative despair that he could find in the
common stuff of human speech adequate means for incarnating,
in the final Canto of the *Paradiso*, the vision of the divine glory so
vividly present to his imagination.

Since its earliest beginnings in the nineteenth century, modern
linguistic science has sometimes encouraged the very opposite
view by enshrining speech, even in its basest utilitarian functions,
among the glories of humanity. We occasionally read, as Edward
Sapir has it in *Language*, that the greatest "poem" is language itself, an inherently aesthetic human attribute. Moreover, the pessimistic attitude may be relieved, though without dispelling the
anomaly, by finding in poetry the one form of utterance capable,

especially in its metrical masterpieces, of transcending the restrictions of its medium. And in fact the poets' occasional frustrations may be outweighed by their frequent celebrations of "words set in delightful proportion," as one of them, Sir Philip Sidney, put it. Most significantly, they constantly feel impelled to speak of poetic language as something awe-striking, *in* the world but not *of* it. We are not surprised to find preternatural powers ascribed to the words of the bard in heroic ages, when the poet was one with prophet and priest. Yet even in the no-nonsense times of the Enlightenment, when history had replaced myth and reason allegedly banished superstition, Fénelon followed ancient usage in calling poetry *le langage des dieux*, an unearthly utterance. So did Alexander Pope. Anyone inclined to shrug off Pope's use of this traditional phrase as a mere form of speech might consider his impassioned imitation of some lines in one of Horace's *Epistles* on the therapeutic power of words in meter. Presumably however, it is more consonant with the Romantic poets' virtual apotheosis of the creative imagination that they should have endowed their language with at least intuitional if not preternatural potency. In *The Prelude,* an epic of his artistic growth, Wordsworth records the moment when his mind first "opened to the charm of words in tuneful order" and absorbed the "Visionary Power" and "mystery" imbuing the language of the great poets he had been reading. Shelley and Keats reported much the same experience.

What is perhaps most worthy of notice is that the habit of characterizing poetic speech as something beyond rational accounting is not an obsolete motif or a mere rhetorical grace note left over from an outmoded piety. Nor is it confined to critical writing of vatic orientation, in which poets are centrally conceived as performing a divinatory function. It persists in critics of the most varied intellectual persuasions, extending beyond the "belletristic criticism" to which W. K. Wimsatt would confine its common occurrence in the phrase "verbal magic." The effect of words in poetry continues to be characterized in preternatural or thaumaturgic terms, even when such terms have no inherent grounding in the most fundamental beliefs of the writer who invokes them. Emerson's exaltation of poetry as a form of utterance instinct with divine energy is readily reconcilable with the transcendentalism of his *Weltanschauung*. But a similar philosophic persuasion seldom underpins the persistent recourse to such terminology in our own century whenever the subject is verse language. Santayana founded the distinction between poetry and prose in the poet's aim to cast a "supernatural spell" over his readers. Thomas Quale concluded from his study of eighteenth-century English verse that poetic diction in any age possesses a "magic force." André Gide spoke unabashedly of its "magic," its "sorcery." For Robert Graves too it was nothing less than a "miracle," something "magic." Even the skeptical scrutiny of a John Crowe Ransom could never really penetrate what he called its "strange secret." Hugh Kenner, hardly the least articulate of our literary intellectuals, contemplated the great poets' "power to charge simple vocables with all they can say"—and joined the rest in pronouncing it mysterious. The reason no one has ever successfully discriminated between poetry and prose, Richard Eberhart wrote, is that the union of thought and feeling in a poem is "a magical fusion." Centuries of speculation have done much to clarify the sources and conditions of the mystery—without finally dispelling it.

In 1819 Coleridge confided to a friend that in the *Biographia Literaria* he had settled the vexed problem of poetic diction as far as it lay within the power of human reason to do. Yet 150 years later Geoffrey Hartman can with equal warrant speak of the problem as "a rich and baffling subject." For, despite the consensus on the crucial issues involved, the whole territory of the four centuries of modern criticism devoted to it is booby-trapped with paradox, antinomy, and terminological ambivalence.

Sometimes these characteristics are mirrored in some detached observation arousing the suspicion that poetic diction operates according to laws entirely foreign to those governing ordinary language. One such is Valéry's notion that poets use an idiom *sui generis,* a "language within a language," one in which, as others have observed, there are, strictly speaking, no synonyms. This aperçu is especially noteworthy in that it lends explanatory support to one of Roman Jakobson's: that untranslatability is part of the definition of poetry. The generic distinction is not confined to arresting aphorisms. It permeates extended examination of the several issues as well, including the method customarily followed in trying to resolve them. Conscious of experiencing in poetry a kind or strength of spiritual enrichment missing in prose, sensitive readers since ancient times have sought to isolate its cause by comparing the two forms of written expression. With differing emphases this method informs the most fruitful theories on the subject. Yet though it has often revealed areas of fundamental agreement, it has by no means produced perfect unanimity. The variety of opinion on the relations of prose and verse (or discursive prose and poetry

in either form) has sometimes led to diametrically opposed conclusions. Some writers have found that the virtues of good verse and
good prose are essentially the same, and some that they diverge. A
radical few even charge that, as one modern poetician put it, prose
is quite simply poetry's enemy. These last represent an extremist
faction of the great majority who have insisted that the conventions
of a metrically segmented linear structure is the essential cause of
poetry's special appeal, if not indeed its defining feature. But on
this point too not everyone has been of one mind. Ever since the
early Renaissance a minority have dissented, most of them on the
soundly Aristotelian premise that meter could be no more than an
adventitious auxiliary factor in the complex mimetic construct that
constitutes a poem. While each side in the debate over meter has at
one time or another made out a good case, neither has made better
than a lame defense against crucial objections lodged by the other.
The disparagers of meter are hard put to it to explain why it is that
every universally acclaimed poetic masterpiece is either metrical or
highly cadenced in movement. On the other hand, those who
make meter definitive have been equally ill at ease when confronted
with perfectly metrical and regularly rhyming verse devoid of poetic
merit. From a theoretical point of view, the still uncertain claims of
free verse, prose-poetry—and its less legitimate first cousin poetic
prose—are only especially fertile speculative provinces of the
broader realm covered by the uncertain relation of metrical form to
poetic quality.

Then there is the much controverted question of poetry's
cognitive status. Being so obviously fictive, so prone to naming
airy nothings, how can poetry vindicate the claim to intellectual
and moral relevance to real human experience made for it by so
many of its champions? What, in the broadest terms, is the nature
of poetry's relation to meaning or truth? No other issue in poetics
has been more bedeviled by elusiveness, ambiguity, and diametric
dissent. Aristotle, in the very treatise in which he ascribed the
efficacy of poetic mimesis to the pleasure we take in learning
something, praised Homer for having taught all subsequent poets
the art of telling lies skillfully. With due allowance for the equivocal meaning of *to lie,* Oscar Wilde two millennia later would enti-
tle a witty lament for the alleged decline of modern poetry "The
Decay of Lying." If Aristotle doubtfully, and Wilde assuredly,
could defend poetic mendacity for its entertainment value alone,
they did so at the considerable cost of trivializing its cognitive
worth. That tactic has a Renaissance variant. Even while staunchly

extolling poetry above philosophy itself for moral edification, when Sidney came to fend off the charge that a poet is a liar, he did so on the ground that he "nothing affirmeth." Scores of other apologists have taken the same stance, which at least removes the sting from the glib dismissal of poetry as both false and useless by the dull positivist lights of a Jeremy Bentham. Before all its vindicators, however, has always hovered the far more discomfiting ghost of Plato, defiant of easy exorcism by either appealing rhetoric or forceful logic. No palliation of the poet's pleasurably deceptive feigning, not even Homer's, could be reconciled with the severity of Plato's idealist brand of truth. Lovers of poetry might wisely prefer not to reply in the philosopher's terms, but to rely instead on a flank attack around his view of reality. If so, however, they do well not to follow the course taken by I. A. Richards when facing the more deadly menace of modern science's exclusive claim to truth. Richards' doctrine that words in a poem which take the form of predications are really pseudo-statements is only a somewhat desperate Benthamite revival of Sidney's denial of poetic affirmation.

What few would have guessed, chronologically interwoven with this train of denunciation and apology were equally vocal glorifications of poets as in fact the supreme purveyors of truth, especially of the kind of truth most profoundly pertinent to the human moral condition. This vindication was not exclusive to those who conceived the poet's office to be centrally divinatory, his words oracular, akin to those of seer and prophet. For a closely related nexus of truth with poetry was proclaimed as well by critics for whom poets, however dependent on ultralogical inspiration, were primarily skilled practitioners of an exacting verbal art (*poiesis*), and thus more fittingly designated by the Greek *poietes* than by the Latin *vates*.

At this point the questions of poetic cognition and poetic language coincide. Especially for critics of the former orientation, truthfulness, if not always truth itself, is somehow entailed in the peculiar commerce poets hold with language, and thus an ingredient inseparable from the aesthetic cast of what they write. It's as though no good poet, *qua* poet, *could* deceive even if he wanted to. Whether a prior disposition to unalloyed candor guarantees stylistic excellence, or a prior determination to write well precludes any incursion of disingenuousness into the product, is unclear. With at least one critic it seems to be the latter case. It is impossible, Northrop Frye concluded of a kind of "poetic" prose many

other readers also disrelish, "to tell the truth in Macaulay's style."
On this premise, perhaps more cogently than on any other, mannerism is deprecated, including the neoclassical poetic diction in
which Wordsworth found nothing more objectionable than its fal-
sity, and so inaugurated sincerity as the cardinal virtue of poetic
style. And here we meet another paradox, which for those who
stress the conventionality of all poetry becomes a dilemma. What
is called mannerism is simply one or another conventional mode of
expression, and this in itself can hardly be considered mendacious.
It is now a long time since any reputable judge has thought that
the stereotyped periphrasis of *The Rape of the Lock* in any way viti-
ates either the moral validity or the accuracy of Pope's portrayal of
the upper-class mores of his day. But why then does the same device so patently fail in, say, Erasmus Darwin's verse? It is a poor
dodge to reply that a mannerism is a "decayed" convention, because that only poses the equally daunting task of defining and accounting for the dry rot.

In any case, I can cite no very conclusive demonstration for an
inherent immunity to dissimulation in poetic utterance. In those
who profess this conviction it operates instead as an axiom of
whatever theory of poetic language they espouse. It seems to be
the gut reaction of some people who, with no ambition to theo-
rize about it, nonetheless put poetry at the head of their literary
preferences. Asked whether she likes poetry, a character in Martha
Grimes's novel *The Old Silent* replies, "Yes . . . because you can
trust the language of it." With a little introspection of what they
feel in recalling scraps of their favorite verse, many devotees of poetry may detect some plausibility in her remark. In the absence of
any explicit alternative evidence, we may surmise that this same intuition prompted Matthew Arnold to declare that the superiority
of poetic speech over any other lay in its enabling humans beings
to come nearest to uttering truth. And certainly Ezra Pound offered nothing better to justify his repeated assertions that a poet's
style, like that of any artist, is good or bad in proportion as it renders truthful reports about the world. Poetic sincerity, he thought,
resided in sound poetic technique, the only reliable recourse for
"telling it like it is."

No probing of poetic utterance, no description of its unique
essence, has ever done full justice to readers' experience of its wondrous ways. Samuel Johnson's opinion—that it is easier to say
what poetry is not than what it is—remains unrefuted. Even those
who have most rewardingly elucidated the problem have shared

Eliot's despair of any definition of poetry commensurate with the phenomenon itself. So it may well be true, as Octavio Paz declared in *The Bow and the Lyre,* that since poetry is on a par with conjuration there is no escaping a belief in "the magical power of words." But to think so by no means relegates to an exercise in futility the centuries of effort to discover, and to formulate in rational terms, the means by which that power is activated. So stultifying a verdict can be rendered only by assuming the nullity of all literary criticism, the most humane of intellectual pursuits. As Wimsatt and Brooks pointed out, the problem of poetic diction is a "good small-scale model" of the enduring issues engaged by the systematic inspection of literature itself.

The Renaissance Setting

UNLIKE LATER PERIODS
of literary history, the English Renaissance subscribed to no generally received conception of poetic style. Though a few of the prefaces, letters, epistles dedicatory, and poetic "arts" and "apologies"
comprising the slender library of its literary criticism address such
aspects of the subject as rhyme and meter, only one, George Puttenham's *Arte of English Poesie* (1589), offers anything like a comprehensive theory of verse language. This deficiency is certainly
not owing to any lack of interest in the topic. Critics at this time
paid close attention to the diction and syntax of verse because
these seemed especially relevant to a broader and more pressing
inquiry into the limits and potentials of the English language itself. Until uncertainty about the quality and stability of their native tongue had subsided, however, no final or terminologically
consistent poetics was possible. The problem, faced by Continental writers as well, was exacerbated in England by the long predominance of spoken French among the educated classes during
the Middle Ages and well into the fourteenth century. Fortunately
for its eventual emergence as the medium of literature, as well as of
refined conversation, English had begun to gain official ascendancy before the Renaissance crossed the Channel.[1]

Yet none of the many themes of Tudor literary discussion is
more pervasive than the state of the vernacular. Virtually throughout the period, despite the increasing use of English in public life,

there was continual debate about its suitability to intellectual discourse. Learned men especially, nurtured on the sonorous periods of Ciceronian prose and the orderly cadences of the Greek and Latin quantitative meters, contemplated with understandable misgivings the syntactical vagaries, grammatical irregularities, and unfixed orthography of English.

Nonetheless, though they seem never fully to have stilled their doubts and perhaps because the patriotic wish fathered the thought, by the final quarter of the sixteenth century poets and critics were voicing a growing confidence that their native tongue was already equal or superior in copiousness to Italian, French, and Spanish. If it came short of the classical languages as an artistic medium—and some denied even this—it could, they argued, be brought to that level by proper cultivation. "What language so hard, harsh, or barbarous," asks one controversialist in 1599, "that time and art will not amend?" How this amelioration could best be attained fostered a debate enlivened by that "incondite exuberance" (in Walter Pater's phrase) peculiar to almost every Elizabethan enterprise. As men have always used words to quarrel about everything else, Samuel Daniel observed near the close of the queen's reign, "wee must nowe at length fall to contend for words themselves." So during this period the inquiry into the adequacy of the English language for composing poetry is fully understandable only as one aspect, though it may be the most important one, of a wider cultural movement.[2]

It would be a mistake to dismiss the Elizabethans' concern as only a symptom of that awe of classical civilization which during the sixteenth and seventeenth centuries motivated the "Ancient" faction in their quarrel with the "Moderns." Here it is instructive to recall the opinion of John Dryden, writing in the next century with the dramatic and epic creations of Shakespeare and Milton behind him. Though the extreme modernist denigration of the past impressed him no more than the ancient party's doctrine of progressive racial degeneration, Dryden was always ready to defend modern literature. Yet his confidence that a literary genius might one day write English poetry equal to the Greek and Roman was limited by the qualification that it could occur "abating only for the language." When he came to translate the *Aeneid* late in his career, he confirmed what many Elizabethans had also felt, that a line of verse entirely in the monosyllables in which English abounds rarely sounds harmonious. Though Dryden was justly proud of what resulted from his three-year effort to make Virgil speak English as though he had been born in modern England, he had to confess that the deficiencies of the vernacular had debarred him from capturing in translation the beauty of Virgil's most exquisite lines.[3]

Considering the long persistence of the linguistic bias which Coleridge was brusquely to censure as Grecomania, the number of Elizabethan writers swelling the chorus of praise for their native tongue may at first seem incongruous. Yet the criticism of the final two decades reveals that though still on the defensive the proponents of English verse were finally winning out. By the early 1580s Philip Sidney's conviction that "our tongue is most fit to honor Poesie, and to be honored by Poesie" was widely endorsed. Especially reassuring was the testimony of those who turned out English versions of classical poetic masterpieces or reputable modern works. Though many of the pioneers—such as Gavin Douglas, Jasper Heywood, Alexander Neville, Thomas Hoby, Arthur Golding, and Thomas Phaer—echoed one another in prefatory apologies for the poverty of English, a few offered their translations in counter-proof. In the epistle before *The Courtyer* (1561), his English version of Baldassare Castiglione's celebrated guide to courtly manners, Hoby saw in translation a means "whereby we alone of the worlde maye not be styll counted barbarous in oure tongue." And by 1598 George Chapman was roundly declaring that English was a perfectly suitable medium for rendering Homer, at the very least "more conformable, fluent, and expressive" for the purpose than Italian, French, or Spanish. William Webbe, discoursing in 1586 on English verse, "demonstrates," at least to his own satisfaction, the poetic potential of the language by juxtaposing memorable passages from the *Aeneid* with Thomas Phaer's English renderings of them.[4]

How reconcile so sanguine an attitude, maintained in the face of quite rational grounds for doubt, with Dryden's soberer estimate three generations later? In part we may ascribe the change to an intervening shift in taste that marked the neoclassical sensibility. The verbal coruscations in which Tudor poets luxuriated were offensive, we know, to virtually every critic from Dryden to Samuel Johnson. But here we deal with imponderables. There are surer and more immediate causes for the Elizabethan critics' defiance of the linguistic anxiety of the time. Apart from the intrinsic force of the apologists' arguments (feebly urged at best), several attendant circumstances conspired to assure their general adoption.

Before examining these, we do well to take a closer look at the obstacles facing English poets who longed to rival in their own nation and speech what Italians since Petrarch had been doing in theirs. Ironically, the heaviest opposition came from the very men whose brilliant intellectual activity had extended the literary Renaissance to England. Those respected cultural emissaries from abroad, Juan Luis Vives and Desiderius Erasmus, along with their English humanist colleagues, sure of the sempiternity of Latin and zealous advocates of its stylistic perfection, regarded the modern languages of Europe as degenerate legacies of a boorish past. Roger Ascham himself, though he wrote in English, could conceive of no other way of raising it to literary quality than by imitating the classics. The only repositories of "the trewe preceptes and perfite examples of eloquence," he wrote, were the works of the choicest Latin and Greek authors.[5] In Italy the fight for the national language (or rather some dialect of it) was more easily won by proponents like Angelo Poliziano and Pietro Bembo. Italians could invoke the revered names of Dante and Petrarch in aid of their cause. Although the great Florentine's *Commedia* was not then regarded, like Petrarch's songs and sonnets, as exemplary in style, it had nonetheless stood the test of time though written in the vernacular. Moreover, Dante had championed Italian verse in his *De volgare eloquentia,* first published in a translation by Giangiorgio Trissino shortly after the appearance of Bembo's own *Prose della volgar lingua* in 1525.[6]

In England, Chaucer's Elizabethan reputation, though hardly overstated when Webbe called him "the God of English poets," made little for the vernacular cause, since the antiquated language of *Troilus and Criseyde* and *The Canterbury Tales* was an all too obvious reminder of the instability of the native idiom. Such in fact it was long to remain, as readers of Pope may discover from the despairing couplet in *An Essay on Criticism:*

> Our Sons their Fathers' *failing language* see,
> And such as Chaucer is shall *Dryden* be.[7]

The largely but not exclusively Puritan campaign for an English Bible numbered among its opponents some of the humanistic decriers of "barbarous" English. A notable exception was Thomas More, who carried his advocacy to a degree of linguistic tolerance rare at the time: "For as for that our tongue is called barbarous, is but a fantasy; for so is, as every learned man knoweth, every strange language to other." Yet the recognition that English was suited to intellectual intercourse did little to enhance its aesthetic standing. Before the last quarter of the century, R. F. Jones concludes, English was still generally regarded "as a mere instrumentality by which knowledge was to be conveyed, and [this] tended to prevent its being considered as a possible medium of artistic expression."[8]

More propitious was the strong patriotism of a heady time, a force motivating the English translators themselves, as F. O. Matthiessen noted. And finally, as the age matured and the productions of a fertile literary era increasingly demonstrated what English authors could do in and with the language actually spoken by Englishmen, it became proportionately harder to adhere to the party of despair. Gabriel Harvey's patriotic pride was stirred by more than his countrymen's "adventurous hartes" and "valorous handes":

> Is not the Prose of Sir Philip Sidney in his sweet Arcadia the embroidery of finest Art and daintiest *Witt?* Or is not the Verse of M. Spencer in his brave Faery Queene the Virginall of the divinest Muses and gentlest Graces?[9]

If the slim record of Tudor criticism is representative, by the final decade of the 1500s the worst forebodings had largely dissipated. The fine work produced by modern poets was valued for more than the pleasure it afforded readers, because in revealing their individual powers these writers had at once adorned and exonerated the national literary medium. Even some of those most prepossessed by the harmonies of classical measures could apparently recognize an alternative music in the rich outpouring of contemporary lyric and dramatic verse, which, Francis Meres wrote in 1598, "makes our language so gorgeous & delectable among us." By the same token, it brightened the promise of future achievment, Meres continued, because by the labors of Sidney, Spenser, Daniel, Drayton, Warner, Shakespeare, Marlowe, and Chapman, English had been "mightily enriched and gorgeously invested in rare ornaments and resplendent abiliments."[10]

Most scholarly accounts of the Elizabethan debate on our language tend, often by mere silence, to obscure the fact that its chief issues were international. After the pioneering Italians, the French in their turn faced the task of defending the living speech of their time and country against charges of inferiority to Greek and Latin for poetic use. English and French literati alike sought to augment their national vocabularies by borrowing from other tongues. Such importation could be less judicious than bold, as when Jasper Heywood rendered *rogae* as "roges" and *stadia* as "stadies" in his 1561 translation of Seneca's *Hercules Furens,* both words quickly becoming obsolete. In both countries there was a movement to settle orthography. Elizabethan writers owed more to French example than they were willing to reveal. Hoby's faith that his translation of Castiglione might make English seem less crude in the eyes of foreigners echoes his countryman Phaer, who three years earlier had also professed to have become a translator "for the defence of my countrey language (which I have heard discommended of many, and estemyd of some to be no more than barbarous)." But the patriotic impulse of either or both may have been spurred by the precedent of Etienne Dolet, writing two decades before them. Dolet had similarly avowed that a main motive for his treatise on the art of translation was so to reform French that foreigners (he meant Italians) would no longer call Frenchmen barbarous ("à fin que les estrangiers ne nous appelleront plus barbares"). Nevertheless, with all due allowance for Continental precedence, the English achievement, at least as English writers themselves assessed it at the century's end, is especially remarkable. Rarely, runs R. F. Jones's account, has a society experienced so rapid a change as that which between 1575 and 1580 replaced Englishmen's despair of their crude vernacular with pride in its eloquence. But the change had been prepared for in the work of vernacular writers exhibited in *Tottel's Miscellany* (1557), *The Mirror for Magistrates* (1559), William Lyly's *Euphues* (1578), and Spenser's *Shepheardes Calender* (1579).[11]

It is impossible not to ascribe the unusual lexical emphases in what Tudor critics wrote in large part to a cultural factor which as manifested in early Shakespeare Professor Harbage has called "verbal effervescence." This tendency too was nourished by the international cultural climate. "You cannot read Renaissance literature," Richard A. Lanham has written, "without noticing everywhere a delight in words, an infatuation with rhetoric, a stylistic explosion."[12]

Nowhere more than in England. There the phonic and semantic resources of the newly expanded English lexicon beguiled the imaginations of educated people to a degree perhaps unequaled at any other time before or since. Besides, as G. D. Willcock has written, they were less inclined than we are to distrust "fine language and direct appeal to the emotions. Now the word *rhetorical,* like the word *artificial,* has acquired a pejorative meaning. The Elizabethan was afraid of neither." It is therefore no accident that this was the age *par excellence* of the poetic pun and of unrestrained and joyous indulgence in alliteration and assonance (letter-hunting, as they called it). In his *Short Treatise on Verse* (1584), Scottish King James VI actually recommended unlimited alliteration and repetitions of the same word up to eight or nine times in a line. He lived in a generation of verbal artists who clearly delighted in the sonorities of their instrument. Spenser's tutor Richard Mulcaster, whose *Elementarie* (1582) displayed what George Saintsbury thought "a Pléiade enthusiasm for the vernacular," was typical. Among other reasons for his love of English, C. S. Lewis notes, was that it admitted more "dalliance with the letter" than any other language he knew. "I favor Italy," Mulcaster wrote, "but England more; I honour the Latin, but I worship the English."[13] He sounds not unlike Shakespeare's Don Adriano de Armado in *Love's Labour's Lost:*

> One who the music of own vain tongue
> Doth ravish like enchanting harmony.

Tastes change. The kind of "music" that so ravished the subjects of Queen Elizabeth simply grated on Augustan ears. Dryden and Johnson deplored it as "bombast." In Shakespeare's punning Johnson saw no less a than a "fatal Cleopatra"; and Dryden's great esteem for Ben Jonson did not extend to the puns in *Every Man in His Humour:* "the lowest and most groveling kind of wit." Not even the bardolatry of Romanticism could vindicate the Shakespearean quibble, though Coleridge made a half-hearted attempt to do so.[14]

Not so in Shakespeare's time. Richard Carew included punning and alliteration ("Agnominations") as among the graces of English prose and verse, naming Sidney master in both forms. But the professed ideals of writers do not always square with their practice. In the *Apologie* Sidney himself dissented from some of his fellows to blame the low state of contemporary poetry on the poets' obsession with fancy verbiage, overdone imagery, and unrestrained alliteration. But Carew's taste for word play could have been nowhere more fully satisfied than in a line from a sonnet of Sidney's own:

> But (God wot) wot not what they mean by it.[15]

Along with the verbal preoccupation the critics shared with the poets, such displays of dictional ingenuity set the whole question of verse style in bold relief. The verbal pyrotechnics of the time, the figurative daring that characterizes song and sonnet and tragic tirade, from the appearance of *Tottel's Miscellany* through the early years of the seventeenth century, did more than merely accentuate the difference between prose and verse. They induced critics to try to define the difference, and so take the first tentative steps toward a theory of poetic language and of poetry itself. The verbal exuberance in which the age delighted allowed George Puttenham to see the poetic mode of expression (in distant anticipation of recent poetics) as a *distortion* of ordinary written and oral discourse by studied violations of grammar and syntax.[16]

A European perspective on the Elizabethans' thinking about poetic language permits a sounder assessment of their contribution than we might otherwise make. Puttenham's notion of poetic style as faulty prose is one example. He may have been recalling, and adapting to his own purposes, the passage in Castiglione's *Il libro del cortegiano* (1528) where Count Ludovico tells the assembled company that the dazzling figures of speech employed by orators are all so many grammatical abuses ("tutte sono abusioni delle regole grammaticali"). In Hoby's translation, readily available to Puttenham, the count is made to say that

> figures of speech which give such grace and brightness to an Oration, are the abuses of Grammar rules, but yet are received and confirmed by use, because men are able to make no other reason but that they delite, and to the verie sense of our eares it appeareth, they bring a life and a sweetnes.[17]

In their efforts to achieve and define a verbal style worthy of their creative ambitions, Tudor poet-critics looked chiefly to ancient poetic and rhetorical theory and modern Italian and French criticism. Ancient poetic lore was of course the common heritage of Renaissance Europe, its impact heaviest and most immediate in cinquecento Italy. Given the reverential attitude toward Greek and Roman authors at the time, it is ironic that the classical poetics was in the main hostile to the centrally linguistic theory many modern inquirers felt compelled to erect. The critical monument ultimately most venerated (following its late recovery), Aristotle's *Poetics,* defined the fundamental principle of mimesis in terms to which the element of diction is no more than tangential. Although in his introductory remarks Aristotle discriminates poetry from the other arts by the medium of its imitation, poetry being the form of art which employs words, whether in prose or verse ("τοῖς λόγοις ψίλοις ἤ τοῖς μέτροις"), what follows largely belies the promise these remarks imply. Of the six parts of tragedy, the genre which occupies the bulk of what has survived as Aristotle's original treatise (or whatever it was), plot almost alone constitutes the imitation and exclusively effectuates the attendant catharsis. Diction, named in fourth place, receives only cursory treatment. In a perfect poetic style, Aristotle held, words in current use are judiciously mingled with unusual words, in order to attain both clarity and distinction. Unusual words are any departure from normal idiom—rare words, lengthened words, metaphors—and these raise the poet's style above the commonplace. Neither in Chapter 22, where this rule is briefly laid down, nor anywhere else in the *Poetics* does he offer any further rationale for its adoption by poets.[18]

Renaissance editors, translators, and commentators found slightly more to their purpose in Horace's breezy verse epistle known as the *Ars poetica*. The Roman poet advocates great care in placing words in a line of verse, as an aid to infusing fresh meaning into a well-worn vocabulary. But his advice is neither explained nor exemplified. Poets are allowed both to coin new words and to revive old ones, though in strict moderation and in sobering awareness of inevitable linguistic decay and of the veto power of current usage ("ius et norma loquendi") in doubtful cases. Horace confirms other classical advocates of a strict stylistic distinction among the several genres and of adapting one's style to the subject being treated or the emotion being expressed. But none of these points is elaborated. Even his references to the sweating labor required to make good verse and his famous stress on revision and polishing ("limae labor") are undercut by the assurance that the right words will come of themselves if the poet has learned wisdom (preferably the Socratic philosophy) and chosen a proper subject. Few lines of the epistle are more quoted by the Italian commentators than those that make good diction an automatic result of the poet's acquisition of sound doctrine.

> Scribendi recte sapere est et principium et fons.
>
> rem tibi Socraticae poterunt ostendere chartae,
>
> verbaque provisam rem non invita sequentur.

[Sound knowledge is both principle and source of good writing. The Socratic pages will furnish you the matter; once the matter is provided, the words will follow readily enough.]

The assurance these lines offer, however, was by no means universally accepted during the Renaissance. Such conscious craftsmen as Ben Jonson, though agreeing that theme (*res*) must be prior to *verba,* clearly did not share Horace's faith in the involuntary accession of suitable diction. The poet who would write well, he noted in *Discoveries,* must "take care in placing, and ranking both matter, and words, that the composition be comely."[19]

Horace's account of the compositional process, one which has had its adherents throughout literary history, would seem to foreclose all necessity and perhaps all possibility of a theory of poetic diction. In every period partly because it tallies with many poets' introspection of their actual experience during composition, Horace's *verbaque provisam rem . . . sequentur* has acted as at least a mild deterrent to stylistic theory and sometimes prompted people to disparage it.[20] Yet Renaissance literati, though conscious that the principle had been laid down by Cicero before Horace and reaffirmed by Quintilian after him, persisted nonetheless in investigating the causes and conditions of successful poetic expression. That they did so owes much to their finding in classical rhetoric the encouragement and guidance in exploring the ways of spoken and written words which classical poetics scantily supplied. Although the texts most often cited, those by Cicero and Quintilian (with rarer glances at Aristotle's *Rhetoric*[21] and the anonymous *Rhetorica ad Herennium*), center on oratory, not poetry, their several contrasting observations on poetic usages had obvious suggestive value at least as starting points for the modern investigator's more concentrated inquiry into the language of verse itself.

Both Cicero in the *De Oratore* and Quintilian in the *Institutio Oratoris* assert the close stylistic affinity between poetry and oratory, the difference between them consisting in the greater lexical and metaphorical license (including archaism and neologism) permitted the poet in compensation for the greater restraint imposed on him by meter.[22] Most heartening to moderns convinced, with Girolamo Frachetta, that metrical discourse was simply the most exquisite of all ("più isquisita dell' altre"), was the rhetoricians' admission that poetic style, though not quite *sui generis,* was a form richer and more striking than even the most eloquent prose, which Cicero thought had originally derived its melody and rhythm from poetic models. Ever ready to assert the orator's mastery of phrase and cadence, he still conceded that the power which rhythmically ordered words can exert on the hearers' minds is at its highest ("summa vis") when the rhythm is that of verse, not of prose.[23]

Quintilian specifies ways in which poetry and rhetorical prose are at once alike and different. Since both aim at delighting (*delectare*) and arousing emotion (*movere*) in their audiences, they share many characteristics of style, a tendency to archaism for example, that raise them above common discourse. But if there is any dominant theme in Quintilian's teaching it is that the orator must steer a stylistic middle course between plain speech and poetic ornateness. Oratory is constrained far more than poetry by the norms of custom, meaning presumably something close to the Horatian *ius et norma loquendi*. But in the *Institutes* that standard becomes one of four criteria of good usage (along with reason, antiquity, and authority). Poets, meter-bound, enjoy the compensatory freedom of not being confined to "currency minted with the pubic stamp" (in H. E. Butler's apt rendering in the Loeb Classics edition). Unlike Cicero, however, who thought even the accidental appearance of metrical regularity to be a blemish in oratory, Quintilian urges aspiring public speakers to study the various meters as effective even in prose. His point is obscure, since he insists that poetry and oratory differ even in the performance, poetry being a kind of song, as the poets themselves, he notes, have always claimed ("se poetae canere testantur").[24]

But ancient rhetorical theory did little to prevent or even mitigate the disagreements and inconsistencies that have ever since plagued Western poetics on the role of meter in distinguishing poetic from non-poetic discourse. The uncertainty, most egregiously encapsulated in Aristotle's provision for a poetry in "bare words,"—the literal meaning of his "λόγοις ψίλοις," usually rendered "prose,"—resurfaces in the earliest modern speculation. The Italian cinquecento writers looked in vain to classical doctrine for help in deciding whether verse form was or was not indispensable to poetic expression. In a discussion of historiography published in 1559, Dionige Atanagi enrolled himself among the orthodox Aristotelians who held that it was poetry's mimetic function and not its metrical form that differentiated it from prose. But in a notable Latin commentary on the *Poetics* which appeared the following year, Pietro Vettori argued that true poetry can exist only in verse ("orationem metricam"). Though Aristotelians of Vettori's persuasion distorted the clear import of the

Poetics on this point of style, they could plausibly have cited its respected author himself in extenuation of their interpretative license.[25] In the more familiar *Rhetoric*, known to scholars throughout the Middle Ages, Aristotle enforces the stylistic distinction between prose and poetry, remarking that the uncommon language of poetry is unsuitable for prose. On the other hand, it is not clear whether "uncommon" includes metrical arrangement as well as the dictional oddities discussed in the *Poetics*. Perhaps so, since he follows Isocrates in asserting that prose should be rhythmical but not metrical, for in that case it would be a poem. But his stand remains ambiguous and the issue has ever since eluded unanimous resolution.[26]

If, as Sidney has it in one passage of the *Apologie*, "one may be a poet without versifying," we are free to wonder why, in that case, "the Senate of Poets hath chosen verse as their fittest rayment . . . not speaking . . . words as they chanceably fall from the mouth, but peizing [i.e., weighing] each sillable of each word by just proportion according to the dignity of the subject." But Sidney's inconsistency is part of an intellectual legacy which he and others have bequeathed in turn to their posterity—willy-nilly, since it seems to be inherent in the enigmatic status of language as an aesthetic medium.[27]

The discussion of poetic language most apposite to the terms of Renaissance inquiry is Book VIII of Quintilian's *Institutes*, devoted entirely to style. It begins unpromisingly enough. After observing that stylistics ("ratio elocutionis") gives both orators and theorists the greatest difficulty, he reiterates the by then familiar doctrines that though eloquence consists in appropriately ornate language, fancy phrase-making and a deliberate aim at gilded verbiage are bad, and that the right words follow unbidden upon right thought. The next few pages constitute the immediate source of the stylistic lore (though not always the poetic practice) dominant in England between the birth of Shakespeare and the appearance of *Lyrical Ballads*. The language of good writing must never be obscene, sordid, or "low." Low words ("verba humilia") Quintilian defines as those beneath the dignity of the speaker or his topic. Theoretically, he is something less than satisfactory. Though he has earlier denied that any word can be better in itself than any other, he asserts that in general the best words are those which are either the most resounding or most delightful to the ear ("aut maxime exclamant aut sono sunt iucundissima")—and then with the reservation that horrible things are best described by words that grate on the ears ("verba . . . audita aspera"). Otherwise, faced with a choice among synonyms, a good stylist will favor the more euphonious ("auditu pulchrius"). In any poem, he notes, theme and diction must match. On humbler subjects, where epic verbal splendor is a blemish, plain words confer the needed poetic grace, as when celebrating country life Virgil spoke of the *exiguus mus* (tiny mouse).[28]

Like other authorities, Quintilian justifies Virgil's archaisms (*olli* for *illi*, *moerus* for *murus*) because they occur in a verse context, whereas, as Ascham was to point out, he condemned this usage in prose. Although in 1549 Joachim du Bellay had welcomed Quintilian's warrant when he urged French poets to cultivate "quelque motz antiques," as Virgil had used *olli* and *aulai* (for *aulae*), his English contemporaries are silent or cautionary on the point. "E. K"'s defense of Spenser's obsolete diction in *The Shepheardes Calender* rests mainly on the prevalent linguistic chauvinism: that by thus restoring long neglected English words to currency the "new Poet" has obviated the deplorable necessity of filling gaps in the native vocabulary by Latin, French, and Italian borrowings. Jonson, a close student of Quintilian and other Latin rhetoricians, also followed him in commending Virgilian archaism to his countrymen but puts stress rather on the Roman master's restraint in using it: "yet how rarely doth he insert *acquai* [for *acquae*] and *pictai* [for *pictae*]!"[29]

The *Institutes* also authorize another motif in early attempts to define poetic style, one stressed by Puttenham. This is the rule that certain figures of speech banned from oratory may be used by poets, since they aim only to give pleasure and are often forced into metaphor by (again) metrical necessity. The examples Quintilian gives are so arresting that one regrets his failure to provide a justifying rationale. Take synecdoche: orators may follow the poets in saying *tectum* (roof) for "house" but not *puppis* (stern) for "ship." Or metonymy: poets may adopt every variety of this figure. But while orators may substitute the container for the contained, as in "civilized cities," only a poet should risk the reverse procedure, as Virgil did in the *Aeneid:* "iam proximus ardet / Ucalegon" (and now his neighbor Ucalegon [i.e., his house] catches fire). In like manner, poets are permitted redundant epithets such as "white teeth" and "liquid wine" ("dentes albos," "humida vina"), the latter cited from *Georgics* III. This liberty too is denied the orator, whose every epithet, he writes, must add something to the *meaning* of what is being said.[30]

It is much that ancient stylists should have noticed a syntactical phenomenon that later analysts would identify as symptomatic of poetic style. Yet neither Quintilian nor Aristotle (who in the *Rhetoric* had instanced the redundancy "white milk") evinced any clear sense that the admissibility of such catechreses may argue a mode of utterance *generically* distinct from prose; or, beyond that, that the generic difference may rest on something deeper, of which these stylistic traits are visible clues.

Sidney's self-condemnation was too severe—that he deserved "to be pounded for straying from Poetrie to Oratorie." That habit he almost certainly acquired, perhaps through the Italians, by the formative influence of the classical rhetoricians. At best, their instruction was a mixed blessing. While their stress on style and diction answered the most immediate need and most pressing interest of Renaissance writers, what they imparted was after all a rhetoric, not a poetics. And so despite the suggestive value of their recognition of notable distinctions between the two modes of verbal composition, the terms of their discussion tended to conflate them. The result was that poetry's marked difference from oratory, despite Aristotle's insistence on it, was blurred. Angelo Poliziano's affirmation in 1498 of Cicero's opinion that "the poet is very close to the orator" was echoed in England by Webbe's assertion that the two were "by byrth Twyns, by kind the same." Even the more discriminating Jonson would later concede their affinity, while insisting that the poet was equal to the orator "in ornement, and above him in strengths."[31]

The tradition of this generic kinship long remained an obstacle to working out a poetic theory per se. In France, as Grahame Castor reports in his study of the *Pléiade,* any view of poetry as a thing *sui generis* was delayed by "the traditional classification of poetry under the head of rhetoric." Prose was "first rhetoric," poetry "second rhetoric." Thomas Sebillet's account in his *Art poétique françoys* (1548) stresses Cicero's qualification that poetry is distinguished only by greater metrical restraint ("plus constraint de nombres que l'autre"). Thus, once again, Elizabethan apologists and theorists wrote in the flow of an international current of thought hard to buck.[32]

CHAPTER TWO

Elizabethan Beginnings

NOTHING WOULD BE MORE
fallacious than to conclude from the heavy stress on the verbal element in Elizabethan poetics that its leading spokesmen were critical formalists. The main bastions of Sidney's spirited defense of
poetry against its perennial detractors are the poets' moral and
civic ministration to humanity, not their artistic prowess. Critics
probed the *dulce* of diction, rhyme, and meter primarily on the assumption that such features of the art were vital for empowering a
utile of intellectual and spiritual nourishment.

Yet that very assumption and the uncertain state of a vernacular medium continued to focus attention on formal issues. Undeterred by the low priority assigned to diction in the ancient critical
texts, or by Quintilian's confession that stylistics is the thorniest
side of literary science, these new critics seem to have been almost
unanimous in endorsing the flat assertion of an early Italian commentator on Horace that no other part of a poem was so poetic as
its diction. If, as Weinberg notes, *verba* received more attention
than *res* in Italy, the same was true of England.[1]

The sprightly *Notes of Instruction* with which the poet George
Gascoigne inaugurated English prosodic theory in 1575 expresses
the Horatian faith that if the poet takes pains with his subject "pleasant words will follow well inough and fast inough." But that didn't
forestall his giving would-be poets considerable stylistic advice. Use
lots of monosyllables, he tells them; don't overdo alliteration; avoid

"rime without reason." This same preoccupation with technique, the conviction that whatever loftier services they may perform poets are chiefly loved for the delightful things they do with words, was a note sounded throughout the period. Given its title, it is not especially remarkable that two-thirds of Puttenham's *Arte* is given over to prosody. Sidney too, though he devotes most of his admired *Apologie* to graver matters, bears spirited witness to the force of style. "For that same exquisite observing of number and measure in words, and that high flying liberty of conceit proper to the Poet, did seeme to have some dyvine force in it."[2]

Since the term *poetic diction,* used to designate a peculiar selection and order of words that sets verse apart from prose, is usually (and justifiably) referred to the neoclassical period, it may be well to declare right off that the Elizabethans, for all the greater heterogeneity of their poetic vocabulary, were at one with classical and Continental critics in never doubting that the poet's language was distinctive.[3] Advocates of stylistic restraint themselves accepted the principle. The conservative Jonson, even as he condemned ornateness, admitted that in a poem the language must "differ from the vulgar somewhat." Daniel, though his own undecorated verse struck his contemporaries as unduly prosaic, was careful to define verse as a "frame of wordes confined within a certain measure, differing from the ordinarie speach." Francis Bacon's characterization of poetry, written after the queen's death, fairly sums up the received thought of the age which bears her name. A famous passage from the *Advancement of Learning* reflects the uncertainty on the role of meter, the *res-verba* division of the subject, and the assurance (under the head of *verba*) of a uniquely poetic style.

> Poesy is a part of learning, in measure of words for the most part restrained, but in all other points extremely licensed. . . . It is taken in two senses in respect of words or matter. In the first sense it is but a character of style, and belongeth to the arts of speech. . . . In the latter it is . . . one of the principal portions of learning, and it is nothing else but feigned history, which may be styled as well in prose as in verse.[4]

Prior to any rationalizing about it inherited or devised, Tudor writers' experience of poetry convinced them that good verse was more *valuable* than even the most artful prose. As mentioned earlier, this conviction was not a postulate of classical provenance, but a major distinction between Greco-Roman and Renaissance poetics. True, Horace and Ovid, to name only two that come readily to mind, affirmed the expressive power and allure of metrical utterance. But for the Greeks and Romans the experience did not, as it did with many Renaissance critics, beget a cardinal item in their poetics. Even Longinus, though he signalizes the sublime as a quality of style that moves audiences beyond mere persuasion to outright transport, drew his examples as much from oratory as from poetry. His citations show that Plato and Demosthenes "transported" him as much as Homer did.

During the Renaissance, conceptions of the poet's language appealed often to what was proved upon the pulses. "Power above powers," the level-headed Daniel rhapsodized,

> O heavenly eloquence,
> That with the strong rein of commanding words,
> Dost manage, guide and master th'eminence
> Of men's affections, more than all their swords.

Not in confirmation of ancient doctrine but under the charm of the beloved lyrics of Petrarch—in which are combined, Ludovico Dolce felt, every beauty of which Italian poetry is capable ("tutte le belleze della Volgar Poesia")—Dolce likened meter and poetic diction to the painter's brush and colors. As the instrumentalities by which he captivates his readers, Dolce reasoned, these particulars of his craft deserve a poet's special care. Neglecting them, he simply fails of his effect.[5]

Unfortunately this instinctive reliance on reader experience failed to generate a consistent theory of poetic style. Puzzling at first, and to the student of English criticism seemingly perverse, the reason for this becomes clear when English critics are studied alongside their Continental compeers. Renaissance readers' lively sensitivity to verbal beauty tended, against established tradition, towards making poetry essentially a *Wortkunst*. Ideally in the form of verse, and irrespective of genre, they sometimes praised it simply as the most resplendent and affecting mode of verbal communication. Accordingly, the words in a poem were frequently likened to precious stones, distinct from the common clay of ordinary speech. This simile, perhaps most conspicuous in the manifestos of the *Pléiade* but employed in England too as early as Stephen Hawes's *Passetyme of Pleasure* (ca. 1505) and Thomas Wilson's *Arte of Rhetorique* (1553), would seem to assign primary value to diction.[6] But the priority was depreciated by the persistent influence of the ancient authorities' relegation of the medium to an ancillary, external, and most often merely decorative role in the total being and function of a poem. The conception that thus prevailed was formulated in a more pervasive and enduring analogy: a poem is to its words as a person's body is to the clothes that adorn it.[7]

The alternate conceptions appear in Sidney's *Apologie,* where the style exacted by meter is given a valuation hardly exceeded in any other critical text. The likening of poetic diction to precious stones appears when he asserts that verse enforces the highest polishing of "that blessing of speech, which considers each word not only . . . by his forcible qualitie but by his measured quantitie, carrying even in themselves a Harmonie." As such it is "the only fit speech for Musick (Musick I say, the most divine striker of the senses)." There is more in the same vein, including the significant recognition that by very reason of this "sweet charming force" poetry, when abused, "can do more hurt than any other Armie of words." And, finally, by the irresistible appeal of "words set in delightful proportion" poets can draw children from play and old men from the chimney-corner. Yet despite this exaltation of their powers, Sidney can speak a few pages later of words, "or (as I may tearme it) Diction," as only "the outside of poetry." Such was the power of ancient preachment to blunt the edge of immediate experience.[8]

One of Sidney's warmest admirers, Harington, in the preface to his translation of Ariosto's *Orlando Furioso,* records what is perhaps the most graphic personal testimony of the time to the power of verse. He tells of being simply bored by his ploughman's accounts of how the fields must be allowed to lie fallow, then burned over, and then harrowed. Yet whenever he heard someone recite the passage in Virgil's first *Georgic* beginning

Saepe etiam steriles incendere profuit agros,

Atque levem stipulam crepitantibus urere flammis

[It has often even been helpful to set the barren fields ablaze, and burn up the light stubble in crackling flames],

something almost miraculous happened. Virgil describes the same processes as Harington's farmer, "but delivered in so good Verse that me thinkes all that while I could find in my hart to drive the plough." The stark disparity between the two verbalizations of identical matter seems poorly accounted for, however, by Harington's complacent recourse to the traditional notion of measured language as "the clothing or ornament" of poetry.[9]

The split between a poem's form and its content implied by classifying its meter and figurative language as merely so much drapery always risks the awkward corollary that the poem *qua* poem would suffer no impairment of its essential being if it dispensed with these things entirely. In Elizabethan England the issue was underscored by the prose of Sidney's *Arcadia,* which Harvey praised for its artful "embroidery." The uncertainty as to the metrical part of it is most explicit in Meres's *Palladis Tamia.* Giving Seneca as his authority, Meres rates the expression of an idea in "the well-knitte and succinct combination [i.e., structure] of a Poem" above its expression in prose. Yet endorsing Sidney's declaration that the prose works of Xenophon and Heliodorus are better poetry than some compositions in rhyme and meter, he adds the further evidence of the English poet's popular romance: "so Sir Philip Sidney writ his immortal poem, *The Countess of Pembroke's Arcadia* in Prose; and yet our rarest Poet."[10]

The affective power Sidney himself ascribed to "words set in delightful proportion" seems to belong to something too deeply involved in its nature to be labeled the "out-side" of poetry. A more satisfactory image than those of clothing and gems to represent its linguistic mode came from the camp of those who held that true poetry cannot exist except in the form of verse. In his *Lezione* delivered at the Florentine Academy in 1573, Agnolo Segni suggested the image of incarnation. Despite his high appraisal of meter, Segni stopped short of the reductive aestheticism that conceives of poetry mainly as an affair of verbal manipulation.[11] He is unswervingly Aristotelian in adhering to the doctrine that it is essentially an imitation of nature. But, he argued, in any given poem this imitation results from a process by which a conceptual "soul" achieves its exclusive and necessary "embodiment" in language. This poetic body, however, cannot be just *any* language; it must be "fixed" speech, metrical, or shaped into verses ("determinata, cio è l'orazione metrica, o fatta in versi"). Segni's position was seconded by Pietro Vettori, who in his great commentary on the *Poetics* had held that meter is enforced upon the poet by a diction peculiar to his art.[12]

Segni's metaphor of miraculous embodiment, allowing for the simultaneous distinction and inseparability of form and content, resurfaces in nineteenth-century references to meter as poetic incarnation. So too with Vettori's formulation of the interdependency of poetic diction and meter, which actually anticipates a crucial point in Coleridge's description of poetic style. One must assume that these ideas were broached ahead of their time, which in this case means before the hegemony of literary organicism, in an intellectual climate inimical to their full development and general reception. Puttenham aside, none of the English critics, not even those who considered meter and a peculiar choice and order of words to be essential to poetic expression, ever allows them more than a sensuous, hedonic function, and then only as ancillary to some cognitive-moral content. True, in Jonson's *Timber* we read that words and their meanings are respectively the body and soul of expression. But there he is speaking of language in general, not exclusively of its use in verse.[13]

Samuel Daniel's *Defence of Ryme* (ca. 1603) contains especially piquant examples of the abortive quality of much Elizabethan thinking about the poet's language. Fresh and acute insights into the subject that cry for elaboration are teasingly left for later criticism to discover and exploit. Daniel knows that the controversy between him and the proponents of an English quantitative prosody turns on "whatever force of words doth moove, delight, and sway the affections of men," since "that is true number, measure, eloquence, and the perfection of speech." The case he makes for rhyme itself includes but goes well beyond the usual hedonic and mnemonic justifications ("for delight and memory"). As a highly conscious poet, he has glimpsed its weightier functions. He anticipates Dryden in finding rhyme to be less an impediment than a spur to invention, a technique salutary to the poet struggling to master the "unformed chaos" of his imagination. These claims are admittedly problematic. The rhyming that was Daniel's and Dryden's creative aid was Milton's detested bondage. But whatever their merits they surely imply that formal devices are rather more than superficial graces—that they belong in fact to the warp and woof of the craft. Yet Daniel reverts repeatedly to the traditional view by ringing the changes on the metaphor which supports it. He alludes to the "attire of Ryme," to measured words as the "habit" of a poem's content, and dismisses the campaign to replace English accentual meter with rhymeless quantity as only finding "other clothes to the same body." Once he even dismisses the "gay words" of poetry as "but the garnish of a nice time," so many "ornaments that do but deck the house of a State."[14] Daniel does better when led by his temperamental pragmatism—if a given metrical scheme works, let it alone. Thus he discovered a principle pivotal in modern theory: that system of meter is best which best comports with "the nature of the language."[15]

Wordsworth's insistence on the substantial identity of poetic and nonpoetic language has slim support in Elizabethan criticism. Daniel does warn against the use of strange and imported words and of coinages. His objection to making "our verse seeme another kind of speach out of the course of our usual practise" is not, however, a demand to erase the generic boundary. It is instead the first English appeal to poets—one to be repeated at later moments of stylistic attrition—to nourish a vital link between how they write and the current spoken idiom. Yet despite Daniel's distaste for flamboyance, the phrase "differing from ordinary speach" occurs in his very definition of verse. Better known are Jonson's calls for stylistic moderation; the poet's language "shall not fly from all humanity," he warned. In a more restricted application, essentially the same point had been made earlier by Nashe when he condemned the "swelling bombast of a bragging blanke verse" (in the first recorded use of that term). These admonitions belong with the repeated pleas that poets avoid the erudite polysyllabic jargon nicknamed "inkhorne terms," a *caveat* sounded at the very outset by Gascoigne.[16]

With reservations no stronger than these, poets and critics unanimously supported King James's including a command of "pithie wordis" in the equipment of the "perfyte poete." Undeterred by ancient wobbling on the question, learned modern Europeans universally endorsed a separation of styles that exalted verse over prose, always in sensuous attractiveness and often in expressive force. In many cases the gap was one of the starkest contrast, extending beyond figurativeness, syntactical deviation, and the use of rhyme and meter to vocabulary itself. Poets, Bernardino Parthenio wrote in his *Della imitatione poetica* (1560) must use words not in common use ("estratto dalla consuetudine"). In France, a central motif of the *Pléiade*'s program for enlarging the lexicon was to acquire, by Greek and Latin borrowings, by archaism, and by coinage, a stock of words specifically poetic. Poets who neglected to do so, Ronsard complained, wrote mere *prose rimée*. To his ears it often sounded no better than chatter ("caquet"), and even at best the result was deplorable because nothing is more destructive of the poetic effect than the tonality of prose. Prose was, quite simply, poetry's deadly enemy ("enemy capital de l'éloquence poétique"). If only because modern, one might say

Wordsworthian, taste in the matter is different, an example of this
scorned "rhymed prose" may afford some sense of what the term
then designated. Ronsard offers one:

> Madame en bonne foy je vous donne mon coeur,
>
> N'usez point envers moy s'il vous plaist de rigueur.

> [Lady, I give you my heart in good faith; please do not treat me
> harshly.]

Only the words *coeur* and *rigueur,* he declares, have no taint of
vulgarity or triviality! In England this degree of *préciosité,* rare in
any case, did not go unchallenged, as we are reminded by Jonson's
warning against language that strays too far from the common.
Since the early Tudor period, as Elizabeth Sweeting found, continued the Medieval tradition that "the diction of poetry was removed as far as possible from the language of everyday life," such
later cautions against artificial excess were wholesome.[17]

For the special topic of this book the most pertinent critical
document is not Sidney's sprightly *Apologie,* but the pedestrian
and more narrowly technical book ascribed to George Puttenham,
The Arte of English Poesie (1589). Dull or no, Puttenham easily
surpassed his contemporaries in what may be called an instinct for
theory. Despite an initially defensive stance (he feels obliged first
to convince his readers that there *may be* an art of vernacular poetry), his account touches on issues of enduring importance in poetics. His sound understanding of mimesis is unique in his time
and rare enough at any time. He sees no contradiction in a poet's
being at once an imitator of nature and an original creator. Having
boldly asserted that the poetry of the Greeks and Romans has no
exclusive claim to rational analysis, "our language being no lesse
copious, pithie, and significative then theirs,"[18] he proceeds to discuss poetry in general, its sources and types. A brief section on
"Proportion" explores the techniques of meter and stanzaic structure. Most of what is relevant to the present study appears in the
pages devoted to "Ornament," especially the chapters labeled "Of
Language" and "Of Style."

As the title of this section leads us to expect, Puttenham's discussion is liberally sprinkled with the clothing metaphor. He contrasts prose with the figured language in which poems are "gal-
lantly arrayed." Fortunately the trite metaphor seems to have been
already too moribund to blur his perception that the linguistic

forms peculiar to poetry are in fact much more than embellishments. Besides the intricacies of prosody, he begins, a good poet must handle

> language and stile, to such purpose as it may delight and allure as well the mynde as the eare of the hearers with a certaine noveltie and strange maner of conveyance, disguising it no litle from the ordinary and accustomed.

Only one phrase in this description is not a flat commonplace of Renaissance stylistics, and it is the most arresting: "as well the mynde." For Puttenham the style of any utterance, including poetry, is no mere added sweetener, like Sidney's sugar-coated pill, tempting readers to swallow the edifying content. Anticipating much said on the subject since, he calls style the image of a writer's mind. As the poet's thought ("conceits") are the stuff of his mental activity, so is "his manner of utterance the very warp and woofe of his conceits."[19]

Moreover, for Puttenham poetic utterance is much more than a perfection of ordinary language. In fact it is more nearly the very opposite. It is figurative speech. Only, as noted earlier, that category entails for him a transformation of syntax often so radical as to amount to a distinct expressive mode. "Figurative speech," he writes,

> is a noveltie of language evidently (and yet not absurdly) estranged from the ordinary habite and manner of our dayly talke and writing, and figure itselfe is a certaine lively or good grace set upon wordes, speaches, and sentences to some purpose and not in vaine, giving them ornament or efficacie by many maner of alterations in shape, in sounde, and *also in sence*, sometime by way of surplusage, sometime by defect, sometime by disorder, or mutation, & also by putting into our speaches more pithe and substance, subtilitie, quicknesse, efficacie, or moderation, in this or that sort turning and tempering them, by amplification, abridgement, opening, closing, enforcing, meekening, or otherwise disposing them to the best purpose.

A tall order!—and a tortuous and mysterious process dimly clarified by a long, pedantic list of the classical names for rhetorical tropes and figures (sometimes with fantastical English equivalents supplied as well, allegedly to make things easier for Puttenham's courtly readers).[20]

And here once again Puttenham assigns to poetic diction a distinctly intellectual function as well as an emotive one. In a tripartite division of figures which he credits to certain unspecified "learned clerks," he identifies a type proper to poetry alone, the *auricular,* having purely sensuous value; a second type, common to poetry and oratory, addressed exclusively to the mind, for which he coins the word *sensable* (careful to distinguish it from *sensible*); and a third type, the *sententious,* combining both functions, proper only to the extended "sentences" (i.e. moral generalizations) of an oration. The terms in this piece of rhetorical taxonomy suggest the classical separation of the figures of thought and speech. His third chapter opens with a further reference to the two kinds of poetic ornament, corresponding to the Greek terms *Enargia* (brilliance) and *Energia* (intensity), one "to satisfie & delight th'eare onely," the other "inwardly working a stirre to the mynde."[21]

It is perhaps regrettable, though in the historical context hardly surprising, that Puttenham neither developed these pregnant insights nor fully realized their implications for poetic theory. His rudimentary terminology makes no provision, for example, for the kind of locution that amalgamates the sensuous and the conceptual. At one point he makes a distant approach to the idea when he finds in the Greek figure of *analogy* a conformity "between the sence and the sensible." But this reference, left unillustrated, is vague and not directly or exclusively posited of poetic style.[22]

Puttenham's adumbrations of aspects of neoclassical poetics are obvious. He endorses the division of styles, accepted by theorists and poets since the *Ad Herennium,* according to the quality of the subject matter—the *high, meane,* and *base,* as Puttenham renders them. He also subscribes to the social source of poetic vocabulary that prevailed in theory, if frequently not in practice, at least until Romanticism. In Puttenham's version, the poet's proper vocabulary and dialect are those in conversational use within sixty miles of London by members of the gentry, preferably courtiers. No critic is more explicit in barring from the poet's lexicon all academic lingo, all provincialisms, and all patois of mechanics and rustics. This strict exclusion is the more noteworthy since Ronsard, whom Puttenham mentions elsewhere with respect, had in the *Abrégé* advised his fellow poets to enrich their stock of diction precisely from the various French regional dialects and the jargon of common workers as well, and not to depend too heavily on courtly speech ("sans affecter trop le parler de la court").[23] The apparent contradiction between this advice and Ronsard's call for a specially poetic diction may be resolved on the assumption that most plebeian words had never entered written prose. The point is doubtful though. In any case Puttenham's dictional exclusiveness remained the norm in theory, even though in England poetic practice often accorded more nearly with Ronsard's judgment.

Puttenham, for whom all "Poesie is a skill to speak & write harmonically," devoted the longest segment of his book to the various English meters, stanza forms, and rhyme schemes in current use. Here again, his recognition of the semantic value of these prosodic features reveals his sense that technique in poetry can belong as much to content as to form. He may be the first critic to notice that in English verse triple rhyme (*serénity, lénity*) works best with comic themes. He points out how the pattern of line lengths in a stanza, "even without respect of the rime," can affect the quality of what is being said. Elsewhere he shows how metrical stress can by itself direct meaning, illustrating the point by quotations from his own verse.[24]

No account of Elizabethan poetics can ignore the attempts by a few poets and critics to abandon rhyme and replace English accentual meter by the Greco-Roman quantitative system. The most elaborate case for this reform is Thomas Campion's meticulous *Observations in the Art of English Poesie* (1602). The weightiest case against it is Daniel's rejoinder in *A Defence of Ryme*.

The reformers' campaign was not the perversion of sanity and good sense suggested by Saintsbury's calling it "the craze for classical metres." It was not confined to England nor did it originate there. In Italy rhymeless quantitative vernacular verse was defended and illustrated in Claudio Tolomei's *Versi e Regole de la Nuova Poesia Toscana* (1539). In France notable advocates included Jacques de la Taille, in *La Manière de faire des vers en francais comme en grec et latin* (1573), and Jean Antoine de Baïf, in *Etrennes de poésie francoise* (1574). Both negative and positive forces enlivened the reformers' enterprise: a distaste for rhyme, thought to be a crudity introduced by "barbarians" after the collapse of Rome, and a genuine and quite reasonable love for the harmonies of classical verse. It was no mere reactionary impulse. Ascham, a defender of the vernacular, initiated the reform in its English phase. Nor was the attempted innovation devised exclusively by learned pedants. Sidney himself tried it in several of the poems in the *Arcadia;* so did Spenser and other good poets. Even after the campaign for it had petered out, Jonson in his *English Grammar* took his countrymen to task for their failure to establish a quantitative versification, "to the end our *Tongue* may be made equall to those of . . . *Italy* and *Greece,* touching this particular."[25]

The experiments with English quantitative verse made by Tennyson, Longfellow, Robert Bridges and Pound, suggest at least a provisional suspension of judgment on what the Elizabethans sought to accomplish. Their results vary greatly in quality. Ascham's specimens in his *Toxophilus* clearly fail, and he later admitted that the classical epic meter "doth rather trotte and hoble than runne smothly in our English tong," which too seldom accommodates dactylic feet. Yet it was he who first gave currency to the distich from Thomas Watson's version of Book I of the *Odyssey* which was frequently quoted by advocates of rhymeless quantity in aid of their cause:

> All travellers doo gladlie report great praise to Ullises,
>
> For that he knew manie mens manners, and saw many cities.

Inspected carefully, the prosody of these lines calls on the reader to respond to a double harmony that without suppressing the natural accent of the words forms them into feet according to the length of the syllables—that is, the *supposed* length as determined by classical rules of orthography and position. Webbe would thus keep the natural accentuation, but would scan *dying* as an iamb. Spenser, in one of the letters he exchanged with Harvey, took the same position. Why, he asks, may we not "measure our Accentes by the sounde, reserving the Quantitie to the Verse?" Campion's system is similar. While protesting that English accent is "diligently to be observed," he held that the name Trumpington in verse must be *scanned* Trumpíngton. Perhaps, as some modern scholars have maintained, Abraham Fraunce, whose hexameter *Lamentation of Amyntas* was highly popular, came closest to realizing Spenser's ideal. Yet that ideal not only runs counter to the natural cadence of English, as Daniel and others at the time noted; it is also self-defeatingly complex.[26]

The success of rhyme then and ever since has tended to overwhelm the force of any reasoning running counter to Daniel's solidly argued defense. Yet if, as most theorists now agree, verse differs from prose by its greater intensity, the Elizabethan case for quantitative meter was not entirely frivolous. Richard Stanyhurst, whose lame English tetrameter version of *Aeneid* I–IV appeared in 1582, put it forcefully. In quantitative verse, he wrote, "everye *foote*, every *word*, every *syllable*, yea everye *letter* is too be observed; in thee other, the last *woord* is onely too be heeded."[27]

Whatever the weight of reason in its favor, the effort to create an English quantitative verse failed. As Samuel Johnson was to caution, there is always an appeal open from critical logic to nature, in this case the nature of English, as Daniel saw. So in part did his chief opponent in the debate. Recognizing that the frequency of English monosyllables prevented the ready formation of dactylic feet, Campion ruled out the hexameter as "altogether against the nature of our language," which he thought would tolerate only iambs and trochees.[28]

For that same reason Thomas Nashe would have none of the classical versification. His ear assured him that the hexameter "goes twitching and hopping in our language like a man running upon quagmires." Yet Harvey, whose opinions he was rebutting, was willing to be "epitaphed" as the inventor of the English hexameter, just as several gifted poets since have thought it well worth trying to bring off, in the hope that readers would come to relish the patterned interchange of syllable lengths over that of stresses. This in fact was Campion's own faith. The ear, he thought, "is a rationall sence," and upon that assurance he finally rested his case:

> Some eares accustomed altogether to the fatnes of rime may perhaps except against the cadences of these numbers; but let any man iudicially examine them, and he shall finde they close of themselves so perfectly that the help of rime were not only in them superfluous but also absurd.[29]

But it was Daniel who spoke for the common taste when he wrote that English verse

> though it doth not strictly observe long and short sillables, yet it most religiously respects the accent; and as the short and the long make number, so the acute and grave [i.e., stressed and unstressed] yield harmonie.[30]

CHAPTER THREE

Neoclassicism I

BETWEEN THE RESTORA-
tion and the French Revolution, English literary thinking retained
several doctrines and opinions prevalent during the Renaissance.
Among them was a relatively low assessment of English as a poetic
medium that persisted despite the ebullient confidence of the
1590s. Though he sought and achieved acclaim as a translator of
classical poetic masterpieces, Dryden himself joined those who decried the inferiority of English to the classical tongues. Believing
that languages were among the cultural institutions subject to cy-
cles of growth and decay, he shared the general sense that English
had long been undergoing an amelioration that was still in progress
during his own time but could never reach equivalence with the
Latin of Virgil and Horace. That hope was frustrated, Dryden
thought, by two inherent deficiencies, one peculiar to English, the
other common to all modern languages: the preponderance of
monosyllables and the almost total lack of inflection, deleterious respectively to the aural beauty and the expressive concision of a line
of verse. The unequaled economy of Virgil's style, he wrote in the
preface to his English *Aeneid,* was made possible by a language that
could convey much meaning in a few words, whereas modern languages like English "have more articles and pronouns, besides signs
of tenses and cases, and other barbarities on which our speech is
built by the faults of our forefathers." Virgil's Latin could comprehend in "one word what we are constrained to express in two. . . .

[T]he word *pater,* for example, signifies not only *a* father, but *your* father, *my* father, *his* or *her* father, all included in one word." Then there was what seventeenth-century writers felt as the melodic limitations of English. Though opposed to promiscuous importation of foreign words, Dryden was therefore driven sometimes to "latinize."

> Poetry requires ornament, and that is not to be had from our old Teuton monosyllables; therefore, if I find an elegant word in a classic author, I propose it to be naturalized, by using it myself; and, if the public approves of it, the bill passes.[1]

Since the Romantic period, English readers have no longer found monosyllabic lines repulsive per se, a shift in taste no easier to explain than many other imponderables of historical change. Critics as diverse as Hazlitt and Saintsbury even regarded the high frequency of monosyllabic verses as a special advantage to English poetry. To the seventeenth-century ear, however, they were simply harsh. Only very rarely, Dryden observes, can one of them sound harmonious, like the first line of his own *Aeneid:*

Arms and the man I sing, who, forc'd by fate.

An even better example, he modestly adds, occurs in Thomas Creech's translation of Manilius:

Nor could the world have borne so fierce a flame.

Little was said to explain the causes of a distaste which lingered into the following century. In supporting Dryden's opinion, Johnson thought that the unpleasant effect was caused by the fact that English monosyllables normally begin and end with consonants. Whatever the source of the irritant, it played a large part in Dryden's gloomy conclusion that "the poverty of our language" thwarted any hope of raising his translation to aesthetic parity with Virgil's universally admired original.[2]

He could not endorse an optimistic faith that great poetry, the product of a human instinct transcending particular cultures and languages, was always possible. Individual literary geniuses, Dryden was sure, were born in vain unless the idiom of their time and place was suited to lofty poetic expression. His contemporaries largely agreed. Greek, William Wotton declared in *Reflections upon Ancient and Modern Learning* (1690), was in this respect above every other language. Great talent is vital, he conceded;

> yet the Language itself has so great an Influence, that if *Homer* and *Virgil* had been *Polanders* or *High-Dutch* Men, they would never in all probability have thought it worth their while to attempt the writing of Heroick Poems.[3]

Although the new century never revived the scheme of a rhymeless quantitative prosody, a few critics continued to damn rhyme itself. They considered this worst of the language's inherited "barbarisms" alone sufficient, despite the much-hailed metrical refinements of Edmund Waller, to defeat any chance that English poetry might one day rival the glories of the ancient. The report is mixed, however, because though rhyme had few consistent defenders, it had its apologists, Dryden (on occasion) among them. Though opposed to rhyme in tragic verse, Thomas Rymer dismissed as a "slender Sophistry" Milton's polemic against "the jingling sound of like endings" in the prefatory note to *Paradise Lost*. Dryden too censured Milton for having written his epic in blank verse, although he later confessed that by rhyming his own English *Aeneid* he had wronged Virgil. Many writers, tolerant of rhyme in the lesser genres, objected to using it in epic (as detracting from its stateliness) and in tragedy (as too remote from live speech). The philosopher Hobbes thought the more intricate rhyming suitable in sonnets out of place in epic, a "difficult toy" apt to force a poet to say what he never intended. Sir William Temple, outspoken champion of the "Ancient" party, predictably condemned the device outright.[4]

It may seem strange that in this first phase of English neoclassicism, when the chief poetic masterpieces were composed in heroic couplets, the most influential purveyors of literary opinion adopted a generally negative stance on rhyme. The fact is a reminder of the frequent discrepancy between the literary theory of a period, or some tenet of that theory, and the best work of its literary artists, the preferences of its readers, or both.[5] In those who were both poets and critics, the clash made for the irony of Ben Jonson's "Fit of Rhyme against Rhyme," which opens with points of indictment echoed throughout the rest of the century in which they were written.

Rhyme, the rack of finest wits
That expresseth but by fits

> True conceits,
> Spoiling senses of their treasure,
> Cozening judgment with a measure,
> But false weight;
> Wresting words from their true calling,
> Propping verse for fear of falling
> To the ground.[6]

The brilliantly effective rhyming of Dryden's great satires and his choice of heroic measures for his epic translations did not prevent his repeated disparagement of the technique. In him the ambivalence produced by the opposition of theoretical conviction and creative experience seems especially sharp. His earliest published pronouncement in 1664 is an unqualified vindication of "the new way" of rhymed staged dialogue, expressed in terms which broaden to a general defense of rhyme in all verse. Besides the interesting heuristic notion that the search for a rhyming word may often "bring forth the richest and clearest Thoughts," as Daniel had also reported, Dryden reasserts the familiar claims that rhyme checks a poet's errant fancy and aids a reader's memory, along with the familiar disparagement of blank verse as only "measured prose." Four years later, in the essay *Of Dramatick Poesie* and the *Defence* of it, came his skillful vindication of rhyming tragedy, which expounds a centrally mimetic theory still compelling despite his subsequent shift to blank verse in his own plays. Yet even during these early years he regretted that the final rhyming syllable sometimes weakened or distorted the rest of a verse line.[7]

Nothing better reveals Dryden's dubiety on the question than the oxymoronic metaphors to which it moved him. In the *Defence* (1668), rhyme appears as a usurper in the kingdom of poetry, but a brave, generous, and delightful usurper; in 1684 he called it a "fair barbarity" in Petrarch's lyrics. When Dryden's praises of rhyme are unqualified, they are often suspect as cases of special pleading, as when he exalts it to "the last perfection of Art" in the preface to his rhyming tragedy *The Conquest of Granada* (1672). He is all too ready to accuse its disparagers, even Milton, of a hostility motivated by their own lack of skill in handling a prosodic device which he himself so abundantly possessed. At times he seems to have seen in "the shackles of modern rhyme" a kind of challenge to achievement, a poet's success in meeting it being proof of superior talent. "Now if a Muse cannot run when she is unfettered," he writes in the preface to the *Aeneid*, "'tis a sign she has but little speed." Anyone who does well in rhyme, he boasts, may do even better in blank verse; the best poets are those who, like Francis Quarles, George Withers, and himself, suffer least under its restraint. Yet he concedes that the unpleasant prosodic game hardly repays the poet's struggle. "What it adds to sweetness, it takes away from sense; and he that loses least by it may be called a gainer."[8]

The weightiest theoretical legacy which antiquity and the Renaissance passed on to neoclassicism was the ornamental conception of poetic style. Till the dawn of Romanticism, writers continued to regard the characteristics of verse as raiment adorning the "body" of a poet's thought. These include meter (usually), syntactical deviations from the prose norm, the sensuous effect of imagery on fancied sight, and of rhyme, onomatopoeia, and alliteration on the ear. As the new century opened, Chapman defined proper poetic translation as a two-step process: first to grasp an author's thoughts and doctrine, and then "to clothe and adorn them with words." Formal prose composition too is sometimes conceived in this way, but here the image of adornment is not always one of approval. A trustworthy historiographer, Edmund Bolton warned his readers in *Hypercritica*, restrains himself in this regard, lest his style, which is only "the Coat and Apparel of matter," cause deception. In duller-minded critics, however, the vestiary conception encouraged the grotesque view that since poetry was an art whose medium was a mechanism for communicating thought, its formal properties were at best a pleasant veneer and at worst an encumbrance. William Alexander's *Anacrisis* (ca. 1634) combines these two notions in a single paragraph of tangled phrasing that helps to assess our debt to the prose of Dryden's essays. "Language," Alexander wrote,

> is but the Apparel of Poesy, which may give Beauty, but no Strength; and when I censure any Poet, I first dissolve the general Contexture of his Work in several Pieces, to see what Sinews it hath, and to mark what will remain behind, when that the external Gorgeousness, consisting in the Choice or Placing of Words, as if it would bribe the Ear to corrupt the Judgment, is first removed, or at least only marshalled in its own Degree. I value Language as a Conduit, the variety thereof to several Shapes, and adorned Truth or witty Inventions that which it should deliver.[9]

A less frequent metaphor for poetic style substitutes the colors of a painting for a body's apparel. By 1701 it had earned sufficient credit to supply a line in George Granville's *Essay upon Unnatural Flights in Poetry:* "Words are the paint by which their [poets'] thoughts are shown." For this analogy English critics had precedent in Renaissance Italy, where, unlike the overworked and more perfunctory image of dress, it was often invoked by writers who assigned a crucial place to the poet's command of language. Unless he cultivates his verbal skill, Ludovico Dolce wrote, the poet labors in vain, because meter and diction are the indispensable brush and colors which he employs to fashion his ravishing portraits of nature ("I versi e le parole sono il penello, ed il colori del Poeta"). For some two centuries this correspondence between the media of poetry and painting continued to draw special force from the popular doctrine of *ut pictura poesis,* the slogan misappropriated from Horace's *Ars poetica* to assimilate "sister arts" which employed different means for their shared imitation of nature. In his authoritative *Reflections on Poetry and Painting* (1719), the Abbé du Bos affirmed the direct correspondence of pictorial colors with "that part of the poetic art that consists in the choice and order of words."[10]

Equating the poet's words to the medium of another art, one so essential as color is to painting, would seem to promise a higher valuation of diction than that implied in the clothing metaphor. Yet although Dryden himself, like Dolce, used the image to argue the central importance of verbal mastery to the poet's success, its occasional adoption by other neoclassical critics did little to dispel the notion that the style of a poem had mainly an ornamental function. One reason for this may be the relatively low status accorded to coloring itself in Renaissance and Enlightenment pictorial theory. It ranked lowest and came last in pictorial creation, after invention (choice and treatment of the subject) and design (delineation and spatial arrangement), as Dolce himself conceded in his *Dialogo della pittura* (1557). The point is duly stressed in Charles Alphonse du Fresnoy's *De arte graphica* (1668), the most respected discussion exploiting the parallel between painting and poetry.[11]

Appropriately, it is in the preface to his translation of Du Fresnoy that Dryden first mentions the correspondence between the media of the two arts: "all that belongs to words, is that in a Poem which Colouring is in a Picture." He appeals to classical authority for this modern idea, freely rendering Horace's "operumque colores" in the *Ars poetica* as "words and elegant expressions." Like other critics, he uses the parallel to depreciate all that poets characteristically do with language.

> The Words, the Expressions, the Tropes and Figures, the Versification, and all the other Elegancies of Sound . . . perform exactly the same Office [as coloring] both in Dramatick and Epique Poetry. Our author calls Colouring the *Lena Sororis;* in plain English, The Bawd of her Sister, the Design or Drawing.

A few pages later he mingles the two metaphors of color and dress in comparing the sister arts. The poet's words clothe his thought "in the same sense as Colours are the cloathing of the [painter's] Design."[12]

Dryden's personal sensitivity to the power of verse language and the high esteem he had for masterly versification were sharply at variance with these sentiments. Nonetheless, they constituted the received opinion on the matter. To discredit those who defended modern poetry by pointing to its stylistic attractions, Temple needed only to remind his readers that even with this advantage it had "at the best but the Beauty of Colouring in a Picture"—by which he was readily understood to mean the beauty of a peripheral if not suspect order. In a letter to his friend Henry Cromwell, the youthful Pope belittled Richard Crashaw's poetry for its lack of design, form, and fable, which are "the soul of poetry," and of structure ("consent of parts"), which is its "Body." Crashaw he classed among mere amateurs whose work offers pretty conceits, striking metaphors, and "something of a neat cast of verse. . . . And (to express myself like a Painter) their Colouring entertains the sight, but the Lines and Life of the picture are not to be inspected too narrowly." In the preface to his English *Iliad*, Pope speaks more favorably of poetic diction. Although he follows the established procedure of treating it as last and least of the epic's constituent parts ("If we descend from hence to the *Expression*. . ."), he now uses the color analogy to convey his delight in Homer's verbal resources.

> We acknowledge him the Father of Poetical Diction, the first who taught that *Language of the Gods* to Men. His Expression is like the colouring of some great Masters.

What was by then a commonplace in poetic discussion had become a faded metaphor by the time Johnson listed an ability "to display the colours of varied diction" among requirements for successful composition.[13]

Another norm held over from the past is the social source of poetic diction. A poet, above all an epic poet, should stock his "magazine of words" (the phrase is Dryden's) from the conversation of gentlemen, the ideal idiom being that of court and city, much as Puttenham had advised. "Elegance of Language," Thomas Sprat observed, is learned from urban conversation, and he reflected complacently that Abraham Cowley did not lose it after his rustication. The neoclassical ideal also authorized archaisms, sparingly admitted, and neologisms, even more sparingly admitted, for lack of a suitable current word. Sharing the common opinion that both Spenser and Milton had overindulged in archaisms, Dryden still justifies those which are more "sounding" and "significant" than any modern alternative.[14]

Despite these overlappings of doctrine, the poetics promulgated by critics in pre- and post-Cromwellian England contrast in important respects only less sharply than do the matter and manner of the contemporary verse and prose. As such things go, the changes were notably deliberate, aspects of a broader cultural mutation that was very much in the forefront of enlightened contemporary consciousness. Dryden and his fellows thought of themselves as literary advocates of a new Augustan age, not so much the continuators of an immediate past as the initiators of something new and better. Their program envisioned a literary order ending the former lawlessness in the republic of letters, an order to match the political Restoration effected by King Charles's return to the throne. Literary and political developments were thus seen as parallel ameliorations, replacing fanaticism and social turbulence with reason and order, the political taken to be ground and guarantee of the literary. Before this happy time, as Dryden wrote early in the new king's reign, his subjects had been "so long together bad *Englishmen* that [they] had not leisure to be good Poets." For all their pride in England's Elizabethan glories, a profound change of taste ruled out any return to the norm of poetic expression prevalent during those fervid times. Perverse as it may sometimes seem to modern students of English poetry, that norm had come to be felt and often described as simply crude. To the relatively fastidious sensibilities of Restoration lovers of verse, the far-ranging polyphony of Elizabethan song and sonnet—the richly varied cadences of a dramatic verse that has captivated generations of readers since at least Johnson's day—seemed downright messy. The four disputants of Dryden's essay *Of Dramatick Poesie* were agreed that "the sweetness of *English* Verse was never understood or practis'd by our fathers." For worthy native models they looked rather to such recent reformers as Edmund Waller and John Denham, and for precept, to ancient authority.[15]

Necessarily responsive to intellectual currents of its own time, English neoclassical poetics is of course no mere replay of classical literary theory. Among contemporary developments especially relevant to this study were the epistemologies promulgated first by Cartesian rationalism and then by the empiricism of Hobbes and Locke, along with the emergence of the scientific method for which they so largely provided the conceptual foundation. Since qualified modern scholars have thoroughly investigated this crisis in Western intellectual history, we need only note here that the improved status of prose as uniquely fit for communicating sound knowledge infused new urgency into the question of what set verse apart from the form of discourse which was now threatening to arrogate any cognitive function exclusively to itself. The resulting change in the perception of the poet's office which this altered valuation of the two age-old modes of written expression seemed to entail materially reshaped poetic theory. The change is directly reflected in the critics' heightened concern with how poets could most effectively employ the medium they shared with writers of prose.[16]

This theme of neoclassical literary theory therefore constitutes yet another defense of poetry, this time against an imminent subversion of the long-established didactic superiority of poetry to prose. The traditional claim was by no means abandoned. Hobbes wrote that a prose writer, like a mere pedestrian traveler, contended in vain against the poet, who had "the strength and wings of *Pegasus.*" Locke cautioned against setting aside the common reader's preference for at least minimum conformity to the norms of graceful expression. He even recognized that

> philosophy itself, though it likes not a gaudy dress, yet when it appears in public, must have so much complacency as to be clothed in the ordinary fashion and language of the country, so far as it can consist with truth and perspicuity.

But such concessions were now asserted in the face of a new criterion of intellectual utility, by which truth and perspicuity required the *least poetic* style. Prose of a transparency unclouded by the impurities of imagery and showy rhythmical patterns therefore gained prestige, necessarily at poetry's expense.[17]

The resulting defense comprised, broadly speaking, two contradictory strategies. One, conceding the justice of the new standard, sought to combine a lexical and syntactical rapprochement of poetry and prose with metrical form. Sprat praised Cowley's Pindaric poems for their "near affinity with Prose" and was glad to think that Cowley's loose meter would not "corrupt our Prose, which is certainly the most useful kind of Writing of all others, for it is the style of all business and conversation."[18] In at least its more simplistic formulations, prone to condemn all but the barest figuration in a poem as "bombast" or "fustian," this response may strike us as too desperate a recourse to the expediency of "if you can't lick 'em, join 'em." It is not even clear, as is sometimes assumed, that the altered valuation played any appreciative role in the rise of that "poetry of statement" so distasteful to Victorian readers but since their day ranked again among the notable achievements of Enlightenment letters. Yet it is this motif of Restoration criticism that literary historians, highlighting such things as Sprat's denigration of metaphor in his *History of the Royal Society* (published in the same year as *Paradise Lost*), have emphasized to the general neglect of the opposing strategy.

Yet that strategy in fact predominated throughout the entire neoclassical period. Variously formulated, its basic tenet, as Sprat summarily expressed it in 1711, was that poetry must be "set off at as great a Distance from Prose as possible." In itself hardly novel, this doctrine was pushed in neoclassical poetics to an extreme typified by its stress on a set of prohibitions and proscriptions. Whatever its effect on the actual practice of poets, the theoretically approved vocabulary of poetry was now smaller than at any other period of English literature. Poetry was to eschew words used in mean conversation and the technical words of trades and professions, as Hobbes, thinking mainly of the epic, told Davenant. Dryden was not long in recanting his early justification of the sea-terms in his *Annus Mirabilis,* instead praising Virgil for keeping his *Aeneid* free of "the Cant of any Profession." Not only in England, but in France too theorists of the epic had all along felt some uncertainty about admitting technical terms. In 1654 Georges de Scudéry confessed in the preface to his *Alaric* a concern that readers unfamiliar with the arts of war, navigation, and hunting must justly object to his use of language peculiar to those pursuits. But as he also suggested, the would-be epic poet faced a dilemma arising from a contradiction within epic theory itself. This greatest of the literary kinds was supposed to be, as was claimed for Homer's, a repository of all learning, a requirement hard to meet without some learned terminology. At the same time, its appeal had to be universal, comprehensible to all sorts and conditions of literate readers, not alone lawyers, mariners, architects, and such. Scudéry elected to honor the epic poet's obligation not to speak amiss of things he "ought to be familiar with," just as young Dryden had chosen to risk bemusing landlubber readers of *Annus Mirabilis* with *oakum, calking iron,* and *marling.* But the choice ran counter to what was to remain a general assumption about poetic speech for over a century thereafter. His later cautious use of salty expressions in his translation of the *Aeneid* did not escape the censure of the young Pope in writing to Cromwell, "because no Terms of Art, or Cant-Words, suit with the Majesty & Dignity of Style [which] Epic Poetry requires." In his *Life* of Dryden (1779), Johnson condemned the stanzas of *Annus Mirabilis* where the sea-terms appear; and he did so by confident appeal to what by then had been expanded from a proscription imposed on epic style to a general rule that all poetry must "speak an universal language."[19]

Edward Phillips, it is true, defends in his *Theatrum Poetarum* (1675) the use of both obsolescent and technical terms in the epic, doubtless with his uncle Milton's daunting example in mind. His tolerance defied a disapproval, however, shared even by Milton's most ardent admirers and all admirers of heroic poetry well into the eighteenth century. Joseph Addison, who devoted eighteen *Spectator* papers to a highly laudatory analysis of *Paradise Lost,* lists among the poem's few faults Milton's free recourse to the jargon of architects and astronomers: *cornice, architrave, ecliptic,* and so forth. On this point as on some others neoclassical stylistic predilection sometimes ran afoul of classical practice, to the special embarrassment of translators. Pope complained in a postscript to his English *Odyssey* that Homer

> seems to have taken upon him the character of an Historian, Antiquary, Divine, and Professor of Arts and Sciences; as well as a Poet. In one or other of these characters he descends into many particularities which as a Poet only perhaps he would have avoided.

His translator, he concluded, can therefore do no better than "to make them as poetical as the subject will bear."[20]

This particular restriction was limited in its practical effects because technical terms are few in any vocabulary and in most genres there is little occasion for them. Yet even terms that might by sound or referential dignity be acceptable were sometimes proscribed. Dryden's use of *diapason* in his first *Ode for St. Cecilia's Day*, which must surely strike many readers today as a happy choice for both sound and sense in a poem celebrating the emotive power of music, did not escape Johnson's censure, despite Milton's prior use of it in "At a Solemn Music."[21]

A much greater retrenchment of the authorized poetic diction came from the ban on "low" words and expressions used in casual talk. Besides embracing a much larger part of the lexicon, this interdiction applied in some degree to virtually every genre of noncomic verse. The century-and-a-half in question never formulated any clear definition of the category or entirely agreed on what words belonged on the prohibited list. Presumably, sensitive readers and poets would no more need an explicit rule to guide them than a well-bred person would need a handbook of good manners for deciding how to behave in any social situation. The broad consensus simply fell short of unanimity. "We are all offended by low terms," Johnson observed in a *Rambler* paper, "but we are not disgusted alike by the same composition because we do not all agree to censure the same terms as low." Still, a perusal of the contemporary discussion provides a rough categorization. The epithets *vulgar* and *low* designated not only slang and scatology, as we should expect, but as well the language of mundane usage that would be readily acceptable in some kinds of prose. Often the criterion is overtly social. The speech of the lower classes, especially the words pertaining to their domestic and occupational activities, was held unfit for serious verse.[22]

Expletives and various connectives and relational words, effective enough in prose, comprised another excluded group. Dryden's water-borne debaters in the essay *Of Dramatick Poesie* derided a wretched versifier who propped his sagging lines "with *For to* and *Unto*, and all the pretty expletives he can find," which Pope in the next age was first to damn in a letter to Cromwell as "meer fillers up of unnecessary syllables" and then to ridicule in deft parody:

While *Expletives* their feeble Aid *do* join.[23]

The gradual elimination of such syntactical deadweight was credited to the prosodic reforms initiated by Waller and Denham. In 1685 Robert Wolseley looked back with complacent scorn at the profusions of *forto*'s, *until*'s, and *thereon*'s, along with "those useful [*ironice*] expletives" in the ill-made verses of his grandsire's day. The Earl of Shaftesbury specifies the main ground of the objection as an adulteration of verse with "prosaic" impurities. In the *Characteristics* (1711) there is the grudging concession that modern poets have in some measure rid themselves of

> the gouty joints and darning-work of wherewith's, thereof's, therewith's and the rest of this kind, by which complicated periods are so curiously strung or hooked-on to one another, after the long-spun manner of the bar and the pulpit.[24]

A critique of one of Waller's poems in John Dennis' early dialogue entitled *The Impartial Critick* (1693)—an example of explicative criticism then very rare—instances the dictional prohibitions enumerated above. Though Dennis shares the universal opinion that Waller had much improved "the Language of our Verse" and taught Englishmen "the Musick of a just Cadence," his fastidious spokesman pronounces the reformer's own poetic *oeuvre* deficient. Even his much praised "To the King, on His Navy," which the finicky Thomas Rymer himself had judged faultless, Dennis blames for dictional blemishes. The words *sped, fray,* and *fishes* are "too burlesque" for the poem's heroic subject, *heretofore* too archaic, and the pleonasm *Liquid main* objectionable because "every epithet is to be look'd upon as a Botch, which does not add to the thought."[25] This last in Dennis's list of alleged blemishes must give us pause for its direct contradiction of earlier opinion, including Aristotle's inclusion of redundancies like *white milk* among the stylistic differentiae of verse. But then defiance of classical authority is not surprising in so outspoken a "Modern" as Dennis.

Despite the vagueness caused by terminological imprecision and idiosyncratic opinion, four overlapping qualities emerge as the basic desiderata in the neoclassical conception of poetic language: *clarity, semantic intensity, propriety,* and *elegance.* Clarity, or lucidity, was especially threatened by technical usages, punning, and unrestrained archaism and coining, and enhanced by avoiding as much as possible the vagaries of live talk. In enjoining lucidity and a ban on vulgar verbiage, the reigning predilection favored the classical ideal expressed by Aristotle's observation in the *Poetics:* "The perfection of style is to be clear without being mean." The rejection of expletives is especially referable to the second quality—semantic weight, intensity, or, in the common designation of that age, *significance.* The "gouty joints" of connective particles, especially such meter-wasting polysyllables as *heretofore,* were felt to contribute no more to the

sense of a line than did redundant epithets. The rationale of their exclusion was expressed most uncompromisingly by Voltaire's declaration that verses which did not express *more* and express it *better* and
faster ("mieux et plus vite") than prose could do, were simply bad
verses. With the advent of Romanticism, clarity yielded gradually to
suggestiveness as a virtue of poetic utterance, even at last to Poe's
ideal of "indefiniteness," and has never since regained its neoclassical
esteem. Eliot's assertion that he could enjoy passages of verse which
he could not understand (Shakespeare's, for example) would have
seemed as ludicrous during the Enlightenment as the obscurity of
modern verse lay outside the ambience of its creative possibilities. In
contrast, semantic intensity has been a staple of theory in every period, more than ever stressed in the poetics of the last half-
century. Because it is now seen that a poem's special aesthetic quality depends on its "being supercharged with significance," in W. K.
Wimsatt's phrase, we can read with renewed approval Swift's self-
deprecating envy of his friend Pope, who

> can in one Couplet fix
> More Sense than I can do in six.[26]

The remaining two qualities, propriety and elegance, show
that the pre-Romantic idea of poetic style was not entirely prohib-
itive. Yet though elegance is conceived as resulting more from
what a poet does with language than what he avoids doing, propriety shows that even the positive norms of the period were often
expressed in proscriptive terms. Although this tendency is never
entirely absent from formulations of ideal poetic style in any age
(think of Ezra Pound's list of "don't's"), neoclassical propriety
marks its heyday. The nice conformity between propriety and the
image of verbal dress is caught in the familiar couplets of Pope's
enshrinement of the accepted literary lore.

> Expression is the Dress of *Thought,* and still
> Appears more *decent* as more *suitable;*
> A vile Conceit in pompous Words exprest,
> Is like a Clown in regal Purple drest.[27]

In their full import, propriety and elegance are best understood as respective correlatives of the decorous and the decorated.

Dictional decorum required that the words of a poem be adapted not alone to the larger contexts of genre and subject but mutually to one another as well. The boy Dryden was much taken by a passage in Joshua Sylvester's popular English version of Guillaume du Bartas's *Divine Weeks and Days* (1598):

> Now, when the Winter's keener breath began
>
> To crystallize the Baltic Ocean,
>
> To glaze the lakes, to bridle up the floods,
>
> And periwig with snow [wool] the bald-pate woods.

But the mature critic came to see it as so much "abominable fustian," the ideas and words in it mutually unsuited. Genuine poetry is distinguished by both conceptual and verbal propriety. Conceptual propriety, Dryden wrote, results when a poet's thoughts are those suggested by his subject; verbal propriety is attained by "the clothing of those thoughts with such Expressions as are naturally proper to them; and from both of these . . . the delight of Poetry results." No tenet of poetics could better illustrate the extent to which poetics itself is dependent on the character of the prevailing intellectual climate. It rests on two assumptions. One is the much discussed belief in a universal psychology. Fundamental truth being common in every age and clime, all readers may agree on the thoughts proper to a given occasion. Individual reactions were simply aberrant or too trivial for communication. The other is a confidence in a correspondence between the objective world and human conception and language that has since attenuated. In the century after Dryden, however, Johnson could still include "impropriety of ornament" in the triad of deficiencies named in *Rambler* 122 as obstacles to a poet's success.[28] In Dennis, who censured Richard Blackmore's image of a "boiling soul" because the two things compared in a metaphor "ought to be *eiusdem generis*," the principle is pushed to pedantic absurdity—as though poor Blackmore hadn't fair warrant (whether he or Dennis recalled it or not) in Shakespeare's phrase "beating mind" (*The Tempest*, IV, I).[29]

Despite their interinvolvement, the ideas of propriety and elegance have to be kept separate because a choice of words proper to a given subject may fall short of elegance, which usually implied figurative embellishment. Yet the two qualities are interdependent in that elegance presupposes propriety, can hardly exist without it. Their subtle coalescence heightens the appeal of many memorable passages of neoclassical verse, as in the exquisite lines from Pope's "To Burlington":

> Another age shall see the golden Ear
>
> Embrown the Slope, and nod on the Parterre,
>
> Deep Harvests bury all his pride has planned,
>
> And laughing Ceres reassume the land.

The association of propriety and elegance is explicit in Dryden's "Apology for Heroic Poetry and Poetic License" (1677). This essay is especially representative of the period's conception of poetic language because its exposition of verse style responds to two diametrically opposed norms of written expression then prevalent. One, hostile to metaphorical elaboration as an obstacle to truth, was generated by the rationalism and empiricism alluded to above. The other came from the new vogue of Longinus's *On the Sublime*, commending an elevated style designed to elicit emotional transport rather than rational persuasion. Dryden's Longinianism is moderate. He values the Greek rhetorician mainly as an ally in defending the poet's traditional liberty (then under attack by a positivistic epistemology) "of speaking things in Verse which are beyond the severity of Prose." But Dryden's argument is no invitation to poets to indulge in unbridled artistic fancy. For him a central theoretical issue was at stake: "that particular character which distinguishes and sets the bound between *oratio soluta* [prose] and poetry." Whether he conceived this distinction to be one of kind or only of degree remains, I think, uncertain in Dryden's critical writing. Clearly, though, he regarded prose as a separate art, that "other harmony" which often answered his creative urge as an alternative choice to metrical composition, as he confessed in the preface to his *Fables* (1700). At the same time there is no doubt that he regarded poetry as the form *par excellence* of verbal art, the product of literary genius, or, as he most often called it in the usage of his day, wit. His pithy definition of this quality exacts a mutual entailment of the two criteria: "a propriety of Thoughts and Words; or, in other terms, Thoughts and Words elegantly adapted to the subject." Like the analogy of clothing which the notion of elegance suggests, this definition remained a critical *point de repère* for a good hundred years.[30]

As the next chapter will show, elegance, as a term subsuming the other three, finally came to designate in France and England alike the compendium of neoclassical stylistic excellence.

The consensus that John Dryden is the representative proponent of the literary criticism of his time obscures an important respect in which he was very nearly the opposite. In his preoccupation with prosodic technique, with metrical skill, and above all with poetic diction, he was unique among his contemporaries and has no worthy counterpart in the eighteenth century. As George Saintsbury accurately put it, Dryden was " a constant critical student of language and style."[31] I think it more than coincidental that for a parallel case we have to go to two other major English poet-critics, Coleridge and Eliot, whose interest in the subject was whetted, guided, and informed by personal creative experience. It is probably significant too that each of them played a major part in initiating a revolution of poetic style. Though it might be argued that the change was less sweeping in Dryden's case, all three began their careers when a momentary exhaustion of poetic vitality forced them to reconsider the perennial problem of how to make works of art out of a medium universally employed for non-aesthetic expression and constantly debased by use—because in all three cases, though perhaps not to the same extent, it came to that. Moreover, when they are closely examined, the "solutions" evolved by the three appear as redefinitions of the relation between the spoken idiom and the language of verse.

Throughout his career Dryden voiced his assent to the doctrine that assigned only an ancillary role to diction in the whole art of poetry. The clothing image is ubiquitous in his pages. Even when stressing a translator's necessary concern with his author's words he dubs them "the more outward Ornaments." To the end, he publicly endorsed the opinion most authoritatively propounded in the *Trâité du poème épique* (1675) by René Le Bossu, "the best of modern critics," that word choice and order deserved the poet's last and least attention. In the preface to the *Fables* Dryden censures Hobbes for having made diction, the mere "colouring of the work," which ranks lowest, the "first beauty of an epic poem." Nowhere in his mature criticism does he recant his opinion of 1672. If you remove Shakespeare's verbal bombast, he asserted, and "dress" him in "the most vulgar words," he loses nothing. His beautiful thoughts remain unscathed. (Our current translators of Shakespeare into modern English prose cannot even claim full originality for their silly project. In Dryden's defense, however, we should remember that his remark occupies a position well below theirs on the scale of literary inanity. He would still have applauded Coleridge's quip that a prose Shakespeare was something like a square circle.)[32]

So incompatible are Dryden's recitals of the accepted credo with his opinions on poetic style whenever he confronts individual cases that they may be regarded as so many prudential obeisances to the official line. Ardent experience gave the lie to theory. Now and then the conflicting impulses appear together. A good playwright, he observes, attends first to plot and character. Only after these have been determined should he turn to scenic structure, "descriptions, similitudes [similes and metaphors], and propriety of language." Yet he immediately adds that these last are the poet's main business, because they afford him the largest play of fancy, which is his "principal quality" and "gives the life-touches, and the secret graces" to his creations. Dryden can hardly discuss any poet ancient or modern without examining his diction, sometimes to the near neglect of everything else. For him even the obvious shortcomings of topic or moral import may be redeemed by a poet's expressive powers. He admits that several subjects celebrated in Virgil's *Georgics*—plagues, battling bulls, bees—lack both importance and intrinsic appeal, "but the words wherewith he describes them are so excellent that it might be well applied to him which was said by Ovid, *materiam superabat opus*" (the execution excelled the subject matter). He could even declare, speaking of translation, that some beauties of verse result exclusively from the poet's linguistic mastery. Not that John Dryden was a formal purist born two centuries before his time. However ravished by verbal fluency, a reader, he knows, is "but half satisfied" if a poem is not informed by the moral truth which poets no less than philosophers are bound to serve.[33]

Freely granting that traditional classical assumption, Dryden can nonetheless affirm that "Versification, and Numbers are the greatest Pleasures of Poetry." At moments they seem to constitute for him the whole attraction. He complains that his predecessors in translating Juvenal (Barten Holyday and Robert Stapylton), though faithful to their author's meaning, missed "the Poetical part of him, his Diction and his Elocution." Dryden's reverence for Virgil is directed almost exclusively to "the *dictio Virgiliana*, the expression of *Virgil*, his Colouring," where every word is so unerringly chosen as to admit no adequate substitute. No other issue so dramatically moves him to break the equable tone of his critical prose. "Good Heavens!" he exclaims in excited delight at a favorite spot in the *Aeneid*, "how the plain sense is raised by the Beauty of the words!" Finely crafted lines inspire him to rapture. Perhaps no other passage in Dryden's literary criticism is more

memorable than one which poignantly mingles the critic's relish
with the translator's despair.

> What Modern Language, or what Poet, can express the Majestic
> Beauty of this one Verse, amongst a thousand others?
>
> *Aude, hospes, contemnere opes, et te quoque dignum Finge*
> *deo . . .*
>
> For my part I am lost in admiration of it: I contemn the
> World when I think on it, and myself when I Translate it.

("Dare to be poor," runs Dryden's felicitous paraphrase, "accept
our homely food / Which feasted him, and emulate a god.")
Often a single Virgilian word or phrase defeats his best effort to
find a worthy English equivalent. The mellifluous interplay of
vowel and consonant in *mollis amaracus,* so delicately suggestive
of the "noble ideas of Cupid's flowery couch," he thinks entirely
lost in his rendition of the phrase as "sweet marjoram."[34]

Dryden judged the stylistic beauty of Virgil's hexameters to be
unrivaled.

> His words are not only chosen, but the places in which he ranks
> them for the sound. He who removes them from the Station
> wherein their Master set them spoils the Harmony. . . . [T]he least
> breath discomposes them; and somewhat of their Divinity is lost.

He places little reliance on the Horatian *provisam rem,* that the
right words will come unbidden to the service of the "invented"
conception. According to Dryden's reformulation of the Renaissance *res et verba* dualism into his definition of wit as "propriety of
thoughts and words," the poet's main effort is directed to the second term. Assured command of his medium he held to be the fruit
of a poet's artistic maturity, a skill painfully acquired, if at all, only
after years of practical experience. The gifted John Oldham never
lived to reach it.

> What could advancing Age have added more?
>
> It might (what Nature never gives the young)
>
> Have taught the numbers of thy native Tongue.[35]

In the preface to the *Aeneid,* Dryden reports having for some
time been gathering materials for an English *prosodia* which in fact
he was never to complete. Meanwhile, pending the appearance of

a work that would presumably have laid down principles of English versification, he offers as a kind of touchstone a couplet from Denham's *Cooper's Hill*,

> Tho' deep, yet clear; though gentle, yet not dull;
> Strong without rage; without o'erflowing, full,

and thus inaugurates the century-long series of citations of these lines by critics who shared his admiration of their "sweetness." To judge from what little he says of it, the projected prosody would have been essentially a technical manual, insufficient to enroll Dryden among the very few who, as he put it, could "find the Reason of that sweetness."[36]

Coleridge elaborated a total theory of poetic diction and Eliot left a number of generalizations which essentially reformulate Coleridge's ideas. Dryden did much less. His contribution lies rather in his insistence that a poet's verbal artistry, embracing both word-choice and meter, is the principal cause of a reader's pleasure; that in the poet's compact with his muse it is accordingly no fringe benefit but a major provision; and that therefore an account of its *modus operandi* must lie at the core of poetic science.

CHAPTER FOUR

Neoclassicism II

IN 1759 SAMUEL JOHNSON noted with misgivings that since Chaucer's day English writers had been aiming at an ever more polished elegance: "every man now endeavours to excel others in accuracy, or outshine them in splendour of style." He feared that literature could hardly escape the natural tendency of all human institutions to degenerate from a perfection long in attaining but brief in duration. "The passage is very short," he observed, "from elegance to luxury." Though his concern embraced all literature, he focused on poetry.[1]

Burlesque verse aside, Johnson's generalization was sound. He sensed, prophetically, that the growing preoccupation with stylistic adornment might now need restraint, "lest care should too soon pass to affectation," though he joined the rest in approving the doctrine memorialized in Pope's familiar couplet:

True Wit is Nature to advantage drest,

What oft was thought, but ne'er so well exprest.

Though later in life Johnson was to censure this pithy definition for reducing wit from intellectual strength to mere "happiness of language," he had never embraced Horace's faith that sound matter guarantees good style. That comforting opinion, he thought, was belied by the many books in which just and noble sentiments are degraded and obscured by unsuitable diction.

Words, therefore, as well as things, claim the care of an author. Indeed of many authors, and those not useless or contemptible, words are almost the only care: many make it their study, not so much to strike out new sentiments, as to recommend those which are already known to more favorable notice by fairer decorations.[2]

There is no better way to reduce misunderstanding of pre-Romantic poetic diction than to determine as far as the evidence permits what quality or qualities of style were then designated by *elegance*. Thoughtful observers at the time were aware that this and other terms of critical approval were as vague as they were widespread. "Every voice is united," wrote David Hume in 1757,

> in applauding elegance, propriety, simplicity, and spirit in writing; and in blaming fustian, affectation, coldness, and a false brilliancy. But when critics come to particulars, this seeming unanimity vanishes; and it is found, that they had affixed a very different meaning to their expressions.

So too in France, where two decades later Etienne de Condillac could still say the same. In constantly speaking of elegance, he complained, critics were using a word whose meaning, subject to capricious usage, has never been fixed ("bien déterminée").[3]

In the critical writing of the time, so far as I have observed, neither *elegance* nor *elegant* bore the faintly pejorative overtone associated with their modern use.[4] Sometimes, especially toward the end of the century, *elegance* named a quality inferior to *sublimity*. But throughout most of the period it denoted quite simply the approved style, apparently subsuming the three other stylistic desiderata identified in the last chapter, and irrespective of the verbal, syntactical, or metrical means used to achieve it. When Thomas Warton called Greek "that inestimable repository of genuine elegance and sublimity" he merely endorsed the received opinion that it had no equal as a poetic medium. In some contexts *elegant* simply meant poetic as against prosaic, with no denial that elegant prose partook of a quality more fully attainable in verse. When prose rises to literary status, as in stage comedy for example, it becomes, Joseph Trapp conceded, though not poetry, "an elegant kind of prose."[5]

If elegance usually implied figurative embellishment, that was because educated readers during this period—as (more or less insistently) in some others—so designated the superior distinction of *belles lettres* in general, especially verse. "Poetry requires ornament," said Dryden. Behind his assertion lay centuries of learned tradition that sometimes extended the requirement beyond the confines of poetry. By Dante's day, Ernst Robert Curtius writes, the "dominating point of view . . . is that discourse must be 'decorated.' The 'ornatus' (Quintilian VIII, 3) is the great desideratum, and it remains so into the eighteenth century." This was true even for proponents of *vraisemblance*. The art of poetry, Du Bos wrote, consists in adorning a representation of things that can really happen with clear and elegant imagery ("par des images nettes et élégantes").[6] Yet well before Johnson's admonition writers had noticed that elegance even in poetry could be attained with minimal adornment, as both classical authority and their own good taste assured them. So Trapp glossed Horace's defense of the plain style.

> By *Sermo pedestris,* the Poet means a more familiar Style, but without meanness; not quite degenerating into Prose, much less into what is vulgar, rude, or scurrilous: tho' plain, it should be elegant . . . graceful, and truly poetical.

But could plain speech *be* elegant? At first neoclassical critics were divided on the question. Simplicity, Dennis argued in angry reaction to Addison's *Spectator* paper praising the ballad *Chevy Chase,* may be an asset in poetry, but simplicity of thought only, not of expression. He cited René Rapin's flat declaration that the flawless Virgil "scarce says any thing in plain Language." Yet increasingly it was seen that some very affecting verse had been written with little or no figuration or deviation from the syntactical order of prose. This kind of verse was given the special label "easy poetry," and Johnson devoted one of his finest *Idler* pieces to a laudatory analysis of its style.[7]

After noting the irony of the label—easy poetry, Horace had noted, is the hardest to write—Johnson offered a needed definition:

> Easy poetry is that in which natural thoughts are expressed without violence to the language. The discriminating character of ease consists principally in the diction, for all true poetry requires that the sentiments be natural. Language suffers violence by harsh or by daring figures, by transposition, by unusual acceptations of words, and by any licence, which would be avoided by a writer of prose. Where any artifice appears in the construction of the verse,

that verse is no longer easy. Any epithet which can be ejected without diminution of the sense, any curious iteration of the same word, and all unusual, tho' not ungrammatical structure of speech, destroy the grace of easy poetry.

Such verse knows no limitation of subject or emotive range. Johnson quotes lines from Addison's tragedy *Cato* that "are at once easy and sublime":

'Tis the divinity that stirs within us;

'Tis heav'n itself that points out a hereafter,

And intimates eternity to man.

Nor does the speech lack elegance, though it is not elegance of the familiar decorative sort, but "gentle elegance," or—in a phrase in which Johnson skirts oxymoron—"naked elegance."[8]

Other writers seconded Johnson's approval of figurative restraint. Even in a detailed exposition of the many devices of exclusively poetic ornamentation, James Beattie conceded the existence of many passages of exquisite poetry containing "not a single phrase that might not occur in prose." With a touch of the psychologism that cripples much pre-Kantian aesthetic speculation, Beattie thought "plain diction without any ornament" was especially adapted to expressing mental distress; he could imagine nothing more moving than Lear's appeal in Act IV, scene 7:

Pray, do not mock me;

I am a very foolish fond old man,

Fourscore and upward, not an hour more nor less;

And, to deal plainly,

I fear I am not in my perfect mind.

Methinks I should know you, and know this man,

Yet I am doubtful: for I am mainly ignorant

What place this is; and all the skill I have

Remembers not these garments.[9]

Whatever the shortcomings of Beattie's disquisition (marred by considerable theoretical wobbling), it is hard to quarrel with his choice of these lines to exemplify verse that combines simplicity with great dramatic and emotive impact. But do the unpretentious diction and unforced cadence of Lear's pathos-laden confession, and Shakespeare's masterly adaptation of the meter to the irregular pulsations of spontaneous utterance,[10] represent the norm of what lettered Britons of Beattie's day meant by elegance—whether naked or in gorgeous array?

It would be rash to give a simple yes or no answer to that question, which I pose only to forestall any automatic inference of the affirmative from the mere fact of Beattie's admiration. Though he can cite the passage to show how the finest verse may on occasion be as undecorated as the simplest prose, he himself would never have accepted Wordsworth's stylistic equation of the two forms of discourse. He is perfectly of his age in relishing poetry for dictional privileges and resources beyond the prose writer's compass. The phrase "build the lofty rhyme" in Milton's *Lycidas* Beattie thought much too daring for prose. Mildly censuring the style of Pope's "elegant version" of the *Iliad* as somewhat too florid, he nonetheless easily prefers it to that by Hobbes and to Trapp's English *Aeneid*, the one downright prosaic, he thinks, and the other tasteless.[11]

Eighteenth-century appreciation of such "easy" poetry as the passage from *King Lear* could occur only when it contained none of the several vulgarisms of word or phrase. To confuse it with our modern recognition of a poet's legitimate recourse to any word or syntactical construction accepted in prose is to overlook strong evidence to the contrary. Neoclassical elegance, even of the simple variety, implied something more circumscribed, as a graphic detail in Beattie's treatise may remind us. For some time readers of Homer were put off by what they felt to be a dictional crudity. René le Bossu, disgusted by Homer's "sauce-pans," "cauldrons" and "animal guts," could only excuse the father of Greek poetry by pointing to similar "grandes bassesses" in the Bible—for who, he asked, will convict the Holy Ghost of bad taste? The word *swineherd*, used in the *Odyssey* of the hero's faithful retainer Eumaeus, was censured by Trapp among others, and even as late as 1789 by Thomas Twining, editor of Aristotle's *Poetics*. Especially shocking was Homer's combination of so "low" a noun with a lofty adjective in "δῖος ὑφορβός" (godly swineherd). Pope thought that in modern languages the phrase was no better than "Burlesque," and would have been as bad in Greek had not Eumaeus been honorable and his occupation at that time equally so. Beattie seconded Pope's historical apology: in heroic times, he observed, pig-raising was a dignified calling. Yet he never would have accepted Richard Lattimore's literal modern rendition ("noble swineherd"). Instead he approves of Pope's decorous circumvention of Homer's catachresis by making it "swain," a word, Beattie notes with evident satisfaction, "both elegant and poetical."[12]

The eighteenth-century concept of poetry as elegant discourse at its finest is thus a final flowering of the idea of a select poetic vocabulary whose seed had been sown in the Renaissance. To what was said of it in the preceding chapters we must add that in its final stages the distinction between prose and verse turned mainly on the narrowest definition of the term poetic diction: a restricted list of words and periphrastic locutions constituting an especially if not exclusively poetic lexicon.[13] The evidence for this conclusion is ubiquitous in the poetry and poetics of the time. Beattie commended Thomas Gray's declaration to his correspondent Richard West in 1741, that poetry must never be the language in ordinary current use. In happy contrast to the French, Gray wrote, English poetry "has a language peculiar to itself" and this language has been successively enriched by the poets, and mostly by the greatest of them, Shakespeare, Milton, Dryden, and Pope. Gray cites examples from Dryden, universally reckoned "a great master of our poetical tongue." In Johnson's view Dryden was not only its master but its founder, before whom there was simply

> no poetical diction: no system of words at once refined from the grossness of domestick use and free from the harshness of terms appropriated to particular arts. Words too familiar, or too remote, defeat the purpose of a poet.[14]

On the face of it, this key pronouncement made by the learned Johnson at the height of his vigorous maturity (ca. 1780) would seem to clash with Gray's derivation of English verse diction from as far back as Shakespeare and even earlier, one supported by modern scholarship.[15] The discrepancy, however, is only apparent, arising from the differing meanings these two writers assigned to the common term. Gray's reference is to certain words and phrases much used in poetry and seldom in prose. Johnson's "system of words" applies only to a final stage in the gradual refinement of poetic style from "the grossness of domestic use." Gray undoubtedly had in mind the kind of poeticisms to which Shakespeare's gave legitimacy. There are the adjectives ending in "y"—"vaulty heaven" and "paly ashes" in *Romeo and Juliet,* "sedgy bank" in *Hamlet;* the stereotypes "salt flood" in *Romeo and Juliet,* "pendent bough" and "nymph" (for a pretty girl) in *Hamlet,* "damask cheek" in *Twelfth Night,* and "glassy stream" in *Hamlet* (cf. "glassy brook" in Goldsmith's *Deserted Village*). Shakespeare also has his full share of personified abstractions like "Concealment" in *Twelfth Night* and "Ambition" in *The Tempest,* the trick of style Wordsworth (despite his own use of it) was to censure as unnatural. In Milton such decorous usages grace almost every page: in *Comus* fish are a "finny drove," sheep "fleecy wealth"; in *Lycidas* flowers are "enamelled," and so forth. Johnson's point is that in Shakespeare these elegancies are too often tastelessly combined with the vocabulary of "domestic" prose ("knife" and "blanket" in *Macbeth*). The result is that the poet's gold, in the image of an anonymous commentator on *Hamlet,* is "strangely mingled with dross in most of his pieces." The luster of Milton's poetic gems too was often obscured in the same way, though in lesser degree, by tortuous syntax and irregular meter, and occasionally by technical and learned jargon. In contrast, the perfected art of Dryden was seen as proof of how thoroughly he had absorbed the lesson that "words too familiar or too remote" would alike have degraded his verse. Before Dryden, Johnson could accordingly generalize, those

> happy combinations of words which distinguish poetry from prose had been rarely attempted: we had few elegances or flowers of speech; the roses had not yet been plucked from the bramble, or different colours had not been joined to enliven one another.

And so it went, repeatedly couched in sets of metaphorical opposites: gold versus dross, roses versus brambles, or—as in another Johnsonian characterization of Shakespeare's style in the preface to his edition of the plays—"gold and diamonds . . . mingled with a mass of meaner minerals."[16]

How far our modern predilection, developed in the aftermath of a stylistic revolution for which Wordsworth's Prefaces to *Lyrical Ballads* provided the manifesto, has diverged from the late neoclassical ideal is plain enough. It leaps to view when we turn from Johnson's denial of poetic potential to words that are domestic, or simply too familiar, to the criterion laid down by a twentieth-century poet. Once a word can be used in conversation, Robert Graves wrote, "without any apologetic accentuation," or in prose "without italics, inverted commas or capital letters, then it is ready for use in poetry."[17]

Johnson was not alone in his concern that the modern poets' aim to raise their verse ever higher above prosaic banality could degenerate into affectation. David Hume detected in France and Britain both an ominous debasement of taste that mistook simplicity for dullness unless it was "accompanied with great elegance and propriety." Joseph Warton agreed. Dryden, he noted, frequently achieved a pleasing effect in his verse with the commonest words. So did Pope. So now Warton can only deplore the "false refinement" deterring poets from using words like "causeway," "seats," "spire," "market-place," "almshouse," and "apprenticed"—all of them found in the admired panegyric on the Man of Ross in Pope's *Epistle to Bathurst*. With current practitioners of "the finical style," according to Beattie,

> a man's only child must always be his *only hope*, a country maid becomes a *rural beauty*, or perhaps a *nymph of the groves*; if flattery sing at all, it must be a *siren song*; the shepherd's flute dwindles into an *oaten reed*, and his crook is exalted into a *scepter*; the *silver lillies* rise from their *golden beds*, and languish to the *complaining gale*.[18]

Among the curiosities of this tide of opinion was a complaint in 1771 by Anna Letitia Barbauld's brother John Aiken, who blamed much of "the insipidity of Modern Poetry" on the descriptive poets' neglect of natural history and their consequent ignorance of the actual details of flora and fauna. Pope, Edward Young, and Thomas Warton were among the offenders. Aiken thought James Thomson's *The Seasons* a happy exception. Most other poets could hardly "conceive of the Morn without dewey locks, or Spring without flowers and showers, loves and groves."[19]

Yet neither Aiken nor anyone else at the time anticipated Wordsworth's wholesale rejection of the style exemplified in Beattie's scornful litany of tarnished poeticisms. As is plain from the general tenor of Beattie's indictment, what they were objecting to was only the dictional disease (by then becoming epidemic) of their automatic use in incompatible topical or tonal contexts where they operated as obstacles to conveying a poet's genuine experience.

Beattie's adherence to the contemporary psychology is signaled in the very title of his *Essays on Poetry and Music, as They Affect the Mind*. His fundamental principles belong to an older tradition, however: that language as the poet's "instrument of imitation" was analogous to the musician's sounds and the painter's colors; and that although the sense of the words must always count more than their sound, verbal harmony, important even in prose, "in verse demands particular attention." He follows the classical doctrine of stylistic levels determined by genres arranged in a descending series: epic, tragedy, lyric, comedy, farce. Thus in a farce or comedy, he notes, the lout Polyphemus might speak "clownishly," but Homer and Virgil are constrained by the epic form to express his loutish thoughts "in their own elegant and harmonious language."[20]

Beattie's argument rehearsed common opinion. Considering the respectable case that can be made for it even today, his rationale is a disappointing mélange of tautology and superficial causality. Words and phrases rare in prose but frequent in verse constitute the resulting poetic diction. The reasons for its growth are that poets readily recall and reproduce one another's language (more deeply implanted in memory than prose), and readers tolerate it because they admire the poets' ingenuity in surmounting the constraints of meter. More instructive is his list of the stylistic traits that characterize poetic language:

1. phrases of classical derivation like Milton's "Shorn of his beams"
2. inversions: Gray's "Now fades the glimmering landscape"
3. words formed by gain or loss of a syllable: *dispart* (for *part*), *affright* (for *fright*), *disport* (for *sport*), *trump* (for *trumpet*), *clime* (for *climate*), *dread* (for *dreadful*), *gan* (for *began*)
4. archaisms: *anon, aye, blithe, brand* (for *sword*), *featly, lay* (for *poem* or *song*), *mead, save* (for *except*), *yon*
5. words never, to Beattie's knowledge, in common use: *appal, car, cates, pinion, courser, noiseless, viewless, shadowy, madding, circlet*
6. contractions: *'twas, 'tis, o'er, e'er*
7. compound epithets: *rosy-fingered, many-twinkling, bright-eyed, straw-built, incense-breathing, love-whispering*
8. nouns turned into verbs: *to hymn, to pillow, to picture, to bosom.*[21]

Like many other theorists, Beattie tried to make provision for the disconcertingly porous nature of the stylistic barrier between verse and prose. He conceded that some of the locutions among these types of "our poetical dialect" also occur in prose, but argued that most of them when so employed are disfigurements: "it is in poetry only, where the frequent use of them does not savour of affectation." Since he also recognized that excellent verse may dispense with them entirely, the question inevitably arises—why do poets continue to use them? Beattie's answers belong more to the history of literary taste than to durable theory. The listed usages, he explains, are melodious and easily adapted to meter. Besides, by long association with sublime and elegant writing they have taken on sublimity and elegance, just as by constant employment on "familiar occasions" some words have suffered qualitative degradation, and a few—from habitual use by "pickpockets, gamblers, and gypsies"—have been made downright repulsive.[22]

The English language, Beattie thought, had been gradually enhanced as an artistic medium by an infusion of tropes and figures. One of these, the periphrasis so groundlessly disparaged by early twentieth-century scholars as a neoclassical "vice," he considered an especially effective constituent of poetic style. Among his examples are "blue serene," "liquid plain," and "sylvan reign." Phrases of this kind, he observes, are useful substitutes for words that are "untuneable and harsh,"[23] the former adjective meaning, presumably, unadaptable to meter. Presumably too, though he doesn't say so, the undesirable mundane words thus elegantly avoided are *sky, sea,* and *rural landscape* (or some equivalent). The case he makes seems uncertain, resting less on a conviction of a positive, expressive efficacy resident in such circumlocutions than on their usefulness in eliminating the "untuneable" alternatives. One thing is clear, however. Far from anticipating Wordsworth's dictional views, the governing drift of Beattie's reasoning, despite all his distaste for the "finical style," suggests that this Scottish poet and rhetorician would have thought something like

Join with the sylvan reign the blue serene

preferable to the English poet's

connect
The landscape with the quiet of the sky.

Later on it will be necessary to detail the sharp disagreement about poetic diction between Wordsworth and Coleridge. But first we must stress the gap which separates these two founders of English Romantic poetry, taken together, from their immediate eighteenth-century forerunners. For despite often noted continuities of poetic theory and practice spanning the two periods, as regards the problem of poetic style it is not inaccurate to assign to Romanticism a revolution in sensibility and conception, taste and theory. To gauge the challenge of Wordsworth's naturalistic ideal of poetic speech, it is enough to set it beside what Joshua Reynolds had said on the subject only fourteen years earlier. The measured words of poetry, the famous painter told his student audience, are a highly artificial construction "such as never is, nor ever was used by men." I shall argue below that the view of poetic diction upheld in the *Biographia Literaria* is certainly more compatible with Reynolds's opinion than with Wordsworth's. Nevertheless, in the judgments rendered on Pope by Coleridge and Johnson, sharply discrepant ideals of poetic style clearly emerge, though perhaps more on the level of taste than of theory. Like his more advanced contemporaries, Coleridge regarded Pope's *Homer* "as the main source of our pseudo-poetic diction." And in a more sweeping condemnation he dismissed the language which characterized English poetry from the time of that celebrated translation (1715–1726) to Erasmus Darwin's *Temple of Nature* (1803) as having no better claim to poetical quality "than that it would be intolerable in conversation or in prose." Yet this pronouncement came only some thirty-five years after Johnson had rendered the diametrically opposed verdict that Pope had

> cultivated our language with so much diligence and art that he has left in his *Homer* a treasure of poetical elegances to posterity.

His whole poetic output, Johnson adds, shows that Pope

> had colours of language always before him, ready to decorate his matter with every grace of elegant expression, as when he accommodates his diction to the wonderful multiplicity of Homer's sentiments and descriptions.[24]

These opposed dictional ideals reflect a divergence of taste even more profound than the ensuing alteration of theory. They also owe something to a corresponding change in how cultural development was thought to affect poetry. Compared with Spenser's style, Pope's "refined diction and harmonious versification" Thomas Warton regarded as the fortunate results of social melioration. The opposed primitivistic motif in Wordsworth's Prefaces, equally a legacy of the eighteenth century, was more congenial to

the Romantic sensibility. But Johnson, like other adherents to the
older and more dominant perfectionism of the Enlightenment,
could not share it. By Elizabeth's reign, he wrote in *Idler* 69
(1759), English translators of foreign verse were obliged to abandon the crudities of their ancestors, having discovered that "elegance was necessary to general reception." In every culture, he
believed, successive ages demand an increasingly elegant and "artificial" style, so that what for Virgil was only an expedient becomes
for Pope a necessity.[25]

The recognition that a poem of the highest order may be *lexically* indistinguishable from prose was not an aspect of English aesthetic liberalism. Though it was subordinate during the period to
the opposite view, it accompanied the whole course of neoclassical
speculation in France as well as in England. In 1758, the dilettan-
tish Parisian Rémond de Saint-Mard saw "une ressemblance par-
faite" between the styles of poetry and prose, and airily dismissed
the exceptions of rhyme and meter as constituting no more than a
"petite différence." Since, according to his own thesis, rhyme and
meter differentiate the passionate language of poetry from the
rational language of prose, they would seem to be rather more
than "petite." But logical consistency on this issue troubled Saint-
Mard even less than it did most other writers of his time. In Malé-
branche's prose and Corneille's verse he finds the same ardor,
vigor, and expression ("même feu, même force, même langage").[26]

The plausible conclusion, that the eighteenth-century critics'
rudimentary terminology was unequal to the complexities of the
problem they confronted, did not then emerge. In casual preface,
learned treatise, and popular manual they are repeatedly led to the
same impasse from the same reductive dichotomy of diction, variously expressed as the plain versus the figurative or the natural versus the artificial. It is also during this period that we first meet with
the familiar modern classroom dogma that abstract words are unpoetic. Homer, Joseph Warton thought, had the good luck to
write "before *general* and *abstract* terms were invented." Henry
Pemberton, when he examined the styles of prose and verse in his
Observations on Poetry (1738), referred the poets' greater dependence on concrete and sensuous language, especially words of visual description, to the different functions of the two modes of
written discourse, prose aiming primarily to instruct the understanding, poetry to "affect the temper." Accordingly, language
that makes us *see*, whether metaphorical or literal, is "equally the
language of poetry." Beattie was in very similar fashion to exalt vi-

sual, tactile, and aural figures over language "merely intellectual."
But the most uncompromising—and absurd—proponent of this
rule was Erasmus Darwin, who regarded it as the only valid distinction between poetry and prose. Even the lone abstraction
renown'd, in Pope's *Windsor Forest*, Darwin condemned as a prosaic blemish, affording a reader no mental picture:

And Kennet swift for silver eels *renown'd.*

He suggested, instead,

And Kennet swift where silver graylings *play.*[27]

Despite approval of "easy" poetry, the prevailing opinion continued to endorse the long-standing preference for decorous circumlocution. In *Les beaux Arts réduits à un même principe*
(1746), an influential treatise widely esteemed in England, Charles
Batteux argued that in poetry words are elevated above their natural condition by sustained similes, bold striking images, lively
repetitions, and unique metaphors. The plain word *dawn* the poet
periphrastically enlivens to "l'Aurore fille du matin, qui ouvre les
portes de l'Orient avec ses doigts de rose" [Aurora, daughter of
the morn who opens the gates of the East with her rosy fingers].
Some years later the industrious bookseller John Newberry
preached the same doctrine to a humbler set of readers. His compendious handbook instructed them that "poetry has language
peculiar to itself." He enforced his point by a simple illustration of
his own devising:

> The prose writer says, *close to her grotto, which is shaded by a grove,
> there is a beautiful lawn edged round with moss.* Which the poet
> would probably have described in this manner.

Close to her grot, within the grove,
A carpet's laid that nature wove;
Which time extended on the ground,
And tuff'd with moss the selvage round.[28]

This stylistic separatism was further underwritten by the varied literary antiquarianism that came to prominence around mid-
century. Collectors of English folk ballads, nourishers of the

Ossianic craze, and scholars of Hebrew poetry certainly found
nothing in the literature they cultivated to contravene it. Quite
the reverse. Robert Lowth, in his *Sacred Poetry of the Hebrews*
(1753), found that the verse of the Old Testament "abounds
with phrases and idioms totally unsuited to prose composition."
And Hugh Blair, writing a *Critical Dissertation* on the Ossianic
poems, similarly rejoices that the very lack of sophisticated terms
in the vocabulary available to the Gaelic bard happily forced him
to employ the figurative expressions "which give a poetical air to
the language." Trapp named *rosy morn* and *roseate East* as examples of a very limited stock of adjective-noun pairings conse-
crated from ancient times to poetic use alone.[29]

Whatever theory may prescribe in any age, a poet's vocabulary
is necessarily restricted. But whereas today we tend to think that
the criterion of inclusion is the poet's private psyche, or the "cosmos" it projects, in the less individualistic orientation of the Enlightenment the selectivity was mainly referred to the craft he or
she shared with other poets. Each art, Batteux wrote, has its peculiar medium: marble, musical tones, or, for the poet, words. But
not ordinary words: the "marble" of poetry is always specially selected, cut, and polished ("c'est le marbre choisi, poli, et taillé").
The magical something which enthralls readers is produced by a
combination of choice words and expressions (*tours*) and by metrical harmony.[30]

The criteria of style were both social and literary. For "low"
words it is almost always social, words designating the trade of
humbly employed persons (*swineherd*), their accoutrements (*knife*),
their patois (the parlance of "pickpockets, gamblers, and gypsies").
The literary criterion takes, generally, two forms. To the classical hierarchy of usage determined by genre was now added the broader
requisite of poetic association, as noted in the case of Beattie.

In most modern discussions of the subject, the categories of
"low" and "familiar" are often thought of as one, no doubt in part
because these epithets were sometimes used interchangeably during the eighteenth century itself, although in strict application
"low" is social and "familiar" primarily literary. Addison's early
piece on Virgil's *Georgics* applies the latter. Book I begins

Quid faciat laetas segetes, quo sidere terram

Vertere, Maecenas, ulmisque adiungere vites

Conveniat. . . .

[What gladdens the growing corn, beneath what star it is proper to till the ground, Maecenas, and join vines to the elms . . .]

Addison prefers *quo sidere* (beneath what star) to *quo tempore* (at what time), the image to the abstraction, not for its greater force but because it is less ordinary. He may also have appreciated the greater visual appeal of the metonymy, but his explicit praise of Virgil is that he chose *sidere* "to deviate from the common form of words." In this instant "familiar" means hardly more than suitable only for prose. Or, going further, it might denote the colloquial. Even a modern reader may sympathize with Addison's sense that the expression "No fear lest dinner cool" in *Paradise Lost* is unpleasantly prosaic, but only as incompatible with the *donné* of the supramundane setting. On the other hand, few can now share the distaste of another critic who in an essay once ascribed to Oliver Goldsmith condemned the phrase "Ay, there's the rub" as "a vulgarity beneath the dignity of Hamlet's character."[31]

In England and France the stylistic exactions of genre set the taste of even the most independent-minded critics. Puns, so succulent to the Elizabethan palate, were now downright disgusting, especially in epic and tragic verse. Voltaire, though with Addison and Beattie a fervent admirer of Milton, was nonetheless shocked like them by the volley of puns fired off by the cannonading devils in the sixth book of *Paradise Lost*. The epic muse was not amusing. "I remember," the fastidious Addison commented by way of salutary contrast to Milton's misplaced frivolity, "but one laugh in the whole *Aeneid*"—thereby providing his less respectful readers with the one laugh in the 279th *Spectator*. Generic stylistic requirements could involve a critic in pedantic absurdity. Beattie thought the rule that the speech of tragic characters must never descend to meanness held even for domestic retainers, who, he solemnly suggests in a glaring confusion of art and life, "may be supposed to have had advantages of education to qualify them for bearing a part in the dialogue." We can guess what he must have thought of the terms in which Shakespeare's Nurse delivered her matrimonial advice to Juliet:

I think it best you married with the County.

O, he's a lovely gentleman!

Romeo's a dishclout to him. . . .

And Batteux too would certainly have included Shakespeare among those ignorant poets who destroy what he calls stylistic harmony by mingling tragic, lyric, and comic verses in the same work.[32]

Another Frenchman, Du Bos, had argued that some words were more beautiful than others because quite independently of meaning they were simply more mellifluous. He approved Jean-Baptiste Rousseau's use of the sonorous *compagnon* in a poem where the aurally less pleasing *collègue* would have been the more accurate. But despite talk of poetic words, English neoclassical theory was generally wary of the fallacy of the inherently poetic. In *Rambler* 168 Johnson expressly rejects it. Verbal ugliness was no more absolute than verbal beauty. The low words that destroy poetic elegance, he wrote elsewhere, were simply those previously "contaminated with inelegant applications." In an ill-tempered critique of Pope's *Homer*, in which he professed to find twenty prosaic lines for every poetic one, Dennis observed that Homer never sinks to the prosaic because Greek had an ample stock of exclusively poetic words, such as certain compounds and dialect terms. But he was careful to ascribe their special aesthetic appeal to association (they never appear in prose), not to any intrinsic quality. The previously cited anonymous author edified his readers with a list of words which in any language he thought "particularly adapted to the poetical expression." By quotations from Virgil, Shakespeare, Milton, and Addison, he highlights the beauty of the verb *to hang* (in all its morphological varieties and foreign equivalents). Other multilingual poetic verbs on his list are *shake, wake, rouse, soothe, flow, rage, shine, blaze*, and *plow*. This is fanciful enough. But he ascribed their allure to the images they invoke, not to intrinsic aural appeal.[33]

Eighteenth-century critics continued the debate on meter, its sources and effects. To the question whether poetry could exist without it the predominant answer of orthodox neoclassicism had always been a clear *no*. But now it was increasingly challenged by a vocal minority. Writing on all poetry irrespective of genre, Richard Hurd took the broad view appropriate to his inclusive topic: "Men may," he conceded "include or not include the idea of meter in their complex idea of what they call a poem." The general opinion, however, was that meter, though obviously never a *sufficient* condition of poetic status, was nevertheless indispensable to its "complex idea." Hurd himself, insisting that the question was no mere logomachy, concluded that at the very least a poem not written in verse would be less than perfect of its kind. It is true that when in 1776 Reynolds pronounced the inseparability of verse

and poetry to be a truth universally acknowledged, he was over-
looking an occasional dissenter like the rhetorician George Campbell, who in that same year declared meter to be no constituent of
poetry but only an unessential appendage. As with other current
literary issues, the received opinion was put most memorably by
Reynolds's friend Johnson.

> . . . versification, or the art of modulating his numbers, is indis-
> pensably necessary to a poet. Every other power by which the un-
> derstanding is enlightened, or the imagination enchanted, may be
> exercised in prose. But the poet has this peculiar superiority, that
> to all the powers which the perfection of every other composition
> can require, he adds the faculty of joining music with reason, and
> of acting at once upon the senses and the passions. I suppose there
> are few who do not feel themselves touched by poetical melody,
> and who will not confess that they are more or less moved by the
> same thoughts, as they are conveyed by different sounds, and
> more affected by the same words in one order than in another.

It should be noted that Johnson's statement contains the two major
claims for verse: as the sole differentia dividing poetry from other
eloquent expression, and as the cause of poetry's superiority. Even
though—somewhat puzzlingly—he is contemptuous of versification
as a branch of humane learning, he nevertheless firmly maintains
that without this "petty knowledge" no one can be a poet, because
it is the key to "that harmony that adds force to reason, and gives
grace to sublimity; that shackles attention and governs passion."[34]

Some of those who shared Johnson's love for numbers considered verse to be less an acquired science, petty or profound, than
a spontaneous accompaniment of poetic utterance, a conviction
not predominant before Romanticism. The hexameter measures
of Homer, hailed as the founder of poetic language itself, Pope
observed,

> instead of being Fetters to his Sense, were always in readiness to
> run along with the warmth of his Rapture; and even to give a far-
> ther Representation of his Notions, in the correspondence of
> their Sounds to what they signify'd.

In the latter point (which Johnson sought in a *Rambler* paper to
prove delusive) we recognize the editor-commentator's sober
confirmation of what the youthful poet had so wittily illustrated in
the *Essay on Criticism*. One example from the notes to his *Homer*

is the narrated action of Chryses, the disconsolate priest of Apollo, rebuffed in his suit to Agamemnon for the return of his captive daughter (*Iliad* I, 34),

βη δ'ἀκέων παρὰ θινα πολυφλοίσβοιο θαλάσσης

[He walked in silence by the shore of the sounding sea],

where "the melancholy Flowing of the Verse admirably expresses the Condition of the mournful and deserted Father."[35]

Samuel Say, in his innovative analysis of the versification of *Paradise Lost*, was to make essentially the same argument. Say was as responsive as Dryden had been to the cadences of prose and like him thought meter to be an acquired regularization of primitive prose rhythms. Yet in that sonic pattern of skillfully chosen words, Say argued, lay "the true magic of verse." It had always been understood by most inquirers that an adequate poetics needed to replace the traditional prose-verse duality with a triad that set non-poetic verse apart from poetic. The concept of non-poetic verse goes back at least to Horace, who in his *Satires* (I, iv) called metrical stage comedy mere prose ("sermo merus"). And of course the idea is implied in Aristotle's denial that Herodotus versified would be poetry (*Poetics*, Chap. 9). But Say's system is unique in that he sought to define the difference in purely metrical terms. Since well-written prose is inevitably cadenced, it shares with verse a certain musical quality. In verse, however, isometry actually imitates even the temporal order of music. And here Say elucidates the difference between the two forms by a crucial terminological distinction: the "Music of numbers" as against the "Power of numbers." The former, involving sensuous delight alone, is felt even in non-poetic verse. For verse to be poetic there must also be the "Power of numbers," which a poet attains only when his meter *collaborates with his meaning*. So manipulated, meter takes on a semantic function beyond its hedonic appeal. The beauty of some lines which Say quotes from the *Georgics* and the *Aeneid* does not

> arise merely from the *Justness* and Simplicity of the thoughts *abstractedly* considered, but as *United* with the *Harmony* and *Power* of the Numbers: And, indeed, it seems impossible to do any tolerable Justice in *Prose* to the Ideas convey'd in the *Verse*.

Most remarkable, considering the date of Say's work, is his claim that meter sometimes functions cognitively in a poem even independently of its words. He noticed that in *Paradise Lost* "many ideas, which necessarily arise in the Mind of the Reader, are convey'd by the very Run and Sound of the Verse, without the Use or Need of Words." The perception of an ultraverbal referential dimension in the rhythm of verse, rare in the eighteenth century despite Pope's early espousal of it, is of course now a commonplace among theorists of versification, who generally agree that, as Harvey Gross has neatly phrased it, "rhythm will rescue for cognition what may never receive articulate verbal expression."[36]

Say's assumption, however, that meter was a civilized refinement on non-metrical expression, was destined for early desuetude and final rebuttal. By the latter part of the century many writers, like Hugh Blair, were pointing to the weighty evidence for the opposite view: that metrical rhythm, like every other feature of poetic expression, was a primitive phenomenon, antedating prose.

Opinions diverged as to how much weight to assign to meter as against other aspects of style in defining poetry. Pemberton, arguing that the role of metaphor had been much overrated, insisted that poetry's peculiarity consisted basically in "disposing the words in a musical measure." Beattie, on the other hand, pointed to what he and others felt to be the undeniable poetical quality of the Book of Job and other prose parts of the Bible to argue that it was not essential. His opinion was facilitated by the deeply ingrained habit of regarding lexical, syntactic, and rhythmic departures from prose style as so much attractive vestiture. That habit especially impeded a firm grasp of the expressive potential of meter. Generally, the prevalent conception that poetry was ornamental discourse was not intended to debase meter. Some critics, however, did dismiss it as merely adventitious, while a few went so far as to decry it as an obstacle to clear communication. So the contradictory positions on meter voiced by Sidney and others during the Renaissance surface anew in neoclassical discussion. In a single paragraph of his *Advancement and Reformation of Modern Poetry* (1701), Dennis moves from a definition of poetry that locates in meter its distinctive nature, to the flat assertion that a passionate and figurative prose is "certainly poetry without numbers."[37]

In a letter to Edward Young prefixed to his *Essay* on Pope's writings, Joseph Warton observes reasonably enough that some poetry is more intense or, as he puts it, "purer" than other poetry. His statement that Boileau's verse *Epistles* are no more poetical than La Bruyère's prose *Characters* might have been taken as a generous tribute to the fastidious artistry with which La Bruyère wrought his admired book.[38] But Warton went further. Emboldened by Horace's refusal in *Satires* I, iv to dignify his own "sermoni propiora" by the name of poetry, he performs an experiment on Pope's first *Moral Essay.* Horace had held that the poetic attributes of a true poem would show themselves even in the fragments left after dismantling its meter ("invenias etiam disiecti membra poetae"). If, however, his own chatty satires were thus deformed, not having issued from the *mens divinior* they would prove to be mere prose. Perhaps too naively taking Horace at his word, Warton rewrites the opening fourteen lines of Pope's poem as prose, removing all inversions, inserting at appropriate points "that is," "perhaps," "of," "so," and "because," and suppressing (for some reason) "at all" at the end of line 8. Now, Warton triumphantly concludes, nothing is left but good sense, no poetry whatever, thus proving the verses to be only measured prose.[39]

Waiving the fact that Warton wrote his own poems in meter, it is hard to defend either his logic or his taste in this exercise. His point is in part to demonstrate the inherent nullity of verse. But the very fact that the alleged poverty of Pope's satire is revealed only by destroying its meter and rhyme is, if anything, an effective argument in favor of those techniques, at least in skilled hands. A more telling strategy—and surely one more consistent with Horace's metaphor of scattered poetic limbs—would have been to show that a passage of admittedly superb verse lost none of its appeal when "demetricized."

This questioning of the role and use of meter cannot be ascribed to the relatively liberal cast of British as against French neoclassicism. For it was in fact among the compatriots of Racine, not of Pope, that metriphobia (if the coinage be allowed) took its most radical form.

French opinion ranged from the position that great poetry might exist without meter, to complaints that it often spoiled greater beauties, and finally to condemnations so sweeping as to threaten poetry itself. The first position found early expression in Bishop François Fénelon's *Letter* to the French Academy of 1714. Fénelon praised the poetry of the Bible, as John Husbands and Robert Lowth were later to do in England. But whereas Lowth found "the poetical diction of the Hebrews" to exist only in such measured lines as the "metrical parts" of *Job,* his French brother of the cloth found Holy Writ poetic in the very places where there is no evidence of meter ("ou l'on ne trouve aucune trace de versification"). Fénelon, whose prose epic *Télémaque* (1699) was long held up as a model of prose-poetry, defined "le langage des Dieux" simply as language enlivened by images, figures, passion, and harmony, whether prose or verse. At some risk to consistency, he regrets that French syntax is so resistant to inversion, the figure indispensable to verse. Destroy the inverted structure of the first five lines of Virgil's *Eclogue* VII, he declares, and their majesty and grace disappear. Du Bos found French versification so barren that it could not exist at all without the prop of rhyme ("Enfin il faut rimer"). Yet rhyme requires for its best effects the inversion that French syntax so awkwardly accommodates. Modern French verse Du Bos therefore sharply depreciated, exalting instead such "poèmes en prose" as Madame de Lafayette's *La Princesse de Clèves* and Fénelon's *Télémaque*. Had their authors been required to compose them in verse, he thinks, these two "beaux Poèmes sans vers" would never have seen the light of day.[40]

Deservedly more notorious are the Cartesian decriers of verse as a bar to clear communication of thought, some of whom seem to have been calling for the total abolition of poetry. In Charles de Montesquieu's *Lettres Persanes,* the Oriental traveler is told with satirical hyperbole that poets make it their business to obstruct good sense and crush reason under fancy verbiage. The Abbé Trublet more soberly imputed to meter a tendency to camouflage shoddy thinking. So did the poet-dramatist Houdar de la Motte, who opined that much of what readers admire in verse is how well poets communicate despite the metrical hurdle ("toute la contrainte des vers"). Since meter obviously contravenes dramatic *vraisemblance,* tragedies should be written in prose. So he "translated" the first scene of Racine's *Mithridate* into prose—an atrocity which Philippe Van Tieghem fittingly laid to an "abolition du sens esthétique." But thus it was.[41]

Although it inevitably recalls the London Royal Society's campaign against metaphorical prose, the French rationalist attack on verse had no English counterpart. Its diatribes were turned on every feature of form or style that since ancient times had been esteemed as means for transmuting the lead of common speech into the gold of verbal song. In his classic discussion of Descartes's influence on French literature, Gustave Lanson suggested that the antipoetic rationalism of the Cartesian system found fertile soil in a profound and permanent tendency of the French mind. Lanson might have cited in support Antoine Rivarol's flat denunciation of metaphor as verbal deception ("ce perpétuel mensonge de la parole"), a source of mental corruption. Meter fares no better. In Rivarol's central argument, infused with royalism and French linguistic pride, we reach the extreme of antimetrical rationalism in Enlightenment literary thought. European civilization, he maintained, had happily emerged from the savagery of gods and verse to the refinements of kingly rule and prose. To deny this, Rivarol was sure, was to defy reason and nature, since especially in France prose and political absolutism had triumphed together because both are rational and natural. Thus Rivarol five years before the storming of the Bastille! With critics of his persuasion what had for so long been the language of the gods became instead the seductive accents of the sirens of unreason.[42]

Less subversive intellectual forces influenced the contemporary English poetics. The rationalism so pervasive in France was felt in English literary speculation only in a comparatively attenuated form. English poetics was much more responsive to two very different, closely related currents of thought: primitivism and Longinianism. Furthermore, whereas Cartesian reason, or so it has been contended, influenced for the worse the quality of French poetry written at the time as much as it redirected critical opinion, in England the cults of the primitive and the sublime affected theory more than practice.

Often named among harbingers of Romanticism, primitivism during the 1700s is a fascinating phenomenon precisely because it runs counter to a fundamental assumption of the Enlightenment, the belief in progress. So pervasive was this belief that it is hard to think of another feature of the ideological map of that period that so clearly marks it off from all others. Although writers subscribed to it with varying degrees of doubt and assurance, the conviction that since the revival of learning civilized institutions had been undergoing and would continue to enjoy a gradual if uneven ameliorative development was shared alike by Christian and agnostic, rationalist and skeptic, conservative and radical. The few dissenters, such as apocalyptic visionaries, enjoyed little intellectual prestige. Faith in the betterment, by reasoned effort, of human knowledge, welfare, and practical achievement makes recognizable contemporaries of such disparate spirits as Johnson and Voltaire, Burke and Paine, Berkeley and Hume.[43]

Universal improvement seemed so incontrovertible that despite a long-standing recognition by a few thinkers (Pascal early among them) that the fine arts were exempt from meliorative change, even poetry and its medium were considered beneficiaries.

Thomas Warton conceived the aim and justification of his *History of English Poetry* (1774–1781) to consist in tracing

> the progress of our national poetry, from a rude origin and obscure beginnings, to its perfection in a polished age. . . .
>
> My performance . . . exhibits without transposition the gradual improvements of our poetry, at the same time that it uniformly represents the progression of our language.[44]

In direct opposition to the governing assumption of Warton's project, a primitivist doctrine held that the very civilization in which Europe gloried, a progressive aggregate of rational institutions, was in fact adverse to the spirit of poetry and to the language which embodied it. A history of poetry, therefore, would have to be one not of advancement but of decline. To the mildly Longinian Thomas Blackwell, an early explorer of the social factor in literary development, it seemed impossible for "one and the same kingdom, to be thoroughly civilized and afford proper subjects for Poetry," or for a language "thoroughly polished in the modern sense" to express the simplicity of manners indispensable to epic grandeur.[45] This depressing conviction was held even by critics, including Warton himself, who otherwise subscribed to the dominant progressivism of the day. But its theoretical implications are more explicit in the writings of his brother Joseph. A sampling of three passages may suffice, the first from an *Adventurer* essay of 1753, the other two from his book on Pope:

> I freely confess I had rather sit in the grotto of Calypso than in the most pompous saloon of Louis XV. The tea and the card tables can be introduced with propriety and success only in the mock heroic, as they have been very happily in the *Rape of the Lock,* but the present modes of life must be forgotten when we attempt anything in the serious or sublime poetry, for heroism disdains the luxurious refinements, the false delicacy and state of modern ages. The primeval, I was about to say patriarchal, simplicity of manners displayed in the *Odyssey* is a perpetual source of true poetry.

> The simple notions which uncivilized nations entertain of a future state, are many of them beautifully romantic and some of them the best subjects for poetry.

> [Pope] stuck to describing *modern manners,* but those *manners,* because they are *familiar, uniform, artificial,* and *polished,* are, in their very nature, unfit for any lofty effort of the Muse.

In 1767 William Duff concluded his study of original genius with a section detailing the several reasons why "uncultivated periods of society," and "cultivated life" were respectively propitious and hostile to poetic composition.[46]

Though Johnson would have none of it, Edmund Burke accepted the idea that progressive refinement entailed expressive enfeeblement. In his influential *Philosophical Enquiry into the Sublime and Beautiful* (1757) he had noted that highly rarefied languages like modern French lacked the "great force and energy of expression" found in those of "most unpolished people" and of Oriental countries. The implications for poetic diction were pressed by several other writers. Texts written or presumed to have been written during the pristine periods of their cultures—notably the Homeric epics, the Hebrew Bible, and the Ossianic poems fabricated by James Macpherson—now took on crucial theoretical importance. The stylistic similarities spanning their differences of language and cultural provenance seemed to point to a vitalizing influence on literary expression by the pre-rational modes of thought and apprehension prevalent during the happy times before cold philosophy arrived to "Conquer all mysteries by rule and line."[47] The languages of primitive peoples, their passions untamed by civilized restraints, Blair asserted in his *Critical Dissertation on The Poems of Ossian* (1763), naturally "assumes a poetic turn." Poetic figures, far from being the "artificial modes of speech" invented by more sophisticated poets and orators (as Dryden had believed), are products of imagination and passion and of the very limitations of the primitive vocabulary. Their allegedly livelier imaginations and a dearth of precise terms for their thoughts forced crude peoples to resort to "circumlocution, metaphor, comparison, and all those substituted forms of expression which give a poetical air to language."[48] Blair's ascription of the chief tropical devices of literary discourse to the pre-civilized state reveals how the primitivist enthusiasm could carry its proponents to the brink—or over the brink—of paradox: refinement suddenly becomes the enemy of "elegance."

With better logic John Husbands saw in the poetry of uncultivated societies the more glorious ancestor of the somewhat denatured style of civilized verse. His grand example is the ancient poetry preserved in the Bible, so much better suited to conveying the "dictates of the Holy Spirit" than the restrained poetic style of more polished ages. For Bishop Lowth, lecturing on sacred Hebrew poetry in 1753, ancient writing is thus *quintessentially* poetic: "Hence the poetry of the Hebrews abounds with phrases and idioms totally unsuited to prose composition."[49]

Meter itself, some thought, was also a spontaneous product of the aboriginal vigor rather than a deliberate contrivance. Some primitivists grounded metrical expression in the same crude social conditions that generated every other feature of poetic style. Blackwell declared that poetry antedated prose because primitive modes of verbal communication "naturally produce Numbers and Harmony." Blair too, conceding the seeming paradox, declared verse to be older than prose. "Music or song has been found coeval with society among the most barbarous nations." In Hurd, however, this primitivist enthusiasm is moderated. In his *Universal Poetry* he found that the cadences originally dictated by nature had been "further softened and improved by art," finally becoming as "ravishing to the ear" as images are to the imagination.[50]

Making no provision in the extant portions of the *Peri hypsous* for meter as a distinctive feature, Longinus had illustrated his quality of "transport" by passages of verse and prose indifferently. Yet the prominent occurrence of the term and concept of sublimity in Husbands's and Lowth's discussions of Old Testament style points to the close collaboration between primitivism and certain doctrines derived from the highly admired Greek treatise. These doctrines, it should be noted, were not strictly speaking those propounded by Longinus. One distortion of his teaching is especially pertinent here. Longinus ascribed τὸ ὕψος to five sources. The two most fundamental, said to be innate, were a capacity for elevated conception and vehement passion. The other three were largely acquired techniques: figurative language, noble diction, and dignified composition. But for these his modern adherents, beginning with Boileau and Dryden, had little use. What appealed to them most, in an age of growing interest in psychology, were the temperamental prerequisites for powerful writing named in Longinus's two innate sources. The true poet, the "genius"—in their interpretation and as that word came to be generally understood—was someone in whose psychical makeup conceptual grandeur was united with emotive depth. The term sublime itself, in Longinus primarily if not exclusively an ingredient of style, thus came to be applied to poems and poets alike. While Johnson, no Longinian enthusiast, was willing to name sublimity as the "characteristic quality" of *Paradise Lost*,[51] others could speak of the sublime Milton, Homer, and Shakespeare (the three poetic giants fortunately born before the polished modern age). For many of Johnson's fellow critics sublimity was also the prevailing quality of primitive literature, precisely because uncivilized people possessed in unusual measure the Longinian vehement passion which, given poetic vent, enthralls readers.

But the chief result for poetic diction theory was that the critics' heretical reading of Longinus only reinforced Horace's precept that the right words for a poem ensued spontaneously from the right prior meditation. Like the aesthetic naturalism of the primitivists, who were in most cases identical with the admirers of *Peri hypsous,* such a conviction argued powerfully for the vanity of theorizing on the subject: no rules were possible, but then none were needed. It is conceivable that Dennis's early intention to write a treatise on verse diction was blocked by the Longinianism which pervaded his critical thought. By the time of *The Grounds of Criticism in Poetry* (1704), he could offer only his own version of Longinus's central concept: great thoughts stimulate in the poet great passion, and great passion in turn generates moving expression. He regards this process as virtually self-evident even without the Greek critic's authority, since no poet in full creative rapture ever "wanted either Words or Harmony." At the other end of the century these motifs are joined in Alexander Knox's critiques (1796) of William Cowper's *The Task*. In one, Knox invokes Horace's dictum and in the next the Romanticist notion that the poet as a particularly sensitized being has only to pour out his genuine feelings in order to arouse a sympathetic reaction in his readers. We are hardly surprised to find him then praising Longinus for demanding certain moral qualities (such as he found in Cowper) in the successful poet.[52]

In Dryden, the Longinian inspiration had no adverse effect on the study of poetic language. In him it managed to coexist with a conscious attention to the attributes of poetic style and a firm belief in the feasibility of a rationale of them. Pope too taught that a poet's knowledge of prosodic science was vital to his attaining verbal skill, despite his intuition of an involuntary causative link between Homer's diction and sentiment. Perhaps Bishop Lowth's paraphrase of Longinus's account of the sublime also reflects Longinus' combination of the innate spiritual conditions of sublimity and the stylistic means to its embodiment. "The word sublimity," he wrote,

> I wish in this place to be understood in its most extensive sense. I speak not merely of that sublimity which exhibits great objects

with a magnificent display of imagery and diction, but that force of composition, whatever it be, which strikes and overpowers the mind, which excites the passions, and which expresses ideas at once with perspicuity and elevation, not solicitous whether the language be plain or ornamented, refined or familiar. In this use of the word I copy Longinus, the most accomplished author on this subject, whether we consider his precepts or his example.[53]

But the powerful empirical psychology of the day occasionally induced writers to minimize the formal aspects of Longinus's treatise. Blair's widely studied *Lectures on Rhetoric and Belles Lettres* (1783) gives due attention to the importance of figurative language in poetry, yet asserts that only the first two of Longinus's five sources, great conceptions and passion, "have any peculiar relation to the Sublime." That quality is never achieved "by hunting after tropes and figures and rhetorical assistances," because its proper region is above the "laboured refinements" of art. And like other British Longinians, Blair posits an opposition between the sublime and "the sublime style" originally set forth in Boileau's preface to his French version of *Peri hypsous* in 1674. The verbal embellishment which made the sublime style, Boileau argued, is actually incompatible with the unadorned conceptual majesty of the sublime itself. To clinch his point, he offered a flowery rewording in "le style sublime" of Jehovah's stark "Let there be light," which Longinus had cited among examples of sublimity.[54]

For Joseph Warton the sublime and the pathetic were "the two chief nerves of all genuine poesy." Neither meter nor diction counted for much. Pope, to Warton's taste, failed to qualify despite the unsurpassed harmony of his versification, whereas Thomson's *Seasons* was truly poetic even though its diction is sometimes "harsh, inharmonious, . . . turgid, and obscure," and its meter often faulty. Warton inconsistently conceded that Thomson fell short of first-rate status only because he lacked a style worthy of his lofty conceptions. Apparently verbal excellence was not, after all, generated by poetic rapture alone.[55]

Warton was by no means insensitive to Pope's polished versification; his book in fact contains several generous appreciations of it. But his wide reading led him to posit two *kinds* of poetry, one greater than the other. The higher quality of the first, proclaimed by Warton's repeated use of the term sublime to describe it (with scattered honorific references to Longinus), is owing to weighty moral and emotive content rather than to prosodic mastery. This "genuine and sublime" species could be careless of diction and utterly dispense with meter.

> It has been the lot of many great names not to have been able to express themselves with beauty and propriety in the fetters of verse in their respective languages, who have yet manifested the force, fertility, and creative power of a great poetic genius in prose.

Warton thought the historian Livy showed himself a great poet in his famous description of Hannibal crossing the Alps. Addison's style evinced the same quality—but in the *Spectator* essays, not in the "professed poetry" of his verse. For this assimilation of the aesthetic potentials of prose and verse Longinus of course provided the sturdiest authority then available.[56]

There is in Warton's observations an ambivalence toward poetic style, implying a disquieting divorce of form and content which threatens to discredit his entire argument. But he evades this impasse—after a fashion—by a split criterion of poetic worth, placing Pope at the head of those on the second level, the prototype being Horace. One interesting effect of this bifurcation of standards is that it initiates the depreciation of the term *elegance*. "Elegance, not sublimity," Warton wrote of Horace (and Pope), "was his grand characteristic." The terminological displacement reflects the turn in the tide of taste setting in at the time, to which the vogues of primitivism and the sublime centrally contributed, and which effectively dissolved the relative consensus of valuation and predilection that had obtained till then. How deeply this change could sometimes operate in practical critical judgment is plain in the contrast between Warton's declaration that no poem in Pope's whole *oeuvre* was in "a strain so truly sublime" as Gray's *The Bard* and Johnson's low estimate of that poem in his *Life of Gray*.[57]

Whether in retrospect one now applauds or deplores the shifting grounds of poetic appreciation that characterized the pre-Romantic Enlightenment, there can be little question that they were not conducive to further progress in understanding poetic language. No other result was possible from an attitude that tended to depreciate formal technique and adopt a general disregard of the poet's medium. Thomas Warton perfectly expressed the altered stance in his judgment that English poets after the Restoration abandoned imagination and sublimity of description for "correctness"; that they paid more attention to words than to things; that "the nicer beauties of happy expression were preferred to the daring strokes of great conception." Dryden's many valuable insights into the technique of his art are actually turned against him in Warton's question-begging conclusion that because he was "blinded by the beauties of versification only" he fell short of a just appreciation of Milton.[58]

From the resulting disorder of prosodic theory English neoclassicism possessed neither the conceptual nor the terminological means to recover. The revival of a reasoned account of the nature and value of the poet's exploitation of his medium came only with the profound renewal of Romanticism, most vitally in the terms provided by the organicist poetics of Coleridge.

CHAPTER FIVE

Wordsworth

THOUGH THE PUBLICA-
tion of *Lyrical Ballads* in 1798 did not by itself open a new age in
English literary history, it did unquestionably inaugurate a new
poetic idiom. The innovative, not to say revolutionary, impact of
the book lay as much in the style of the poems themselves as in the
principles set forth in the prefaces which Wordsworth supplied for
the second edition (1800, 1802). The ensuing controversy, however, has for decades been directed almost exclusively to Wordsworth's arguments and Coleridge's later rebuttal.

The present study must of course attend less to the kind of poetry written than to the critical doctrines propounded in each age.
Yet confronting so profound an upheaval as Romanticism requires
a prior awareness of contemporary poetic taste and practice. A
handy way of attaining this may be to glance at the poetry of
Lyrical Ballads in that context by comparing two samples of descriptive blank verse. One is James Thomson's admired depiction
of the snow storm in "Winter," from *The Seasons* (1726), the other
the exordium of "Tintern Abbey." Here is Thomson:

> Lo! from the livid East, or piercing North,
>
> Thick clouds ascend, in whose capacious Womb,
>
> A vapoury Deluge lies, to Snow congealed:
>
> Heavy, they roll their fleecy World along;

And the Sky saddens with th'impending Storm.

Thro' the hush'd Air, the Whitening Shower descends,

At first, thin-wavering; till, at last, the Flakes

Fall broad, and wide, and fast, dimming the Day,

With a continued Flow. See! sudden, hoar'd,

The Woods beneath the stainless Burden bow,

Blackning, along the mazy stream it melts.

And here Wordsworth:

Five years have passed, five summers with the length

Of five long winters! and again I hear

These waters, rolling from their mountain-springs

With a soft inland murmur.— Once again

Do I behold these steep and lofty cliffs,

Which on a wild secluded scene impress

Thoughts of a more deep seclusion; and connect

The landscape with the quiet of the sky.

For some time during the 1700s leading critics thought blank verse to be ill-suited to nondramatic verse, especially in the humble genre of descriptive poetry. Johnson found it unduly dependent on "bold figures and striking images," and as late as 1806 Richard Payne Knight pronounced it no better than prose unless it was crammed with inversions and other departures from normal syntax. Johnson did concede that in *The Seasons* blank verse was preferable to rhyming pentameter couplets. Yet granting all that is due—a good deal—to Thomson's verbal landscapes, we can see that the critics' low estimate of the form's potential was neither gratuitous nor excessive. Even more readily can we appreciate Coleridge's calling Thomson's blank verse "rhyme- craving" five-foot iambics.[1]

Nor are these reservations challenged by even the best in that kind written later in the century. William Cowper's recourse in *The Task* (1785) to recognizably Miltonic phrasal structures like "devious course uncertain" (Book III, line 3) gives his lines an air of calculation. Perhaps for this reason Leigh Hunt was to deny him a claim to having been a pioneer in "the true way to nature and a natural style" finally achieved in his day.[2]

By juxtaposing the passages from "Winter" and "Tintern Abbey" we can see that the restrictions imposed on blank verse by the critics were no longer tenable after 1798. And from the contrast in diction and phrasal cadence we can see why it is no exaggeration to speak of a revolution, and why in the "Advertisement" to the first edition of *Lyrical Ballads* the authors anticipated the consternation of readers: "they will look round for poetry . . . and inquire by what species of courtesy these attempts can . . . assume that title."[3]

To set "Tintern Abbey" beside its nearest possible metrical and generic counterparts lends point to Wordsworth's repeated prefatorial references to "the real language of men." The eighteenth-century manner was too consciously literary. In Thomson's reference to the woods "bowing" beneath the snow's "burden" many educated readers of Wordsworth's time would have caught the silent allusion to Horace's almost identical image for depicting the same natural phenomenon in Ode 9 of Book I ("candidum / . . . sustineant onus/silvae laborantes"). Wordsworth's protest is his version of the principle that all good verse is vitally related to the spoken idiom. Had he grounded his polemic against "vicious" poetic diction on that doctrine alone (one on which he and his collaborator fully concurred),[4] most of the controversy triggered by his observations would have been obviated.

Yet the core of Wordsworth's argument confirms Alexis de Tocqueville's thesis in *l'Ancien Régime et la Révolution:* that no revolution, whether political, intellectual, or artistic, ever fails to retain some features of the past. Scholars have pointed to the primitivistic theories of late neoclassicism that lie behind Wordsworth's statements about the virtual identity of common or rustic speech and good verse style, and the role of fastidiousness and refinement in its degeneracy into "poetic diction." The novelty of Wordsworth's views consists chiefly in the centrality he gave them and the bold terms in which they are formulated. (To have converted Dennis's honorific "poetic diction" into a term of abuse is perhaps revolution enough.)

Wordsworth's echoes of primitivistic ideas are most explicit in three familiar passages which it will be convenient to quote in full. The first appears in both the 1800 and the 1802 prefaces:

> Low and rustic life was generally chosen because in that condition, the essential passions of the heart find a better soil in which they can attain their maturity, are less under constraint, and speak

a plainer and more emphatic language; because in that condition of life our elementary feelings exist in a state of greater simplicity, and consequently may be more accurately contemplated; and, from the necessary character of rural occupations, are more easily comprehended; and are more durable; and lastly, because in that condition the passions of men are incorporated with the beautiful forms of nature. The language, too, of these men is adopted (purified indeed from what appear to be its real defects, from all lasting and rational causes of dislike or disgust) because such men hourly communicate with the best objects from which the best part of language is originally derived; and because, from their rank in society and the sameness and narrow circle of their intercourse, being less under the influence of social vanity they convey their feelings and notions in simple and unelaborated expressions. Accordingly, such a language, arising out of repeated experience and regular feelings, is a more permanent, and a far more philosophical language, than that which is frequently substituted for it by Poets, who think that they are conferring honour upon themselves and their art, in proportion as they separate themselves from the sympathies of men, and indulge in arbitrary and capricious habits of expression, in order to furnish food for fickle tastes, and fickle appetites, of their own creation.

The two other passages were added in the "Appendix" to the 1802 preface:

The earliest Poets of all nations generally wrote from passion excited by real events; they wrote naturally, and as men; feeling powerfully as they did, their language was daring, and figurative. In succeeding times, Poets, and men ambitious of the Fame of Poets, perceiving the influence of such language, and desirous of producing the same effect, without having the same animating passion, set themselves to a mechanical adoption of those figures of speech, and made use of them, sometimes with propriety, but much more frequently applied them to feelings and ideas with which they had no natural connection whatever. A language was thus insensibly produced differing from the real language of men in *any situation.*

Thus the English poets' gradual buildup of a "language peculiar to itself," which sixty years earlier Thomas Gray had hailed as a boon, is now, in radical evaluative reversal, deplored. The linguistic abuses thus spawned, Wordsworth continued, spread across national boundaries, and with the progress of refinement this diction became daily more corrupt, thrusting out of sight the plain humanities of nature by a motley masquerade of tricks, quaintnesses, hieroglyphics, and enigmas.[5]

The link between Wordsworth's declarations and the primitivist ideas reviewed in Chapter 4 is obvious. It is equally obvious, however, that his use of them is selective and freely adapted to his personal program. Wordsworth did not share the primitivists' dispiriting persuasion that civilized poets could not hope to emulate the giants of pristine ages. His frank acknowledgment of how much he owed to Bishop Percy's collection of folk ballads is made with no hint that his own compositions were not poetically superior to anything he found there. He was also admirably immune to an Ossianic mania so strong that it captivated the imaginations of European poets, musicians, and painters for decades.[6] The very style of *Ossian*, the enthralled Herder wrote, proves its antiquity; its inner spirit assures us in vatic accents that Macpherson himself could never have written it because such poetry is impossible in modern times ("so was lässt sich in unserem Jahrhundert nicht dichten"). Wordsworth was as far from such adulation as Johnson had been. But even if he had not seen Macpherson's "Celtic" fabrication for what it was, Wordsworth's temperament and convictions were proof against such fervent reverence for the heroic past and the historical determinism it fostered with such chilling implications for modern poetry.[7]

It is precisely because he considered the debased diction of contemporary verse to have resulted not from blind historical forces, but from a culpably willful compliance by fame-thirsty men with "the progress of refinement," that Wordsworth was able to level an indictment where the Duffs, Blairs, and Browns had usually voiced only a lament. To charge two whole generations of English poets with creative debility or betrayal may seem a desperate tactic in Wordsworth's struggle to create a taste necessary to a favorable reception of his own poems. Yet in one respect his charge is more than a protest made in personal interest; it formulates the prevalent socialization of a motif of late neoclassicism, its depreciation of the long-honored compositional "rule" of model-imitation in favor of "original genius." By 1750 this theme had become common in European discussions of poetry and the fine arts. Its relevance to poetic style was perhaps most summarily expressed in Germany by J. G. Sulzer, whose four-volume encyclopedia of aesthetics (1771–1774), which draws heavily on British and French speculation, is an erudite compendium of reigning opinion. Under the heading "Gedicht" Sulzer includes an account of the derivative, artificial style which in several respects parallels Wordsworth's diagnosis. It affirms that genuine poetic expression results only from spontaneous natural feeling. Lacking this essential, now and then some "would-be poet ["vermeinte Dichter"] decks out the most vulgar parlance in the garments of poetic art."[8]

But Sulzer's would-be poet is still only an occasional transgressor, relatively innocuous. By the rationale of a more thoroughgoing primitivism, however, he becomes a common type, owing ironically to the very refinement of versification and the esteem it enjoyed in enlightened society. Blair's diagnosis provides a closer anticipation of Wordsworth. "In after-ages," he wrote, "when Poetry became a regular art, studied for reputation and for gain, Authors began to affect what they did not feel, counterfeiting passion by displays of "artificial ornaments."[9]

The kind of meretricious verse that occurred only occasionally ("bisweilen") according to Sulzer, and more generally according to Blair, becomes epidemic in Wordsworth's account. Poetic diction, still not in itself reprehensible by Blair's reckoning, he identifies as both the hallmark of the venality and the instrument of its propagation. The debased currency of "tricks, quaintnesses, hieroglyphics, and enigmas" had through the operation of a stylistic Gresham's law driven the honest coin of natural expression out of circulation.

A more crucial difference between Wordsworth and the earlier decriers of refined adornment is that in his opposition of genuine poetic language to "adulterated phraseology" the "horizontal" temporal terms of the primitivist rendering are superseded by "vertical," societal terms. The favored barbarians of a real or suppositious golden age are converted into modern rustics, and civilization as a whole is reduced to its well-educated, urban, elite sophisticates. Eliot felt that Wordsworth's "social interest" explained both the formal novelty of his verse and his "explicit remarks on poetic diction."[10]

Perhaps so. It should be noted though that the shift from a historical to a societal schema, hardly unique to Wordsworth, was a conceptual mutation experienced by a whole generation nurtured on Rousseau and the democratizing tendencies of the French Revolution. The ideational progression is traced with Gallic clarity in that engaging if highly personal celebration of Romanticism, Madame de Staël"s *De l'Allemagne* (1813). A man "d'esprit supérieur," she wrote in her chapter on poetry,

> used to say *that prose was factitious and poetry natural;* in fact nations scarcely civilized always begin with poetry, and whenever a strong emotion agitates their souls the most vulgar men unconsciously use images and metaphors. . . . Common folk are much nearer to being poets than people in good society, because good breeding and witty banter can act only as barriers, and can inspire nothing.[11]

By this reasoning the social dimension of dictional theory is reversed. The poet's verbal "magazine" is no longer Puttenham's speech of urban courtiers, a norm only slightly relaxed in the later Enlightenment to the conversation of "honnêtes hommes." Now it has become that of Wordsworth's "middle and lower classes." Defenders of his theory have been most embarrassed by his further social abasement of the source of poetic language to the speech of rustics. No one needs the prompting of Coleridge's critique to ask how rural laborers, most of them illiterate, could have been possessed of "a far more philosophic language" than that used even by the least talented versifiers. Yet here too Wordsworth may only have been pressing to literal absurdity an aesthetic pastoralism rooted in eighteenth-century primitivism. The genius, Duff had written, shunning the din of cities, flourished in "the peaceful vale of rural tranquillity."[12]

There is an intimate connection between Wordsworth's veneration of uncultivated speech and his conception of his proper role as modern poet. The social impulse of which Eliot spoke was also a moral one. Wordsworth's avowedly didactic purpose was nothing less than the spiritual regeneration of society. Since as he envisioned it this aim depended for its success on a bond of fraternal sympathy linking the poet, as "a man speaking to men," with his readers, what more natural than that the language of his compositions should as nearly as possible approximate theirs, and so carry an intrinsic warrant of communal feeling? With this ideal other Romantic poets were to be in general accord.[13]

Unfortunately, Wordsworth's formulation of this principle raises questions never resolved anywhere in his critical writings. Since no one, rustics surely included, ever really talks poetry, the phrase "common language of men" invites other than a literal construction. Wordsworth's reservations, designed no doubt to forestall this objection, are not very helpful. Only "a selection" of common speech would be used, the language taken from rustics would be "purified . . . from . . . real defects and from all lasting and rational causes of dislike"; and the poet would besides "throw over" the residue "a certain colouring of the imagination" in order to endow common objects with dignity and allure. Some of Wordsworth's modern apologists would have it that these provisions sufficiently distance his position from anything like the parroting mimicry it seems to advocate. Even if so, however, questions remain. What are the criteria of the required selection? What words, phrases, or syntactical or grammatical idiosyncrasies, repugnant to reasonable taste, would suffer the winnowing process? And finally, does not the poet's imaginative manipulation of his subject matter entail a degree of stylistic alteration sufficient to preclude any assimilation of his verse to common talk that could have theoretical significance? From no reading of Wordsworth's prose, however attentive and however willing to make allowance for what M. H. Abrams called his "peculiarly dark and equivocal" statements, can we extract any clear answers.[14]

Since "real language" is so emphatically a phrase of approval, and since for Wordsworth the words suitable for genuine poetic expression, in contradistinction from "poetic diction," were inspired by real passion, it is not implausible to gloss "real" as "ingenuous" or "sincere." This reading certainly accords with a preference for the speech and feelings of semiliterate country folk over those of cosmopolites. Postponing for a moment the questions whether sincerity is ever a proper artistic virtue, and how without intimate acquaintance with a poet anyone can *tell* whether his poem is sincere or not, we are faced here with a further puzzle. As one commentator has noticed, Wordsworth's claim that rustics convey their feelings in "simple and unelaborated expressions" clashes with his assertion that passion yields a language that is "dignified, variegated, and figurative."[15] It can hardly help to point out that this very contradiction was already present in Wordsworth's legacy from the primitivists and Longinians. Blair, to call again on their most influential proponent, had lauded in his fourth Lecture the simplicity of pristine sublimity: the "native and unaffected simplicity" in Homer, the "plain and venerable manner of ancient times" in *Ossian*. To show that Milton is worthy to be classed with these giants, he quotes a passage from *Paradise Lost* that is written "entirely in a style and versification, easy, natural, and simple, but magnificent." Yet in Lecture XIV, to support his claim for the natural superiority of pre-civilized poetry, his readers are told that

> the most illiterate speak in Figures, as often as the most learned. Whenever the imaginations of the vulgar are much awakened, or their passions enflamed . . . they will pour forth a torrent of Figurative Language, as forcible as could be employed by the most artificial declaimer.[16]

What is nevertheless clear in Wordsworth's doctrine is the generative nexus between a poet's emotion and a valid style. If his own verse style is now figured and now plain, that is apparently because either type may be released by a given affective state. At one time the poet's sincerest feelings may give us

And never lifted up a single stone;

at another,

Have sight of Proteus rising from the sea.

In other words, there is (we may infer) no predicting what degree of tropical complexity, what level of vocabulary from the most ordinary to the most recherché, will suggest itself (during that creative interval that in Wordsworth's famous account of poetic germination follows tranquillity) as a proper embodiment of the overflow of emotion. Wordsworth's description, which again recalls the aesthetic psychologism of the century just ending, is couched in terms readily adaptable to Romanticism's expressivist critical orientation. The principle that poets must in some sense or other participate in the emotion they verbalize is at least as old as Horace's warning against the vanity of trying to draw readers' tears for a grief dispassionately described:

> si vis me flere, dolendum est
Primum ipsi tibi.

[If you wish me to weep, you must first grieve yourself.]

But as understood by most pre-Romantic critics, Horace's counsel insists only that a poet must achieve a prior imaginative realization of the emotion he seeks words for, not that he must have experienced it. Du Bos, for example, invokes "la maxime d'Horace" to argue that a reciter of poetry, like an orator, must be able to allow the relevant emotions to kindle his imagination ("s'échauffer l'imagination") and so take on the affective state of his *personae* ("se mettre à la place de ceux qu'il veux faire parler"). Anything but a requirement of sincerity, the ideal envisioned in neoclassical thought is closer to Keats's chameleon poet, having no character of his own.[17]

The ideal of sincerity gives almost exclusive importance to the criterion of propriety, at the same time altering its definition from an essentially formal to an ethical one. Traditionally, propriety had designated dictional suitability to subject or genre or both. Without entirely dropping this requirement from its total import, romantic poetical propriety is conformity of style not to the form or content of a poem, but to the psychic state of the poet; in a word, *sincerity*. David Perkins has ably shown how this "elevation of sincerity accompanied the profound change that led us to think of poetry as something close to self-expression. It has resulted in far-reaching revisions of poetic content and style, of the process of composition and the basis of enjoyment." In this spirit the young Byron honored the few poets of his day as those

> Who, least affecting, still affect the most:
> Feel as they write, and write but as they feel.[18]

Whatever else may be said for or against this Romantic revamping of an item of the neoclassical critical lexicon, it had an obvious attraction in the century which ultimately raised the hitherto humble lyric genre to virtual identity with poetry as a whole, a position it still largely occupies. Once a poem is considered to be less, or less centrally, a representation of some external object or event than a kind of *cri de coeur*, a corresponding alteration is almost inevitable in the role allotted to conscious craft in its creation and in the idea of what makes for valid poetic expression. Though priority in this regard must be given to Wordsworth, the new norms quickly became fundamentals of Romantic poetic theory. William Hazlitt put it with his usual pithiness. The artificial diction initiated, as he saw it, by Beaumont and Fletcher, caused the vapidity of so much later English verse,

> by not leaving the moulds of poetic diction to be filled up by the overflowings of nature and passion, but by swelling out ordinary

and unmeaning topics to certain preconceived and indispensable standards of poetical elevation and grandeur.[19]

Such a conviction raises anew with special urgency two closely related questions: what part, if any, is played by "art" in the making of good verse? and *wherein* does the desired natural idiom differ from the repellent artificial variety? Both questions are inherent in every poetics ever devised, but they are better addressed in those propounding an essentially mimetic poetic function, such as the neoclassical, rather than an expressive one. Both systems, however, allow some necessary involuntary psychic activity both before and during composition to consist with a certain amount of conscious craftsmanship. In the commonest account the procedure comprises two stages, inspiration first providing the materials, *including at least provisionally the words and their arrangement,* followed by the deliberate alteration, improvement, confirmation, or rejection of the lexical and metrical details of what was freely given. It is doubtful whether what happens is always, if ever, so neatly sequential, whether it is not rather an intermingling of both activities simultaneously or in undetectable oscillation. But every poetics provides for some collaboration of voluntary and involuntary cerebration.

From one point of view, the species of inspirational theory which is expressionism in its purest form, assumed in some of Wordsworth's most emphatic declarations, does not sit easy with the notion of craftsmanship. In naive expressionism the generating emotion is supposed to be real, that is, an emotion actually felt by the poet as a recollection of real experience, not of something merely heard of or imagined. On such an assumption, any manipulation, any conscious adjustment of the outpouring of unpremeditated utterance, is suspect. All formal verbalizing carries the taint of insincerity, tacitly acknowledged and perfectly acceptable in certain linguistic forms of social intercourse. In asking "How do you do?" one is not usually supposed to be especially concerned about another's welfare. Since by any theory, including the Romantic, poetry is in fact a verbal *art*, the result is an impasse which gravely questions sincerity as a valid criterion of poetic style.

Yet if a poet's conscious labor is directed not toward finding an alluring form for some fancied state of mind, but instead, as Pater believed, toward finding the right words, and the right order of words, for most faithfully representing his psychic state, the assumption of a necessary incompatibility between technical contrivance and authorial candor largely disappears. Late in life

Wordsworth himself put the case for conscious artistry in terms startlingly emphatic in someone who had raised the role of natural expression in the creative act to near self-sufficiency. "Again and again," he wrote to a correspondent,

> I must repeat that the composition of verse is infinitely more of an art than men are prepared to believe. . . . Milton talks of 'pouring forth his unpremeditated verse.' It would be harsh, untrue, and odious to say there is anything like cant in this; but it is not *true* to the letter, and tends to mislead. I could point out to you five hundred passages in Milton upon which labour has been bestowed.[20]

At the heart of this issue lies a perennial dilemma. As Wordsworth here insists, verse, inasmuch as it differs from other forms of utterance, obviously implies a certain degree of manipulation (or distortion) even if this is alleged to result not because the poet deliberately adopts certain devices but merely from activating his creative instinct. Yet, expressionists are the first to point out, a poem or passage often displeases us to the extent that it strikes us as contrived. As the classical saw reminds us, without the *ars celare artem*, the creative finesse for avoiding this impression, an artist's technical mastery goes for nothing. The fault, however, is more complex than it is usually represented to be. Its unpleasant effect is not caused simply by visible or audible evidence of craft, because that is apparent in all verse good or bad which is richly figurative or strongly metered. Less than any other is the theory of passion-motivated expression adapted to resolve this dilemma. Its criterion of sincerity, genetic rather than ontological, is ultimately referable not to poetic style but only to the subjective conditions of its formation. In that respect the very definition of the opposed terms natural and artificial is problematic, including whether they are in fact mutually exclusive.

This limitation of expressionist and psychologistic poetics in some measure accounts for Wordsworth's failure to make clear what be meant by "poetic diction." In his efforts to do so he meant to supplement the genetic argument with an objective theory of value or, in this case, disvalue. His procedure was not to excogitate an abstract definition of the evil à la his friend Coleridge, but to give examples of what he had in mind. Besides these, there is only the suggestive metaphor of *incarnation*, which he was apparently the first English critic to hit upon. In the third "Essay on Epitaphs" Wordsworth cites the baneful effect of Pope's style as a prime example of the awesome power which, for good or ill, words have over thought. They should therefore not be trifled with, as happens whenever they are not "an incarnation of the thought, but only a clothing for it."[21] Since he considers meretricious writing less in its aesthetic than in its moral implications, Wordsworth's sentiments here indicate the depth of his revulsion from the vicious verse diction which by argument and example he set himself to supplant. "Language," he explained,

> if it do not uphold, and feed, and leave in quiet, like the power of gravitation or the air we breathe, is a counter-spirit, unremittingly and noiselessly at work to derange, to subvert, to lay waste, to vitiate, and to dissolve. From a deep conviction then that the excellence of writing, whether in prose or verse, consists in a conjunction which must be of necessity benign; and that it might be deduced from what has been said that the taste, intellectual Power, and morals of a Country are inseparably linked in mutual dependence, I have dwelt thus long upon this argument.

Moreover, in what seems like only an ad hoc analogy, Wordsworth in fact overturns the centuries-old way of envisioning the relation between thoughts and the words used to communicate them. For his body-and-soul metaphor, applied specifically to the language of verse, tends to replace the largely decorative conception of figures, syntactical deviations, and meter by a structural conception, providing a more satisfactory interinvolvement of form and content. It is therefore regrettable that although Wordsworth resorted to that metaphor again in the 1815 "Essay, Supplementary to the Preface" and, according to De Quincey, used it in conversation, he failed either to elaborate it or to modify his earlier remarks about the language of verse to suit its implications.[22]

Abrams observed that in any expressionist poetics the question of diction is crucial because the poet's feelings are thought to manifest themselves not in plot or character but in words. Therefore "it becomes the major task of the critic to formulate the standards by which the language of poetry is to be regulated and judged."[23] If so, it was Coleridge and not Wordsworth or any other Romantic writer who most successfully fulfilled the program—but, as will appear below, in mimetic rather than expressionist terms. Nevertheless, what Wordsworth essayed in that direction, his several citations of poems and passages said to be marred by vicious diction, deserve attention in any account of modern thought on the poetic idiom.

To begin with, he was clearly not talking about nothing. Throughout literary history readers have borne witness to the sharp divergence of delight and disgust they felt from reading different poems, or even single lines. And some readers have accordingly tried to determine what it is that makes the difference, to isolate the stylistic traits that mark off bathetic verbiage from "the true voice of feeling"—to put it in the Keatsian phrase that neatly figures Wordsworth's genetic orientation. The problem is as pressing and baffling for the creator as for the critic, owing in good part to the refractoriness of the medium the poetic artist is condemned—and privileged!—to work in. "Remember also," Wordsworth pleaded with his public in 1815, "that the medium through which, in poetry, the heart is to be affected—is language; a thing subject to endless fluctuations and arbitrary associations." But whatever the poet's creative frustrations, the theorist cannot elude his corresponding burden of elucidation. Wordsworth's remarks consistently pose the question, however unsatisfactory the answer they provide. In what is still one of the most penetrating and informed explorations of the issues involved, Wimsatt and Brooks highlighted the two essential questions raised by the Wordsworth-Coleridge debate on poetic language, which they rightly called "a significant event in English literary history." The first, the genetic question, has occupied us for most of this chapter so far. The second, discussed above in relation to its recalcitrance to genetic solution, is the *critical* question: "How is 'poetic diction' in the sense of something undesirably artificial to be distinguished from the valid language . . . of poetry?" [24]

To answer it Wordsworth in the 1800–1802 Prefaces first quotes a sonnet by Gray, a poet he considers more "curiously elaborate in the structure of his own poetic diction" than any other.

> In vain to me the smiling mornings shine,
>
> And reddening Phoebus lifts his golden fire:
>
> The birds in vain their amorous descant join,
>
> Or cheerful fields resume their green attire.
>
> These ears, alas! for other notes repine;
>
> *A different object do these eyes require;*
>
> *My lonely anguish melts no heart but mine;*
>
> *And in my breast the imperfect joys expire;*
>
> Yet morning smiles the busy race to cheer,

And new-born pleasure brings to happier men;

The fields to all their wonted tribute bear;

To warm their little loves the birds complain.

I fruitless mourn to him that cannot hear

And weep the more because I weep in vain.

He then pronounces only the five lines he has printed in italics to be of any value.[25] Unfortunately, it is frequently pointed out, this verdict only further muddies an argument already unclear. The so-called good lines, for example, Wordsworth declares to be indistinguishable from prose except for the rhyme and an alleged faulty adverbial use of the adjective *fruitless.* Yet even waiving the total disregard of meter and the casual dismissal of rhyme, many readers will wonder whether an inversion and a personification in the first of the approved lines, two other personifications in the next two, and the antithetical phrasing in the last do not pretty well set them apart from normal prose. And what, in the nine "bad" lines, exemplifies the vicious poetic diction? We are left to guess. One early twentieth-century student of Wordsworth's dictional theory did so, with dubious results. What Wordsworth meant to condemn, she wrote, was simply bad imagery, specifically the pathetic fallacy, the false and frigid personification of valleys and rocks as "creatures" displaying emotions.[26] In one line, for instance, the mornings are made to smile. But if anything so easily identifiable as this was the evil, why didn't Wordsworth say so? And if, despite his silence on the point, he did object to mornings smiling, why in the "good" lines did he overlook eyes "requiring," anguish "melting," and joy "expiring"?

Understandably concerned that he had failed to give an exact notion of what he meant by "poetic diction," he added to the 1802 Preface an appendix of several pages devoted to that purpose. It comprises three parts: the sketch quoted here earlier of the historical regression by which originally passionate language gave way to an "adulterate phraseology" willfully imitative of genuine poetic expression but devoid of its "animating passion"; a citation of four eighteenth-century poems said to be written in that phraseology; and a brief critique of two stanzas of Cowper's "Verses by Alexander Selkirk," the one pronounced deplorable, the other admirable.[27]

Gray's sonnet is once more criticized, though this time for faults "not of the worst kind." Then, as affording the clearest "notion of what I mean by the phrase *poetic diction,*" he names Pope's

"Messiah," metrical paraphrases of Holy Writ, including Matthew Prior's of "Though I speak with the tongues of men and angels . . ." (I Corinthians 13, 1), and Johnson's of "Go to the ant, thou Sluggard" (Proverbs 6, 6). This last he quotes in full, calling it a "hubbub of words," and then sets beside it the prose of the King James version.[28]

Whatever immediate assent to the disparagement of these poems may have obtained during the nineteenth century no longer prevails. Reviewing hostile comments on Pope's "Messiah," its modern editors protest, apparently with Wordsworth especially in mind, that "the assumption that the Messiah can be honored 'sincerely' only in a diction of rugged simplicity scarce merits consideration." As for Johnson's "Turn on the Ant thy heedless eyes," exactly why so skillful an adaptation of the biblical prose should suffer denigration as "hubbub" must puzzle even a reader not especially fond of heroic couplets. Presumably Wordsworth hit on paraphrases as a sure-fire means of eliciting unfavorable contrast between a justly admired original text and inferior versions. But in fact readers may rate the originals higher without regarding Prior's and Johnson's imitations as in any respect contemptible. More to the point, we are once again left wondering just what in their diction, or in Pope's, is offensive. In Johnson's case we might suppose that three personified abstractions ("sloth usurp," "solicitation courts," "want . . . Shall spring") are among the blemishes, since they exemplify the one stylistic trait specifically condemned in the body of the Preface as an "ordinary device to elevate the style, and raise it above prose." Yet we are given pause by the recollection of those that occur in the five lines of Gray's sonnet that passed muster.[29]

And so we come to "Alexander Selkirk." The first stanza quoted is condemned en bloc. The epithet "church-going" is numbered among the "strange abuses" which modern poets have affected. Why this rather tame instance of the familiar device of the transferred epithet should offend readers Wordsworth does not explain. Saintsbury's scornful comment on the cavil was to suppose Wordsworth himself never spoke of a "dining-room." In the two final lines of the closing sentence, where it appears,

> But the sound of the church-going bell
> These valleys and rocks never heard,
> Ne'er sighed at the sound of the knell,
> Or smiled when a sabbath appeared,

he sees "an instance of the language of passion wrested from its proper use . . . applied upon an occasion that does not justify such violent expressions." Since among his illustrations of vicious diction, this is the only reference to its genetic source, the citation alerts our interest. The trouble is that few readers, as Wordsworth is frank to admit, will either discover much violence in the personifications of hearing, sighing, and smiling, or find the somewhat shopworn trope of empathetically sentient landscape inappropriate to the emotional state of a castaway fondly recalling tokens of civilized life. The second quoted stanza is praised for its "natural language," but no examples of it are specified.[30]

Wordsworth and his modern academic disciples seem to have grasped the problem by the wrong handle. The academic habit of ascribing the inadequacy of neoclassic poeticisms to the fact that they are stereotypes, or have become trite, is open to two crippling objections. It cannot explain why this "trite" idiom continues to please modern readers of Pope and several other poets of that period. And it fails to consider that all language is by its very nature stereotyped—perhaps none more so than the "plain speech" touted alike by Wordsworth and eighteenth-century celebrants of "easy" poetry.

Despite the challenge of Coleridge's incisive refutation in the *Biographia,* no aspect of Wordsworth's prosodic theory has been less adequately treated in modern commentary than his denial of any essential difference between the language of verse and well-written prose. One can only suppose that modern dissenters have seen no need to supplement Coleridge, while those disposed to favor Wordsworth's side in the exchange have been embarrassed by ambiguities and inconsistencies, especially on the subject of meter, similar to those that becloud other aspects of his poetics. To his credit, he does avoid the usual equivocation inherent in the word *poetry* itself, which in some contexts obscures the opposition *prose* versus *poetry.* This is implied in his denial of "any *essential* difference between the language of prose and metrical composition."[31] Besides, he openly asserts that *poetry* properly designates the more inclusive opposite to *science,* not to *verse.*

On superficial view, this admission may make Wordsworth appear to have been endorsing the arguments of eighteenth-century critics who denied that meter was necessary to poetry. A late spirited version of this position, contributed by the Reverend William Enfield to the *Monthly Magazine* in 1796, has even been suggested as Wordsworth's immediate source. Abrams saw striking parallels between the two men's thinking. Actually, however, they shared little beyond the proposition that some prose may have poetic quality. Enfield's purpose was to deflate what to him were arrogant claims for the superiority of metrical expression over its rival, much in the vein of the anti-metrists discussed in the previous chapter. Although he admits (somewhat damagingly to his whole thesis) that verse is "certainly the fairest dress of poetry," he does not hesitate to maintain that Milton "would have written a magnificent fable concerning the loss of Paradise, and Butler a witty tale of Hudibras, had they only expressed their conceptions in prose." Nothing could be further from the opinion of Wordsworth. He argues at length against those who "underrate the power of metre in itself," and asserts that of two equally skilled portrayals of passions, manners, or characters, one in prose, the other in verse, "the verse will be read a hundred times where the prose is read once." And as noted earlier, he thought Pope had been able by the power of verse alone to invest mere common sense with passion. As with others of his aesthetic persuasion, Enfield's main exhibit in support of his case against meter is the so-called prose poem, a form which never much impressed Wordsworth despite his acceptance of the wider definition of poetry. Enfield ends his account by invoking the usual examples, ranging from parts of the Old Testament, through *Ossian*, to *Télémaque*.[32]

If it is hard to make consistent sense of Wordsworth's poetics as a whole, we may nonetheless glimpse its motivation in the same healthy impulse to humanize the art that led him to exalt common speech. Poetry had too long been called and too often treated as the language of heaven. It was time to restore it to earth, and to humanity.

> Poetry sheds no tears "such as Angels weep," but natural and human tears; she can boast of no celestial Ichor that distinguishes her vital juices from those of prose; the same human blood circulates through the veins of them both.[33]

One can hardly think of a poet from whom this might have come with better grace than the author of "Tintern Abbey."

The difficulties with his line of reasoning begin to appear in the confident claim that it would be easy to prove

> that not only the language of a large portion of every good poem, even of the most elevated character, must necessarily, except with

reference to the metre, in no respect differ from that of good prose, but likewise that some of the most interesting parts of the best poems will be found to be strictly the language of prose, when prose is well written.

This sweeping statement not only impairs his vindication of the power of meter; it must also immediately contravene the experience of most readers of poetry. It fairly cries out for support by the passages from Milton which he affirms he could readily have cited, instead of the unavailing evidence of a few inoffensive lines in Gray's mediocre sonnet. It does at least serve to differentiate Wordsworth's view from that implied by the proponents of poetic prose. Whereas they hold that some poetry is written in prose, his position is that some of the finest *verse* is *stylistically identical* with good prose, a proposition radically divergent in its theoretical implications. Assuming the general validity and perhaps, as Wordsworth claims, the demonstrability of his assimilation, it would suffer no serious damage from the qualifying phrase "except with reference to the metre," if meter is depreciated to a trivial decoration, a troublesome impediment, or an outmoded affectation, as it sometimes has been. When, however, it is given the efficacy ascribed to it by Wordsworth, it is difficult to conceive how an otherwise stylistic conflation of prose and verse can be tenable, or even what it could mean. The contradiction surfaces again in the 1802 Appendix when he praises the last stanza of "Alexander Selkirk." It would, he thinks, be equally good in prose, "except that the Reader has an exquisite pleasure in seeing such natural language so naturally connected with metre." Anyone may wonder how an equal value can inhere in two forms of expression when one of them lacks an "exquisite pleasure" which the other provides. The discrepancy is especially grave in a critic who repeatedly rated poets' capacity to please among their prime assets.[34]

Wordsworth's most extended discussion of meter aims to reconcile his own use of it with his conviction of the essential identity of prose and verse. Poetry arouses pleasurable excitement in readers. But this excitement is unruly, and without "the co-presence of something regular," namely meter, to temper the expressive ardor and often painful imagery produced by the poet's passion, it may "be carried beyond its proper bounds." He also claims for meter the aesthetic framing or "distancing" often valued since as a technique whereby repellent subject matter becomes tolerable.[35]

There is good reason to think that he owed part of his argument to Coleridge, who confided to Southey that the Preface of *Lyrical Ballads* was half his own brainchild. The probability of Coleridgean influence is strengthened by Wordsworth's reference to metrical language inducing the pleasurable experience of "similitude in dissimilitude," a principle he declared to be "well known to those who have made any of the Arts the object of accurate reflection." It is further strengthened by what Coleridge wrote to William Sotheby in 1802:

> . . . metre itself implies a *passion*, i.e. a state of excitement in the Poet's mind, & is expected in that of the Reader—and tho' I stated this to Wordsworth, & he has in some sort stated it in his preface, yet he has [not] done justice to it.

And so Coleridge suspects a "*radical* difference" of opinion between himself and his friend which he was to elaborate years later in the *Biographia Literaria*. The radical difference included Wordsworth's assumption that meter was a purely voluntary feature of poetic utterance. Alone among the properties of poetic language, and in direct contradiction of Coleridge, it has no ground in passion and thus no place in the originating emotion posited in Wordsworth's account of the creative process. He therefore always speaks of it as something "superadded" to the kind of language that is dictated, as he has it in the Appendix, by genuine passion: "if metre be superadded thereto"; "to superadd the charm" of meter. To superadd, *Webster's Dictionary* informs us, means "to add over and above: add something adventitious, superfluous." Wordsworth accordingly refers to the metrical form of "Alexander Selkirk" as a "mere circumstance" with no bearing whatsoever on its faults or beauties. The ideas and feelings expressed, "whether the composition be in prose or in verse, . . . require and exact one and the same language. Metre is but adventitious to Composition." A few years later he characterized the *choice* of meter in preference to prose as a "vehicle" for epitaphs, expressly excluding it from the "modes of fiction" generated by strong passion.[36]

Wordsworth's refusal to allow meter a place among the emotive data tranquilly recollected during the creative process is puzzling. What seems especially incongruent with the rest of Wordsworth's creative doctrine is that in the heightened state of receptivity prevailing during composition poets should be considered impervious to the emotive agency of a rhythmic impulse to which their less sensitized readers are allegedly so responsive. Moreover, since he was elsewhere so insistent that poetic phraseology is what the body is to the soul, why should meter have no part in that "sensuous incarnation" which, in the "Essay, Supplementary to the Preface" in the 1815 edition of his poems, he adjudges to be indispensable to poetry's very existence? Surely the opposite view would tally more closely with the experience recalled (among other places in his own verse) in the "Prospectus" of *The Recluse*, lines 10–13:

> To these emotions, whencesoe'er they come
>
> Whether from breath of outward circumstance,
>
> Or from the Soul—an impulse to herself,
>
> I would give utterance in numerous verse.[37]

The formalizing tendency of the creative urge has been attested to by poets throughout history.

With their testimony Wordsworth's denial of any role to meter in the genesis and growth of a poem or in his conception of genuine poetic language stands in startling contrast. The omission is the more glaring since meter figures centrally in the primitivist aesthetics by which he was otherwise influenced. Blackwell thought that primitive poetic fables "naturally produce Numbers and Harmony," and John Brown wrote that "*Rythm* [sic], *Numbers*, and *Verse*" arose naturally from the love of "measured Melody" prevalent in savage society. Meter, these writers would have it, is born with poetry itself.[38]

A more discriminating version of the process held that though formal meters themselves came about through gradual improvement in the poetic art, their root principle is natural and primitive. Sulzer's German phrase perhaps most deftly labels the distinction. The poet's passion gives birth to a crude rhythm which he calls "der Ursprung des Verses" (the starting-point of verse). As the art became more refined, this inchoate cadence was gradually regularized. In this sense, Sulzer concluded, it could be said that meter is inherent to poetry ("dass der Vers dem Gedichte natüralich sei").[39]

Sulzer's "Ursprung des Verses" finds an equivalent term in Coleridge's "elements of metre" when he converts the stages of the primitivists' historical progression to steps in the psychology of poetic composition:

> As the *elements* of metre owe their existence to a state of increased excitement [in the poet], so the metre itself should be accompanied

by the natural language of excitement. . . . [And then] these elements are formed into metre artificially, by a *voluntary* act.

To see how mutually remote the two poets' concepts of versification were, we need only compare this passage from the *Biographia* with another from Wordsworth's Appendix. Having alluded again to the natural language of primitive poetry, he adds:

> To this language it is probable *that metre of some sort was early superadded*. This separated the genuine language of poetry still further from common life. . . . This was the great temptation to all the corruptions which have followed."[40]

Briefly put, both agree that formal meter separates the spoken idiom from poetic expression. But whereas for Coleridge, despite his high estimate of poetic prose, it was a prime condition of poetic value, for Wordsworth it was an ambivalent adjunct, as much a contrivance as the deplored poetic diction. But of the two, meter, governed by known rules, was much less pliant to the arbitrary caprice of each poet's authorial vanity. Though no necessary ingredient of a poem, it may therefore in itself be an innocuous attraction, like the maraschino cherry which may or may not, at the diner's choice, top an ice-cream sundae. But it is no more than that. How such a trivialization can be squared with Wordsworth's early defense of its power against detractors is not readily apparent.

CHAPTER SIX

Coleridge I

SINCE THE 1930s COLE-
ridge's poetic theory has enjoyed a unique reputation. Dryden and
Arnold (Johnson is a doubtful third) were what Remy de Gourmont called *créateurs de valeurs*,[1] critics who established the literary taste and conceptual priorities of their generations. Coleridge
was not one of these. What sets him apart from them is that as regards poetic theory he came to share that honor with T. S. Eliot in
his time, during which, and for some time after, Coleridgean concepts were confirmed, reformulated, or otherwise kept viable.

A survey of what had been said on the subject before him reveals that Coleridge's analysis constitutes a watershed in the development of poetic diction theory analogous to that represented by
Kant in aesthetics.[2] This has nothing to do with the German
philosopher's influence on Coleridge's thinking. I mean rather
that he arrived at his new departure point in poetics by what
amounts to a critique, in the sense of a resumption and reordering
of past doctrine—specifically of literary mimesis—just as Kant had
revolutionized epistemology, ethics, and aesthetics via critiques of
the established empiricist bases of these sciences. Coleridge's initial concern simply to refute Wordsworth's faulty notions of poetic
language occasioned a fundamental restructuring of all that had
gone before. The resulting theory profoundly conditioned a vibrant era of twentieth-century Anglo-American poetics inaugurated by I. A. Richards's acceptance of Coleridge's primacy in

poetics. For Richards, Coleridge, having for years explored poetry
with unrivaled "assiduity and enterprise," was a literary Galileo
who "initiated a new era for criticism."[3]

Wordsworth sought in his Prefaces to win public approval for
the innovative style of his own poems by replacing what he regarded as a degenerate taste with an appreciation of natural expression. Coleridge, ultimately, undertook a far more ambitious
task. While sharing his friend's immediate purpose, from the outset he felt obliged to dissociate himself from the faulty reasoning
used to advance it. And yet the issues Wordsworth had raised were
weighty ones. So, driven according to his wont by an instinct for
grounding every intellectual opinion in solid theory, Coleridge
soon realized that an effective refutation of Wordsworth's miscon-
ceptions of verse language would require a fresh investigation of
the nature of poetry itself. Accordingly he thought it expedient

> to declare once for all, in what points I coincide with his opin-
> ions, and in what points I altogether differ. But in order to render
> myself intelligible I must previously, in as few words as possible,
> explain my ideas, first, of a POEM; and, secondly, of POETRY itself,
> in *kind*, and in *essence*.[4]

The ensuing explanation is set forth mainly in seven brilliant
chapters of the *Biographia Literaria*. In them Coleridge defines
poetry's verbal ontology as essentially congruent with those of the
other fine arts, being rooted in the same creative psychology and
having the same humanizing function. To grasp his multifaceted
program, the account in the *Biographia* must be supplemented by
passages in the letters, the notebooks, the lectures, the marginalia,
and the table talk.[5]

These supplementary sources reveal how constantly during
the fifteen years between the 1802 *Lyrical Ballads* and the *Biographia* Coleridge had excogitated the issues of prosodic theory,
including the most crucial and most baffling: "the long continued
controversy concerning the true nature of poetic diction." On the
eve of its publication in 1817 he informed his correspondent
William Sotheby of his gratification at having done so "as far as
Reasoning can settle it."[6]

None of the celebrated doctrines propounded in Coleridge's
writings, such as the imagination's reconciliation of opposites or
the separate definitions of poem and poetry, adequately explains
what sets his critical thought apart from that of his contempo-

raries. Its real distinction and enduring appeal lie rather in his subordination of the literary expressionism dominant in his time to a fundamentally mimetic orientation which includes and transcends it. His reformulation thoroughly revises the classic imitation theory (or theories) to which he and Wordsworth were necessarily heirs. It is hardly surprising that this revision makes allowance for the expressionism which, as M. H. Abrams demonstrated in *The Mirror and the Lamp*, determined the orientation of the critical thought of early Romanticism. No one so ardently immersed in the intellectual currents, native and German, of his day could have entirely escaped the implications of so profound a shift of critical focus as that from the poet's song to the soul of the singer. The redirection was powerful and pervasive, facilitated by the cult of genius predominant in the late eighteenth century. Whereas a poem had long been conceived as a picture, pleasing and instructive, of some aspect of the world real or fancied, it was henceforth regarded more and more as the precious emanation of a rare spirit. In Coleridge's poetics the new expressionism appears mainly in his description of the creative process. The same imagination which fuses opposites to form the dynamic, organic unity of its product is also the faculty which empowers the vital "infusion" of the poet's own thought and feeling into his creation.[7]

A favorite axiom of Coleridge held that all intellectual progress depended on "desynonymization," the detection of distinct meanings for two terms till then considered synonymous. The best known example is his separation of *fancy* and *imagination*. His idea of artistic representation is based on another, a compelling redefinition of the old mimetic terms *copy* and *imitation*. Though far less noticed, this latter discrimination is in fact the cornerstone of his critical edifice. We have Coleridge's own word for it. The qualitative distinction between a copy and a true imitation, he wrote, is nothing less than "the universal principle of the fine arts."[8]

To take the full measure of Coleridge's enrichment of the term imitation, it will be helpful to review how it had been understood in neoclassical criticism. Before doing so, however, it must be made clear that the word imitation is here used exclusively as Coleridge used it, to designate artistic mimesis, not the process of emulating masterpieces.

The classical origins of mimesis are of course in Plato and Aristotle. Imitation as a term for emulation of the great imitators of nature derives mainly from Longinus and Horace, a doctrine revitalized in our time by Eliot, Northrop Frye, and others. But whatever its merits, it is important to remember that Coleridge's copy and imitation are terms of exclusively mimetic reference, naming alternate and radically disparate versions of the nexus between art and reality.

There's no need to review here the complexities of the classical mimesis debated by modern interpreters.[9] But since it is germane to Coleridge's dictional theory, one or two generalizations about the ancient usage are in order. For centuries before Coleridge's birth the classical formula "Art copies nature" expressed a universally accepted aesthetic dogma.[10] That this general acceptance never prevented definitional disagreement is traceable in part to a divergence between what Plato and Aristotle themselves intended by it, one rooted in their differing epistemologies and ontologies. To state it simply, in Plato's idealist conception of truth and reality imitation is essentially a pejorative term, whereas in the empiricism of "solider Aristotle" it names a valid means to one kind of knowing. Our delight in an imitation, Aristotle maintains, arises from the pleasure of learning something. For Plato, however, the poet's claim to teach is fraudulent. Coming by way of the senses, his imitation of reality can only deceive, since truth and real being reside not in sensible objects but in immaterial Forms, or Ideas, which are apprehensible only by the intellect.

Whatever the profound implications of Plato's argument for subsequent philosophy (which I am unqualified to determine), its main influence on Western critical theory lies mainly in one of his assumptions: that the poet aims at no more than a simulacrum of what strikes his senses. His mimesis is a copy of the lowest order, often pleasing to contemplate but after all only a slavish mimicry of common perception. In the *Republic* Socrates belittles the procedure involved by likening it to catching a bare reflection of the visible world in a mirror. And so the poet whom Plato bans from his perfect state as deceiver and corrupter of the soul is denied creativity as well.

Mimesis as described in the *Poetics* is something very different. Perhaps because of the fragmentary state and doubtful form of that treatise, some of Aristotle's references to it are less than clear and some seem inconsistent with others. There can be no doubt, however, that he meant to distinguish poetry from the nature or reality it "imitates." It is something produced, not *re*produced, by a poet who is a maker, not just a recorder. However startling to modern readers (as S. H. Butcher had to admit), the object of this imitation is exclusively "men in action." Like every other aspect of

real life, human activity is essentially disorderly, lacking both coherence and limits. What the poet makes of it, a "plot," is both
unified and bounded. It has a beginning, conceived as that which
has nothing preceding it, and an end conceived as having nothing
following it, the two causally linked by a middle. Unlike life, it
admits of nothing accidental. It may admit impossibilities, which
reality of course cannot admit, provided they are "probable."
The poet, Aristotle declared, should even prefer probable impossibilities (ἀδύνατα εἰκότα) to improbable possibilities (δυνατὰ
ἀπίθανα). Since the former phrase is a paradox in real experience,
it sets up a further and sharper distinction between Aristotle's
mimetic construction and the world it imitates.[11]

But what can his arresting oxymoron mean? Aristotelian commentary shows that *probability*, like other crucial terms in the
Poetics (*hamartia*, *peripeteia*, above all *katharsis*), is of debatable
import. But the commonest ingredient in the various explications—and the one most answerable to the distortions of an imagined cosmos—takes "probable" to mean consistent with the conditions of a given work's fictive world. Thus Cinderella's proving
to be the one young woman in an entire kingdom whose foot fits
a particular slipper is acceptable in a world where her gorgeous apparel can revert to rags on the stroke of midnight. Even if this is a
heretical reading of Aristotle's idea, it gains force from repeated
independent confirmations by later critics. It reappears notably, for
example, in Henry James's essay "The Art of Fiction," where he
argues that we must freely grant the artist his *donné*, the initial assumptions of his fable, however discrepant from quotidian experience, provided only that all that follows conform to the imaginative environment they define. Coleridge's conception of mimesis is
perfectly congruous with this aesthetic law. Its importance lies in
what it implies for the critical judgment of a work of art, whatever
its medium, by enforcing an evaluative norm in which the criterion
of representational fidelity, even where admitted, is subject to a
prior and overriding requirement of intrinsic structural coherence.
Wordsworth's dictional naturalism, even when most favorably construed, represents a reversal of this priority.

Hardly any neoclassical writer took an artistic imitation to be
the mindless facsimile of the perceived world described by Plato.
When Robert Howard condemned the use of rhyme in tragedy
because people do not speak in rhyme, Dryden, we recall, replied
that on stage nature must be "wrought up to an higher pitch."
Addison said the same of descriptive poetry, in which a natural

scene is so enlivened by art that "the real landscape pales in comparison with the poet's imitation of it."[12]

The distinction between life and mimetic art, elusive enough at any time, seems to have been especially hard to maintain during the Enlightenment against the double current of rationalism and empiricism. Its shifting status is reflected in the pair of quasi-polar critical terms adopted by Boileau, *le vrai* and *le vraisemblable*. The very beauty of a poem was conditioned on its conformity to truth because, as his ninth verse Epistle had it, nothing false can be beautiful ("Rien n'est beau que le vrai"). Yet this claim was hard to reconcile with an equal stress on the formal coherence of the *vraisemblable*, "probability." Never clearly defined, this concept at least bears witness to the neoclassical sense of the aesthetic vacuity of photographic imitation. The third Canto of Boileau's *Art poétique* warns against a point-for-point correspondence of a literary work to reality: "Le vrai peut quelquefois n'être pas vraisemblable."[13] What is true may sometimes not *look* true.

A sketchy aesthetic category enduring well into the eighteenth century, *vraisemblance* figures crucially in Batteux's treatise on fine art. In Aristotle's *Poetics* Batteux found support for contending that in a proper artistic imitation the resemblances do not accord with nature but only appear to do so. Batteux tried to vindicate *vraisemblance* by equating it with the notion of "la belle nature." Poets and painters delight us with a perfection of beauty never found in what we perceive around us, by forming their imitations according to a process of selective realism. They copy nature right enough, but only those aspects of it which are in themselves immediately pleasant to contemplate. But this way of assuring artistic verisimilitude exposed the arts once again to the age-old charge of deceptiveness, especially since Batteux himself accepted the essentially positivistic implications of the reigning conception of what is true. At the core of his apologia lies the discrediting concession that poetry is a constant lie bearing all the marks of truth ("un mensonge perpétuel, qui a tous les caractères de la vérité").[14]

Nonetheless, Batteux's book retained its appeal. Within a few years, its thesis was given a subtler, vaguely Neoplatonic treatment by Johann Joachim Winckelmann, who envisaged a similar procedure as the means whereby the Greek sculptors had endowed their human forms with ideal grace and beauty. They combined into a single statue imitations of the finest bodily features as they had observed them distributed among several living persons.[15]

Broadly speaking, these Continental eighteenth-century formulations differ in no essential from what Coleridge could find in his countryman Dryden, who early asserted what many readers easily discover. Poetry should in some sort serve truth, "but to affect the Soul, and excite the Passions, and, above all, to move admiration . . . a bare imitation will not serve." Later he anticipated the doctrine of *la belle nature:* a single work of art comprises "the scattered beauties of nature united by a happy Chymistry, without its deformity or faults."[16] But though neoclassical poetics firmly underwrote Coleridge's rejection of what he would call the copyist's "idle rivalry" with nature, he would surely have detected in Dryden's "happy Chymistry" of selective combination, and in Batteux's and Winckelmann's more elaborate versions of it, an all too apt instance of the fancy's substituting a mere aggregation of discrete elements for the fused unity attained through the imagination.

The nearest approach to Coleridge's poetic mimesis among older critics is found in Reynolds, one of the very few eighteenth-century figures of whose opinions Coleridge spoke highly ("An artist, whose writings are scarcely less valuable than his works"). In number 13 of the *Discourses on Art* Reynolds adduces characteristic features of the mimetic arts to argue that, except for painting in its most primitive phase, each of them is valued for offering us not "a natural expression of a given object" but a new creation naturally calculated to delight the imagination. How closely Reynolds approaches the organicism of Coleridge's genuine imitation appears precisely in what he said of verse. Having noted the "violation of common speech" effected by meter, he defended it by a justifying principle,

> the sense of congruity, coherence, and consistency, which is a real existing principle in man; and it must be gratified. Therefore, having once adopted a style and a measure not found in common discourse, it is required that the sentiments also should be in the same proportion elevated above common nature, from the necessity of there being an agreement of the parts among themselves, that one uniform whole may be produced.[17]

The originality of Coleridge's separation of copy from imitation does not preclude all intellectual ancestry. Some scholars have detected a source for Coleridge's idea in Plotinus, who in the Eighth Tractate of the fifth *Ennead* defended artists' imitations because "they give no bare reproduction of the thing seen," but imbue their works with ideal elements drawn from their own souls. But this conception bears so slender a relation to Coleridge's line of reasoning that we can hardly suppose his theory would been other than it is had he never heard of the *Enneads*. Though the same may be said for Winckelmann, he does provide one of the very few instances before Coleridge of a desynonymization of the hitherto interchangeable terms. But the fact is almost certainly coincidental. Though Coleridge probably knew Winckelmann's work he never mentions him, and the terminological distinctions the two men draw notably differ. Winckelmann does exalt one kind of imitation ("Nachahmung") over another which he labels a resembling copy ("eine ähnliche Kopie"). But whereas Winckelmann's "Kopie" is only the much less valuable of two quite legitimate modes of artistic representation, Coleridge's "copy," only an "idle rivalry" with nature, is worthless.[18]

Earlier critics were of course fully aware that the horror and moral outrage they would feel at witnessing the deeds of a real regicide and tyrant would have been allayed by their grim satisfaction at the spectacle of his final defeat, but with nothing like the pleasure afforded by a reading or staging of *Macbeth*. They also saw that a circumstantial, factual report of the real tyrant's crimes and ultimate punishment would fail in the same way, except that in the verbal surrogate of a text (the "copy") the painful emotions elicited by an immediate perception of the real thing would be much attenuated. As neoclassical opinion shows, however, the theory commonly adopted to explain this latter difference postulated an artistic imitation that came to little more than one or another kind of prettification of unpleasant realities. This could be accomplished by deletion or addition: by suppressing insurmountable ugliness or dullness in the original, and thus highlighting its less objectionable ingredients; or by the supervention of such formal palliatives as meter and figurative language. The most cogent exposition of the latter option, by David Hume, represents a kind of mid-position between the former and Coleridge's mimetic theory, which in fact it imperfectly resembles.[19]

Coleridge inherited a critical tradition that sought to solve the mimetic question not by moving from psychologically grounded critical principles to the poetic work's mode of existence, as he was to do, but in the reductionist terms of the reigning faculty psychology itself. The older critics had been inclined to regard the difference between the passions aroused by a real occurrence or object and those aroused by its imitation as one of degree, not of kind.

This appears clearly in the French work which achieved wide repute in England and Germany, Dubos's treatise on poetry and painting. These two arts, he explained, must excite in us impressions identical in kind with those aroused by the objects they depict, but weaker. He thus posits a crudely psychologistic theory of aesthetic value. Passionate excitement, even if painful, Dubos argued, affords a welcome relief from the dysphoria of affective torpor. But artificial passions have the additional advantage of being devoid of the painful aftereffects left by most real passions. When the fictive experience ends, the impression quickly dissipates ("disparoit sans avoir des suites durables"). Racine's *Phèdre* provides him with a celebrated instance. The sight of a young princess, sick with remorse and expiring in convulsions, would be simply repellent. But the play, he argues, draws tears which "will end with the presentation of the ingenious work of fiction that caused them to flow."[20]

In virtually every crucial particular Coleridge's genuine imitation diverges from Dubos's account. No vicarious substitute for actual experience, it differs *in kind* from the "life-stuff" it manipulates. And the value of what the artist creates, the total psychic activity it affords us, is consequently—as leading aestheticians have since affirmed—*sui generis*.

So envisioned, a poem's relation to reality is less one of likeness than of "commentary." Its formative value does not stop with that honing of our perceptive powers sometimes claimed (plausibly enough so far as it goes) as a benefit of artistic representation.[21] Coleridge's imitation implies a morally and intellectually enriched conception of poetry that more fully answers to a thoughtful reader's experience of it. Putting this another way, his mimesis makes provision for our finding in poetry the Arnoldian "criticism of life" for which Arnold himself offered no satisfactory theoretical ground. In this regard, however, it is imperative to keep constantly in mind that for Coleridge the "criticism" in question derived both its form and its cognitive value from its aesthetic mode, in the creative imagination as distinct from the rational understanding. His steady grasp of this distinction belongs with so much else that has made him seminal and congenial to the most fruitful poetic theory of the present century.[22]

CHAPTER SEVEN

Coleridge II

AGAINST WORDSWORTH'S theses that genuine poetic language is ideally derived from rustic speech and that there is no essential difference between the languages of poetry and prose, Coleridge directed a bi-level refutation in the *Biographia*. On the first level are several denials of these assertions themselves or of assumptions they entail. Thus he retorts that the best part of any language comes not from the countryman's habitual communion with unspoiled nature but from the intellectual and imaginative activity of cultivated minds.[1]

It is on the more fundamental level, however, his idea of a genuine artistic imitation, that his theory of verse language ultimately rests. He skillfully applied his copy-imitation antithesis to the drama, opera, painting, sculpture, and acting, as well as to poetry. It is further supported by the affinity of imitation to such other major tenets of his aesthetic as "multëity in unity" (i.e., artistic beauty) and the polar action of the creative imagination. The fatal flaw in Wordsworth's remarks about good and bad poetic style lay in a misconstruction of artistic mimesis. Taken literally, his choice of rustic speech as the norm of poetic expression would yield only a mimicry of colloquial usage. His equation of prose and verse confuses two generically distinct modes of relation to perceived reality. Prose—here meaning nonfictional writing, since it aims at objective reports of the experiential world ("facts experienced and recorded, as in history") or, in philosophic or scientific writing, of conceptual truth ("truth absolute and demonstrable")[2]—could reasonably be labeled a copy of nature (though all but the barest notation must be something more). Verse, however, which inevitably subjected the reality it represented to various formal distortions and patternings as a condition of attaining aesthetic quality, was fittingly classified as imitation. Although Coleridge's conception is essentially Aristotelian and hence traditional, his exposition of it was new, both as a general aesthetic principle and as an enduringly compelling elucidation of a cardinal theoretical issue. By redefining artistic imitation to consist with his aesthetic of polarities, he developed a mimetic analysis of poetic language that is salutary in largely avoiding the impasses and contradictions of previous speculation.

Nor can it be fairly objected that Coleridge's account is flawed by neglect of the excluded middle occupied by "poetic" prose. Far from relegating stylistically attractive prose to the status of a mere copy, he declared it to be at its best poetry "of the highest kind." The wide embrace of his key terms—ranging from the graphic to the histrionic arts—equally precludes the inference that he would deny genuine mimetic quality to novels, which moreover he is at pains to classify with poems under a shared function: "the communication of pleasure may be the object of a work not metrically composed . . . as in novels and romances."[3]

Nevertheless, it might have eased the burden on his interpreters had Coleridge made it explicit that an adequate response to Wordsworth's reasoning required him to apply his mimetic categories exclusively to linguistic and stylistic considerations. A successful novel's representational efficacy may depend equally on other components of its structure, and in many cases so marginally on its verbal style that the well justified objection to translations of verse holds with less force against translations of prose fiction. In a poem, by contrast, the conditions of genuine imitation inhere in the very texture of the discourse, in meter and in figurative and syntactical peculiarities, mutually validated.

Two notebook entries vie for the honor of recording Coleridge's first mention of copy-versus-imitation. One of these, applying it to stage plays and operas, Kathleen Coburn refers to 1805. The other, printed in *Anima Poetae,* E. H. Coleridge assigned to 1804, followed in this by Shawcross. Conceding that date to be probably correct, Miss Coburn shows 1808 to be the very latest the evidence permits. The dates of these earliest references to it would seem of themselves effectively to refute the notion that Coleridge owed his distinction to Friedrich Schelling, because that philosopher's *Philosophische Schriften*, which Coleridge certainly read and from which he closely paraphrased other material, was not published until 1809.[4]

In the first pre-Schelling notebook entry Coleridge gropes for the elusive etiology of the copy-imitation distinction.

> Hard to express that sense of the analogy or likeness of a Thing which enables a Symbol to represent it, so that we think of the Thing itself—& yet knowing that the Thing is not present to us.—Surely, on this universal fact of words & images depends by more or less mediations the *imitation* instead of *copy* which is illustrated in very nature *shakesperianized* / that Proteus Essence that could assume the very form, but yet known & felt not to be the Thing by that difference of the Substance which made every atom of the Form another thing /—that *likeness* not identity—an exact web, every line of direction miraculously the same, but the one worsted, the other silk.

His effort hardly succeeds. But it does provide an unusually subtle delineation of the age-old mystery of mimetic art reducible to a set of paradoxes: first, that a segment of experience (alias life, nature, reality) can be recognizably represented in a medium—words—totally alien to the substance of the represented object; second, that that representation takes on a value not discernible in the object itself; and third—and most puzzling—that its value seems to depend on the degree to which it *avoids exact duplication*. The second entry merely declares that complaints about the unreality of opera assume that it is a copy of nature, whereas like other dramatic works it is an imitation.[5]

Given these prior observations of his own, Coleridge must certainly have been gratified to come on Schelling's censure of artists who "reproduce the existent with slavish accuracy" and thereby create not works of art but mere masks ("Larven"). Schelling, too, confronts the third paradox. "How does it happen," he asks,

> that to every person of reasonably cultured sensibility imitations of what is called reality which are pushed to the point of illusion appear in the highest degree false, even conveying the impression of phantoms, whereas a work in which the idea predominates grasps him with the full force of truth and carries him for the first time into the genuinely real world?

Admittedly Schelling's question pinpoints the same anomaly from which Coleridge's speculation starts—the vapidity of photographic realism. But there the similarity between them ends. Coleridge omits the very heart of the German's reasoning, that by embodying and revealing the idea ("Begriff") genuine art conveys truth, whereas slavish mimicry is mendacious, and for that reason repulsive. Nor does he oppose to the deceptive copy ("die bis zur Täuschung betriebenen Nachahmung") any polar term for the valid mimesis.[6] Most important, both his statement of the issue and his solution are idealist and epistemological, whereas, for all his own idealist orientation and his faith in the cognitive value of poetry, Coleridge's formulation is fundamentally empirical and psychological. In a word, on this issue Schelling is Platonic, or Neoplatonic; Coleridge, more nearly Aristotelian. True, in his division of humanity into Platonists and Aristotelians Coleridge placed himself among the former. But in the *Biographia* he adopted "with full faith the principle of Aristotle that poetry as poetry is essentially ideal."[7]

The differing conceptions of mimesis held by the German thinker and his English admirer appear in the very essay, "On Poesy or Art," which is otherwise made up of distressingly close paraphrases of Schelling's oration on the plastic arts and nature, from which the above quotations are taken, eked out by hints from the same philosopher's *System of Transcendental Idealism*. In every true imitation, as distinct from copy, Coleridge argued,

> two elements must coexist, and not only coexist, but be perceived as coexisting. These two elements are likeness and unlikeness, or sameness and difference, and in all genuine creations of art there must be a union of these disparates. The artist may take his point of view where he pleases, provided that the desired effect be perceptively produced,—that there be likeness in the difference, difference in the likeness, and a reconcilement of both in one.

Perfectly consistent with every other reference he makes to copy and imitation, this account is equally foreign to Schelling's. So with Coleridge's explanation of why trompe l'oeil art is repellent:

> If there be likeness to nature without any check of difference, the result is disgusting, and the more complete the delusion, the more loathsome the effect. Why are such simulations of nature, as waxwork figures of men and women, so disagreeable? Because, not finding the motion and life which we expected, we are

shocked as by a falsehood, every circumstance of detail, which before induced us to be interested, making the distance from truth more palpable. You set out with a supposed reality and are disappointed and disgusted with the deception; whilst in respect to a work of genuine imitation, you begin with an acknowledged total difference, and then every touch of nature gives you the pleasure of approximation to truth.[8]

Though both men invoke "truth," Schelling means Truth ideal and absolute, Coleridge the empirical truth of verisimilitude.

From earlier writers Coleridge did borrow illustrations of his governing principle. Reynolds had attacked the fabricators of waxwork figures as mere "copiers," not to be classed with men of genius. Moses Mendelssohn and Adam Smith had also deplored waxworks and artificial fruits and flowers as examples of tasteless mimicry. Though Coleridge acknowledges Smith as source, he never alludes to Mendelssohn. Yet in making his case he must have had the German writer in mind as well, because his chief objection to waxwork statues, the viewer's shock at not finding life and motion in them, paraphrases Mendelssohn's: "so vermissen wir mit Widerwillen das Kennzeichen des Lebens, die Bewegnung." And elsewhere Mendelssohn contrasts a rose cast in metal or glass with one admirably painted by Van Huysum, whose fruit paintings Coleridge ranks among genuine imitations in a letter quoted below.[9]

Nonetheless, as with Schelling's indictment of the aesthetic nullity of facsimiles, Coleridge's rationale is otherwise totally discrepant from Mendelssohn's. Whereas Coleridge condemns outright the "idle rivalry" of naturalistic duplications, Mendelssohn, like Winckelmann, allows them a certain minimal degree of pleasure-giving quality—figures done in plaster of paris, for example. Nor do his reasons for the greater value of imitations accord with Coleridge's. In one Mendelssohn closely parallels Plotinus in ascribing such artistic worth to the beholder's perception of the artist's soul in his creation. In another, he reiterates Winckelmann's doctrine that the art work embodies a transcendent ideal by bringing into concentrated unity several "beauties" scattered among real objects. All this is irrelevant to the dynamic organicism of conflicting likeness and difference expounded in Coleridge's theory. [10]

If either of these earlier writers was of any material use to Coleridge it was the one he himself cites. In perhaps the most enlightening illustration of his mimetic theory he applies it to the contrasting effects of stage scenery and landscape painting. Like wax effigies or the marble peach on a mantle, stage scenery aims at delusion; the painting, an imitation, does not. Whether or not we *are* deluded in either case, with the painting "it is a condition of all genuine delight that we should *not* be deluded. See Adam Smith's *Posthumous Essays.*"[11]

Yet even in the case of Smith the discrepancies between him and Coleridge easily outweigh the similarities. For one, nowhere does Smith use the term *copy* as opposed to *imitation*. More important, no more than Mendelssohn does he see any important aesthetic value in the kind of mimesis he desiderates, his pleasure arising mainly from a recognition of the artist's skill in mastering material recalcitrant to replication. Although he concedes that song enhances what it imitates (discourse and sentiments) through melody and harmony, Smith does not find that statuary and painting add any new beauties of their own to those already discernible in nature. Coleridge's profound experience to the contrary was in fact the initiating raison d'être of his desynonymization of these two primary items in the terminology of mimetic thought.[12]

One scholar has charged that both copy and imitation, as Coleridge conceived them, deny the artist's creativity. But besides the contrary import of what has already been said above, a single observation in the *Biographia* suffices to silence this objection. There Coleridge praises the naturalness of Wordsworth's poetic representations of rustic life, "as raised and qualified by an imperceptible infusion of the author's own knowledge and talent, which infusion does, indeed, constitute it an *imitation* as distinguished from a mere *copy*." Knowing that no peach was ever marble and that the doings of people in real life are modally discrepant from the fictional conventions of stage setting and acting, the copy-maker does his best to avoid a further marring of fidelity by any such infusion of authorial manipulation. Even if, as Father Apple-yard would have it, Coleridge's copy and imitation designated only two degrees of representational fidelity, their disparity is palpable in experience. However logically impeccable, no theory can claim our assent that fails to allow for the vast superiority of *Hamlet* over the most skillful television soap opera, though the latter is in many respects the more faithful rendering of real life.[13]

A full account of why this is so is impossible. Having grasped the indispensable conditions of a mimetic etiology, Coleridge never claimed to have opened the arcanum of poetic art to the daylight of full comprehension. His imitation remains a mysteriously value-fraught phenomenon, a *tertium aliquid,* as he is obliged to call it, generated by the beneficial antagonism of the imagination's fusion of polar opposites and validated only in aesthetic experience.[14] "Imitation," Coleridge explained,

> is the mesothesis of Likeness and Difference; the Difference is as essential to it as the Likeness; for without the Difference, it would be a copy or facsimile. But, to borrow a term from astronomy, it is a liberating mesothesis; for it may verge more to Likeness as in Painting, or more to Difference, as in Sculpture.

This passage from *Table Talk* is probably his most succinct definition of the "universal principle." In the art of landscape gardening he saw a type of the mimetic restructuring of nature which we enjoy in a good drama.

> "How natural!" we say; but the very wonder that furnished the *how* implies that we perceived art at the same moment. We catch the hint from nature itself. Whenever in mountains or cataracts we discover a likeness to anything artificial, which we yet know was not artificial, what pleasure! So in appearances known to be artificial that appear natural.

So, that is, in works of art, whose appeal depends upon their *being perceived as artificial.* A symptom of the inanity of copyist "art"— transcripts of the language of common men in poems as well as marble peaches in fruit bowls—is the fabricator's solicitude to conceal all evidence of contrivance.[15]

Coleridge underscores the heterogeneity of Shakespearean and modern drama by observing that the distance between life and art that is an essential element in Shakespeare appears as an unintentional defect in the inept naturalistic productions of the current stage. "We should think it strange," it occurs to him, "if a tale in *dance* were announced, and the actors did not dance at all. Yet such is modern comedy."[16] The mimicry of a copy, in other words, constitutes a breach of mimetic promise, a disappointment of a set of expectations aroused in the audience by the very conventions of the drama. In like fashion Coleridge will condemn prosaic phraseology in verse as a violation of the linguistic conditions implied by the poet's choice of metrical form.

That most of the modern plays Coleridge had in mind were not metrical meant that even in prose the representation of conversation must be an imitation, not a copy. Coleridge led the way in recognizing that prose, though less intensely than verse, was alike a convention. Others have confirmed his point. Henrik Ibsen revitalized European drama, Georg Lukacs observed, by writing "a dialogue which was in a much deeper sense true to life than any mere copy of everyday conversation could be."[17]

Acting too, Coleridge assured the comedian Charles Matthews, must always be an imitation, which

> of necessity implies & demands difference—whereas a copy aims at *identity*. What a marble peach on a mantlepiece, that you take up deluded, & and put down with pettish disgust, is compared with a fruit-piece of Vanhuysen's, even such is a mere Copy of nature compared with a true histrionic *Imitation*.

He praised a Shakespearean actress named Hudson for avoiding both overstressing the iambic beat and the opposite fault of "substituting *copy* for *imitation*" by mimicking natural talk.[18]

Coleridge's thought is notoriously eclectic, blending ideas of multiple intellectual ancestry to form his own doctrines. Though this is perhaps more evident in his philosophical and political thinking, his aesthetic speculation too lacks the systematic seamlessness of a Kant's or a Croce's. Its virtue lies not so much in perfect internal consistency as in the imaginative brilliance by which ideas of varied philosophical origin are made to collaborate in the elucidation of an issue lying at the heart of literary theory.

Appleyard and Bate have both suggested a kinship between Coleridge's imitation and *symbol*, defined in *The Statesman's Manual* as something which is always an actual part of what it stands for. That poetic language is in this sense symbolic may be inferred from his locating Shakespeare's language in a mean between, or blend of, human speech and the "language" of nature, such that it becomes "itself a part of that which it manifests." Other Coleridgean conceptions fit more readily into his mimetic theory. Surely it is easy to see how the pretence to literal fidelity that characterizes the copy must inhibit that momentary suspension of disbelief—to invoke his most parroted formula—on which artistic illusion (not delusion) depends. Among Wordsworth's poetic defects Coleridge condemns a matter-of- factness produced by a labored minuteness of representation often necessary to win assent to statements in real life but offensive in poetry, where the reader "is willing to believe for his own sake." The negative faith in poetic illusion, which enables us willingly to suspend judgment as to the real existence of poetic images, is estopped by the intrusion of "words and facts of known and absolute truth." In Shakespeare's *The Tempest,* he finds an admirable interdependence of dictional imitation and the qualities of "poetic probability" and dramatic illusion, unmarred by any intrusion of "copyist" literalness.[19]

As regards poetic language, the most crucial link joins imitation to organic unity and the creative imagination. His several references to imitation make it clear that the vital "mesothesis of likeness and difference" that structures it is an instance of the opposites which the poet's imagination reconciles in dynamic tension. "All imitation in the Fine Arts," as in one place he lays it down, "is the union of Disparate things." How mimesis relates to the doctrine of reconciled opposites is most impressively argued in Chapter 18 of the *Biographia,* and precisely in refutation of Wordsworth's claim that no essential stylistic difference exists between verse and prose. Meter, Coleridge reasons, far from being the merely pleasant but unessential superaddition of Wordsworth's supposing, is "the proper form of poetry," lacking which it is simply defective. As Wordsworth himself had admitted, poetry implies passion, Coleridge supplying the refinement that the very act of poetic composition generates this passion, which in turn demands (and in fact produces) a language correspondingly different from that of prose. He then adds that a closely related principle, "if not the same argument in a more general form," states that every part of an organized whole must be adjusted to the more important parts. Finally, he emphasizes, this whole chain of reasoning rests on the principle that poetry is an imitative art; and—in yet another version of his basic idea—

> imitation, opposed to copying, consists either in the interfusion of the SAME throughout the radically DIFFERENT, or of the different throughout a base radically the same.[20]

If poetry is quintessentially an imitative art in this dynamic sense, then Coleridge's identification of verse as the ideal form of poetry answers perfectly to his understanding of meter itself. Meter effects a "salutary antagonism" between the emotion contemplated by the poet in the excitement of creation and a spontaneous effort to hold it in check. It is a technique of mimetic mastery available to the creative imagination, which, we recall, reconciles among other discordant elements an exceptional emotion with an exceptional order, in this case the order imposed by the isometric segmentation of the verse line.[21]

To arrive at this conception, Coleridge relied on the traditional strategy of distinguishing the styles of verse and prose, which he considered indispensable to a sound resolution of the whole *quaestio vexata* of poetic diction (as Thomas De Quincey was despairingly to name it). But in the greater precision, complexity, and depth of his treatment he carries it far beyond its earlier limits. In past poetics meter figures either as one of several distinguishing marks of verse, on a par with its various syntactical peculiarities, or else as *the* addendum uniquely making both for poetry's distinction from and superiority to prose. In his vital recasting of these conventional views, meter for Coleridge, though nugatory in isolation, becomes the temporal or rhythmic condition in which the other stylistic traits of versification (inversion, figurative language, the aural devices of rhyme, assonance, and so on) attain their fullest effect. As the artificial regularization of instinctual rhythmic utterance, meter is the sensuous correlative, as it were, of the verbal *ordonnance* permitted in verse. He likened it to yeast, valueless or even disagreeable in itself, but enlivening the liquor in which it is contained. Considered alone, he affirms, meter

> is simply a stimulant of the attention, and therefore excites the question: Why is the attention to be thus stimulated? . . . Neither can I conceive any other answer that can be rationally given, short of this: I write in metre, because I am about to use a language different from that of prose.[22]

The difference in question has of course nothing to do with a special poetic vocabulary. It is stylistic but not lexical: "Poetry justifies, as *Poetry* independent of every other Passion, some new combination of Language, & *commands* the omission of many others allowable in other compositions." This sentence sums up Coleridge's theory in its three interdependent heads. First, verse is a mode of expression characterized by a unique verbal ordonnance. Second, the passion that generates both that ordonnance and its accompanying metrical form is primarily the passion of the mimetic activity itself, not an emotion aroused by the subject or occasion of the poem. Meter is thus the sensible manifestation of the polar tension that marks off imitation from copy. Third is the express denial that metrical form can "naturalize" an inherently prosaic ordonnance. Here, then, is the clearest ground of Coleridge's dissent from Wordsworth's notion of verse as a mere "superaddition" to an essentially prose order of discourse. There is also an obvious consonance between Coleridge's prosody and Roman

Jakobson's doctrine that "poeticalness" is not a rhetorical supplement to discourse but a total "re-evaluation" of all its components. In the *Biographia*, the most nearly corresponding sentence runs: "If metre be super-added, all other parts must be made consonant with it." But Jakobson also held that in verse every word was "converted into a figure of poetic speech." In Coleridge no such automatic conversion occurs, a fact borne out by the occasional presence of prosaic lines in otherwise good poems.[23] Between the species of style, one peculiar to verse and one proper only in prose, he did discern a neutral third common to both which may have been susceptible of Jakobson's poetic conversion. Conjecturally too, that style may have prompted Coleridge's equivocal observation that "a poem of any length neither can be, nor ought to be, all poetry." Some admirable poems—he offers in evidence narrative passages from Chaucer's *Troilus* and George Herbert's verses—he adjudges to be entirely in the neutral style. But Coleridge and Jakobson do not perfectly agree: Daniel's *Civil Wars*, Coleridge thinks, is marred by a "frequent incorrespondency of his diction to his metre."[24]

Coleridge's failure to produce a sequential exposition of his total prosody and the incoherence of the relevant chapters of the *Biographia* have occasioned dubious interpretation or openly avowed perplexity. The assertion that a poem of any extent neither can nor *should* be poetic throughout is a notable instance, worth our consideration if only because it is the probable source of Poe's dogma that poems must be short—the most notorious misreading of Coleridge's point. Shawcross flatly, and not unfairly, accused Coleridge of leaving his assertion unsupported. A modern theorist hazards the guess that by the "non-poetry" of a poem Coleridge meant "pseudo-poetry (reflections of other faculties [than the imagination] that are made to resemble poetry in their superficial arrangements)."[25] But it is hard to imagine Coleridge favoring *pseudo*-poetry in any composition, let alone a poem.

My own reading may be no better. I can only surmise that here as elsewhere Coleridge may have been led astray by the imprecision of the words *poetry* and *poetic*, sometimes used to designate not a kind of writing but a superior degree of expressive excellence. If so, he should perhaps have said that a long poem is the better for not being everywhere equally poetic. This, as we shall see later, was the alternative formulation adopted by Eliot.

Coleridge's rejection of Wordsworth's argument in the Prefaces rests on his contention that there are "modes of expression" natural to prose but detrimental to verse, which profitably accommodates an alternative mode detrimental to prose. This does not mean that metrical style must be exclusively poetic. But it does require that "whatever else is combined with *metre* must, though it be not itself *essentially* poetic, have nevertheless some property in common with poetry, as an intermedium of affinity" with the meter. The very strength of his conviction on the matter makes it regrettable that Coleridge nowhere cites an example of the stylistically vitiated prose he has in mind, to balance his citations of prosaic verse. But for all his exaltation of poetry Coleridge was far from indifferent to what Dryden had called "the other harmony." He closely studied the evolution of English prose. His esteem for it is signalized by his tripartite division of human utterance: verse, prose, and conversation, the first two set firmly apart from the last. This stylistic trichotomy, we should note, also exposes the contradiction between Wordsworth's essential identification of rustic parlance with poetic language, and his stylistic equation of verse and prose.[26]

Two crucial aspects of Coleridge's theory still want clarification despite the scholarly attention given them. One relates to the separate definitions of *poem* and *poetry* in the *Biographia*. Allen Tate once damned the passages in question as "probably the most confused statement ever uttered by a great critic." Though Coleridge holds that verse is the most perfect form of expression and that any hint of meter in prose is undesirable, he has unqualified praise for poetic prose. From this it would appear that he was no more successful than earlier writers in evading the old dilemma. If metrical form is the perfection of poetry, how can many parts of the Book of Isaiah be, as he declares, "poetry in the most emphatic sense"? So superlative a characterization surely precludes the inference that its poetical quality would have been enhanced by metrical form.[27]

For enlightenment we turn to the *Biographia*. In Coleridge's most theoretically compacted sentence, a poem is defined as

> a species of composition, which is opposed to works of science, by proposing for its *immediate* object pleasure, not truth; and from all other species (having *this* object in common with it) it is discriminated by proposing to itself such delight from the *whole*, as is compatible with a distinct gratification from each component *part*.

Despite the distracting personification of a poem "proposing" its ends, this definition is couched in strictly ontological and functional terms. It is therefore disconcerting—at first—to find Coleridge quite deliberately shifting to psychological terms when he comes to define *poetry,* though without abandoning the functionalism. Unlike a poem, which is "a species of composition," poetry is not limited in its material form. It is instead whatever results from the peculiar nature of the poet's creative activity. Its definition is therefore tantamount to a description of that activity, a process which, "in ideal perfection," engages the whole human psyche. The poet

> diffuses a tone, and spirit of unity, that blends, and (as it were) *fuses* each into each, by that synthetic and magical power, to which we have exclusively appropriated the name of imagination. This power, first put in action by the will and understanding, and retained under their irremissive, though gentle and unnoticed, controul (*laxis effertur habenis*) reveals itself in the balance or reconciliation of opposite or discordant qualities: of sameness, with difference; of the general, with the concrete; the idea, with the image; the individual with the representative; the sense of novelty and freshness, with old and familiar objects; a more than usual state of emotion, with more than usual order; judgement ever awake and steady self- possession, with enthusiasm and feeling profound or vehement; and while it blends and harmonizes the natural and the artificial, still subordinates art to nature; the manner to the matter; and our admiration of the poet to our sympathy with the poetry.[28]

From these two celebrated passages we might infer, with misgivings, that Isaiah, being poetry, must reconcile opposing elements; and that *not* being a poem, its component parts (if such are even identifiable) do not produce a distinct gratification from that of the whole (if any). But in what would this reconcilement consist, if not in those very features which mark off the poetic from the prose style? They are precisely the attributes that, by Coleridge's insistence, at once require the rhythmic pulsation of meter for their consummation and justify its use.

Moreover, the dilemma seems only deepened by the reflection that, for all Coleridge tells us to the contrary, a given piece of poetic prose may contain proportionately more poetry than a given poem (unless very short), because his interdiction against an exclusively poetic texture throughout a poem is nowhere entered against a passage of poetic prose. So a reader may reasonably assume that Coleridge judged poetic prose to be, potentially at least, a richer form of expression than poems properly so called. Since in the total context of his dearest convictions this would be patently absurd, the only possible conclusion is that Coleridge's terms *poetry* and *poem*, the *poetic* and the *poematic*,[29] designate not merely degrees of expressive power but *distinct orders of utterance*, of which the poematic is the more intense.

The term "poetic diction" is too blunt for the precision of Coleridge's analysis, by which poems are subject to criteria of usage not binding upon poetry. He apparently assumed that he had rectified the situation in the second volume of the *Biographia*, which, he assured Edward Coleridge in 1823, contained "the true principles of judgement respecting Poetry, *Poem*, poetic & *poematic* Diction."[30] Regrettably, the ambiguity of the word *poetry* still on occasion muddied his argument, for example his assertion that without meter poetry is simply defective. To be faithful to his desynonymization, and to his obvious intent, he ought to have said that meter was the form proper to the poematic ordonnance. Tate's indictment of Coleridge's exposition is surely excessive. Still, its author's own lexical carelessness is almost certainly the major reason why it has not been instead, as it becomes when rightly understood, an invaluable contribution to modern poetics.[31]

In 1811 Coleridge informed a lecture audience that poetry was the language of heaven, its "exquisite delight" giving a foretaste of the celestial joy. That such rhapsodic praise was meant only for metrical poetry emerges when he invites us to compare a beautiful passage describing the Indian fig tree, in Book IX of *Paradise Lost*, with its prose source in Gerard's *Herball;* or Shakespeare's depiction of Cleopatra in her barge with the prose version of that spectacle in North's *Plutarch*. Either comparison, Coleridge wrote, would clearly show

> the charm and *effect* of metre and the art of poetry, independent of the thoughts and images—the superiority, in short, of *poematic* over *prose* composition, the poetry or non- poetry being the same in both.[32]

The second knotty point in Coleridge's poetics has to do with the relation of passion and meter. In the *Biographia*, he grounds the origin of meter in an antagonism between passion and a spontaneous, countervailing, mental impulse to hold it in check. In its first stage, this impulse is as natural as the passion which occasions it, just as the primitivist account from which Coleridge takes off currently held. But in a second stage of the creative process (because this is what he is ultimately seeking to explain), the poet's conscious will organizes this inchoate impulse into meter proper. From these data, no doubt first glimpsed in his own creative experience, he deduces the two "legitimate conditions" required for metrical composition.

> First, that as the *elements* of metre owe their existence to a state of increased excitement, so the metre itself should be accompanied by the natural language of excitement. Secondly, that as these elements are formed into metre *artificially,* by a *voluntary* act, with the design and for the purpose of blending *delight* with emotion, so the traces of present *volition* should throughout the metrical language be proportionally discernible. Now these two conditions must be reconciled and co-present. There must be not only a partnership, but a union; an interpenetration of passion and of will, of *spontaneous* impulse and of *voluntary* purpose.[33]

This remarkable explication is further evidence (highlighted by his italics) of how consistently Coleridge's metrical theory conforms to his governing doctrine of the imagination as a reconciler of warring forces. But to grasp its full significance is to understand as well its conformity with his fundamental concept of a genuine imitation, in which, he insists, "the traces of present *volition* should throughout be . . . discernible." But the phrase most pertinent to our chief concern provides that meter "be accompanied by the natural language of excitement." In such narrative pieces as Wordsworth's "Simon Lee," "Alice Fell," and parts of "The Sailor's Mother," Coleridge could discover no such justification for their being in metrical form.[34]

Verse diction and meter spring from an identical passionate movement of the psyche. Unless the distinctive features of poetic syntax are prompted by mental excitement, they are only tasteless verbal posturings. Forgetting this, Coleridge surmised, Walter Scott had marred his *Lady of the Lake* by resorting to inversions only to accommodate his meter and rhyme or disguise colloquial phraseology. Shakespeare and Milton, he predictably observes, never do so. In *Paradise Lost,* where syntax and metrical cadence so superbly correspond in mutual tension, a style thought unnatural by Johnson and Eliot among others Coleridge praises as "exquisitely artificial: for the position [of the words] is rather according to the logic of passion, or universal logic, than to the logic of grammar." Meter too, though consciously manipulated, properly arises only "where the feeling calls for it." In a corresponding state

of receptiveness and expectancy, a good reader assumes his author
to have been rapt in sustained emotional excitement whence
"arises a language in prose unnatural but in poetry natural." Coleridge also readily intuited what some linguists have since affirmed:
that "the poet's rhythms," as Edward Sapir put it, "can only be a
more sensitive and stylized application of rhythmic tendencies that
are characteristic of the daily speech of his people." Coleridge regarded his countrymen as fortunate heirs of a tongue so rhythmically expressive that it "will, in a strong state of passion, admit of
scansion from the very mouth."[35]

Few problems of literary theory are more elusive than those
encountered in differentiating prose from verse. Not even the precision of Coleridge's dissection could entirely eliminate some blurring of the generic line between the two styles of written discourse. In one place he provides for degrees of passion, so that
where it is too weak for formal meter it will at least result in a "language more measured" than usual. Certain affecting passages in
the English Bible, he told a lecture audience in 1811, follow, if admittedly not the tidy iambics of a Pope, a rhythmic undulation occasionally scannable as classical hexameter:

> God went / up with a / shout,
> our Lord with the / sound of the / trumpet.

"So true it is," he concluded, "that wherever passion was, the language became a sort of metre." Yet Coleridge thought any conflation of prose and verse cadence was finally precluded by a disparity
in their affective sources. Poems, he conceded, shared with vivid
prose an emotive ground. But a poem proper can result only from
"that pleasurable emotion, that peculiar state and degree of excitement, which arises in the poet himself in the act of composition."[36]

So apparent to sensitive readers is the link between the beauty of
poetic lines and their measured structure that some investigators
have actually devised tests to determine how far the aesthetic quality
inhered in unaided meter. Warton's experiment with Pope's couplets
was repeated in reverse when Cohen turned a terse newspaper report of an auto crash into free verse. Though such tests seem justified by the very nature of the theoretical question, they neglect the
negative effect for which Coleridge's account makes due allowance:
that sometimes meter not only fails to give pleasure but positively
repels. In addition to the examples of this culled from Wordsworth's
poems, he dared, if only in a marginal jotting, to bring a similar indictment against the ten-line section of Milton's *Comus* beginning

> And not many furlongs thence
> Is your Father's residence. . . .

With a histrionically exaggerated acknowledgment of his presumption—prostrating himself at Milton's feet—he would ask

> in a timid whisper whether rhymes and finger-metre do not render poor flat prose ludicrous rather than tend to elevate, or even to *hide* its nakedness.

If meter is to be used at all, all else must be, in the phrase which he borrowed from pictorial criticism, in *keeping* (*OED:* "the maintenance of harmony of composition"). And this includes, before all else besides, the language. Poets are fastidious. "The sole difference, *in style,* is that poetry demands a *severer keeping*—it admits nothing that Prose may not often admit; but it *oftener* rejects."[37]

To Coleridge's mind, a prime condition of that keeping is a heightened emphasis on the words themselves in the poematic as distinct from the prose ordonnance. That attention of which he declares meter to be the stimulant promotes in the reader of a poem the fullest realization of its words' sensuous weight and designative force. And words are obviously chief among the "parts" forming the whole of its organic structure.

Organic unity and Coleridge's theory of verse diction most immediately coincide in his definition of a poem as a species of composition yielding "such delight from the *whole* as is compatible with a distinct gratification from each component *part.*" This organic part-whole relation he locates between the complete discontinuity of a series of striking lines or couplets, each of which absorbs the reader's exclusive attention, and a monolithic unity whose component parts are devoid of individuality. And as usual with Coleridge, the objective structure so described is provided with a subjective, psychological grounding:

> the reader should be carried forward, not merely or chiefly by the mechanical impulse of curiosity, or by a restless desire to arrive at the final solution; but by the pleasureable activity of mind excited by the attractions of the journey itself.[38]

The full savoring of the details of diction, imagery, syntactic components, and so forth which an attentive reader enjoys in fine verse is here given a theoretical justification imperfectly realized in the neoclassical notion of artistic unity epitomized in a couplet of Pope's *Essay on Criticism:*

> 'Tis not a lip, or eye, we beauty call,
>
> But the joint force and full result of all.

To this the organicist critic retorts that in fact we *do* call the lip or eye individually beautiful, just as, simultaneously, we relish the whole these "parts" unite to comprise.

Romantic organic aesthetics arose in Germany, where Schiller, the Schlegel brothers, and Schelling were its chief proponents. But it is the description of organic unity given by the philosopher Hegel in his posthumous *Lectures on Aesthetics,* published in the year following Coleridge's death, that most deserves our present notice, if only because the near identity of its terms with those of his English contemporary's definition of a poem had never been pointed out, so far as I could discover, before my own earlier mentioned study. The parallel is the more noteworthy since in this case no influence, in either direction, can be in question.

In a unified work of art, Hegel explains, there must be a particularization of its individual parts, which must each seem to be cultivated for its own sake in order to attain to organic unity ("um in eine organische Einheit zu kommen"). A prose discourse engages the mere understanding ("Verstand"), which hurries over details to the *Endresultat* (cf. Coleridge's "final solution") of an intellectual abstraction or a practical purpose. In the poetic mode of thought, however, and in the part-whole relationship it entails, each part is given independent importance. Every moment is, in varying degrees, vibrant and interesting in itself ("für sich interessant, für sich lebendig"), so that the imagination delights to tarry over it, to paint it lovingly, savoring its autonomous charm. Poetry, Hegel's ponderous personifications continue, makes its way more slowly than the judgments and conclusions of the understanding, which cares contrastingly less for the path along which it travels to its destination ("weniger dagegen auf den Weg, den er entlanggeht"), indifferent, in Coleridge's similar image, to "the attractions of the journey itself."[39]

The parallel of physical and mental progression seems a clear advance over all earlier attempts to distinguish the stylistic conditions of verse from those of prose, perhaps because it is so well adapted to a poem's temporal mode of realization. The Abbé Bremond adapted the simile to the poetics of mystical idealism which he elaborated in *La Poésie pure*. To an exquisite passage in a great poem, he wrote, we exclaim "Stop! let me take in the delights of this beautiful line"; whereas to prose we say impatiently, "Get on with it! Hasten to the outcome" ("Marche! marche! *Ad eventum festina*"). There is also Valéry's image of "walking" prose and "dancing" poetry, divergent from Coleridge's envisagement in positing a non-telic poetry. This disagreement between them reflects the French poet's radical purism, to which Eliot was to take telling exception. The contrasting tendency of more recent theory to preserve some cognitive and referential status for poetry is a return to Coleridge's view that though verse and prose both move toward a communicative goal, in verse getting there is half— or rather more than half—the fun. "Prose," writes Howard Nemerov in the latest version of the idea, "is a way of getting on, poetry a way of lingering."[40]

Again like Coleridge, though in terms encompassing a larger frame of reference, Hegel envisaged a poetic structure that avoids the opposite extremes of an undifferentiated unity and a total disunity.

> For the autonomy [of each part] must not be so firmly established that it is absolutely disjunct from the others; the independence asserts itself only enough to show the various aspects and portions of the work as having achieved their own vital representative status.

These relatively autonomous parts nonetheless form a whole because the fundamental theme of the work ("Grundbestimmung") is severally developed and exhibited in each of them. A poem deficient in this kind of dynamic unity, Hegel declared, tends to fall from the region of free poetry into the realm of prose ("der Bereich der Prosa").[41]

The linguistic aspect of poetry, Hegel observed in the *Lectures on Aesthetics*, "could provide us with material for endlessly extensive and complex discussions"—a statement which the course of recent poetics has endowed with something like prophetic force. His perception of the centrality of the verbal medium to poetics, however, did not shake his conviction that the ultimate difference between prose and poetry lay not in the stylistic norms characteristic of each, but more deeply in "two different spheres of consciousness ("zwei überschiedene Sphären des Bewusstseins"). And in what sits uneasily with his organicism—and directly contradicts Coleridge—Hegel extends his idealist conception to declare that a poem suffers no essential loss when translated into another language or even into prose.[42]

When the mimetic conception separating imitation from copy is applied to verse language it generates a prosody uniquely poematic. The corresponding ordonnance is one in which meter, aural devices, and deviant syntax are converted into constituents of an aesthetic end. In doing so they enhance the part-whole relationship defining Coleridge's organic unity, in which the pleasure conferred by the whole must consist with a separately felt pleasure from its component parts. In order to reveal itself, he told a lecture audience, the spirit of poetry must take on a living body, which is "of necessity an organized one,—and what is organization, but the connection of parts to a whole, so that each part is at once ends and means!"[43]

In Coleridge's poetic imitation, the reconciliation of opposites effected by the creative imagination is anything but peaceful. Because the opposites are polar, the reconciliation is dynamic, not static, and thereby productive of a tension felt by the reader of a poem as the essential ingredient of his aesthetic response. In Coleridge's literary aesthetics this notion is ubiquitous, as the warring elements variously manifest themselves in the stages of the creative process, in the structure of the finished work, and in the psychology of the pleasurable experience it evokes. Meter sets in dynamic tension the polar extremes of "more than usual" emotion and order, first in the poet and then in his readers.

More than anything else, this grounding in a major tenet of modern aesthetics accounts both for the superiority of Coleridge's idea of an imitation over all those expounded in earlier mimetic theory, and for the twentieth-century viability of his poetics. The kinship of Coleridge and modern poeticians consists in the fundamental fact that he and they alike propound a "poetics of tension," to borrow the phrase applied by Wimsatt and Brooks to I. A. Richards's critical system.[44]

Tension,—a term alternating in modern theory with *ambiguity, conflict,* and *irony*—names a quality increasingly identified as indispensably characteristic both of the arts and of the unique experience they incite. Leonard Bernstein did not hesitate to affirm that ambiguity or tension (he used both terms) "has always inhabited musical art (indeed all the arts), because it is one of art's most potent functions."[45] Bernstein's generalization has distinguished lineage in confirmations by Schiller, Schopenhauer, Nietzsche, and Bernard Bosanquet, among others less well known.[46]

Coleridge's true congeners are not the critics of his day but the ablest analysts of poetic language writing in our own. These include, significantly, investigators of quite varied disciplines: Cleanth Brooks, defining the language of poetry as "the language of paradox"; Philip Wheelwright, locating the essence of metaphor in the "semantic tension" among its heterogeneous elements; Nelson Goodman, venturing the generalization that wherever there is metaphor there is conflict.[47]

Most Coleridgean in his supporting rationale, Paul Ricoeur describes "a specific kind of tension" operative in metaphor:

> To see *the like* is to see the same in spite of, and through, the different. This tension between sameness and difference characterizes the logical structure of likeness. Imagination, accordingly, is this *ability* to produce new kinds of assimilation and to produce them not *above* the differences, as in the concept, but in spite of and through the differences.[48]

It would be hard to come by a more arresting reformulation (though it aims at much more) of Coleridge's imitation as a likeness which "of necessity implies and demands difference."

The theory of poetic tension, part of the larger aesthetics of dynamic polarity, has long seemed to me to depend for its acceptance less upon logical exposition than upon confirming experience, the silent testimony of persons with the imaginative capacity for strenuous introspection of the *form* taken by their psychic transactions with great art. Since I could recall no hint of this surmise anywhere else, it was gratifying to find one in Owen Barfield's study of Coleridge's thought. After analyzing the polarity expounded in the *Biographia*, he wrote that readers are required "not to think about the imagination, but to use it . . . , that the apprehension of polarity is itself *the basic act of imagination.*" Turning later to the poet's verbal medium, Barfield observes that experiencing "metaphor *as* metaphor . . . is to experience likeness as a *polarity* between sameness and difference; and there is a similar contrast [in Coleridge] between allegory and symbol, or allegory and myth."[49] Might not one add copy and imitation? In any case Coleridge encourages us to conclude that in the balanced or countervailing masses in painting, in the harmonic and melodic tensions and their cadential resolutions in music, no less than in the thrust and counterthrust of metrical pulsations against syntactic groupings in verse, polarity is intuited.

CHAPTER EIGHT

The Younger Romantics

WORDSWORTH WAS THE presiding spirit of nineteenth-century English poetic theory. His ideals of spontaneous expression, sincerity, and moral purpose reigned virtually unchallenged except by the momentary aesthetic amorality of the coterie headed by Oscar Wilde during the nineties. Yet Wordsworth's dominance did not extend to the issue of poetic style. Despite the plaudits of Mill and De Quincey for the ideas put forth in the Prefaces to *Lyrical Ballads*, by his immediate successors Wordsworth's stylistic principles were either rejected outright or accepted only in versions so diluted by reservations as to degrade the principles themselves to marginal status. His conflation of verse and prose was apparently meaningless to younger poets of the time, convinced almost to a man that the language of verse was a mode of using words that was special, precious, "magical" even. What the master had decried as poetic diction *could,* they conceded, be meretricious, as frequently it had been. But not always—and not necessarily.

Certainly the poetry they wrote defied Wordsworth's precepts. In his last, unfinished poem Shelley describes the dawn heralded by bird-song when

> at the birth
> Of light, the Ocean's orison arose,
> To which the birds tempered their matin lay,

oblivious of the scorn Wordsworth had poured on the "vicious" phrasing Gray had indulged to describe the identical natural phenomenon. Wherein is Shelley's "tempered their matin lay" a less objectionable circumlocution than Gray's "their amorous descant join"? Shelley's stated convictions about poetic language consist well enough with such "elegant paraphrases" and thus necessarily depart fundamentally from Wordsworth's. This is not to deny either the great difference between the neoclassical and Romantic poetic styles or Wordsworth's pioneering contribution to the latter. Yet without minimizing his debt to the older poet's revitalizing example, Shelley could not find in Wordsworth's stylistic pronouncements a sound validation either for his own style or for how good poets had ever written. No more could his contemporaries.

The position that was generally to prevail was early taken by Hazlitt. As already noted, Hazlitt was fully cognizant of the enervation of modern poetry Wordsworth had denounced. But he saw in it only an exacerbation of a perennial tendency, which in 1818 he traced back to Beaumont and Fletcher. In 1825, while freely acknowledging his limited accord with the "great outcry" that "has prevailed for some time past against poetic diction," he argued eloquently that this legitimate objection must never prevent us from luxuriating in the linked beauties of voluptuous fancy which adorn the poet's "fairy fabric of thought." Nor should any theory-spawned indifference suppress our rapture at the "occasional lines of inconceivable brightness" streaking his page.[1]

Hazlitt's position had in fact been particularized in his truculent review of the *Biographia* in the *Edinburgh Review* in 1817. He declares Wordsworth's "ingenious project" of forming poetic language from rustic speech, out of "horror or contempt for the abuses of what has been called poetic diction," to have been so ill-conceived that only "a pitiful affectation of singularity" could have triggered the ensuing controversy. Then comes his own contribution to it, combining limited concession to Wordsworth, adoption of notions from the book under severe review, and flowery replay of neoclassical ideals of poetic style.

The plain language familiar to all classes, Hazlitt admitted, was the stuff of impassioned expression in good poetry and prose alike. But this is

> not the exclusive language of poetry. There is another language peculiar to this manner of writing which has been called *poetic diction*—those flowers of speech, which, whether natural or arti-

ficial, fresh or faded, are strewed over the plainer ground which poetry has in common with prose.

It is the very reverse of the "slang phrases" Wordsworth condemned.

> Upon the whole, therefore, we should think this ornamented and coloured style, most proper to descriptive or fanciful poetry, where the writer has to lend a borrowed, and, in some sort, meretricious lustre to outward objects, which he can best do by enshrining them in a language that, by custom and long prescription, reflects the image of a poetic mind. . . . The pleasure derived from poetic diction is the same as that derived from classical diction.

There follows a faintly question-begging attempt to distinguish the "words dipped in 'the dew of Castalie'" that properly "varnish over the trite and commonplace" from those that only encumber natural and passionate expression. But whereas poetic diction, being "borrowed and artificial," was accordingly reprehensible to Wordsworth, Hazlitt forthrightly vindicates its proper place and function.[2]

Much impressed by the Wordsworth-Coleridge debate on the issue, Shelley sided largely with Coleridge. His agreement with those who commended familiar language to poetic use contains the reservation that it be "the real language of men," not that of any one social class. In the preface to *Prometheus Unbound* (1820), he appeals to the practice of the Greek poets and of Dante and Shakespeare as precedent for having taken much of his poem's imagery "from the operations of the human mind, or from those external actions by which they are expressed." His phraseology immediately recalls what Coleridge had laid down in the *Biographia* (which, Mary Shelley recorded, her husband had finished reading on December 8, 1817): that the best part of language is "derived from reflection on the acts of the mind itself. It is formed by a voluntary appropriation of fixed symbols to internal acts, to processes and results of imagination." Shelley's claim to having adapted classical expressions to his own verse is no perfunctory gesture of literary piety. The Platonism so pervasive in his writings is only the central strand of an impassioned Hellenism which made it hard for him to imagine how modern European culture could have evolved without the ancient aliment. "We are all Greeks," he wrote in the preface to *Hellas* (1822).[3]

No item of Wordsworth's poetics was more questioned in his generation than his stylistic assimilation of prose and verse. The young Byron knew that many readers of his *English Bards and Scotch Reviewers* (1809) would enjoy his gibe at the poet

Who, both by precept and example, shows

That prose is verse, and verse is merely prose.

The Romantic writers' considerable preoccupation with poetic language, their fascination with what struck them as its special power and allure, in itself distanced them from Wordsworth's depreciation of it. From all they wrote on the subject it is clear that except in the reductive sense that Coleridge himself had easily conceded—that poet and prose writers shared a largely common vocabulary—they found the two styles to contrast in virtually every respect. Some of them rested the distinction mainly on differing psychological sources of prose and verse, some on formal features, others on discriminations of function—moral, cognitional, social.

Here we should note a fundamental change in critical terminology. Whereas in earlier ages *poetry* had meant primarily if not exclusively a kind of discourse, by the 1800s it had become bewilderingly inclusive. Immemorially of course it had on rare occasions, and often in the archaic form *poesy,* designated a poetic or artistic quality. In Romantic criticism it was stretched further, to cover as well every conceivable cause and occasion of beauty or emotive appeal in art or nature. A spirited formulation of this broadened conception occurs in Friedrich Schlegel's *Gespräch über die Poesie* (1800), which bears to European Romanticism as a whole roughly the same inaugural link as that between the exactly contemporary Preface to *Lyrical Ballads* and English literary Romanticism. What are the things we call poems, Schlegel asked, compared "to the amorphous and unconscious poetry ("formlose und bewusstlose Poesie") that stirs in the plant, irradiates in the light, laughs in the child, shines in the bloom of youth, glows in the loving breast of women?—But this is the original, primordial kind, without which there certainly would have been no poetry of words." Schlegel's restriction of such wordless poetry to a primordial category was easy to overlook. This is what happens in "On Poetry in General," the introductory lecture of Hazlitt's popular series published as *The English Poets* (1818), in which the expanded designation of *poetry* is indulged with tiresome abandon. Two or three of the dozen or so definitions of his topic, generally in the simple formula "Poetry is . . . ," do make it a kind of language, but only in the vaguest figurative terms: "the language of the imagination and the passions," "the universal language" of the heart, and the like. In Herschel Baker's paraphrase of a contemporary review of Hazlitt's book, the critic "makes poetry mean so much—a certain kind of composition, the talent that produces it, and the subjects that are treated—that he blurs distinctions essential to a definition." Hazlitt's aim, however, was precisely to dispel the notion that poetry is "found only in books, contained in lines of ten syllables," and to proclaim its presence "wherever there is a sense of beauty, or power, or harmony," as in ocean waves or growing flowers. Fear, hope, and love are poetry—and so, he adds, are contempt, jealousy, remorse, admiration, wonder, pity, despair, and madness.[4]

Nonetheless, Hazlitt deserves attention for scattered remarks on how verse and prose differ. In poems, he found, one delightful image suggests another, a process that would be objectionable in prose because there, the author seeking only to win our assent, "nothing can be admitted by way of ornament or relief, that does not add new force or clearness to the original conception." As often happens when the contrasting natures of the two kinds of writing are referred to their differing functions, Hazlitt here posits a too narrow notion of prose, a great deal of which in every age and culture has aspired to something more or other than intellectual persuasion—nowhere more than in the colorful tapestry of his own criticism. Some of his opinions on the subject seem only barbs by perhaps the ablest English prose stylist of his time against the several gifted poets of his acquaintance—"those jealous votaries of the Muses," as he called them. In "The Prose Style of Poets" he maintained that poets write bad prose. Habituated to metrical beat and rhyme, they cannot manage the less orderly cadence of the "other harmony." Whereas verse, he thought, is artificial, prose is the perfection of the most natural kind of utterance, conversation. Coleridge, followed by a parade of poets since, argued the alternative filiation, which makes verse the artistic refinement of live talk. But Hazlitt thought "the natural measure of prose" to be controlled, as in social intercourse, by the speaker's sense of his theme and his articulative address, talents remote from the external exactions of the number and arrangement of syllables in a verse line. In *The Round Table* he deplores the intrusion of a rhyming effect into prose rhythm. Johnson's prose he thought vitiated by a constant "rhyming on the sense" by balancing two halves of a sentence against each other. Whatever the local validity of these strictures, they hardly justify charging poets with a trained incapacity (in Thorstein Veblen's useful oxymoron), given the excellent prose written by several of them besides Dryden.[5]

Discussing *Coriolanus* in *Characters of Shakespeare's Plays* (1817) led Hazlitt to distinguish the two forms of written discourse according to the contrasting societal principles which, he held, they epitomized. Verse, the product of the imagination, is aristocratic; prose, the instrument of the understanding, democratic. Because the imagination is "an exaggerating and exclusive faculty," the idiom of poetry, "right royal," readily adapts itself to the language of power. Given Hazlitt's egalitarianism, this ideological dichotomy is possibly dismissible, like others, as a veiled form of social advocacy. But perhaps not. His opposing ideologies do *not* correspond to degrees of verbal ornateness and simplicity, Hazlitt being among the first to challenge the long-held prejudice against monosyllables in verse. In the essay "On Familiar Style" he ascribes the excellence of much of Christopher Marlowe's versification precisely to an effective use of them. And elsewhere, after citing several passages from Marlowe's plays which "leave a track of golden fire behind them," he remarks on how many of that poet's mighty lines are made up entirely or predominantly of words of one syllable.[6]

The central motif in the negative primitivism of Thomas Love Peacock's *Four Ages of Poetry* (1820) is stylistic. Crude passion, barbaric manners and superstitions, in Peacock's blunt positivism, are best depicted in figurative language, whereas the rational communication of dispassionate truth on which civilization depends would be absurd if made in verse, as anyone can see "by versifying one of Euclid's demonstrations."[7] Shelley's celebrated answer to Peacock, *A Defence of Poetry* (1821), accordingly focuses on what poets do with language. His fervently held convictions about it are, moreover, underpinned by a persuasion that language is the chief index of mankind's dignity, power, and glory—as we are reminded by Asia's praise of Prometheus, the archetypal hero of Shelley's cosmic poetic drama:

He gave man speech, and speech created thought,
Which is the measure of the universe. (II, 4, lines 72–73)

And later in the drama the Spirit of Earth celebrates language as among the brightest of human attributes,

> a perpetual Orphic song,
> Which rules with Daedal harmony a throng
> Of thoughts and forms, which else senseless and shapeless
> were. (IV,1,lines 417–19)

Fully sharing his adversary's belief in the primeval source of poetry, dance, and song, Shelley insisted that poets retain a sense for the pristine linguistic vitality that is indispensable to the spiritual well-being of civilized society.

> Their language is vitally metaphorical; that is, it marks the before unapprehended relations of things and perpetuates their apprehension, until the words, which represent them become, through time, signs for portions or classes of thoughts instead of pictures of integral thoughts; and then, if no new poets should arise to create afresh the associations which have been thus disorganized, language will be dead to all the nobler purposes of human intercourse.

How the formal or technical features of poetic utterance effect its fulfillment, though not specified, is suggested in his assertion that as this "vitally metaphorical" language loses its quality the verbal "pictures" atrophy to mere "signs" in the dearth of new poets.[8]

Shelley's interest in poetic language was by no means confined to its culturally inspiriting potency. In favorite poets he prized nothing more than their verbal élan. "His very words are instinct with spirit," he wrote of Dante. Nor did he acclaim this quality only in the few major deities of the poetic pantheon whom he especially revered. A letter to T. J. Hogg in 1817 tells of his special admiration for the "irresistible energy of language" in the *De Rerum Natura* of Lucretius; and many modern poets, often in spite of the spiritual blindness he found in some of them, startled him with the "electric life which burns within their words." Even a single word, though buried in a prosaic context, may be "a spark of inextinguishable thought," and so poetic.[9]

In Shelley's appreciation, however, more is involved than a personal sensitivity, or hypersensitivity, to expressive verve for its own sake. The soaring rhetoric of the *Defence* is in the typical

manner of vatic criticism. Shelley exalts not only the poet's function and inspirational sources but, more markedly than other celebrants of bardic revelation, his medium as well. "A poet," he proclaims,

> participates in the eternal, the infinite, and the one; as far as re-
> lates to his conceptions, time and place and number are not. The
> grammatical forms which express the moods of time, and the dif-
> ference of persons, and the distinction of place, are convertible
> with respect to the highest poetry without injuring it as poetry.

It is largely for this reason that he ranks language highest among
artistic media. Sculpture, painting, and music retain their honors,
but poetry is queen over them all because its words constitute a
mirror which reflects, whereas plastic materials, colors, and tones
are so many clouds dimming the celestial light which as media
they all seek to disseminate.[10]

Shelley was no formal purist. For him, the real value of poetry
is ultimately cognitive and moral, not terminally aesthetic. In this
respect—and it is an important one—he must be set apart from
later theorists of a Romantic cast whom in other respects he resembles, like Poe and such of Poe's *Symboliste* progeny as Paul
Verlaine and Valéry, who exalted music as the quintessential art. As
Shelley wrote in the *Defence*, the "great instrument of moral good
is the imagination; and poetry administers to the effect by acting
upon the cause," that is by nurturing the organ of man's moral nature.[11] Regrettably, Shelley's vatic turn often led him into the kind
of rhapsodic extolment which tends to smother the dispassionate
anatomy of poetry's verbal efficacy essential to respectable theory.
That he was nonetheless capable at times of perceptive analysis will
appear later in this chapter.

Equally unpropitious is the idealist aesthetics to which Shelley
subscribed. Like aesthetic idealists in general, he regarded a work
of art as only an imperfect embodiment of its maker's inward vision. All pictures and statues are cripples, in Emerson's shocking
metaphor. The idea took milder form in Shelley, whose Neoplatonism enforced the belief that even the most consummate artistic
creations were so many domes of many-colored glass staining the
white radiance of a forever unrealizable Beauty. A much cited passage in the *Defence* holds that the most glorious poetry is hardly
more than "a feeble shadow of the original conception of the
Poet." If so, then the most penetrating critic's fullest description

of a poem's linguistic mode becomes a science of shadows and can have only limited interest and appeal for readers curious about its ontology. Idealist and incarnationalist conceptions of art works notably differ. Briefly put, the critic who envisages a poem as "incarnating" its ideational content escapes the theoretical impasse faced by the idealist because he considers that the full value of the poem *does not exist before its realization.*[12]

To judge from the penetrating remarks in John Keats's letters, the eloquence of poetry was from the outset the main cause of his infatuation with it. In a paper contributed in 1817 to the *Champion* he found Edmund Kean's chief excellence as a Shakespearean actor to be his elegant and musical elocution, a poetic melody alive with sensuous and spiritual delights. The depth of Keats's unremitting attention to verbal detail shows even at moments of his most engaging self-deprecating humor. In a letter to his brother and sister-in-law he copied out a stanza as it stood in the first version of "La Belle Dame sans Merci":

She took me to her elfin grot,

And there she wept and sigh'd full sore,

And there I shut her wild wild eyes

    With kisses four.

Anticipating their possible objection to the arbitrary specification of *four* kisses, he pleads in defense his wish

to restrain the headlong impetuosity of my Muse—she would have said 'score' without hurting the rhyme—but we must temper the Imagination as the Critics say with Judgment. I was obliged to choose an even number that both eyes might have fair play,

and so on jocularly. But the jokes veil serious purpose. Elsewhere he writes of finding the beauties of Shakespeare's sonnets and other poems to inhere in the many "fine things said there unintentionally—in the intensity of working out conceits." He offers his friend J. H. Reynolds examples from Sonnet 12 and from *Venus and Adonis,* venting his admiration in mock envy: "Is this to be borne?" In 1819 he wrote Benjamin Bailey that Shakespeare and *Paradise Lost* seemed more marvelous to him with each passing day, because "I look upon fine Phrases like a Lover." In *The Fall of*

Hyperion, in lines he quotes in a letter to Richard Woodhouse, he had just expressed his faith that poetry alone, "With the fine spell of words," can free the imagination from the prison-house of inarticulateness.[13]

Like others, Keats believed that a poet's native language affected the quality of his poetry. For a time, he disparaged French in this regard, explaining to his sister Fanny that "the real use and greatness of a Tongue is to be referred to its literature." In the resources of English he reveled, and like other poets sensed the vital bond connecting effective verse and the contemporary spoken idiom, best realized, he felt, in Thomas Chatterton's poems: "general English idiom in English words." In *Paradise Lost* he found the faulty opposite, concurring with an assessment of it occasionally made by others: a splendid corruption of the language. Milton's uniquely "beautiful and grand Curiosity" was a baneful model for young poets because its English was denatured by adaptation to Greek and Latin cadence and syntax. Although Keats rejoiced in the "power" he was acquiring by learning foreign languages, he vowed to keep his verse free of their influence. As it is, he thinks the example of Milton's seductive masterpiece has spoiled his *Hyperion.* The highly inverted style of *Paradise Lost* requires in its author a mood of sustained artistry. "I wish to give myself up to other sensations. English ought to be kept up."[14]

Keats's homely admonition epitomizes the experience of poets who sense that what they have to say can only be said by a rapprochement between their style and the English they daily speak and hear spoken around them. Each major artist thus faces the problem of evolving a mode of expression calculated to effect the desired naturalness, to which the solution will—paradoxically—require a future generation of poets to repeat the identical revitalizing effort.

Not alone the stylistic manner of a past master but as well a conventional verse or stanza form—whether heroic couplet, blank verse, or rhymed tetrameter—has been found unsuited to the altered intonations of an ever-evolving spoken language. By Keats's day the sonnet, reintroduced around the time of Pope's death after long desuetude, had attained to splendid new life at the hands of Wordsworth. Yet despite his success in both its Petrarchan and English varieties, Keats hankered after a form more attuned to the structural limitations and potentials of modern English. Like some readers even today he was put off by the often unnatural effect of the closing couplet of the Shakespearean sonnet and at the same time felt the "pouncing rhymes" of the Italian pattern to be awkward in English. His sonnet beginning "If by dull rhymes our English must be chained" belongs with two or three others that resulted from his groping for something better, in which the English muse would at least be "bound with garlands of her own." Admirers of his magnificent odes will agree that his efforts were anything but fruitless.[15]

A profound intuition informs Keats's prosodic opinions. A casual reader of his correspondence may find nothing momentous in his phrasing of what he especially admired in Shakespeare's sonnets: "the *intensity* of working out conceits." Yet the word I've italicized is rich in theoretical implication. It encapsulates what he soon discovered about good verse: its semantic concision and, beyond that, the quality of tension as its crucial aesthetic condition. Keats would have been quick to agree with an able modern student of poetic language who has found tension "at every level of poetic organization," aptly describing it as "language at full stretch." This is clear in his famous advice to Shelley to "be more of an artist, and 'load every rift' of your subject with ore." It shows too in the experimental sonnet just mentioned, which attempts a more satisfactory fitting of the rhyme scheme to English. There poets are called upon to

> inspect the lyre, and weigh the stress
> Of every chord, and see what may be gain'd
> By ear industrious, and attention meet;
> Misers of sound and syllable no less
> Than Midas of his coinage, let us be
> Jealous of dead leaves in the bay wreath crown.

With this appeal Keats joins hands across the years with his scorned counterpart in aural "industry" and syllabic frugality, Pope, who once described true poets as those who "show no mercy to an empty line." And so the poet who during the last years of his brief life fashioned some of the most ore-packed verse in our language added his voice to the small but perceptive company of those for whom poetic utterance is set apart from all other discourse by that greater semantic loading and sonant density said to be best conveyed by the German words for the art, *Dichtung* and *Gedicht*.[16]

The second theoretical implication emerges most clearly in two other remarkable passages in Keats's letters. The earlier, of December 1817, instructs his brothers Tom and George that

> the excellence of every Art is its intensity, capable of making all disagreeables evaporate, from their being in close relationship with Beauty & Truth—examine *King Lear* and you will find this exemplified throughout.

We may regret that Keats failed to explain *how* a work of art effects this wonderful "evaporation of disagreeables." On the other hand, it should be apparent that in *Biographia Literaria,* published just five months before Keats wrote this letter, his remarkable intuition was given as cogent a supporting rationale as it is ever likely to receive.[17]

But we can find the nub of Keats's intuition in a later letter. Even so repulsive a sight as a street brawl, he wrote in 1819, partakes of an attractive "grace" from its display of sheer energy. Then follows a flight of analogical fancy. "This is the very thing in which consists poetry; and if so it is not so fine a thing as philosophy— For the same reason that an eagle is not so fine a thing as a truth." Keats's parallels have the mind-jolting quality of "metaphysical" conceits and prompt a conundrum-like query: How is poetry like an eagle? He doesn't say, but the most plausible answer is that poems and eagles alike embody power in pleasing forms. Though by an ideal standard such incarnations are cruder than philosophic abstractions, they often have an immediate experiential cogency more salubrious to the psyche than even the most logically impeccable argument can provide.[18]

Keats's choice of philosophy as the rival discipline is felicitous, recalling the never-ending animus between philosophers and poets already of long standing in Plato's day. Of course philosophy in its Platonic garb was regarded by many Romantic poets as friend and ally, something very different from the bloodless intellection spawned by Cartesian rationalism—the "cold philosophy" whose mere touch could destroy fancy's "charms" (*Lamia,* II, lines 229–30). Although his argument is hardly original, Keats's graphic treatment turns it into a thumbnail defense of poetry as an art forever exposed to intellectualist detraction for an alleged misappropriation of language, the jealously guarded instrument of the thinker's dialectical road to truth. No Romantic poet was more delicately responsive than Keats to the efficacy of language as the poetic medium. "A melodious passage in poetry," he wrote, "is full of pleasures both sensual and spiritual. The spiritual is felt when the very letters and points of charactered language show like the hieroglyphics of beauty; the mysterious signs of our immortal freemasonry."[19]

From time to time there have been those, at least until very recently a minority, who deny that poetry has any special aesthetic worth, or any expressive advantage whatever beyond what may be found in all verbalizing. With some current theorists, the "deprivileging" of verse is entailed in their reduction of all writing to so many undifferentiated "texts." Since these stylistic egalitarians seem deaf to any abstract counterargument, their opponents do better to appeal to a very common experience of readers throughout history, one never more eloquently celebrated than by the spokesmen of Romanticism. I allude to the plain fact that certain brief passages of fine writing, mainly in verse, stick willy-nilly in memory and so are endlessly quoted. Many of them are so felicitous that they charm readers of the most divergent types and often survive even the most profound shifts of taste. Such are the extracts from several masterpieces which Matthew Arnold commended as "touchstones" for the sound assessment of new verse. When they are in a foreign language they seem to suffer more in translation than poetry usually does. One of Arnold's choices, Dante's "E la sua volontate è nostra pace" (*Paradiso*, III, line 85), is a good example of this. "In his will is our peace" is by no means irretrievably prosaic; but it is unlikely to have been stored up in anyone's treasury of poetic gems. A more telling instance may be one Arnold omitted, Virgil's "Sunt lacrimae rerum et mentem mortalia tangunt" (*Aeneid*, I, line 462), where the semantic density and emotive force owe so much to the synergy of sonant modulation and concise Latin syntax as to elude any translation that is not a near total betrayal (as the despairing Dryden confessed of another Virgilian passage). Only in the original do the words combine to make readers delightedly catch breath, by leaving behind them "a track of golden fire," in Hazlitt's splendid image.[20]

Though perhaps worth only a footnote in a literary history, this phenomenon relates intimately to our topic. It is therefore worth comparing how a few Romantic writers justified their shared admiration of the line in *The Merchant of Venice* opening Lorenzo's speech to Jessica on the music of the spheres:

How sweet the moonlight sleeps upon this bank.

Nor should we assume that it had no appeal to pre-Romantic taste. For in terms that suppose a similar admiration in his day,

John Gilbert Cooper, in his *Letters Concerning Taste* (1755), singled out the line for special praise. For the student of poetic diction theory it may be instructive to set his judgment beside those
recorded in the following century by Hazlitt, Francis Jeffrey,
Leigh Hunt, and Shelley.

> *Cooper:* "That Verb [sleeps], taken from animal Life, and trans-
> fer'd by the irresistible Magic of Poetry, to the before lifeless Ob-
> jects of the Creation, animates the whole Scene, and conveys an
> instantaneous Idea to the Imagination what a solemn Stillness is
> requir'd when the *peerless Queen* of Night is in the full Splendor
> of her Majesty, thus lull'd to Repose."

> *Hazlitt:* " . . . I think the effect of moonlight is treated in an
> *ideal* manner in the well-known line in Shakespeare—

See how the moonlight *sleeps* upon yon bank.

> The image is heightened by the exquisiteness of the expression
> beyond its natural beauty, and it seems as if there could be no end
> in the delight taken in it."

> *Jeffrey:* "What other poet has put all the charm of a Moonlight
> landscape into a single line?—and that by an image so true to na-
> ture, and so simple, as to seem obvious to the most common ob-
> servation?—

See how the Moonlight *Sleeps* on yonder bank!"

> *Hunt:* "The happiest instance I remember of imaginative meta-
> phor is Shakespeare's moonlight 'sleeping' on a bank."

Hunt includes Lorenzo's whole speech in the select specimens of
English verse which comprise the bulk of his book, the famous line
printed, as in Jeffrey's case, with a minute but damaging error:
"How sweet the moonlight sleeps upon *the* bank."[21]
    The comments of Hazlitt, Jeffrey, and Hunt differ in details.
But these arise mainly from divergences of illustrative purpose outweighed by their agreement with Cooper in ascribing the magical
effect chiefly to the poet's metaphor of *sleep*. (In the cases of
Hazlitt and Jeffrey the point is made mainly by typographical emphasis.) Yet the personification alone, effective though it be, cannot merely as personification account for the line's universal appeal. This is sufficiently obvious when we see how much is lost in

the imperfectly recalled versions supplied by Hazlitt and Jeffrey, even though they retain the personification.

What these four critics had to say can hardly do full justice to the effect produced by Lorenzo's muted ejaculation. The more exquisite the verse, the more futile will seem anyone's attempt to pluck out the heart of its mystery. These truisms granted, a more circumstantial explication offered by Shelley of how Shakespeare's line works its magic is an obvious advance over the others. It occurred in a colloquy between him and Byron purportedly recorded *verbatim* by a third person, first published in 1830 and later included as an appendix to W. E. Peck's life of Shelley. "Now," Shelley observes of Lorenzo's utterance,

> examining this line, we perceive that all the parts are formed in relation to one another, and that it is consequently a whole. *Sleep,* we see, is the reduplication of the pure and gentle sound of *sweet;* and as the beginning of the former symphonizes with the beginning *s* of the latter, so also the *l* in *moonlight* prepares for the *l* in *sleep,* and glides gently into it; and in the conclusion, one may perceive that the word *bank* is determined by the preceding words, and that the *b* which it begins with is but a deeper intonation of the two *p*'s which come before it; *sleeps upon this slope,* would have been effeminate; *sleeps upon this rise,* would have been harsh and inharmonious.

When Byron objects that "the beauty of the line does not lie in sounds and syllables, and such contrivances" but in the metaphor of sleeping moonlight, Shelley replies:

> Indeed, that is also very beautiful. In every single line the poet must organize many simultaneous operations, both the meaning of the words and their emphatic arrangement, and then the flow and melting together of their symphony; and the whole must be united with the current of the rhyme [i.e., assonance].

Conceding that a poet may be unconscious of these "simultaneous operations," Shelley asserts that since ultimately they all depend on reason he does better to bring them to consciousness. "But what," he continues,

> makes this metaphor beautiful? To represent the tranquillity of moonlight is the object of the line; and the sleep is beautiful, because it gives a more intense and living form to the same idea; the

rhyme [assonance] beautifully falls in with this, and just lets the cadence of the emphasis dwell upon the sound and sense of the sweet word *sleep;* and the alliteration assimilates the rest of the line into one harmonious symmetry. This line, therefore, is it not altogether a work of art?[22]

Probably what first strikes a reader of these observations is how closely they anticipate modern explicative demonstrations of how sound and sense collaborate in good verse to form organic wholes. Though Shelley neglected the larger contexts of speech, scene, and play, his limited purpose is skillfully attained, omitting only the role of meter—especially in this case the effect of a cadence which only gently strains against the regularity of the iambic pentameter pattern. Clearly for him and others who pondered poetic words in the wake of *Lyrical Ballads* and its iconoclastic Prefaces, they were still the stuff of an art, a medium manipulated to create something more compelling than anything else produced by the use of language.

CHAPTER NINE

Early Victorian Opinion

BETWEEN COLERIDGE'S death and the early twentieth century, English discussion of poetic style was all but barren of theoretical innovation. With few exceptions, for the first time since the Elizabethans vindicated the vernacular as a poetic medium, English writers, when they had occasion to ponder the question, were content mainly with perfunctory rehearsals of the conventional ideas.

It is not that Victorian writers denied the central role which a mastery of his medium plays in the poet's art. Many of them affirmed that poets were first and foremost lords of language. In 1825, T. B. Macaulay called poetry the art of "employing words in such a manner as to produce an illusion on the imagination," just as painters do with colors. A generation later John Henry Newman, in his *Idea of a University*, had recourse to the same trite analogy to raise the question with more rhetorical force. Rejecting the popular romantic heresy that artists of genius need never take pains, he pointed to Michelangelo's and Raphael's use of preliminary sketches in the evolution of their masterpieces of statuary and painting. And why, he asked, "may not language be wrought as well as the clay of the modeler? why may not words be worked up as well as colours?" Put by a man of more intellectual independence than Macaulay possessed, these questions promise some studied probing of the issues they raise. But instead, like Macaulay and others, Newman takes refuge in Duke Theseus's celebrated lines on the poetic imagination's free-ranging power to shape and name "airy nothing"—as though theorizing could do no better.[1]

Yet it is less than accurate to speak of the early Victorian critics' "almost total lack of interest in the problems of the medium" of poetry. Newman's chapter on literature in *The Idea of a University* deals predominantly with its language. The words of a scientific work, he argues, dealing with things, constitute little more than a semiotic notation, whereas literature, dealing with thoughts, "uses language in its full compass, as including phraseology, style, composition, rhythm, eloquence." In this somewhat heterogeneous list of linguistic features Newman does not distinguish verse from oratory and other kinds of artistic prose. That he appreciated the distinction, however, is plain enough in a youthful essay misleadingly titled "Poetry, with Reference to Aristotle's Poetics" (1829). Noting that meter is the form common to poetry in every language, he saw in it not a restraint but rather, in genuine work, both an outward manifestation of a poem's "music" and "the suitable index of its sense." Almost every one of Newman's contemporaries—heirs as they were to the Romantic exaltation of lyric poetry—record their sensitivity to poetic expression. The youthful John Stuart Mill locates the surest proof of a true poet in a certain quality discernible in "his words, or the mode of their arrangement." Carlyle's characterization of poets adverts constantly to their style of utterance. De Quincey wrote prolix essays on "Style," "Language," and "Rhetoric," referred often to the Wordsworth-Coleridge dispute on poetic diction, and restated, without acknowledgment, Coleridge's cardinal dicta on meter, prose versus verse, and related topics. Matthew Arnold's *On Translating Homer,* (1861), easily his most sustained examination of dictional quality, turns throughout on painstaking discriminations of poetic style. Reviewing Saintsbury's *Specimens of English Prose Style* in 1886, Pater ascribed the "indispensable qualities" of prose and verse to contrasting modes of thinking. He thought the qualities of order, precision, and directness showed to best advantage in an artistic prose equally free of the opposite faults of purple-patch gaudiness and a "bare *sermo pedestris.*" But neither in this review nor anywhere else did he identify the contrasting qualities of verse.[2]

The stagnation of Victorian poetics may owe something to the persistence in most Victorian poetry of the diction and idiom established during the Romantic revolution. But its main cause was a collaboration of several cultural currents setting strongly against theoretical innovation. One was, quite simply, the supersedure of formal speculation by other critical concerns, most vigorously pressed early in Victoria's reign by Carlyle's literary journalism, in which moral, social, and historical considerations predominated. In the more urbane Arnold too, questions of style and structure yielded in urgency to the central role he assigned to poetry and criticism in sustaining culture against the corrosive hostility of contemporary philistinism. Though he exalted poetry as "the most perfect speech of man," the poetician in Arnold was usually the servant of the social advocate and, ultimately, the moralist, whose alternate definition of poetry was a "criticism of life." Even the "aesthete" Pater evinced a related if etiolated species of this critical displacement. The formal aspects of art, so appealing to his fastidious sensitivity, finally interested him less for their own sake, or for their importance in determining the *differentia specifica* of poems or paintings, than as agencies of ethical utility. (The resulting asceticism of personal amelioration is propounded in *Plato and Platonism*, 1893). Neither Pater nor Arnold can quite be classed with the utilitarian moralist who asked, in scathing paraphrase of Théophile Gautier's preface to *Mademoiselle de Maupin*, "In the presence of such grave concerns, can one be bothered with style or rhyme?" Yet to both men the erection of a systematic theory of verse language could only have seemed a matter of secondary importance and no urgency.[3]

Another factor, already mentioned, was the tendency to conceive of poetry fundamentally as a precious spirit infused into all fine art from sources in natural beauty and human passion. This Romanticist motif became more pronounced as the century advanced. Especially erosive of theory was the consequent shift of attention from what poets created to the intellectual and psychological equipment which enables creation in the first place and determines the relative worth of its products. Carlyle's enshrinement of the poet as hero and Emerson's vision of him as "representative man" are celebrated examples of this preoccupation. Though never quite overlooked by either critic, the formal qualities of poetic expression were most often taken as tokens of beings endowed with unusual powers of intuitive vision and emotive depth which made them a race apart. A great poem was a revelation to the less percipient public of the author's spirit-quickening experiences and of otherwise ineffable truth. Bad poems were condemned more for prophetic or confessional dissemblance than for shoddy workmanship. According to Whitman's rhapsodic preface to *Leaves of Grass,* technical ineptitude is always transcended by the sterling artlessness of revelatory bardic utterance. "All faults may be forgiven him who has perfect candor." Thus sincerity replaced expressive acumen as a cardinal poetic virtue, becoming as the century progressed a tacit premise in the work of influential critics. Its ancestry is obvious in both Wordsworth's diatribes against "artificial" diction and the Romantic expressionism best labeled by Keats's "true voice of feeling."[4]

There was also a renewed stress on the deep-seated English distrust of any direction of thought leading to metaphysical speculation. Willing ears received Pater's warning, in his early essay on Winckelmann (1861), against a taste for metaphysics, "if we mean to mould our lives to artistic perfection." From the idea of aesthetic criticism detailed in his preface to *The Renaissance,* Pater excluded all abstract inquiry into beauty "as unprofitable as metaphysical questions elsewhere." To confirm the Victorian depreciation of the *Biographia,* Leslie Stephen in 1888 had only to accuse the author "of infecting English thought with the virus of German metaphysics." British writers were quick to deplore the baneful example of modern Germany, where poetics had become the province of philosophers. The tendency was hard to check, since most traditional issues in literary theory seemed inherently amenable to the categories of philosophic thought; none more so than that of poetic language, whose elusiveness inevitably tempted vigorous intellects to seek ontological solutions. Alexander Gottlieb Baumgarten, the founder of aesthetic science, had initiated the trend. Ernst Cassirer has shown how Baumgarten's experience as reader and would-be writer of verse taught him to distinguish poetic from scientific themes. "It is a step of equal importance," Cassirer continues, "that, in order to formulate this difference, Baumgarten went back primarily to the form and special character of the language of poetry."[5]

For their distrust of abstract definitions of poetry Victorian writers could find support in German Romanticism itself. "Nur Gestalt und Farbe," wrote Friedrich Schlegel in *Gespräch über die Poesie,* "können es nachbildend ausdrücken, wie der Mensch gebildet ist; und so lässt sich auch eigentlich nicht reden von der Poesie als nur in Poesie" [Only shape and color can convey a visual image of a human being; similarly, strictly speaking, nothing can be said about poetry except in poetry.] This motif is sounded in an early display of Carlyle's visceral vitalism entitled "Characteristics" (1831), where he declares that poetry can only be spoken of "*mu-*

sically, or in the language of poetry." The very attempt to do otherwise, he argues elsewhere, risks the "disease of metaphysics . . . a perennial one." Though in some respects a healthy reaction against academic pedantry, the Victorian impatience with abstract reasoning often promoted a terminological imprecision that hobbled the logical rigor of what they themselves had to say. Arnold is a notable case in point. What his temperamental realism could effect was limited by an aversion not alone to metaphysics but even to less abstruse levels of abstraction in every field of intellectual endeavor. In *Literature and Dogma* (1873) he relegated Plato's argument for the immortality of the soul to the "futilities" of demonstration he contemned, and intemperately brushed aside the doctrine of the Trinity as "the fairy-tale of the three supernatural persons no man can verify." Yet with an insouciance exasperating to his most respectful readers, he felt no obligation to define the mysterious "laws" of *poetic truth* and *poetic beauty* invoked at crucial moments of his poetics.[6]

A final deterrent to fresh scrutiny of verse language in Arnold's time was the relatively diminished prestige of poetry as against prose fiction and other forms of belletristic prose, with an ensuing blurring of the boundaries between them. In their very different ways Carlyle and Pater especially championed this development. Carlyle urged both Tennyson and Browning to give up verse for prose and hailed Boswell's *Life of Johnson* as a heroic poem and Goethe's *Werther* as a "poetic (and prophetic) utterance of the World's Despair." Carlyle's personal contribution to this altered literary taxonomy was the poeticization of historiography in his *French Revolution.* Reviewers tended to "aesthetize" the work, Carlyle's biographer reports, responding to it as one might to *Paradise Lost.* In "Style" Pater tried to differentiate the unique properties of several prose artists. Bacon's prose is "coloured," Livy's and Carlyle's "picturesque," Cicero's and Newman's "musical," Plato's, Jules Michelet's, and Thomas Browne's "mystical," Milton's and Jeremy Taylor's "exalted." Prose, Pater thought, had become the "privileged artistic faculty" of the hour, an "instrument of many stops, meditative, observant, descriptive, eloquent, analytic, plaintive, fervid." Given a prose so versatile, what room or need for verse? And what call to press further than past critics had already ventured into the quagmires of verse theory?[7]

Neither the changes in literary and critical priorities nor Victorian writers' coolness toward reasoned theorizing, however, reduced them to silence on verse language. No survey of the subject can fairly neglect even their reiterations of Romantic doctrines, because in these there is often an accrual of meaning or shift of emphasis induced by altered historical conditions. Romanticism had achieved a revolution of poetic taste and creed. For the generation of Carlyle and De Quincey the major tenets of the Romantic program subversive of long-standing views were now become premises of whatever further observations of their own the Victorians had to offer.

Whereas the Victorians were, generally speaking, continuators of Wordsworth's rather than Coleridge's ideas, Leigh Hunt was the reverse. He deserves our notice for his attention to "the claims of the medium" rare in his day, as Alba Warren pointed out, and for his sympathetic response to Coleridge's principles of poetic diction. For despite their reluctance to accept Wordsworth's views, Hunt's younger contemporaries never gauged the profundity of what he himself had in *Imagination and Fancy* (1844) hailed as Coleridge's "masterly expositions of the art of poetry." In that book he garnered, for the pleasure and edification of common readers, scraps of what he considered quintessential English verse, taken from several Elizabethans, Milton, Coleridge, Shelley, and Keats.[8]

In an introductory chapter, "What Is Poetry?" Hunt staunchly defends meter as a necessary ingredient of poetic expression. He begins by flatly branding it "a prosaic mistake" to think that prose serves as well as verse for writing poetry. His rationale is largely Coleridgean. Meter is demanded by "the perfection of the poetical spirit," fully revealed by the poet's natural inclination to use it. Erroneously called a clog, meter is in fact a stimulus to composition, springing from the same inspirational source as the poet's other creative impulses. It is "no dominator over the poet," he argues,

> except inasmuch as the bond is reciprocal, and the poet dominates over the verse. . . . What great poet ever wrote his poems in prose? or where is a good prose poem, of any length, to be found?

Nor is rhyme, in Hunt's view, a mere aural decoration. He recalls Dryden's remark that searching for a rhyming word often gave him a thought; and the tenor of Hunt's preceding argument shows a firm grasp of the theoretical implications of that experience.[9]

Hunt's account conforms to a gradual shift of emphasis in the definition of poetic language at last fully established in Romantic poetics. Conceived first as primarily a matter of genre-determined choice of vocabulary, it was later envisaged less as a *selection* than an *order* of words discrepant from that of prose. In Johnson the second stipulation is mentioned—barely—when he alludes to "a happy combination of words" in a passage which lays the main stress on a poetic lexicon with no "vulgar" or technical terms. The change is completed in Coleridge's summary lexical characterization in the *Biographia:* "A poem contains the same elements as a prose composition; the difference therefore must consist in a different combination of them, in consequence of a different object proposed." Meter, then, in post-Romantic discussions of poetry, is often defended on the grounds that it promotes a salutary intensification and—potentially at least—facilitates the formal perfection of Coleridge's "different combination."[10]

Hunt's discipleship to Coleridge was anything but submissive. On the perennially mooted issue of prose poetry he dissented not only from Coleridge but from his revered friend Shelley as well, both of whom had committed the "prosaical mistake" Hunt would correct. He had a firm grasp of the principle first explicitly enunciated by Samuel Say that a poem's versification is an active ingredient in the compound of thought and emotion the poet communicates. Perhaps echoing Carlyle (see below), he asserts that poetic subjects (the category is never clearly defined) are those adaptable to "song, or metrical excitement." Hunt's whole rationale is clinched by the declaration that he knows "no very fine versification unaccompanied with fine poetry; no poetry of a mean order accompanied with verse of the highest."[11]

These opinions support the statement in Hunt's review of Shelley's *Prometheus* in the *Examiner* (1822) that poetry "has a music—and often a language"—distinct from that of prose. Like Coleridge in the *Biographia,* he shows that if the words of a common greeting are tricked out in measured lines and inversions the result is not poetry but the worst doggerel:

Yourself how do you find?
Very well, you I thank.[12]

Whenever poetry was his subject, Hunt emphasized its verbal medium. As early as 1818, in *Foliage,* a volume including translated passages from the *Iliad,* he joins in the familiar lament over the unfitness of "Teutonic" English, with its ubiquitous monosyllables, to render "the long organ music of Homer." In *Imagination and Fancy* Spenser and Marlowe are prized mainly as the first English poets "who perceived the beauty of words not as apart

from their significance . . . but as a habit of the poetic mood."
Ever responsive to stylistic delicacy, in the review of *Prometheus
Unbound* he aimed a deft riposte at the more obtuse reviewers'
ridicule of the line (not yet made memorable by frequent citation),

> Pinnacled dim in the intense inane.

"The *intense inane*," Hunt noted, "implies excess of emptiness, and
is a phrase of Miltonic construction like 'the palpable obscure' and
'the vast abrupt.' Where is the unintelligible nonsense of all this?"[13]

Hunt is further unusual in his time for some rudimentary models of close textual explication that lend candor to his exaltations of
poetic language. *Imagination and Fancy* contains a bit of analytical
dissection that might have led the American New Critics to name
him their forerunner in practical criticism as fairly as they acknowledged Coleridge their ancestor in theory. One exegesis highlights
the subtle variation of vowel sounds in Shelley's "To a Skylark"; another shows how the diction in Keats's *Eve of St. Agnes* "fuses the
imaginative and the spiritual, the remote and the near."[14]

A single stanza of Shelley's poem occasioned the kind of detailed analysis he would have welcomed:

> Like a high-born maiden
>
> In a palace tower
>
> Soothing her love-laden
>
> Soul in secret hour
>
> With music sweet as love, which overflowed her bower.

"Not a sound of a vowel in the quatrain," Hunt points out, "resembles that of another, except in the rhyme."

> Observe, for instance (for nothing is too minute to dwell upon in
> such beauty), the contrast of the *i* and *o* in "high-born"; the dif-
> ference of the *a* in "maiden" from that in "palace"; the strong
> opposition of *maiden* to *tower* (making the rhyme more vigorous
> in proportion to the general softness); then the new differences in
> *soothing, love-laden, soul,* and *secret,* all diverse from one another,
> and from the whole strain.

Hunt's exegeses are not grounded, as ideally they should be, in
any poetic ontology, though they accord well enough with the

qualities of *Unsuperfluousness* and *Variety* which in "What Is Poetry?" he names as essentials of good verse. But like Shelley's
analysis of "How sweet the moonlight . . . ," Hunt's explications
assume the dynamic organicism, or holism, he had absorbed from
Coleridge. His declarations that *variety* consists in the avoidance
of monotony by distributing pauses, retardations, and accelera-
tions of tempo, and so on, and that "the whole secret of
versification is a musical secret" detectable only "by the ear of genius" may not take us very far. But they crossed the frontiers of a
rich and hitherto hardly explored analytical province.[15]

Though rare in his day, Hunt's exercises in close reading were
not unique. There is De Quincey's eloquent demonstration of 1847
in *Tait's Magazine* showing how "metrical pomp" and "pomp of
sentiment" are embodied in a swelling "roll of dactyls" culminating
in the "deep spondaic close" of the exordial lines of *Paradise Lost:*

> That to the height of this great argument
>
> I may assert eternal Providence
>
> And justify the ways of God to men.

De Quincey had the good sense to recognize that demonstrations of
this kind can only show *how* metrical movement is efficacious, never
why it is: "for mysterious," he remarks parenthetically some pages
later, "is the life that connects all modes of passion with rhythms.[16]

No such diffidence troubled Edgar Allan Poe in his explication
included in "The Rationale of Verse" (1848) to illustrate what he
laid down as the basic principle of all versification: *equality*. For
this pervasive feature of technique, Poe assigned a psychological
foundation, verse having its origin in "the human enjoyment of
equality, fitness." All the familiar prosodic properties, which Poe
curiously labels *moods* of verse—such as rhythm and meter, stanzaic structure, rhyme, alliteration, and the refrain—are alike so
many manifestations of this equalizing tendency. To show how the
"various systems of equalization" can be called almost simultaneously into play, he invented an ad hoc dactylic stanza:

> Virginal Lillian, rigidly, humblily dutiful
>> Saintlily, lowlily,
>> Thrillingly, holily
>>> Beautiful!

"Here we appreciate," he instructs his readers,

> first the absolute equality between the long syllable of each dactyl
> and the two short conjointly; secondly, the absolute equality of
> each dactyl and any other dactyl, in other words, among all the
> dactyls; thirdly, the absolute equality between the two middle
> lines; fourthly, the absolute equality between the last two syllables
> of the respective words "dutiful" and "beautiful,"

and so on through a tally of fourteen such phrasal, syllabic, and
aural "equalities," in a numbing display of analytic precision.[17]
How seriously, readers may wonder, are we to take this merciless
exercise in prosodic calculus? Poe seems not to have been merely
indulging his propensity for hoaxes. On the sober opening page of
his treatise he had declared that nine-tenths of versification belongs to mathematics. The dissection of his sample stanza is perhaps now most interesting as an anticipation of the method of
structuralist explication applied so ingeniously by Jakobson to
sonnets by Baudelaire and Shakespeare. Poe foresaw the same objection to his enumeration of correspondences that has been made
to Jakobson's more sophisticated exegeses: that no one can take
them all in while reading the poem. Poe insists, to the contrary,
that an alert reader should indeed immediately (and pleasurably!)
"appreciate . . . each and all of the equalizations detailed."[18] His
monotonously homogeneous string of sonic and rhythmic parities
makes pretty thin gruel beside the rich heterogeneity of Jakobson's and Lévi-Strauss's multileveled dissection of Baudelaire's
"Les Chats." Nevertheless, Poe's *equality* can be taken as a crude
precursor of Jakobson's *equivalence*.

The very excess of Poe's enumeration highlights an issue central to any theory of verse discourse but seldom given adequate
treatment: evaluation. Poe boasts of the complexity in his stanza.
Yet the concentration of no less than fourteen sonant and rhythmic "equalities" within ten words can only deepen a reader's sense
that their poetic value must be slim. Worse yet, Poe's demonstration assumes that formal patterns in poems can be valuable apart
from any collaboration with an intellectual content trivial or
weighty, depending only on degrees of technical complexity.
Jakobson and Lévi-Strauss show that "Les Chats" is admirable for
an unusually skillful concurrence (however elusive) of its technical
structure with a structure of "argument." In Poe's exegesis the latter has no more than a phantom existence.

The rare nineteenth-century specimens of poetic explication may tentatively be regarded as casual and unsystematic harbingers of what some literary historians think was initiated as a recognized critical method by I. A. Richards's *Practical Criticism* in 1929. If so, why did it not appear before then, since its theoretical ground in holistic organicism had already been established? The most likely answer is the critical agenda prevailing from antiquity through neoclassicism. Modern explication of poems focuses on their stylistic features, especially in lyric verse, whereas on the hierarchical ladder of genres and structural "parts" bequeathed by Greece and Rome to modern Europe lyric verse and diction occupied the lowest rungs. With one dubious exception, the surviving corpus of ancient criticism contains no models of textural literary anatomy. The dubious exception is a brief analysis in Longinus of one of Sappho's poems, which Allan Tate saluted as a forerunner of New Critical close reading, "probably the first example in criticism of structural analysis of a lyric poem." But in fact Longinus dealt there exclusively with the referents of Sappho's words, not with her words as such.[19]

An unusual amount of self-contradiction and changes of mind on crucial issues marks the critical writings of De Quincey, Mill, and Carlyle. The epoch-making Wordsworth-Coleridge debate over·poetic diction long preoccupied De Quincey, who was closely acquainted with both men. At first, though he recognized that Coleridge's contribution to it was easily the best part of the *Biographia,* he favored Wordsworth's argument as "the most finished and masterly specimen of reasoning" on any fine art ever produced, one which Coleridge had utterly failed to discredit. But this fulsome encomium was not to stand. Years later, presumably after further pondering what in the essay "Rhetoric" he dubbed "the thorny question of the *quiddity,* or characteristic difference, of poetry as distinguished from prose," he issued a sharp and still cogent challenge to Wordsworth's denunciation of neoclassical poetic style. Remarking first that in much of their verse Dryden and Pope actually did write in the natural idiom Wordsworth valued, and then conceding that in both there is also "much of the unfeeling and prescriptive slang" he had censured, De Quincey exposes the fatal flaws in Wordsworth's thesis.

> Spenser, Shakespeare, the Bible of 1611—how say you, William Wordsworth—are these right and true as to diction, or are they not? If you say they *are*, then what is it you are proposing to

change? . . . [I]f you say, no, they are *not;* then, indeed, you open a fearful range to your own artillery, but in a war greater than you could, apparently, have contemplated. . . . [I]f the leading classics of the English literature are, in quality of diction and style, loyal to the canons of sound taste, then you have cut away the *locus standi* for yourself as a reformer: the reformation applies only to secondary and recent abuses. . . . [I]f they also are faulty, you undertake an onus of hostility so vast that you will be found fighting against the stars.[20]

De Quincey adds that Wordsworth should have supplied extensive illustration of good and bad diction, because without it "the whole dispute is an aerial subtilty beyond the grasp of the best critic and the worst."[21]

As he suggests, the kind of diction Wordsworth deplored occurs in some of the finest passages not only of Dryden and Pope but of Shakespeare and Milton as well—not to mention Wordsworth himself. (See his "Ode Composed on a May Morning," which has "purpling East," "Blithe Flora," "pearly shower," "dewy gleams," and "balmy air.") It is one thing to recognize such stereotypes to be characteristic of a period style, quite another to represent them as *in se* vices.

Reading it today, we might take De Quincey's dissatisfaction with Wordsworth to imply an endorsement of Coleridge's refutation. But no such thing. The two contenders, he concluded, had combined to yield a "barren result, leaving the whole question as far from solution as ever."[22]

J. S. Mill, though much steadier than De Quincey in his esteem for Wordsworth, nonetheless also sensed the shakiness of the reasoning in the Prefaces. He began as an ardent Wordsworthian. In a letter to John Sterling in 1831 he prized in the poet to whose verse he owed his personal recovery from spiritual malnutrition the rare double gift of creative power and critical acumen. On Coleridge's critical achievement he was by contrast totally silent, even in the later essay hailing him as the century's one worthy philosophic alternative to Jeremy Bentham. In "Thoughts on Poetry and Its Varieties" (1833), Mill reverted to a comparison of poetry and oratory as the basis for his own conception of the psychological sources, lexical character, and effects of those two verbal arts. His formulation departs from older ones only in being more emphatically lyricist and expressionist; poetry is in the strictest sense an "act of utterance," and lyric poetry, Mill contended, is both the oldest and most "poetic" variety. Poetry and oratory are alike emotive expressions. But whereas the orator's words are means to the end of persuasion, the poet's are ends in themselves. Oratory breaches the thin and porous wall separating it from poetry not when the speaker's emotive fervor begins to issue in images, but when feelings rise to consciousness in an associative train, each one blending with or giving way to the next. When this psychological condition has been reached, the "words, or the mode of their arrangement, are such as we spontaneously use only when in a state of excitement, proving that the mind is at least as much occupied by a passive state of its own feelings, as by the desire of attaining the premeditated end which the discourse had in view."[23]

Yet this explanation of the inception of poetry redirected Mill not to Coleridge but to Wordsworth, because it seemed to him, as he reported in a footnote, to point to one substantial fault in the latter's theory of poetic diction. Granting that all natural expression of feeling may issue in language devoid of conventional phraseology, Mill nonetheless adds that whenever a given culture has offered a poet a choice among modes of conveying the same emotion, the stronger that emotion is the more instinctively he has preferred "the language which is most peculiarly appropriate to itself, and kept sacred from the contact of more vulgar objects of contemplation."[24]

What is immediately striking in Mill's account is not its similarity to Hazlitt's on this same point, but its reversion to a neoclassical norm. It thus tends, possibly beyond Mill's intention, less to a mere corrective of Wordsworth's deficiencies than to a virtual rejection of the naturalism from which they stem. But most salient in the context of poetic diction is that it is not a theory of verse, still less of verse language. Mill's ostensible aim is to delineate *poetry*, to discriminate its embodied form from other literary forms adjacent to its domain. "For where everyone feels a difference, a difference there must be." But this aim dissolves as his inquiry is diverted into the current of the prevailing Romantic conviction that poetry conceived in essence is not a department of formal discourse but a quality common in varying degrees to all the fine arts, not excluding architecture. Even when, at times, *poetry* for Mill is more restrictively synonymous with Coleridge's *poesy*, he fails to isolate within the global term the separate provinces of the "poetic" (pertinent to verse and prose alike) and the "poematic" (pertinent to verse alone). In this youthful essay on the subject Mill may well have been among those whom Hunt disparaged as perpetrators of

the "poetical mistake," since he had begun by scorning the equation of poetry with metrical composition as a "wretched mockery
of a definition." A mere five years later he was to speak more appre-
ciatively of the aesthetic value of meter.[25]

The best known—and most overrated—distinction Mill deduced from his separation of poetry from oratory was that orations are heard, poems overheard; speakers address an audience,
whereas poets talk to themselves. He held all poetry, even dramatic and narrative, to be in essence a species of self-communing.
"All poetry is in the nature of a soliloquy." The nearest contemporary parallel to this discrimination is found in the work of the Reverend John Keble. Between 1832 and 1841, as poetry professor at
Oxford, Keble delivered a series of Latin lectures on poetry's
restorative power ("De poeticae Vi Medica"), dedicated in adula-
tory terms to Wordsworth. In them Keble affirmed his hearty
agreement with "those who refuse to limit the divine gift of Poetry to the manufacture of verses." He did not, however, accord
poetic rank to all artistically admirable prose. Cicero's orations,
though they stir our feelings with subtle cadence and ornate
phraseology, are not poetry, nor would they have been so in verse.
Neither are those of Edmund Burke. On the other hand, the prose
of Plato and Jeremy Taylor *is* poetry. The difference closely restates Mill's distinction between the heard and the overheard.
Plato and Taylor, caught up in their subjects, wrote only to please
themselves (which certainly would have discomfitted both of them
to learn); orators by contrast are rhetorical, their words being
"over-carefully framed to appeal to an audience." Keble also supports Mill's early envisagement of poetry as at bottom a psychic
state, not a compositional form. But he pushes it to an extreme
which Mill at no time sanctioned. Beauty of language, Keble declared, was no source of poetry; words and meter are lifeless instruments. He doubts whether any poet cried up for rich and
beautiful diction can be classed with those who are poets by nature
and genuine feeling. Wordsworth's Prefaces could never have inspired a more stark severance of form and value.[26]

In Mill's discrimination of the heard and overheard we have
an instance of the suggestive insights into the nature of poetry that
imperfectly compensate for the Victorian theoretical stasis. The
terms of Mill's catchy image, again consistent with his expressionism, are affective rather than objective. Their tenuous relevance to
modes of the literary medium is all too apparent when he immediately applies them to the graphic arts and music, where *hearing*

and *overhearing* become increasingly metaphorical and analytically unavailing. Rembrandt's portraits, being "poetic," are overheard. But the figures represented in modern French portraiture and statuary are "in the worst style of corrupted eloquence." In Rossini there is only a kind of musical oratory, whereas in Mozart we have genuine poetry. "Who," Mill asks about one of Mozart's most beautiful arias (begging more than one question in the complex ontology of a performing art), "Who can imagine 'Dove sono' heard? We imagine it *over*heard."[27]

Mill distinguished between poetry and prose fiction in cognitive rather than affective terms. *Poetry* in this case designated both verse and poetic prose; *fiction,* prose narrative. Both can communicate truth, but of separate areas of experience. The poet's truth, drawn from introspection, portrays the human soul; the novelist's, garnered from observation, represents only external reality, a delimitation which even then, before the novel's claim to artistic status had been assured, must have seemed to some readers demeaning. Nowhere in his discussion is there the slightest hint that the cognitive efficacy of poetry demands meter or any lexical or syntactical departure from prose norms. In his *Autobiography,* Mill reports having profited from Carlyle's prose not as "philosophy to instruct," but as "poetry to animate."[28]

Yet Mill was certainly not unresponsive to meter. In a generally laudatory review of Tennyson's early poems, he faulted the young poet for not making the aural qualities of his versification more suitable to his themes. In the *Autobiography* he tells of having been well equipped by early training to savor poetry in its traditional form. He recalls that his twenty or thirty readings of Pope's *Homer,* that "brilliant specimen of narrative and versification," began in his eighth year. His father set him to writing verse, in the familiar Enlightenment faith that some things could be better expressed that way than in prose. By 1838 he had reversed his earlier view to accept the traditional valuation of metrical composition as supreme in the hierarchy of verbal expression. Prose, he wrote in a piece on Alfred de Vigny, serves well enough for whatever one has to say. There are no so-called poetic subjects inaccessible to prose treatment. Nonetheless, we resort to verse for

> what is worth saying better than prose can say it. . . . A thought or feeling requires verse for its adequate expression, when in order that it may dart into the soul with the speed of a lightning-flash, the ideas or images that are to convey it require to be

pressed closer together than is compatible with the rigid grammatical construction of the prose sentence. One recommendation
of verse, therefore, is, that it affords a language more *condensed*
than prose.

One could hardly ask for a more apt gloss on Wordsworth's dictum
that poetry "carries truth alive into the heart by passion." But Mill
adds a second "recommendation" of verse when, like De Quincey
and Eliot, he refers to some law of the human mind, in obedience
to which all profound and sustained feeling has from time im-
memorial "tended to express itself in rhythmical language.[29]

Mill preceded Poe in the conviction that such passion, inherently transient, requires that poems generally be short. Long
poems, except in the hands of a Homer, Dante, or Milton, will always strike readers as beyond their capacities for sustained perusal.
And, like others who have considered the subject, Mill sees that the
universal grounding of verse in the human psyche is insufficient of
itself to guarantee its rare glories. The peculiar character of a poet's
native tongue may enhance or debase the quality of what he can do
in it. Mill joined others in thinking French, so well suited to prose,
inferior as a prosodic medium to the other major European languages. De Vigny, Mill laments, had to make his verse out of "the
most prosaic language of Europe," a language "essentially unmusi-
cal," in which, because it permits only one type of sentence for
both prose and poetry, "all the screws and pegs of the prose sentence are retained to encumber the verse." Thus the monotony, to
Mill's ear, of De Vigny's alexandrines in *Eloa*. (But how then did
Racine attune this same verse form to a tragic magnificence that
still captivates theater-goers at the Comédie Française?)[30]

The question involved certainly cannot be settled by consulting history. The German progenitors of Romanticism discovered
through antiquarian and comparatist research new evidence for
the natural union of poetry and meter. For a resoundingly affirmative answer to whether meter is essential to poetry ("Ist das Silbenmass der Poesie eigentlich?"), August Schlegel confidently
pointed to its temporal and geographical universality. No rational
invention, meter is a phenomenon as deeply implanted in human
nature as poetry itself, found in every clime and culture.[31] Yet
while what poets accordingly produce, critics discuss, and readers
of poetry delight in is almost entirely metrical composition, total
unanimity on the role or necessity of meter itself, as we have seen,
has never prevailed. Earlier challenges to it were strengthened

under Victoria when the novel rose in artistic respectability, when some writers extolled the aesthetic merit of non-fictive prose, and a few even suspected that though poetry might be immortal, meter was on its deathbed. Certainly this period planted the aesthetic seeds that were to flower in the theory and practice of free verse—in Arnold's "Dover Beach" actually supplying twentieth-century prosodic rebels a telling exhibit for their cause. Yet an even stronger case was to be made for regarding free verse not as an abandonment of meter but a radical renovation of it to accommodate profound changes in the modern social psyche.

Faced with the complexities of the metrical question, Mill simply changed his mind, declaring in 1833 that at passionate moments even non-poets "speak poetry," then five years later exalting meter in the eloquent terms quoted above. De Quincey was uncharacteristically more consistent on the *quaestio vexata* of what distinguishes verse from prose. He strongly implies, without I think ever stating it in so many words, that poetry and verse are inseparable. He came closest to doing so in a note added in 1859 to his much earlier essay "Rhetoric," where he makes meter the cardinal distinction of poetry. Most of what he wrote on meter itself in the long essay on literary style (1840–1841) rehearses the main Coleridgean ideas on the subject. Prose was a late literary "discovery," verse the primitive mode in which, for example, oracles were delivered. "Whoever heard of a prose oracle?"[32]

De Quincey's separation, in "The Poetry of Pope" (1848), of writing into the "literature of knowledge" and the "literature of power," aiming respectively to *teach* and to *move,* does little to clarify the issue. As a replacement of the traditional account, which yokes pleasure and profit in individual works of genuine literary art, De Quincey's harsh segregation is not very satisfactory. In "Letters to a Young Man" (1823), which contains a sketchy version of the dichotomy, he makes an abortive attempt to relate it to formal categories. Proffering the idea of power in place of pleasure in its customary coupling with instruction, he identifies it with the emotions aroused in readers rarely if ever by real, extraliterary experience, but inevitably by poetry. In every mind, he explained, countless modes of feeling lie dormant until they are articulated by some poet. He makes no attempt to connect this process to metrical order beyond what is suggested in naming *King Lear* and *Paradise lost* as notable instances of it. These works imbue with vitality the "lifeless form" of the world postulated in geometry, which has no more affective reality for us "than the square root of two."[33]

Although in the later essay all the works named as examples of "power" literature—the *Iliad, Prometheus Bound, Othello, Hamlet, Macbeth,* and *Paradise Lost*—are in verse, the category is stretched to include "the commonest novel." Presumably then, the "deep sympathy with truth" to which such works move us may be aroused by fictive literature in any form. Elsewhere, however, there is both positive and negative evidence that he thought the power of this "higher" literature resided largely in poetry. Like most of his generation, De Quincey denigrated didactic verse. For the merely informative literature of knowledge he thought prose the proper instrument. Why, he asks, should an author aiming at edification or instruction be so silly as "to handcuff himself, were it only by the encumbrances of metre, and perhaps of rhyme?" True, two decades earlier he had conceded that, in didactic verse treating mechanical arts, a reader does admire the poet's skill in modulating materials recalcitrant to metrical expression "into the proper key for the style and ornaments of verse." But, he quickly adds, this achievement is not much better than rope-dancing (funambulism figures prominently in De Quincey's lexicon of pejoratives).[34]

His essay on Pope contains an extended dirge on the inadequacy of man's limited stock of words to communicate the infinity of his thoughts. But this gloomy reflection is offset, in the essay on Wordsworth, by what reads very much like a tribute to the power of verse to transcend the expressive limits of ordinary utterance. "How often," he asks,

> must the human heart have felt the case, and yearned for an expression of the case, when there are sorrows which descend far below the region in which tears gather; and yet who has ever given utterance to this feeling until Wordsworth came with his immortal line:

—Thoughts that do often lie too deep for tears"?[35]

De Quincey sometimes came close to erasing the boundary between the literatures of knowledge and of power, as when he allowed a didactic role to poetry with the proviso that the instruction it imparted be only indirect, "by hieroglyphic suggestion," and always "masked in deep incarnations." The latter image apparently held greater significance for De Quincey than it did for Wordsworth, whose prior use of it he declared to be the weightiest thing he had ever learned about style. "Never, in one word," he wrote, "was so profound a truth conveyed." In using it, De Quincey thought, Wordsworth was thinking of poetry, his own and others'. For in a literary context the notion of incarnation serves more aptly than rival conceptions to dispel the rift between thought and expression conveyed by the clothing metaphor. With "poetic" thinking, De Quincey joined others in arguing, the severance would be as fatal as with the union of soul and body. Like that "mysterious incarnation," poetic thought and its verbal materialization coexist not in juxtaposition with each other but *in* and *through* each other. In De Quincey's writings, however, this conception of the unity of form and content is extended to fine composition other than verse. In "Language," he recognized as quite legitimate the kind of style that is in fact only a separable decoration of the thought. But his full approval is reserved for the other kind, in which imagery, for example, "is the coefficient that, being added to something else, absolutely *makes* the thought as a *third* and separate existence." Like Coleridge's *tertium aliquid*, which it inevitably recalls, De Quincey's way of putting it must strike many readers as most appropriately descriptive of the ultrarational vibrancy of great verse. But, precisely in the essay on Wordsworth, it is in Taylor's and Burke's prose that he finds the consummate incarnation of the figurative and conceptual, a revelation by imagery alone of truths otherwise beyond expression.[36]

It was left for De Quincey's younger contemporary George Henry Lewes in 1842 to apply the idea of incarnation exclusively to verse. Rhythm, no mere contrivance, Lewes wrote in refutation of Wordsworth's equation of prose and poetry, is a natural emanation from the human soul, as August Schlegel, whose criticism Lewes knew well, was among the first to declare. Meter, as Lewes sums it up, therefore constitutes "the form of poetry; not the form as a thing arbitrary, but as a thing vital and essential; it is the incarnation of poetry." Prose, Lewes thought, though it may be emotive and, as often claimed, even poetic, can never be poetry properly understood. Four years later, calling Shakespeare "the touchstone of poetic art," he invoked the term *Gestaltung* as an equivalent to the incarnational mode achieved by words in a poem.[37]

Lewes extends the moribund ban on "unpoetic" words to cover proper names. He asks us to imagine the *Iliad* opening with "John Thompson's wrath to us the direful spring," or the *Orlando Furioso* with "The Wilsons, Smiths, the Wigginses, and Browns." He then censures Wordsworth for having actually done the equivalent in his thirty-two-line apostrophe to a spade, beginning

"Spade! with which Wilkinson hath tilled his lands." Lewes's objection was not to the poet's calling a spade even in verse a spade. He even overlooks the bathetic ascription of aesthetic sensibility to a garden tool ("How often hast thou heard the poet sing"). What Lewes cannot abide is the *name*, Willkinson, one which "the gods have not decreed . . . poetical," as they have the name Achilles.[38]

Some proper names, personal and geographical, have been admired as effective elements of poetic diction, many in *Paradise Lost* for instance. But if, as we may surmise, their resonance comes from historically conditioned attitudes to certain races, social classes, and cultures, does Lewes's disapproval only reflect the snobbery of a classically educated Victorian gentleman? One recalls immediately the outburst of mingled disgust and pity with which Arnold reacted to a newspaper account of a child murder committed by a factory girl surnamed Wragg. He deplored the

> touch of grossness in our race . . . the original shortcoming in the more delicate spiritual perceptions . . . shown by the natural growth among us of such hideous names,—Higginbottom, Stiggins, Bugg! In Ionia and Attica they were luckier in this respect . . . ; by the Illisus there was no Wragg, poor thing!

And J. R. Lowell reported that "all England laughed" at Wordsworth for specifying "dear brother Jim" in "We are Seven" (suppressed in later editions). Had the poem been a translation from the Turkish naming "one *Ibrahim*," Lowell contended, no reader's taste would have been offended.[39]

In a chapter of *Heroes and Hero Worship*, Carlyle propounds a more or less transcendental view that one may be a poet whether one writes in prose or verse—or not at all! Yet it also contains one of the most penetrating characterizations of verse form to be found in English criticism. It reads like an enrichment and extension of his friend Emerson's doctrine that poems are made not of meters but of a "metre-making argument," by a process, according to Emerson, in which thought and form are simultaneous, but thought, "in the order of genesis," is prior to form. In Carlyle's vatic account, the poet's visionary power *inevitably* yields the compelling speech and even the metric form of verse—the "song," in the old usage he affected. Emerson too was to assert in *Representative Men* (1850) that the secret of Shakespeare's meter is that "the thought constructs the tune." But in Carlyle the metaphor is deepened to symbolize a unique creative gnosis that inspirits every stage of the poet-prophet's activity.

> A *musical* thought is one spoken by a mind that has penetrated into the inmost heart of the thing; detected the mystery of it, namely the *melody* that lies hidden in it; the inmost harmony of coherence which is its soul. . . . All inmost things, we may say, are melodious; naturally utter themselves in Song. . . .
>
> Poetry, therefore, we will call *musical Thought*. The Poet is he who *thinks* in that manner. At bottom, it turns still on the power of intellect, it is a man's sincerity and depth of vision that makes him a Poet. See deep enough, and you see musically; the heart of Nature *being* everywhere music; if you can only reach it.[40]

For Carlyle, poetic words are a kind of hieroglyphics communicating the "heroic" Truths that cannot be delivered by any manipulation of the notational system of a given language. The poet's transactions with these Truths are far grander than the mere portraiture of the human soul which Mill considered a sufficient justification of the poet's office. The death in 1832 of Goethe, whom Carlyle esteemed above every other modern author for his "singularly emblematic intellect," occasioned the boldest formulation of his mantic poetic faith. Goethe embodied the true poetic seer, empowered to "discern the godlike Mystery of God's Universe, and decipher some new lines of its celestial writing." In him dark things become clear, and present and future are harmonized; "thereby are his words in very truth prophetic; what he has spoken shall be done." Such mystical terminology fits easily with an incarnational view of poetic diction. Carlyle credited Coleridge with the observation that a musically constructed sentence, "of true rhythm and melody in the words," is a sure sign of some profound truth. "For body and soul, word and idea, go strangely together, here as everywhere."[41]

Given convictions of such cosmic grandeur, the questions usually raised about poetic style, its peculiar syntax, its measured ordonnance, and so forth, seem almost beside the point. At worst, even to pose them may profane a sacred mystery. At best, an investigator ought to give the linguistic medium only what attention it deserves as instrumental to something else of transcendent value. Around that, such artistic conventions as allegory and the stylistic devices gather willy-nilly "as the fit body round its soul." Inquiry

into the poetic art was further depreciated in Carlyle's writings by
his repeated assimilations of literary merit to nonliterary "hero-
ism." Commanding figures like Mohammed and Napoleon are intrinsically "poets." And Cromwell *could have been* a writer had he
not been called to worthier and more arduous tasks than literary
composition. All are united by *sincerity*, the master merit. So persuaded, Carlyle is ultimately carried beyond the realm of criticism
entirely. "Speech is great," is his desperate conclusion, "but Silence is greater."[42]

Elsewhere Carlyle is simply self-contradictory. A sensitive and
compelling protest against ornamental excess in poetic phraseology in one review, for example, is discredited by the outright denial in another of any merit whatsoever to a poet's manner of
expressing himself. Validly enough, he praises the sparsity of
Goethe's figurative diction, especially his avoidance of "coloured-
paper metaphors," his frugally employed tropes being "the genuine new vesture of new thoughts." When, however, he adds that
some part of Luther's poetic character shows in his great hymn
"Eine Feste Burg," though "it jars upon our ears," it seems fair to
protest against a blurring of criteria. If the heroic valor Carlyle dis-
covers in the hymn can subsist with verbal cacophony, in what
does it consist? If in a Longinian grandeur of conception, then
why did it fail to incarnate itself in "song" in the case of Luther,
whose divinatory powers, Carlyle asserts, enabled him to occupy
the very center of "the sphere of poetry?" Carlyle doesn't say.[43]

Carlyle's hero-worshiping enthusiasm led him to an obscuran-
tist extreme of another notion he shared with Emerson, who held
that Art aimed at something higher than the arts. In an essay of
1830 on Jean Paul, Carlyle displaced Emerson's belief that no
poet ever equals his poem by declaring instead that no poem was
ever fully worthy of its creator. Accordingly, the judgment he
reaches after fifty rambling biographical pages is that Jean Paul,
though he wrote no verse, must be ranked among the greatest
poets—not for his prose fiction but for the heroic tenor of the life
it graphically manifests.[44]

Emerson's distinction between Art and the arts has a better
claim to theoretical significance. Grounded as it is in a transcendental variety of Neoplatonism, whatever its limitations it is at
least more amenable to rational inspection than Carlyle's hyperbolic formulations. Like Shelley, Emerson divined that what an
artist "makes" is necessarily a lesser thing than the prior conception in his mind.[45] It is in this sense that his works are thus so

many "abortive births . . . cripples and monsters." But Emerson does not on that account summarily dismiss the one in the exclusive prizing of the other. His plea is not for the dispensability of the arts but for a recognition of what in their original conception was bound to suffer debasement in the process of material realization, though less so in the verbal than in the other media. To even the finest creative intellect, he wrote in *Society and Solitude,* the materiality of "the stuff on which it works" constitutes an insuperable obstacle to perfection. Yet what he says of the poetic medium is not entirely unfavorable:

> The basis of poetry is language, which is material only on one side. It is a demi-god. But being applied to the common necessities of man, it is not new-created by the poet for his own ends.[46]

Emerson's idealist aesthetics has since been vigorously controverted. In much empirical aesthetics, a work of art has no existence prior to its embodiment in a medium, which, moreover, far from being an impediment, is often a catalyst of inspiration.

Yet Emerson's complaint is far from being a personal whimsy. It is one often heard, most poignantly in Dante's lament over the inadequacy of speech to describe the effulgence of the paradisal glory, in the last Canto of the *Commedia.* In any case, the overarching idealism that obliged Emerson to speak of artistic cripples must be balanced by his idea of a "metre-making argument," which Herbert Read called one of his occasional deep insights. This Emerson defined as a thought so impassioned and organically vital that it "has an architecture of its own, and adorns nature with a new thing." Whatever Emerson may have thought of the graphic arts (very little in Henry James's opinion), he would seem to have accorded glory enough to the "cripples" produced by poets, artists whose words were like deeds, "modes of divine energy."[47]

In nineteenth-century America, Emerson's and Whitman's vaticinal poetics stand in sharp contrast to Poe's ideal of the poet as craftsman (*poeta,* not *vates*). As propounded in his "Philosophy of Composition," a poem's diction is produced by deliberate forethought, words chosen and arranged to induce in readers a particular affective state. Poe's understanding of poetic language is based on a division of the mind into the three faculties of intellect, moral sense, and taste. Poetry belongs exclusively to the last. This reductive mental partitioning, designed primarily to discredit what Poe dubbed the didactic heresy, allowed him to secure for poetry a function independent of those proper to science, history, philosophy, or any other discursive discipline. In his lecture "The Poetic Principle," where these ideas are promulgated, Poe made no reference to the prosodic scheme set forth in "The Rationale of Verse."

He entertained the prevalent notion that the "poetic sentiment" runs through all the arts, including landscape gardening. But it is most perfectly manifested in music. Poetry, "its manifestation in words," is nearest to music both in form and function. Both arts are means to the creation of that "supernal beauty" which the human soul thirsts after. In neither the composition nor the enjoyment of poetry, he maintained against most other theorists, does emotion have any part. Engaging not the heart but the soul, poetry, like music, provides us intermittent glimpses of eternity. His one statement of a strictly formal bearing advocates the supreme importance, if not quite the "absolute essentiality," of music in poetry. The term music here designates a complex condition particularized in the "various modes of metre, rhythm, and rhyme." His argument is finally epitomized in the succinct recapitulation which registered on Baudelaire (who plagiarized it), and through him on the *Symboliste* poets, an impact which Poe could not have foreseen:

> I would define, in brief, the Poetry of words as *The Rhythmical Creation of Beauty*. Its sole arbiter is Taste. With the Intellect or with the Conscience, it has only collateral relations. Unless incidentally, it has no concern whatever with Duty or with Truth.[48]

As with other purist theories, Poe's conception of verse language as a rarefied aesthetic idiom ultimately trivializes it. Once its aural and rhythmic delights have been duly savored, it appears to be a curiously emasculated discourse. To have envisaged poetry as something which cannot without radical injury to its nature be judged solely by cognitive and moral norms is a salutary achievement for which Poe deserves special but not exclusive credit. But the uncompromising terms of his analysis virtually annul poetry's value as spiritual nutriment by largely closing it off from the moral and intellectual substance without which its verbal felicities operate to scant avail. In practice the ideal is unattainable. In Poe's own verse it is violated even by so delicate a theme as a beautiful woman's death, which he held to be the most poetic of subjects.[49]

Another ambiguity in Poe's theoretical position is equally hard to dispel. In the very year in which he was proclaiming in lecture halls up and down the Northeast Coast that meter was all but indispensable to poetry, that beauty, not truth, was its province, and that a long poem was a contradiction in terms, he published in New York the book-length cosmological fantasy *Eureka,* subtitled *A Prose Poem.* This he addressed in a preface to the few readers who could appreciate it "for the Beauty that abounds in its Truth; constituting it True." To this elite group he proffered the book "as an Art-Product alone . . . or, if I be not urging too lofty a claim, as a Poem." Many people are inclined to dismiss this work as bogus science or (no more charitably) bogus mysticism. Two exceptions are Valéry and W. H. Auden, both of whom found *Eureka* praiseworthy. Auden, however, though willing to rank it with the cosmologies of Hesiod and Lucretius, was understandably disconcerted because by its very existence it violated "every article of his [Poe's] creed." Yet what Auden overlooked is that some theoretical justification for *Eureka* and for Poe's prefatorial characterization of it may be found in words which the poet had put into the mouth of one of the two angelic creatures in his brief celestial fantasy entitled *The Colloquy of Monos and Una* (1841). In their postapocalyptic conversation the two resurrected spirits review the gradual dissolution of the world, finally annihilated by the nemesis of an overweening *libido sciendi* in its inhabitants. During its decline, Monos recalls, only the poets now and then gave warning that knowledge would be fatal to man "in the infant condition of his soul." Their prophetic power is described in language more appropriate to the vatic orientation of Carlyle than to the purist formalism expounded in "The Poetic Principle." Poe's stance in his cosmic playlet is recognizably a version of the by then well established Romantic vindication of intuition against the tyranny of pure reason, with all that it implies for the status of poetic discourse. Monos pays tribute to the poetic intellect—that intellect which we now

> feel to have been the most useful of all—since those truths which to us were of the most enduring importance could only be reached by that *analogy* which speaks in proof-tones to the imagination alone,—and to the reason bears no weight.[50]

A language which delivers truths of the greatest significance in such imaginative "proof-tones" is no ordinary language. In his mythic phraseology Monos expresses the honorific conception of poetic utterance which Arnold, in his more restrained manner, was later to characterize as the most nearly perfect mode of conveying the truth. Regrettably, neither poet-critic succeeded in constructing a set theory of this precious idiom, as exemplified in the best poetry they knew. As for Poe, the very different tenor of the principles he advanced with such dogmatic assurance shortly before his death may make us wonder whether he ever shared, *in propria persona*, the views of his fictive speaker in that celestial colloquy.

CHAPTER TEN

Matthew Arnold

DESPITE THE TEMPERA-
mental hostility to rational analysis so often deplored in Arnold's
literary, social, and religious thought, his pervasive influence on
Anglo-American academic literary study faded only with the advent
of the New Criticism. As regards poetics, his enduring authority
owed much to the impressive ancestry of his persuasion that abstract formulations of how poets use words were fruitless. Earlier
versions include the Renaissance "je ne sais quoi," Pope's "nameless graces which no precepts can declare," and the Romantic sense
of the ineffability of poetic beauty most arrestingly exemplified in
Schlegel's dogma that it could be articulated only in poetry.

Since, however, it is widely assumed that the mysteries of versification are best made less mysterious by reasoned analysis,
Arnold's disinclination to apply it may well have contributed to a
certain undervaluing of his abiding concern with the subject. This
was actuated by a personal sensitivity to "the consummate felicity
in diction" of which he deplored the lack in Byron, and which in
one of its many varieties he labeled "natural magic." Students of
Arnold are surely right to stress in his criticism the cognitive and
moral themes which he himself made central; but in doing so they
have tended to slight the aesthetic qualities which he considered
equally requisite to the weighty cultural mission which he thought
poets were uniquely called upon to fulfill. Cardinal Richelieu, he
observed in "The Literary Influence of Academies" (1864), wisely

saw in the French Academy an instrument for strengthening and perpetuating "the *ethical* influences of style in language," influences exerted most powerfully in great verse. In Homer's epics Arnold found nothing more edifying than their style, and in his General Report of 1878 as school inspector he stressed the invaluable formative effect the diction and rhythm of good poetry could have even on readers uncertain of its meaning.[1]

With some impatience toward those less aesthetically percipient, he prided himself on an ability to detect "the ring of false metal" in the tinny rhetoric of Macaulay's *Lays of Ancient Rome,* in which he could hardly read the lines,

> To all men upon this earth
>
> Death cometh soon or late,

"without a cry of pain." The intemperate tone occasionally evident in the bill of complaint against what struck him as the detestable style of Francis Newman's English *Iliad* measures the depth of its affront to Arnold's sensibilities, just as the matchless language of Homer himself moved him to one of his rare lyrical effusions.

> For Homer's grandeur is not the mixed and turbid grandeur of the great poets of the north, of the authors of *Othello* and *Faust;* it is a perfect, a lovely grandeur. Certainly his poetry has all the energy and power of our ruder climates; but it has, besides, the pure lines of an Ionian horizon, the liquid clearness of an Ionian sky.[2]

An appraisal of Arnold's opinions about poetic language can usefully take as *points d'appui* two dicta from the last decade of his life. The later one maintains the inferiority of prose to verse in "power." More importantly, it commits him to the idea that verse constitutes a distinct category of utterance, a commitment from which Arnold never shrank. Admiring Johnson's *Lives of the English Poets* for its admirable conformity to "the true law of prose," he was careful to discriminate.

> Prose requires a different style from poetry.
>
> Poetry, no doubt, is more excellent in itself than prose. In poetry man finds the highest and most beautiful expression of that which is in him. . . . Poetry has a different *logic,* as Coleridge said, from prose; poetical style follows another order of evolution than the style of prose.

In Arnold's conception the distinction is generic. Poetic simplicity, "that perfectly simple, limpid style, which is the supreme style of all," is not a rarefied variety of the simplicity of prose. It issues rather from a momentary remission of the emotive intensity which characterizes poetic composition as a whole. In Shakespeare this relaxation yields "the golden, easeful, crowning moments of a manner which is always pitched in another manner from that of prose, a manner changed and heightened."[3]

None of this should be allowed to obscure Arnold's very real sense of the aesthetic virtues of prose, to which he paid tribute in "Maurice de Guérin" (1863). Guérin's *The Centaur,* "a sort of prose poem," he found more instinct with "the magical power of poetry" than the same poet's work in the staple alexandrine meter. Metrical forms, even those which have served as proven vehicles for the monuments of poetic art—such as Greek hexameters, English blank verse, and French alexandrines—can sometimes impose unacceptable restrictions on a poet's freedom of expression. Worst of all in this regard, Arnold thought, was the alexandrine. A poet of genius had better adopt "a more adequate vehicle, metrical or not," for conveying his thoughts.[4] Arnold was not the first champion of metrical utterance to find his faith challenged by the allure of one or another piece of imaginative prose—nor the last.

Yet his sense of a generic gap between prose and verse, however vaguely conceived at times, was always in the forefront of his consciousness, even in casual judgmental remarks. Of a passage of lush natural description by Ruskin he suggests that the author was trying to do in prose what can only be well done in verse. The "key" in which verse is pitched even justified to his mind the traditional poetic locutions on which some critics in the previous century had founded the crucial difference between the two forms. Archaisms like *spake* for *spoke, aye* for *ever, don* for *put on* constitute "the poetic vocabulary, as distinguished from the vocabulary of common speech and of modern prose." Twentieth-century readers inclined to balk at such archaisms as passé might reflect on Hart Crane's recourse to them in his verse and Owen Barfield's theoretical approval of them as features natural to poetic expression.[5]

The earlier of Arnold's two dicta might stand as topic sentence to an account of his entire thought about the poet's use of language. "Now poetry is nothing less than the most perfect speech of man, that in which he comes nearest to being able to utter the truth."[6] Occurring in an essay on Wordsworth, who regarded the poet primarily as one human being addressing others, Arnold's definition is framed appropriately to his immediate subject. Otherwise though, his summary generalization is thrown out without either supporting justification or the badly needed clarification of its terms. In what does "perfection" consist? and what, here, is the precise import of "truth"? In default of clear answers to such questions, we are forced to contrive shaky inferences from the evidence scattered throughout Arnold's critical writings. Of this more below. For the moment it is worth noting that the two clauses of his sentence comprehend the twin aspects of poetry on which Arnold from first to last dwelt with increasing emphasis, and which he came more and more to conceive as interdependent coordinates of its mode of being. These are a unique manipulation of the verbal medium and a cognitive-moral value for which no other kind of discourse provides an adequate substitute. The nature and evaluation of this discourse leads, in Arnold, directly to his "touchstones."

Almost two decades before he introduced *touchstone* into the English critical lexicon, in "The Study of Poetry" (1880), Arnold made extensive use of the device itself in a series of lectures delivered during his tenure of the Oxford Professorship of Poetry and printed in 1861 as *On Translating Homer.* He knew no more effective means of conveying to his hearers some sense of the superlative qualities that constituted the "grand style." After quoting two stanzas from Walter Scott's *Marmion,* which he thought below that level of excellence, he offers a defense of his procedure.

> I may discuss what, in the abstract, constitutes the grand style, but that sort of general discussion never much helps our judgment of particular instances. I may say that the presence or absence of the grand style can only be spiritually discerned; and this is true, but to plead this looks like evading the difficulty. My best way is to take eminent specimens of the grand style, and to put them side by side with this of Scott.

He chose four such specimens for the purpose, from the *Iliad,* the *Aeneid,* the *Divine Comedy,* and *Paradise Lost:*

ἀλλά, φίλος, θάνε καὶ σύ; τί ἦ ὀλοφύρεαι οὕτως;

κάτθανε καὶ πάτροκλος; ὅ περ σέο πολλὸν ἀμείνων.

[But come, friend, die yourself; why lament in this way? Patroclus also died, a far better man than you.] (*Iliad,* XXI, 106–7)

Disce, puer, virtutem ex me verumque laborem,

Fortunam ex aliis.

[Learn valor and true toil from me, my boy; from others learn good luck.] (*Aeneid,* XII, 435–36)

Lascio lo fele, e vo per dolci pomi

Promessi a me per lo verace Duca;

Ma fino al centro pria convien ch' io tomi.

[I leave the gall and seek after the sweet apples promised me by the true Guide; but first I must fall to the very center.] (*Inferno,* XVI, 61–63)

His form had not yet lost

All her original brightness, nor appeared

Less than archangel ruined, and the excess

Of glory obscured.(*Paradise Lost,* Book I, 591–94)

Like the touchstones given in "The Study of Poetry," these fragments all exhibit Arnold's penchant for expressions of heroic resignation, self-denial, and stoic acceptance of tribulation. Except for the *Aeneid,* the works they represent were all to supply additional samples for the later list. The absence of any from Shakespeare, who was to provide two touchstones in 1880, suggests that Arnold had yet to slough off a youthful disdain for his verbal exuberance. The inclusion of Virgil is somewhat surprising, since elsewhere in *On Translating Homer* Arnold treats the long-cherished Virgilian "elegance" as inferior to the Homeric grandeur.[7]

He gives no hint of how grandeur and elegance differ except to insist that grandeur subsists independently of a corresponding dignity of subject matter. In total contradiction of Le Bossu two hundred years earlier, for Arnold the lowliest particulars of the action—eating, drinking, going to bed—occasion no falling off in a nobility of manner which, Arnold never tires of repeating, pervades the entire *Iliad.* He recalls that William Cowper, one of Homer's translators, had complained of how hard it was to render these homely episodes without a lowering of style. In Homer's surmounting that difficulty Arnold sees the main proof of his mastery. Strangely, he makes no reference to Addison's praise of Virgil's ability to describe the manuring of a field with no loss of verbal elegance. Equally strange, since he set such store by the point, is that he never cites a Homeric example. The one doubtful exception is "a passage of the simplest narrative" describing Hector addressing words of encouragement to his allies in battle (*Iliad,* XVII, 216ff.), an instance of "the level regions" of Homer's narrative, which Arnold defends against complaints that they are discords in the heroic strain. The four citations of poetic grandeur deal exclusively with moral elevation, heroic action, or tragic fatality.[8]

Only reluctantly, and still protesting the futility of "verbal definition," did Arnold attempt to formulate his concept, goaded to do so by complaints about the vagueness of his terms *noble* and *grand.* The grand style, he explained, "arises *when a noble nature, poetically gifted, treats with simplicity or with serenity a serious subject.*" This somewhat tautological effort prompted in Arnold's editor W. H. D. Rouse the sobering reflection that no one could improve on Longinus's definition of stylistic grandeur as the expression of a lofty soul. Nonetheless, it becomes clear as he proceeds that he is not merely indulging in the rhetorical gush that sometimes passes muster on the lecture podium. Some of what he says is clear enough. The grand style may never admit the comic. Simplicity and serenity are two of its most important characteristics. Homer is the special master of simple grandeur, while Milton supplies the "best model of the grand style serene." Arnold not only points to examples of each type in Dante, who excels in both, but makes a stab at explaining their peculiar psychological sources. Serenity results from the poet's "saying a thing with a kind of intense compression," as if his mind were burdened with thoughts too numerous and weighty for explicit naming. In one triplet of the *Purgatorio* he finds "a beautiful specimen of the grand style in simplicity, where a noble nature and a poetical gift unite to utter a thing with the most limpid plainness and clarity:

> Tanto dice di farmi sua compagna
>
> Ch'io sarò là dove fia Beatrice;
>
> Quivi convien che senza lui rimagna." (XXIII, 127–29)

"So long he [Virgil] saith he will bear me company, until I shall be there where Beatrice is: there it behooves that without him I remain"—so Arnold translates, but with the despairing admission that no words of his can convey the "noble simplicity" of Dante's Italian. Then, as though carried away by that consummate example, he declares that the simple style is in fact preferable to the serene, being "the more magical." Arnold cites Pope in support of his own opinion that the *Iliad*'s alliance of consummate expressive simplicity with perfect nobleness is rivaled only in the English Bible. The severe style, he adds somewhat disconcertingly, manifests an intellectual agility that can exist with little or none of the "exquisite faculty" so evident in a simple style: poetic talent.[9]

One might have thought intellectual prowess a prime requisite for the profound application of ideas to life which Arnold exalted in these very lectures and elsewhere as the poets' chief claim to esteem. And yet it was Homer's superb command of the simple variety of stylistic grandeur, he assured his fellow Oxonians, that empowered him in his epics to attain that essential of the poet's moral office with a perfection never since surpassed. All good poetry can stir the heart, but the few masters of the grand style do more: "they refine the raw natural man, they transmute him." Despite the kinks and twists of Arnold's unmethodical presentation, he leaves no doubt that the recipe for his grand style requires a balanced blend of moral, intellectual, and aesthetic ingredients. At no point does he seek to enforce it by an indiscriminate conflation of the revered epic masterpieces. Though they are equally "grand," the styles of Homer and Milton, he notes, are widely discrepant. The movement of *Paradise Lost* is labored and "self-retarding"; that of the *Iliad*, "flowing, rapid." The opening invocation to the muse in each case alone suffices for illustration, Homer's "ἄειδε, θεά" [sing, goddess] coming in the first line, whereas Milton's "Sing, heavenly muse" is suspended until the sixth. Arnold says little on the role of diction in effecting the grand style, though clearly he thinks it relevant to his thesis. Much of these lectures is given over to a minute destructive analysis of the English vocabulary in which Newman had vainly sought to render the tone and spirit of Homer's Greek. At one point Arnold pronounces Hamlet's image of *grunting* and *sweating* under life's burdens, which Newman adopted in his *Iliad*, to be offensive; at another, he censures George Chapman's "Poor, wretched beasts" as an unsuitable rendition of "ἀ δειλώ," Zeus's apostrophe to Achilles' immortal horses, in a passage to be chosen as a touchstone. The alternative "poor wretches," good enough for a ballad, travesties Homer. (Arnold's own suggestion was "unhappy pair.")[10]

Arnold's recourse to scraps of verse for testing the quality of poetry has had at best a mixed reception. Eliot and Wellek are among those who have objected that lines isolated from their contexts can have little poetic value. Wellek goes so far as to deny that one of Arnold's most prized touchstones, Dante's "E la sua volontate è nostra pace," is even verse.[11]

Though these strictures have merit, they do not justify disparaging the touchstones as an evaluative gimmick. Arnold saw in them an antidote to two fallacious poetic estimates, the historical and the personal. Using the historical estimate, a reader mistakes for intrinsic merit the crucial contribution of a given poet or poem to the development of a nation's poetry. The personal estimate results when a reader overestimates a piece of poetry simply because it happens to appeal to a temperamental idiosyncrasy or stirs memory of an emotionally charged experience. Both estimates impede the sound evaluation which Arnold calls the real one. He claimed that in each of his model passages a tactful reader would find, once it was well lodged in memory, "an infallible touchstone" for ascertaining the worth of any poetry whatsoever. It was probably with Arnold in mind that Arthur Symons, noticing how hard it was for critics to appreciate contemporary poetry, denied that it could be done by "the mere testing of Mr. Yeats or Verlaine by Milton or by Virgil." Though his point is a sound warning against pedantry, one might reply that of two critics otherwise equal in evaluative armament we do well to trust the judgment of the one more thoroughly acquainted with Milton and Virgil, among much else. It is easy to depreciate Arnold's device, with its disquieting suggestion of talismanic powers. It is equally easy to overlook the significant point that by using lines of verse as criteria he grounded his real estimate on the linguistic stuff of which verse is made. His valuation is therefore neither pragmatic, as in the historical estimate, nor unduly affective, as in the personal, and more objective than either.[12]

It is hard to see why John Eels should have concluded that Arnold was insensitive to the aesthetic value of his touchstones, since Eels himself praises their perfection as notable examples of poetic concision and economy, "the best words in the best order" for conveying certain moods. Eels is surely right that the favored excerpts chime with Arnold's pessimistic view of life; right also that as they are taken entirely from tragic drama and epic they reflect the limits of his poetic taste, including his coolness toward the comic. But assuming that their aesthetic quality, with one exception, played no part in Arnold's selection of them, Eels neglects their formal excellence. It is far more likely that Arnold chose them not for their "philosophic" soundness but for their excellence as *poetry*, defined in the essay which introduced them to the public as "thought and art in one"; and that he chose those rather than others of equal poetic merit because they happened to have the additional advantage of embodying what he most deeply felt about human experience. Focusing on this latter motive alone, Eels finds Arnold guilty of his own "personal estimate." But this charge is blunted by the fact that other critics have also praised most of the touchstones, although Arnold may have predisposed a few of them to do so. In a grudging estimate of Arnold's criticism, Eliot, no mean "touchstoner" himself, conceded "the felicity of his quotation: to be able to quote as Arnold did is the best evidence of taste."[13]

The ultimate justification of Arnold's resort to the touchstone method is the pragmatic one validated by his social purpose. He aimed to improve the public's poetic taste, and so dilute the philistinism of the great British middle class to which he himself belonged. What in "The Scholar Gypsy" he had deplored as "this strange disease of modern living" required that men and women be taught how to *benefit* from poetry, how to tap the deepest wellsprings of its consolatory and sustaining power.[14]

The eleven nuggets of verse Arnold culled in 1880 from Homer, Dante, Shakespeare, and Milton are certainly as remarkable for euphonious diction and movement as for emotive depth or arresting thought. They consist perfectly well, though in varying degrees, with H. F. Lowry's assertion that "with Arnold, as with Carlyle, poetry is musical thought." Yet for Arnold all poetic style, including the grand variety, comprises moral and intellectual content as well. True, he could speak of style as a value-neutral element, a poet's personal cachet, as when he wrote that Wordsworth "has no style," nature seemingly having written his poems for him. But generally, when the subject in any way touches on poetic evaluation, overall excellence and stylistic distinction are synonymous in Arnold.[15]

The citation of Shakespeare among the touchstones is best explained by Arnold's having outgrown his Hellenic fastidiousness of taste. In the Oxford lectures Shakespeare is still of the "so-called" golden age of Elizabethan literature, one "steeped in humours and fantasticality up to its very lips." Much muted in *On the Study of Celtic Literature* (1867), this bias virtually disappears by 1879. Arnold now joins his countrymen in naming Shakespeare and Milton, equally and without reservation, as "our poetical classics," proudly quoting the verdict of a French critic who had recently pronounced the verse of England's greatest dramatic poet to be the most varied and harmonious since the Greeks.[16]

Yet it sometimes appears—the evidence is too inconsistent to be conclusive—that in Arnold's mind two characteristics of the grand style set it off from other poetry of the highest quality, Shakespeare's included. One is a clarity and immediacy of conception conveyed in a limpid nakedness of wording that made him relish Homer's simplicity above Milton's serenity; the other is the capacity to sustain that manner throughout a whole poem, even one of epic length. Coleridge, Eliot, and—notoriously and reductively—Poe denied the possibility or desirability of a lengthy poetic composition being pitched throughout at a high level of intensity. Not so Arnold, who admired the "immortal" lines of Robert Burns's "Farewell to Nancy,"

> Had we never loved sae kindly,
>
> Had we never loved sae blindly,
>
> Never met, or never parted,
>
> We had ne'er been broken-hearted—

only to complain of the author's inability to hold to their level everywhere in his poem. "The rest," he said, "is verbiage." Arnold had no patience with Horace's tolerant concession that Homer himself nods off now and then. On Arnold's reading of him Homer composes "always at his best," is never "quaint and antiquated, as Shakespeare is sometimes." As for grandeur, only in flashes does Shakespeare display the lofty Homeric simplicity, as in Cleopatra's terse invocation of death, "Poor venomous fool, / Be angry and despatch!"[17]

Arnold scorned the judgment of an eminent scholar who found in Tennyson's blank verse the very attributes Arnold had named as the determinants of Homer's greatness, especially *"plainness of words and style, simplicity and directness of ideas."* Against what he saw as a typical instance of English blindness to the genuine Greek simplicity, Arnold protested that in Tennyson there is instead

> an extreme subtlety and curious elaborateness of thought, an extreme subtlety and elaborateness of expression. In the best and most characteristic productions of his genius, these characteristics are most prominent. They are marked characteristics . . . of the Elizabethan poets; they are marked, though not the essential characteristics of Shakespeare himself.

Though distinct from the Shakespearean, it is, he argues, the same fault, manifested in the imagery of such a line as "Now lies the Earth all Danaë to the stars." His main objection is concisely summarized. "In Homer's poetry it is all natural thoughts in natural language; in Mr. Tennyson's poetry it is all distilled thoughts in distilled words." One scents here, as in other Victorian critics, a whiff of Wordsworthian naturalism. But the contrast between Arnold's classically conditioned idea of poetic expression and Wordsworth's is much greater than any shared taste. The two men are separated by the distance between Wordsworth's declared ideal of rustic idiom and what for Arnold constituted the "most perfect speech of man." No one can ever imagine the author of the Prefaces to *Lyrical Ballads* looking with much favor on anything that could be called stylistic grandeur in verse.[18]

Arnold's stress on the simplicity of Homer's stylistic grandeur reflects more than his general disapproval of decorative and ornate verbiage and involuted phrasal structure in poetry. It was also as a poet, concerned with the survival of poetry in the modern world, that he warned against figurative indulgence. This line of argument first appears in the correspondence with his friend Arthur Clough, where it forms part of a youthful dialogue between the two poets on the art in which they hoped to make their marks. At first Arnold pleads for a plain style only because he thought it best suited the maturity of the cultural moment. He flirts here with a historical relativism that would have been hard to reconcile with his later notion of touchstone verses enshrining universally relevant criteria. He is sure that if Shakespeare and Milton had lived in modern England neither would have indulged in "the taking, tourmenté style" then cried up on every hand. Good poetic style is the clearest possible expression of whatever the times demand. This argument reappears a few years later with greater emphasis when he indicts Shelley and Keats for trying to reproduce Elizabethan "exuberance of expression." But now Arnold goes further, to a position that threatens to reduce the dictional component of poetry to the lowly status it had occupied in classical poetic theory. Modern poetry, he thinks, "can only subsist by its contents"; and if it is to become once again the "complete *magister vitae*" that it was in ancient times, it must adopt a style and vocabulary of the most unadorned simplicity. Whether, as Lionel Trilling believed, the expressive baldness of some of Arnold's own poems resulted from this opinion need not concern us here.[19]

A year later these views were absorbed into the critical polemics occasioned by the 1853 edition of his *Poems*. In the preface he invoked both the practice of the Greek poets and the principles Aristotle propounded in his "admirable treatise" to support the view that in a poem it is always some significant human action, its structuring, its over-all *architectonicè*, that matters, not the local attractions of diction, cadence, and image. Modern English poets, he complained, have been led astray in this by the seductive precedent of Shakespeare's verbal profusion. Though Shakespeare had chosen plots admirably adapted to poetic and dramatic treatment, he too was on occasion betrayed by his gift for ornate phrasing, and by a certain "irritability of fancy" that prevented him from allowing his characters to speak plainly even when the dramatic situation called for it.[20]

If these charges seem excessive, they can be excused by the reflection that Arnold was then writing as a critic pressed by the need to vent precepts salubrious to Arnold the poet. Yet even when full allowance is made for the exigencies of Arnold's creative needs, a problem remains. Detractors of the touchstone method may well point to the place in the 1853 preface in which he pours scorn on

> poems which seem to exist only for the sake of single lines and passages; not for the sake of producing any total impression. We have critics who seem to direct their attention merely to detached expressions, to the language about the action, not to the action itself.

Granted, Pope too had condemned among his "partial" critics those who valued poems exclusively for their language. But could there be a more glaring instance of judgment by "detached expressions" than that which advocates the touchstone as criterion? Carefully considered, however, these strictures of Arnold the young poet conflict less with the evaluative method of the mature critic than at first appears. To recall two of the touchstones: not even by the most perverse reading of *Hamlet* or *Paradise Lost* will the complex structure of human action and passion which they represent seem no more than contrivances to provide the troubled prince an opportunity for voicing the lyrical pathos of "Absent thee from felicity awhile," or the epic narrator an occasion for the exquisite phrasing of his reflection on the loss "which cost Ceres all that pain." The Arnold of 1853 was perhaps only offering his personally felt endorsement of the organic interdependence of parts and whole established in Romantic theory. The later Arnold may perhaps be faulted for not making it explicit that in proposing the use of touchstones he was not abandoning that principle. But the thrust of his whole critical output makes it highly probable that nothing in the eleven touchstones recommended them to his choice so much as their symbolic status, each one instinct with the poet's moral vision, which vitalized with varying degrees of intensity almost every strand of his poem's texture. If Arnold was mistaken, if the symbolic charge of the touchstones was a delusion of personal taste, then their validity as evaluative tools is seriously diminished.[21]

Though still reluctant in "The Study of Poetry" to inquire "what in the abstract" makes for the finest poetry, he cannot entirely avoid the attempt. Poetic excellence, he explains, is to be found in *both* "matter and substance" and "manner and style." The matter and substance provide the profound truth and high seriousness that distinguishes the greatest poetry, but only to the extent that they are accompanied by a fit style and manner, constituted of the two elements of diction and movement. This complex of paired abstractions comes short of conceptual precision; while the doublets *diction* and *movement* clearly, and *truth* and *seriousness* vaguely, name related qualities, *matter* and *substance*, like *style* and *manner*, seem to be only synonyms. But the imprecision does not lessen his firm grasp of the mutual interdependence of form and content that characterizes the products of metrical mastery. The two "superiorities" subsist in "such steadfast proportion" to each other, he writes, that a deficiency of truth in a poem quite simply forecloses any distinction of diction and movement.[22]

So far so good. Yet there are other statements in Arnold's criticism, a few quite original and richly suggestive, that require a special effort of explication for clearly understanding them. One such, from *Essays in Criticism (First Series)* (1865), expanding on his central doctrine that poetry interprets life, adumbrates his later definition of it as the most perfect possible expression of truth. "I have said that poetry interprets in two ways," he recalls;

> it interprets by expressing with magical felicity the physiognomy and movement of the outward world, and it interprets by expressing, with inspired conviction, the ideas and laws of the inward world of man's moral and spiritual nature. In other words, poetry is interpretative both by having *natural magic* in it, and by having *moral profundity*. In both ways it illuminates man; it gives

him a satisfying sense of reality; it reconciles him with himself and the universe.

Arnold could hardly have assigned a loftier mission to poets and poetry than that spelled out in the final clauses of this passage, correspondent with his conviction that modern humanity stood in sore need of such satisfaction and reconciliation.[23]

What remains problematic are the more technical implications of this excerpt. Can either natural magic or moral profundity, though collaborative in all really first-rate poetry, exist separately in mediocre works? So much seems to be implied in his initially assigning them respectively to objective and subjective experience. In the 1880 critique of Keats, Arnold rated him supreme in "the faculty of naturalistic interpretation." Recalling the dying poet's hope to be among the English poets after death, he remarks with moving concision: "He is; he is with Shakespeare." But to this generous estimate he immediately adds that Keats was never "ripe" for the second mode, the faculty of moral interpretation. And here the serious student of Arnold's poetics encounters an impasse. In the essay on Wordsworth, published in the year immediately preceding that on Keats, he was at pains to explain "the large sense" in which he was using the term *moral*, that is, to comprehend anything dealing with the question of "how to live." Casting about for the relevant touchstone he finds one ready to hand in Milton's

Nor love thy life, nor hate; but, what thou liv'st,

Live well; how long or short, permit to heaven.

But Keats too, he adds, just as surely "utters a moral idea" when he consoles the lover depicted on his Grecian urn, eternally denied his kiss, with the words,

Forever will thou love, and she be fair—

no less surely than does Shakespeare's Prospero musing on "such stuff as dreams are made on."[24]

Arnold's key terms *natural magic* and *moral profundity* are not simple equivalents of the more familiar form and content, or style and matter. As he sometimes speaks of it, natural magic is, to be sure, a stylistic quality, a compelling manner of rendering the natural world. But no critic was ever more insistent than Arnold that good poetic style of any kind was an index of intellectual maturity, all genuine poetic utterance embodying a moral vision, whether the poet sing of a lover's despair or an autumnal scene. Yet this conviction is blurred whenever he alludes to natural magic as a purely autonomous formal grace. Once at least the two views met in direct collision. Shelley, he observed, had natural magic in his rhythm, but possessed neither the intellectual power nor the sanity to compass it in his diction.[25]

Arnold normally implies that in the greatest poetry the magical and moral kinds of interpretation of life are inextricably fused. Yet in Aeschylus he could detect both separately identifiable even in brief phrases. In the *Choephoroi* "δράσαντι παθεῖν" [let the doer be done by] interprets morally; in *Prometheus Bound* "ἀνήριθμον γέλασμα" [multitudinous laughter (of ocean waves)] renders nature. Presumably the desired fusion obtains in two citations from Shakespeare:

> Full many a glorious morning have I seen
> Flatter the mountain tops with sovreign eye,

and

> There's a divinity that shapes our ends,
> Rough-hew them how we will.

Arnold's syntax would imply that the two quotations, from Sonnet 33 and from *Hamlet*, each embody *both* modes. Their themes, a sunrise and human destiny, might make it seem more likely that the first exemplifies natural magic and the second moral profundity. Yet in the line from the sonnet the morning is so heavily personified as to qualify as moral in Arnold's broad designation of anything pertaining to human existence. But surely the same plea might be made for Aeschylus's image of laughing ocean waves, which, however, Arnold offers as a rendition of nature innocent of moral import.[26]

The weight of evidence favors, barely, the conclusion that the quality for which Arnold could find no more fitting name than natural magic was a stylistic element, not a thematic one. Though little of his poetics is given over to mimesis, he was well aware of its crucial role. In terms which recall Coleridge on the subject, he censured Byron's "copyist" manner of promiscuously adopting for poetic use everything that life offered him, too often forgetting "the mysterious transmutation to be operated on this matter by poetic form." If we take our cue from Arnold himself and pay greater heed to what the touchstones tell us on this issue than to his foggy generalizations about it, we shall be even more convinced that the magic is produced by the linguistic resourcefulness of the poet. He is the magician, not the experiential stuff he labors to "interpret." In *On the Study of Celtic Literature* (1867) Arnold may at first seem to ascribe the faculty not to the poet but to his subject, when he praises the natural magic of Keats's

> White hawthorn and the pastoral eglantine,
>
> Fast-fading violets cover'd up in leaves.

But we are brought up short by the final exhibit in that book, from *The Merchant of Venice:*

> in such a night
> *Stood Dido with a willow in her hand*
> *Upon the wild sea banks, and waft her love*
> *To come again to Carthage.*

The italics here are Arnold's, who closes his discussion by observing that the lines are "so drenched and intoxicated with the fairy-dew of that natural magic which is our theme, that I cannot do better than end with them." Fair enough. But any reader may add that the main theme of the lines is not the external features of the setting but unrequited love, which in human experience belongs as surely as anything else to the question of "how to live"; and that the magic lies in the poignancy of Shakespeare's moving portrayal of the forsaken Dido's anguish.[27]

Arnold's poetic percipience too obviously outran his capacity for communicating the finer aesthetic subtleties to which he so delicately responded. His own awareness of the frustration involved was revealed in *On Translating Homer,* when he observed that the critic of poetry needed a poise so perfect that the slightest imbalance—of temper, personal crochet, or even erudition—could destroy it. The perception of "poetic truth" is so elusive that even by "pressing too impetuously after it, one runs the risk of losing it." Yet half a dozen years later we find him yielding to a personal inclination toward that very impetuosity. In *Celtic Literature,* readers with an abiding interest in poetic style are alerted by his emphasis on four of the many modes of "handling" nature in verse: the *conventional,* the *faithful,* the *Greek,* and the *magical.* Striking illustrative samples, from Greek, Latin, and English poetry, follow. But only the first of those in English is of any help in defining the mode to which Arnold assigns it. Pope's pompous lunar metaphor, "refulgent lamp of night," makes reasonably clear the manner of the conventional mode. But wherein Keats's

What little town by river or seashore
Or mountain-built with peaceful citadel,
    Is emptied of this folk, this pious morn?

is Greek (apart from setting), "as Greek as a thing from Homer or Theocritus," it is impossible to fathom, even when Arnold points to an accession of radiancy. Even more cryptic is his confidence that readers will be "disposed" to label "Greek" (not "magical"!) the speech from *A Midsummer Night's Dream* beginning

I know a bank where the wild thyme blows.

There is more of the same—all of it, we should have the humility to admit, perhaps obvious enough to those who share Arnold's schooling in Greek verse. The earnestness of his concern with poetry as an institution vital to cultured living makes it unlikely that he did not himself perceive the stylistic distinctions he names. It is therefore the more regrettable that the terms he adopted to convey them must strike most readers as vague and perversely arbitrary.[28]

Though irretrievably ambiguous, the perfunctory phrase "poetic truth" gains renewed import when used by a critic who believed poetry to be man's most nearly truthful form of utterance. For Arnold the truth in question is truth of a special kind, special and "higher," requiring an idiom suited to a cognitive order alternative to that of science. He thus adopts a major tenet of Romantic poetics, though somewhat reductively defined. Arnold's poetic truth eschews the purely abstract numeration and quantification which, as he thought, contemporary science employed to present the world to human comprehension. His fullest discussion of this idea occurs not in his critical prose but in *Literature and Dogma,* where he exalts the style of the Bible, which "keeps to the language of poetry," over that of theology, which employs as much as possible the abstract jargon of science. Wordsworth's personification of the earth as "the mighty mother of mankind" thus contrasts with the geographer's "oblate spheroid." The poet conveys something people feel about the planet they inhabit. The literary language of the Bible functions in the same way. It is

> language *thrown out* at an object of consciousness not fully grasped, which inspired emotion. . . . [T]he language of figure and feeling will satisfy us better about it, will cover more of what we seek to express, than the language of literal fact and science. The language of science about it will be *below* what we feel to be the truth.[29]

Arnold here renews a theme that had taken on special urgency since the Enlightenment, the defense of poetry against positivist detraction. In its original form the threat had been idealist, coming at the very outset of recorded criticism in Plato's indictment of poets as deceivers. The best known later apologists, Sidney and Shelley, had responded mainly by making poetry's sensuous attractions, which Plato thought baneful, ancillary to its cognitive utility. But by Arnold's time the stakes had been raised. Ineffectively challenged by the religion of the day, the triumph of scientific "truth" seemed to entail not only the loss of a "world of fine fabling," but the virtual dehumanization and alienation of human beings reduced to "absurd" inhabitants of one of the myriad "oblate spheroids" of an indifferent universe. Though Arnold was by no means the originator of this brand of cosmic pessimism, a motif common in Romantic literature, no one could have felt more personally affected by it than the poet whose most famous lyric envisaged a world having neither "certitude, nor peace, nor help for pain." Moreover, it is Arnold's formulation of this cultural crisis that has been most influential as an intellectual legacy to modern defenders of poetry like John Crowe Ransom and I. A. Richards. Richards credited Arnold with having foreseen that poetry would one day fill the emotional void left by science's "neutralization of nature," and thus save us from the impending chaos. Self-professed Benthamite positivist, Richards cannot admit any such category as *poetic* truth, truth for him being exclusively an affair of science. But he follows Arnold in grounding his analysis of poetic language, in function and form, on an alleged discrepancy from scientific discourse. "In its use of words," as he put it in *Science and Poetry* (1926), "poetry is just the reverse of science." In Richards's thinking, the difference between the two uses becomes so nearly total that poetry is denuded of any cognitive value whatsoever; its salutary working is purely emotive, even neurological. Not so Arnold. For him the emotion attaches first of all to the way the poet thinks, and only because of that does it condition his style. Poetry as much as science "gives the idea, but gives it touched with beauty, heightened by emotion."[30]

Arnold can nonetheless claim for poetry a kind of truth *above* that of science, one indispensable to its special function of "criticizing," which must always be performed "in conformity to the laws of poetic truth and poetic beauty." He came nearest to clarifying these vague terms in the essay on Wordsworth, by quoting a passage from *The Excursion:*

> One adequate support
> For the calamities of mortal life
> Exists, one only;—an assured belief
> That the procession of our fate, howsoe'er
> Sad or disturbed, is ordered by a Being
> Of infinite benevolence and power;
> Whose everlasting purposes embrace
> All accidents, converting them to good.

Arnold has no quarrel with the faith in divine guidance expressed here. He objects only that the lines have "none of the characters of *poetic* truth, the kind of truth which we require from a poet," and find in abundance elsewhere in Wordsworth.[31] Since he fails to say what aspects of the passage—diction, rhythm, syntax, or nonformal ingredients—make for the deficiency, we are left to guess *what* the linguistic modalities of poetic truth might be. Arnold cited Wordsworth's lines as a negative touchstone, which for him was all that was required to convey a certain lapse from the ideal he named poetic truth. To ask for more would be to ask that the method of the touchstones be replaced by an ontological procedure for which Arnold had neither the taste nor the gift.

CHAPTER ELEVEN

Pater and Others

WALTER PATER'S OPINIONS
on poetic art are crucial to those concerned to fix his proper place
on a scale of judgement that runs from P. E. More's intemperate
denial that he was a critic at all to William E. Buckler's recent ranking him among the half-dozen or so "indispensable" English critics, the very best between 1880 and 1920, the year (one notes) of
Eliot's critical debut with *The Sacred Wood*. Buckler's assessment is
surely nearer the truth. Apart from intrinsic merit, Pater is outstanding for his Janus-like historical role as both the last typically
Victorian critic and the largely unwitting exemplar of a generation
of gifted writers who well before the queen's death were to reorder
the literary and aesthetic ideals honored during the heyday of her
reign. Recalling their activity in 1936, W. B. Yeats described it as a
revolt against Tennyson's moral discursiveness, Swinburne's political eloquence, Browning's psychological probings, "and the poetic
diction of everyone." With no fundamental change in theory, this
revolt encouraged a priority of the aesthetic over the moral and intellectual constituents of art works which stimulated a fresh
scrutiny of the verbal medium of poetry. In the closing sentence of
Appreciations (1889), Pater assigned to every critical school and
age the duty of contending "against the stupidity which is dead to
the substance, and the vulgarity which is dead to form." But his
disciples, if not indeed their mentor himself, expended far more effort against the vulgarity than against the stupidity.[1]

For the history of English speculation on the poet's medium the most salient feature of the critical orientation initiated by Pater was that it elevated prose to aesthetic parity with verse or at least to a comparable status. This result he may have effected as much by the example of his own essays as by critical argument. Wilde recalled Pater's asking him at their first meeting why he did not direct his efforts to prose instead of to poetry. "Prose," he told his pupil, "was so much more difficult." Not until he came to read *The Renaissance* (1873) did Wilde fully apprize Pater's advice and realize "what a wonderful self-conscious art the art of English prose-writing really is, or may be made to be. Carlyle's stormy rhetoric, Ruskin's winged and passionate eloquence, had seemed to me to spring from enthusiasm rather than from art. I don't think I knew then that even prophets correct their proofs." For Wilde though, the consummate master in this wonderful art was Pater himself. Yeats headed his Oxford anthology with an excerpt from the famous meditation on da Vinci's *Mona Lisa* in *The Renaissance*, rearranged in vers libre to emphasize its "poetic" quality. He did so because that passage had, as he explained, "dominated a generation."[2]

The growing prestige of prose induced a corresponding change in the critical method of treating the problem of poetic language. Despite the recognition throughout Western criticism of an intermediate prose kind—oratory from the beginning and stylistically ornate or fictive prose by the late 1600s—the traditional comparisons of verse and prose had been made mainly to distinguish the artistic and nonartistic (discursive) modes of communication. This procedure was by no means abandoned. Now, however, verse and imaginative prose were sometimes juxtaposed in critical scrutiny as alternative species of an identical poetic genus, in order, by a more exacting analytical discrimination, to isolate the stylistic traits imposed or (as verse apologists would have it) made possible by metrical form. One result of this altered focus on the problem was a fresh look at the enigma of verse itself, although not one taken by Pater.

The appearance in 1885 of Saintsbury's *Specimens of English Prose Style* is evidence of the growing late Victorian tendency to regard prose as an artistic rival to verse. By 1912 he could match his *History of English Prosody* (1906) with a *History of English Prose Rhythm*, confident of continued public appeal. As we should expect from the man whose *Renaissance* was to convince the young poet Arthur Symons that prose too could be a fine art, Pater's review of the *Specimens* honored this new valuation. Yet, in reversal of his earlier opinions, he used the occasion to argue that in their "indispensable qualities" the styles of prose and verse were actually opposed. Emphatically put, the point is more than a polite momentary concession to Saintsbury's more moderate view of the prose-verse distinction. Pater made no attempt either to reconcile his position here with his career-long habit of blurring or minimizing the difference, or to clarify his assertion that it was what writers should chiefly bear in mind. For verse, he offered no counterparts to the "order, precision, and directness" which he named as the special criteria of good prose. Surely Pater of all critics could not have intended his readers to infer that verse was impaired by disorder and vagueness, if not by obliquity. And in fact a principal theme of his much admired essay "Style" in *Appreciations* is that all the good qualities of prose and verse alike are so many instances of expressive precision—of which more below.[3]

For all its uniquely Paterian nuances of discrimination, "Style" is a repository of the main tenets of the Romantic literary aesthetic, the more memorably worded because written by one who had put them to the test of his own experience as reader and writer. He knew a reader's special delight in being attuned to his author's conscious artistry, in prose certainly but in poetry as well, because in the latter, he says, that mark of "constructive intelligence . . . is one of the forms of the imagination." Thinking of Wordsworth's jarring lapses from sublimity into bathos, Pater offers his own version of poetic organic unity on the lexical level. Great moments are possible only when in the poet's imagination word and idea are joined

> inseparably one with the other, by that fusion of matter and form, which is the characteristic of the highest poetical expression. His words are themselves thought and feeling; not eloquent, or musical words merely, but that sort of creative language which carries the reality of what it depicts, directly, to the consciousness.[4]

What he thinks Wordsworth and Coleridge intended as the "imaginative" style in poetry he finds in a passage from Shakespeare's *Henry V* (Act IV, scene 6):

> My cousin Suffolk,
> My soul shall thine keep company to heaven:
> Tarry, sweet soul, for mine, then fly abreast.

Here Pater detects an infusion of the figure into the thought

> so vividly realised, that, though birds are not actually mentioned,
> yet the sense of their flight, conveyed to us by the single word
> 'abreast,' comes to be more than half the thought itself.

This he takes to be an example of what Coleridge meant by imagination as distinct from fancy, which Coleridge himself had illustrated by the lines from *Venus and Adonis* memorialized by his citation. Actually though, despite Pater's perception that it was in
his aesthetics and poetics that Coleridge came "nearest to principles of permanent truth and importance," he nowhere explicitly
identifies them. Pater is a prime illustration of Buckler's generalization that English literature made poor use of its "one great theorist, Coleridge" (a neglect, however, amply redressed after World
War I). On one point Pater's misreading of the *Biographia* seems
merely willful. He anticipated Orsini's mistaken impression that in
Coleridge's organic form the artist becomes "almost a mechanical
agent" devoid of purposive activity during composition. The
"philosophical critic," as Pater's solemn pronouncement has it,
will value even in intuitive and imaginative works "the spectacle of
a supreme intellectual dexterity which they afford"—as though
the discernible presence of that very dexterity were not a much-
stressed and indispensable constituent of Coleridgean mimesis.[5]

On poetic diction Pater sided—after his subtler fashion—with
Wordsworth. With reservations needed to adjust them to what
readers were accustomed to, he endorsed Wordsworth's dictional
naturalism and stylistic equation of verse and prose, along with the
attendant depreciation of meter. As Pater interprets him, Wordsworth sought in verse to approximate the real language of men
"not on the dead level of ordinary discourse," but as "winnowed
and ennobled" in choice moments of heightened emotion. His
concept of meter is a less crudely dismissive reformulation of
Wordsworth's notion of the "superadded charm." It differs in
pushing Wordsworth's rationale to the extreme of asserting the
aesthetic equality of verse and prose. In effect Pater was really making the case in "Style" for his own convictions by a studied fine-
tuning of Wordsworth's. Adapting the views set forth in the 1800
preface to his own sense of the matter, Pater finds the meter in
Wordsworth's verse to be

> but an additional grace, accessory to that deeper music of words
> and sounds, that moving power, which they exercise *in the nobler*

> *prose no less than in formal poetry.* It is a sedative to that excitement sometimes almost painful, under which the language, *alike of poetry and prose,* attains a rhythmical power, *independent of metrical combination,* and dependent rather on some subtle adjustment of the elementary sounds of the words themselves to the image or feeling they convey.

Pater spices his rejection of the sharp dividing line between verse and prose, drawn by Dryden and his contemporaries, by ironically contrasting Dryden's allegedly prosaic verse with his prose, so "fervid, richly figured, poetic, as we say," that it was often defaced by the intrusion of scannable lines. It is a very Paterized Wordsworth who on dubious historical evidence is here made the champion of poetic prose, the pioneer who substituted for the merely technical and possibly accidental distinction of meter an "essential" dichotomy between "imaginative and unimaginative writing." This preferred ground of difference Pater likens to De Quincey's distinction between the literatures of knowledge, or fact, and of power, or the "imaginative sense of fact."[6]

It was, as he confessed, "under sanction of Wordsworth" that Pater propounded his theory of style. In part obviously an apologia for the kind of prose he so meticulously cultivated himself, the ideas in "Style" are equally inductions from his wide reading of other prose writings and so propounded as universally valid. From his earliest maturity, as he reported in his essay on Winckelmann (1867), the term *poetry* had meant to Pater all literature designed to please by form apprehended separately from content. As "high examples" of it he singled out not the usually invoked metrical masterpieces but Goethe's prose romances and, as even more representative, Victor Hugo's novels. Clearly this evaluation went beyond merely acknowledging the stylistic graces of prose. It expressed Pater's belief that some discrimination of the differing ways poets and prose writers manipulate their common medium was crucial to any sound concept of good writing. "I propose," he wrote in "Style,"

> here to point out certain qualities of all literature as a fine art, which, if they apply to the literature of fact, apply still more to the literature of the imaginative sense of fact, while they apply indifferently to verse and prose, so far as either is really imaginative— certain conditions of true art in both alike, which conditions may also contain in them the secret of the proper discrimination and guardianship of the peculiar excellence of either.

We may only regret that Pater never chose to direct the light of his delicate percipience into whatever dark place he thought the discriminative secret lay hidden.[7]

He is with those who hold that well-written history, the work of a Livy, Tacitus, Gibbon, or Michelet, falls within De Quincey's imaginative sense of fact. To those who deplore any imaginative intrusion into historiography as a betrayal of the historian's necessary objectivity, Pater offers the usual retort: however determined to confine themselves to a bare recording of the "facts," historians must select among them, so that their "objective" portrayal of past events cannot help being colored by the "vision within." In Pater this commonplace is envisaged within a fundamentally expressionist theory. Truth and beauty are ultimately related, in that all beauty is "only *fineness* of truth," and, in the verbal arts, "the finer accommodation of speech to that vision within." It may be permissible to speak of Pater's theory as mimetic (he refers to art as imaginative transcription), except that his mimesis is almost entirely solipsistic, all literature being good in proportion to how accurately it represents an author's subjective state, which he calls the "soul-fact." And verse is only one department of it, one Pater was disinclined to exalt above others, the more so since prose had become for many discriminating readers the preferred belletristic form.[8]

Since in any use of language there is a "translation" from within to without, the quality of literary language, whether prose or verse, resided for Pater in expressive precision. Symons recalled his advising young writers to read the dictionary in order to discover what words to avoid. In "Style" this advice is repeated in good earnest, as a procedure by which an author may winnow his stock of words until "he begets a vocabulary faithful to his own spirit." Whatever is written, unless it directly conduces to a faithful "portraiture of one's sense," must be sacrificed to the ideal of a communicative precision devoid of otiose "surplusage." Not a poet, but instead Gustave Flaubert, whom he would canonize as "the martyr of literary style," is Pater's supreme model in this endeavor. In the French novelist's relentless search for *le mot juste* he saw not primarily a struggle to delineate a fictive world (as Flaubert represented his chief aim), but a dramatic enactment of Pater's own ideal of lexical precision, fidelity to an author's psychic state. "The problem of style was there!—the unique word, phrase, sentence, paragraph, essay, or song, absolutely proper to the single mental presentation of the vision within."[9]

Pater never seems to have doubted that language was capable of the required *justesse*. His calls for communicative precision were made with no hint of the occasional frustration confessed by even the greatest masters, who have at times found their medium too intractable for the "absolute" propriety he demanded. Pater need not have recalled Dante's anguished cry in the *Paradiso*, "O quanto è corto il dire . . . !" He could have found a cautionary example provided by Flaubert himself in the musings of Emma Bovary's seducer Rodolphe, ruefully likening human speech to a cracked cauldron on which we beat out tunes for dancing bears when we long instead to move pity in the stars ("attendrir les étoiles").[10]

What Pater mainly valued in fine writing was its *uniqueness,* which Austin Warren found to be "almost the central term for Pater's quest." In *The Renaissance* he takes pointed exception to Winckelmann's admiration of Greek sculpture for its *Allgemeinheit* (universality), because that quality entailed an impoverishment of "what we call *expression.*" Pater preferred the more individualized masterpieces of Michelangelo. The comparison evoked his most peremptory statement on the issue. Any art work "not concerned with individual expression, with individual character and feeling, the special history of the special soul, was not worth doing at all."[11]

For all the subtlety and penetration of its exposition, his argument is vulnerable to two lines of dissent. The first is essentially a logical objection to uniqueness as a prime aesthetic quality, especially in the verbal arts. Strictly speaking, whatever is unique in anyone's private consciousness would be incommunicable to anyone else because language is a social institution, intersubjective, shared on every level, phonemic, lexical, syntactical, within a given speech community. A reader's very response to the precision of a *mot juste,* recherché or trite, depends on its collective import. A totally idiosyncratic item of consciousness would defy verbal embodiment.

Pater himself anticipates the second objection, corollary to the first, that to limit the subject of artistic expression to the "vision within" was to relegate "style to the subjectivity, the mere caprice, of the individual." No rule of good practice, let alone any stylistic theory, would be possible. Cryptically brief, his discussion offers no clear rebuttal of this objection. The fog of vagueness seems—momentarily—to lift when he alludes to his conviction that the most nearly perfect art is music, because in musical compositions form and substance are virtually identical. Though Pater does not explain exactly how a literary expressionism as subjective as the one he advocates can attain to impersonality by simply assimilating to the condition of music, we may plausibly conjecture what he had in mind. There is an important sense in which the style of a fine musical composition is at once unique to its composer and impersonal. Experienced music lovers can usually tell from style alone that a given composition is, for example, Chopin's. Yet though his style is his alone, it bespeaks nothing of the man himself beyond his creative mode. It is, in a homely metaphor, his trademark, but not his fingerprint. To this line of argument, however, it will be rightly objected that the crucial difference between the musician's intellectually pure medium and the literary artist's ideationally freighted words prevents the latter from ever reaching the impersonal "purity" of music.[12] As with other ideas he took from Wordsworth, Pater adapted the norm of sincerity to his aestheticism, altering it from a moral quality to a technical corollary of his expressionism. As he remarks in passing, this ran counter to the eighteenth-century feeling that poetry "rejoices" in abstract terms. The Paterian conception of artistic sincerity, virtually synonymous with expressive precision, demands instead a language in which concrete particulars predominate. He praised the perfect sincerity of D. G. Rossetti's poems, manifest in "a structure and music of verse, a vocabulary, an accent, unmistakably novel," yet free of mannerism; a speech that accurately reveals things that were especially vivid in the poet's private experience—in short, a verse style that is an "exact equivalence to those *data* within."

There is, I think, some shuffling in Pater's conception of how literary artists compose. In Rossetti's case and others, it requires that the perfect word or phrase be "always, one could see, deliberately chosen from many competitors" to enable unique transcription. Yet in the same volume he had endorsed Wordsworth's "imaginative mood" for spontaneously generating its own verbal equivalent. He says the same in *Plato and Platonism:* "the line, the colour, the word, following obediently, and with minute scruple, the conscious motions of a convinced intelligible soul.[13]

The discrepancy in Pater's various statements about the issue may be reduced if we take them as describing successive steps in composition. First the mood, inspiration, or "occasion" must be vividly realized; then only can an answerable style ensue. Even on this interpretation, however, any version of Flaubert's search for a *mot juste* and Horace's reliance on the *provisam rem* are mutually exclusive etiologies. Most damaging to the notion of a purely deliberate verbal manipulation is the position Pater took in "The School of Giorgione," locus of the famous aphorism that all art aspires to the condition of music. There he rejects the classical two-step *res-verba* creative process in favor of the unitary Romantic conception. In art, he wrote, "form and matter, in their union or identity, present one single effect to the 'imaginative reason,' that complex faculty for which every thought and feeling is twin-born with its sensible analogue or symbol."[14]

In his excellent book on Newman, Arnold, and Pater, David J. DeLaura convincingly argues the close dependence of this crucial passage in "The School of Giorgione" on one in *The Idea of a University,* where Newman represents not only the words of a poem but its rhythm and meter too as "the contemporaneous offspring of the emotion or imagination" by which the poet is possessed during composition. DeLaura noted that Pater even adopted Newman's "key metaphor" of imaginative reason. But he overlooks what in relation to poetic theory is one important difference between the two men's thinking. Unlike Newman and others before him noted above, Pater never includes metrical form among the workings of the "complex faculty." Neither is there a suggestion anywhere that he agreed with Newman that meter was the outward manifestation of a harmony in the poet's consciousness and an index of his meaning.[15]

In Pater's constant call for lexical "sincerity" we have the best explanation of his poor opinion of meter and his consequent failure to evolve an adequate theory of verse diction. For like all artistic conventions, meter is inherently "insincere," more so even than language itself, because less susceptible of individualizing manipulation, as Wordsworth had noted. Although (according to the most trustworthy testimony we have) in verse, and impassioned prose, rhythm and an *impulsion toward* meter inhere in the psychology of composition, metrical patterns themselves are traditional, a conventional legacy from outside anyone's personal sensibility. Meter can therefore never fail to dilute, or transmute, the "sincerity" of a style minutely correspondent to an idiosyncratic inward vision, which Pater extolled. Like Baudelaire, the author of *Petits poèmes en prose,* Pater dreamed of the "miracle d'une prose poétique" that, as Baudelaire described it to his patron Arsène Houssaye, should by its emancipation from meter and rhyme be more delicately attuned to "the lyrical motions of the soul, the undulations of revery, the abrupt springings of consciousness ("soubresauts de la conscience")."[16]

In Pater's work, especially at its cruces, it is beauty in *visual* manifestations, "some form . . . perfect in hand or face; some tone on the hills or on the sea . . . choicer than the rest," that most intensely ministers to the "life of constant and eager observation" depicted in the notorious "Conclusion" to *The Renaissance*. In his criticism painters and sculptors loom larger than writers, and prose predominates over verse. It is hard, in fact, to down the suspicion that imaginative prose simply moved Pater the more deeply. Nothing in his few published essays on poets evinces the relish for verbal artistry that appears in his piece on Pascal's prose in *Miscellaneous Studies*, for example. "What quality of expression, how brief, how untranslatable!" he writes of the *Provincial Letters*. And in the *Pensées* he finds the epitome of the stylistic concision peculiar to French itself, "the brevity, the discerning edge, the impassioned concentration of the language"—terms surely apposite to Pascal's mastery, but most often evoked by unusually alembicated passages of lyric verse.[17]

Pater implicitly accepted Coleridge's central insight of an artistic mastery of chaos through order. In his thinking, though, it is extended to accommodate his sense that life itself—the perfected life—is a work of art. As he interprets Plato's rarefied polity, it is the duty of every citizen of an ideal republic "to escape from, to resist, a certain vicious centrifugal tendency in life." For Pater, Plato's brand of idealism was exemplary in the aesthetic mode formulated in Coleridge's definition of beauty as *Multëity in Unity*. "To realize unity in variety," Pater reasoned," to discover *cosmos* . . . below and within apparent chaos is from first to last the continuous purpose of what we call philosophy." The Platonic theory of Ideas, in Pater's understanding of it, aimed only to undergird the Pythagorean τὸ πέρας (limit), pitting the "unity-in-variety of concerted music" against τὸ ἄπειρον, "the infinite, the indefinite, formless, brute matter of our experience of the world." Thence ensued, for many like-minded critics, almost as a logical step, a perception of meter as the central agent among the centripetal forces. Pater, however, never took this further step.[18]

His failure to do so is the more notable in that Plato would seem to encourage it. "And Platonic aesthetics, remember!" Pater cautioned his students, "are as such ever in close connection" with Plato's ethics. He took special note of Plato's belief that poetic meter and rhythm play a vital moral role in the education of youth, the decorous and indecorous in human behavior being consequences of good and bad rhythm respectively. In Pater's reading of it, Plato's doctrine is asserted

> with immediate reference to metre and its various forms in verse, as an element in the general treatment of style or manner (λέξις) as opposed to the matter (λόγοι) in the imaginative literature, with which as in time past the education of the Perfect City will begin.[19]

Yet even though Pater's aestheticism shared with Platonic pedagogic theory the faith that artistic harmony was salubrious to the soul, nowhere in his discussion of poetry is meter assigned any more vital function than that of a "sedative" to the undue excitement of rhythmical language, the notion he took from Wordsworth.

This omission holds in *Marius the Epicurean* despite a passing reference to language "delicate and measured," in the chapter on euphuism. There, through the thinly imagined personage of Marius's friend Flavius, Pater meditates on the poetic art. Inspired especially by the example of the tale of Cupid and Psyche, as recently recast in Apuleius's novel *The Golden Ass,* Flavian is obsessed by a vocation. No doubt with some sense of a parallel between the decadent Rome of Marcus Aurelius and his own historical moment, Pater depicts the young man's enthusiasm entirely in terms of the linguistic medium of the art by which he dreamed of exerting power over his compatriots. Flavian, for whom delicately controlled expression is to be the battle gear of his future triumphs, is an "indefatigable student of words, of the means or instruments of the literary art." Pater touches briefly but sensitively on perennial questions raised inevitably by the problem of poetic language, most arrestingly the relation of verse to the contemporary spoken idiom. Flavian is cast as a kind of Antonine Roman Wordsworth, whose literary program aims, *inter alia,* to vindicate "the rights of the *proletariat* of speech." But, a Wordsworth of decidedly Paterian sensibility, he

> would make of it a serious study, weighing the precise power of every phrase and word, as though it were a precious metal, disentangling the later associations and going back to the original and native sense of each,— restoring to full significance all its worth of latent figurative expression, reviving or replacing its outworn or tarnished images. Latin literature and the Latin tongue were dying of routine and languor; and what was necessary, first of all, was to reestablish the natural and direct relationship between

thought and expression, between the sensation and the term, and restore to words their primitive power.[20]

Pater's euphuism embraces every conceivable resource making for "effective expression at all times." But this raises the familiar protest: why can't writers, poets or not, say what they have to say in plain, direct language? More than a philistine complaint, the query has respectable historical bearings. Flavius himself envies earlier times when the plain and the poetic seemed to coexist, as in some lines he cites from Homer:

οἱ δ' ὅτε δὴ λιμένος πολυβενθέος ἐντὸς ἵκοντο,
ἱστία μὲν στείλαντο θέσαν δ'ἐν νηὶ μελαίνῃ, . . .
ἐκ δὲ καὶ αὐτοὶ βαῖνον ἐπὶ ῥηγμῖνι θαλάσσης

[Now when they had gotten within the deep harbor, they furled the sails and stowed them within the black ship . . . then they came ashore at the edge of the surf.] (*Iliad*, I, 432–33, 437)

"And how poetic the simple seemed, told just thus!" Pater marveled, as readers at ease in Homer's Greek have always done. And thinking perhaps of Arnold's having taken Homer as prime example of the grand style, he wonders whether that style did not owe something to the quality of the primitive language itself, in "a time in which one could hardly have spoken at all without ideal effect," making of the sailors and their ship "a picture in 'the great style,' against a sky charged with marvels."[21]

In the last two decades of the century only Gerard Manley Hopkins materially advanced our ideas of poetry as a verbal art. Oscar Wilde's contributions, greater in range, are valuable more for witty and arresting paraphrases of earlier doctrine than for fresh ideas. Nevertheless, the subject continued to attract the attention of writers with motives and viewpoints as varied as those of Ruskin and Swinburne in England and Lowell in America. There was no proper debate; critics spoke *past* each other, as it were, though in most cases to the same public. If there is any pattern discernible in the chorus of variable opinion, it is a very rough—and unequal—division between a majority influenced by Wordsworth and a minority whose ideas, consciously or not, aligned them more closely with Coleridge. The latter insisted more on a clear separation of prose and verse, adhered in one version or another to an organic poetics of tension, and advocated tempering spontaneous effusion with conscious art.

Harold Bloom's assertion that Ruskin's idea of the imagination is "largely derived" from Coleridge, wants qualification. It would be more accurate to say that imagination in Ruskin is Coleridgean only in those broad assumptions shared by both authors of *Lyrical Ballads*. Beyond that, in the fundamental principles that directed his thinking about poetry, and in the terms he used to communicate it, Ruskin was as much as Arnold and Pater an intellectual heir of Wordsworth. For what might be loosely identified as an abortive late Victorian neo-Coleridgean poetics, we must look instead to Wilde, Swinburne, Hopkins, and R. L. Stevenson.[22]

Though he is understandably best remembered for his work on the graphic arts and architecture, Ruskin's several unmethodical observations on literature evince a genuine delight in fine verse. His many books, studded with choice quotations from the English poets and from Dante and the Greek and Roman classics, show a lifetime of varied and devoted reading. In his earlier work especially, his taste suffers somewhat from the Victorian deafness to even the finest neoclassical poetry. But this limitation was largely overcome in his maturity, as his editors Cook and Wedderburn observe. Even during the time of his youthful denigration of Pope, whose lack of passion he deplored in *Modern Painters*, Ruskin already admired in him a mastery of the "absolute art of language" which he thought rivaled only by Virgil's. In this he stands apart from Arnold and other contemporaries, whose Romanticist viewpoint seldom if ever allowed them to grant full poetic status to the poems of Dryden and Pope. The change in Ruskin's taste seems to have proceeded roughly *pari passu* with his increasing attention to metrical language as such. Whatever the reason, in the *Lectures on Art* (1870) Pope's earlier alleged cold-hearted hypocrisy has been supplanted by the "serene and just benevolence" that informs a couplet from the *Essay on Man* which Ruskin hails as "the most complete, the most concise, and the most lofty expression of moral temper existing in English words:

Never elated, while one man's oppress'd;
Never dejected, while another's bless'd."[23]

Ruskin referred the aesthetic as well as the moral qualities of great verse to its linguistic medium, a view unusual in so willing an heir to the Romanticist conceptions of poetry which are least conducive to that theoretical premise. One such was the parity between the verbal and pictorial arts in value and function. "Understand this thoroughly," Ruskin wrote; "know once for all, that a poet on canvas is exactly the same species of creature as a poet in song." The nonstylistic cast of his evaluation is further assured by a similar assimilation of the literary genres. A play, poem, or novel are all three really "poems," whether written in meter or in prose. And (asserting a Carlylian vaticism) all literary creation is apportioned between Thinkers and Seers, as we read in *Modern Painters:* "To see clearly is poetry, prophecy, and religion—all in one." In addition, Ruskin's writings are infused with an abiding moralism whereby poetry's traditional amendatory virtues are inflated in a way that enforces an undue narrowing of poetic subject matter while identifying a poem's worth with the edifying qualities of its content, to the virtual exclusion of its formal excellence. Poetry, runs an early and confessedly tentative definition in *Modern Painters*, is the imaginative suggestion "of noble grounds for noble emotions." Indignation is a proper "poetical feeling" only if it has been aroused by serious injury, not by being cheated in some petty financial transaction. However "energetic," the admiration excited in some people by a fireworks display or a street of handsome shops is not a poetical feeling. A budding flower on the other hand is poetic because it manifests "spiritual power and vital beauty" surpassing admiration.[24]

To these counsel-darkening conceptions we might add the notion of the "Pathetic Fallacy," the most notorious instance of Ruskin's unfortunate tendency to "ériger en loi" some personal gut reaction. Ruskin's excoriation of such tried and true imagistic devices as the transferred epithet and personification, illustrated respectively by Charles Kingsley's "cruel, crawling foam" and Coleridge's dancing red leaf (from *Christabel*), may well spring from Wordsworth's criterion of sincerity, which Ruskin early embraced.[25]

Given his anti-analytical bent, it is refreshing to find here and there in Ruskin a discerning attention to verse as a unique use of words, elevated above the prosaic by departures from standard syntactical usage and by the conventions of meter, lineation, and rhyme. His efforts to define the difference in set terms lack precision. He handles the problem more effectively in *The Elements of English Prosody* (1880), where he explicates a parenthetical couplet from *The Rape of the Lock* (Canto IV, lines 123–24) to show the advantages of iambic pentameter over prose:

(*Sir Plume*, of *Amber Snuff-box* justly vain,
And the nice Conduct of a *clouded Cane*).

This kind of verse, Ruskin wrote,

> admits . . . of no careless or imperfect construction, but allows
> any intelligible degree of inversion; because it has been consid-
> ered to the end, before a word is written, and the placing of the
> words may afterwards be adjusted according to their importance.
> Thus, "Sir Plume, of amber snuff-box justly vain" is not only
> more rhythmic, but more elegant and accurate than "Sir Plume,
> justly vain of his amber snuff-box"; first, because the emphasis of
> rhyme is laid on his vanity, not his box; secondly, because the
> "his," seen on full consideration to be unnecessary, is omitted, to
> concentrate the sentence; and with a farther and more subtle rea-
> son, . . . that a coxcomb cannot, properly speaking, *possess* any-
> thing, but is possessed by everything, so that in the next line
> Pope does not say, "And the nice conduct of *his* clouded cane,"
> but of *a* clouded cane.[26]

The plausibility of this dissection, especially of its final point,
grows with repeated perusal. Neither the method of Ruskin's
analysis nor the terms of his argument involve any theoretical advance. Yet his exegesis is doubly remarkable: for revealing how
flawlessly Pope can adapt stylistic niceties to the moral and tonal
requirements of his narrative, and for such meticulous attention to
metrical syntax in a critic who had inherited, and retained, attitudes hostile to sustained critical focus on technique as a pedantic
concern with mere mechanics: the letter killeth. . . .

As Ruskin's writings during the eighties and nineties suggest,
Pater ultimately failed to dislodge poetry from its privileged position in the literary hierarchy, though he certainly raised prose to an
unprecedented level of critical esteem. Not even Wilde, Pater's
most ardent disciple, was willing to challenge the primacy traditionally accorded to verse. If the age paid more frequent tribute to
the prose writer's art, it also continued a deliberate concern with
versification, manifest in the Pre-Raphaelite school, in William
Morris, and most notably in A. C. Swinburne.

Swinburne must without hesitation be put on the Coleridgean
side of the dictional debate. Granted, his explicit assessments of
Coleridge as critic are vague and inconsistent. The essay on Coleridge, an effusive tribute to his creative genius, joins a casual disparagement of his poetic theory in its text with a footnote reference to his "matchless fragments of metrical criticism." Written in
Swinburne's typically unrestrained manner, the preface to *Miscel-
lanies* (1886) simply denies sanity to anyone who questions the

"incomparable value" of Coleridge's criticism at its best. But given Swinburne's passionate, often strident, celebration of the marvels of verse, there is no reason to doubt the candor (however tiresome the hyperbole) of his applause for the poetician who had refuted Wordsworth's assimilation of verse and prose.[27]

Throughout his criticism, Swinburne harps on metrical skill as his principal criterion. He was no formal purist, certainly no consistent one, since he now and then makes allowance for a poet's soundness of thought and on at least one occasion even avowed a quasi-Emersonian dependency of metrical efficacy on prior psychic activity. "Where the thought goes wrong," he wrote in an 1867 review of Arnold's last poems, "the verse follows after it." He was gratified to find in Arnold's latest offering less of the flimsy matter that had marred his earlier work and therefore less of "feeble or faulty metre." But generally with Swinburne it was a mellifluous flow of language alone that won his esteem, the sole "indispensable test" of really great poetry being the poet's "consummate mastery of his instrument." Although willing to concede that, in some sense of the Arnoldian phrase, a "criticism of life" may be found (and valued) in the work of all good poets, he denied that that can ever determine their relative rank. Rating Keats's *Grecian Urn* at least as highly as Arnold had done, Swinburne rejected outright Arnold's declaration that it anywhere embodied a morality comparable to that of Shakespeare. Keats, he thought, was one of the most "nonmoral" poets who ever wrote—and none the worse for it.[28]

Swinburne's idea of the technical mastery he held to be indispensable to poetic success included both diction and meter. The criteria of good diction he left largely unspecified. He rejoices to find Arnold's "sublime" meter enhanced by the "miraculous" effects of "his choice or chance of language casual or chosen." But this pleonastic approval is unsupported by illustration in the review. He does cite Arnold's use of *convey*, in "The Buried Life," as a successful adoption of a word found mainly in prose, but thought it only a "Wordsworthian trick" which could be either beauty or blemish.[29]

Swinburne is clearer on what he meant by good meter, unvaryingly exalting its unique aesthetic potential. As one might infer from his poetry, he delighted in strong metrical regularity, what in inappropriate applications is disparaged as sing-song. Whether in verse formed of iambs, trochees, dactyls, or anapests, what he especially relished was an isochronic rhythm, as in musical measures, where monotony was relieved and meaning enlivened not by departures from the strict metrical pattern but by tempo changes and judiciously deployed *rubati,* further enhanced, in lyric verse especially, by rhyme. "Rhyme is the native condition of lyric verse in English," he wrote;

> a rhymeless lyric is a maimed thing, and halts and stammers in the deliverance of its message.
>
> To throw away the natural grace of rhyme from a modern song is a wilful abdication of half the power and half the charm of verse.[30]

Swinburne was least sensitive to the subtler, more subliminal rhythmic life of blank verse. Coleridge's lilting "Kubla Khan," the perfect example of Swinburne's ideal versification, he gloried in as "perhaps the most wonderful of all poems." The same poet's rhymeless Conversation Poems he dismissed as embryonic and malformed; even the exquisite "Frost at Midnight" is damned with the faintest of praise. To Swinburne's taste, any relaxation of cadence toward the less predictable movements of prose, the style of *sermoni propiora,* was prosodically noxious. In a discerning essay on John Webster, he is willing to admit that the loosened meter of Bosola's speeches in *The Duchess of Malfi* suits well enough with that character's necrophilic turn of mind, but still deplores it as a fatal tendency toward the "negation or the confusion of all distinctions between poetry and prose." This complaint is given a semblance of plausibility by the sound mimetic argument—recalling Dryden and presaging Eliot on dramatic verse—that if real people don't speak in good meter, neither do they speak in bad. Byron, though equal to Shelley in their common passion for natural beauty, is inferior to him by his faulty meter. His verse, Swinburne wrote in *Essays and Studies* (1875), stumbles and halts where excellence requires "a swift and even pace of musical sound."[31]

No critic has ever been more unshakable than Swinburne in the conviction that meter was not an impediment to creativity but the exact opposite: an instrumentality of psychic invigoration in the struggle to compose. He castigates such rebels against conventional versification as Whitman, who, he says, have never been able to rejoice in the "sublime liberty of expression" conferred by the laws of meter. Truly gifted poets have always been "happy in the acceptance of that immortal and immutable instinct whose impulse is for law, whose passion is for harmony, and whose service is perfect freedom."[32]

Swinburne's unusual prizing of metrical regularity and rhyme—and on the evidence of his own practice we should add profuse alliteration and assonance—are subsumptions of his central persuasion that verse language was—above, beyond, and before all else—verbal *music*. His pages bristle with musical terms. It is in this respect that Shelley represents his poetic ideal. Poetry, Swinburne proclaims, has seldom soared to empyrean heights "on wings of more perfect music" than in the first and fourth acts of *Prometheus Unbound*. Coleridge's supremacy, and his superiority to Wordsworth, consist in his being our finest "melodist," above all in the "absolute melody and splendour" of "Kubla Khan." Coleridge used his combination of creative instinct and subtle prosodic science to make it "the supreme model of music in our language," rivaled only by Shelley's. William Collins is exalted above Gray and every other English poet coming after Pope solely for his "purity of music," for being "content to sing out what he had in him—to sing and not to say, without a glimpse of wit or flash of eloquence." Swinburne could even forgive the most obvious relaxations of meter (though they pained him) in a poem where he found a predominance of clearly apparent rhythmic and melodic effects. Though the cascade of musical terms in his criticism can sometimes cloy, the aural sensitivity they evince sometimes guided him to perceptive assessment. Whitman's "dirge" for Lincoln he pronounced "the most sweet and sonorous nocturne ever chanted in the church of the world." Similarly, "Dover Beach," despite its lack of rhyme and its metrical irregularity, he picks out as the best offering in Arnold's *New Poems*, pleasing for its "grand choral cadence . . . regular in resonance, not fitful or gusty but antiphonal and reverberate."[33]

In America Lowell was attentive both to the stylistic qualities of Coleridge's and Wordsworth's verse and to Wordsworth's ideas of what those qualities should be. In Coleridge's verse the commonest words become "magical" by the skillful placement of their vowels. "The most decrepit vocable in the language throws away its crutches to dance and sing at his piping." Lowell's essay of 1875 on Wordsworth is a repository of useful commonplaces. The "prosaic" discords in his verse are produced by confounding poetic and nonpoetic "ideas." Lowell heartily seconds the Romantic rejection of the decorative theory of poetic style. "For in all real poetry the form is not a garment, but a body."[34]

Though also made up largely of post-Romantic truisms on the subject, the chapter on poetic diction in Lowell's posthumous

Lowell Institute *Lectures* (1894) contains an account of the "double meaning" of the term, and of Wordsworth's responsibility for it, more succinct than the often turgid discussions found in modern textbooks. There are, Lowell explained, two kinds of poetic diction, "the one true and the other false, the one real and vital, the other mechanical and artificial." Wordsworth, Lowell continued in a comic vein which hardly detracts from the justice of his account,

> for a time confounded the two together in one wrathful condemnation, and preached a crusade against them both. He wrote, at one time, on the theory that the language of ordinary life was the true dialect of poetry, and that one word was as good as another. He seemed to go even further and to adopt the Irishman's notion of popular equality, that "one man is as good as another, and a dale better too." He prefers, now and then, prosaic words and images to poetical ones. But he was not long in finding his mistake and correcting it.

Where this unspecified correction occurred, whether in the poet's theory or practice, Lowell does not say. "Poetical" to Lowell does not mean ornate, fanciful, or recondite—least of all when a poet aims at passionate expression, for then "the simpler the language and the less removed from the ordinary course of life the better." His aptly chosen illustration of that maxim is the much admired line from Webster's *Duchess of Malfi:*

Cover her face; mine eyes dazzle; she died young.

The perfectly conveyed horror, Lowell shrewdly notes, is enhanced by Webster's segmenting the line to prevent the meter from diluting the impact of the bare emotion on a reader.[35]

As in Lowell, the organic relationship of meter and meaning is a major motif of John Addington Symonds's essay *Blank Verse* (1875), defending rhymeless pentameter against neoclassical detractors. Conceding that the sad stuff often cobbled together in that form deserved censure, Symonds reasoned soundly that properly managed the five-beat line can dispense with stanza and rhyme by becoming "an organic body of vital thought" with a "melodious structure" of its own. Because no other meter quite succeeds in working this compelling effect, he concluded, blank verse has been the most powerful English poetic vehicle, a form

potential in English speech since Chaucer and rescued by Marlowe
from the stilted experiments of Surrey, Sackville, and Norton.[36]

An ampler range of thought and reading enlivens R. L.
Stevenson's "On Some Technical Elements of Style in Literature,"
published in 1885. Stevenson tolerated Whitman's aim to display
in verse a fresh stock of words to "shake people out of their indifference." But for conveying any more than a fraction of one's experience, he thought, no vocabulary was large enough, not even
Shakespeare's. Pater's ideal of a precise equivalence of a writer's
style to his psychic state was therefore illusory. Besides, what
words we have are so encrusted with associations acquired
through long use that they make "a travesty of the simplest
process of thought" whenever we seek to give it utterance. Of the
celebration of social equality in Whitman's *Leaves*, he observed
that only someone devoid of literary tact would have used the
word *hatter* in verse aspiring to serious emotive appeal.[37]

Fortunately, only the faintest shadow of this lexical despair
falls over the pages of "Elements of Style," even when Stevenson
reflects that whereas its sister arts are blessed by the use of choice
ductile materials, literature must work with a vulgar social instrument. The rest of the essay is mainly a lively statement of familiar
views on the nature of prose and verse then being broadcast by
Saintsbury and others to an ever-widening sector of the British
public. Both literary forms require good judgment (or instinct) in
word-choice. Both being arts, they involve the mastery of tensions
and impediments required to achieve a dynamic structured pattern. But the pattern of verse is the more complex. In prose, each
sentence first ties a knot of suspended meaning, then resolves it.
So the prose artist, as Stevenson graphically puts it, "juggles with
two oranges." The poet, playing metrical pattern against both
phrasal rhythm and the "logical texture" formed of syntactical
units, must juggle with three. Stevenson had learned from the *Biographia*, if he did not discover it for himself, that prose is no more
a natural utterance than verse is; all style is "synthetic." Though he
believes "reasonably interesting prose" to be a rarer thing than
"fairly pleasing verse," he sides with the majority who find verse
aesthetically richer. With rare exceptions lexically indifferent, the
two arts represent distinct orders of verbal creation. The "merits"
of prose are at once inferior and different in kind; the prose writer
rules over "a little kingdom, but an independent."[38]

Stevenson confirms the transcultural law proclaimed by the
ancients from Isocrates to Quintilian, and by Saintsbury and other

contemporaries, that asserts an antinomian relation between rhythm and meter in the prose ordonnance. "Prose must be rhythmical," he wrote,

> and it may be so as much as you will; but it must not be metrical. It may be anything, but it must not be verse. A single heroic line may very well pass and not disturb the somewhat larger stride of the prose style; but one following another will produce an instant impression of poverty, flatness, and disenchantment.

Since this often noticed effect is seldom explained, Stevenson's quite plausible accounting is the more welcome. A line of verse, he notes, is uttered as a single phrase; and a succession of them in prose quickly becomes wearisome. He instances the iambic pentameter groupings in Dickens, the inevitable whipping boy in this matter. But why is this so?—because anyone aiming at prose, not verse, but inadvertently falling in with "the inherently rhythmic strain of the English language," produces only the weak side of verse, its regular beat. "A peculiar density and mass," he continues,

> consequent on the nearness of the pauses, is one of the chief good qualities of verse; but this our accidental versifier, still following after the swift gait and large gestures of prose, does not so much as aspire to imitate.

Therefore, Stevenson concludes, the metrical prose writer, not intending verse, entirely neglects

> those effects of counterpoint and opposition which I have referred to as the final grace and justification of verse, and, I may add, of blank verse in particular.

Thus he followed Coleridge's lead in founding the vital differentia of verse utterance in a dialectical interplay of meter and syntax, emotion and thought.[39]

With the debatable exception of G. M. Hopkins, the most impressive writing on the poet's art during the closing decade of Victoria's reign was Oscar Wilde's. Given the fact that Wilde was the period's most blatant cultural iconoclast, the glib deflater of hallowed pretensions in art and life, it is curious that no writer was more insistent than he that a just assessment of the culture of one's own time be grounded in traditional thought. "For he to whom the present is the only thing that is present," he wrote in a review of Pater's *Appreciations,* knows nothing of the age in which he lives. To realise the nineteenth century, one must realise every century that has preceded it.[40]

As Professor Wellek noticed, and what a student of twentieth-century literary criticism could hardly miss, Wilde's valuation of tradition here anticipates Eliot's in "Tradition and the Individual Talent." In critical power and scope Wilde is no match for Eliot. But in their poetic principles—as distinct from their judgments of individual poets, their taste, and their critical tone and style—the two men agree more than they differ. It must not be forgotten that Eliot too was iconoclastic, more profoundly so in fact, since he mounted his attack from outside the literary establishment, whereas Wilde had lodged his protests from within it. Richard Ellmann, one of the few students of the period to take a proper measure of Wilde as critic, identified three phases of late nineteenth-century criticism, placing Pater in the second, transitional between Arnold and Wilde. In theory, however, especially that branch of it dealing with poetic style, Wilde took nothing from Pater. It is only in his care to make the critical essay itself an art that Wilde emulated his teacher. Though they concur in endorsing Coleridgean organicism, Wilde scarcely alludes to Coleridge himself. He abandons Pater to revive the principles of Aristotle, whose *Poetics* he called a "perfect little work of aesthetic criticism," and to whose concept of mimesis Wilde's pronouncements on verse style almost everywhere conform.[41]

Pater's expressionism, his artistic "sincerity," is not Wilde's. In a phraseology almost verbatim from Pater, Wilde spoke of the artist's constant search for "the mode of existence in which soul and body are one and indivisible, in which the outward is expressive of the inward; in which form reveals." But they adopted the incarnational envisagement to enforce radically different doctrines. Pater's artistic truth consisted in a perfect match of a writer's language with the content and condition of his consciousness. The "soul" which Wilde's artist would display is that of the work he is creating, one not necessarily akin to his own. By this conception, artistic truth consists in "the unity of a thing with itself: the outward expressive of the inward: the soul made incarnate: the body instinct with spirit." With any show of loyalty to his own stylistic creed, Pater could never have written approvingly of Swinburne, as did Wilde, that he was "the first lyric poet who tried to make an absolute surrender of his own personality, and he has succeeded." The remark severs Wilde from Pater to link him, again despite their mutual antipathy, to Eliot, whose prime requirement of "a continual extinction of personality" in art it strikingly adumbrates. "All bad art," in Wilde's shocking version, "springs from genuine feeling." It is no coincidence that Eliot also found Swinburne's "world" to be "impersonal, and no one else could have made it."[42]

True, Pater's tutelage shows in Wilde's declaration that the critic's sole aim is "to chronicle his own impressions." But in "Pen, Pencil, and Poison" he makes those impressions only "the first step in aesthetic criticism," which cannot terminate in sound judgment unless it has been unconsciously "guided and made perfect by frequent contact with the best work." The implied debt to Arnold becomes explicit when Wilde adds that the true critic cultivates a "disinterested curiosity" about "the best that is known and thought in the world."[43]

Like others, Wilde took language to be, as he put it in *Intentions* (1891), "the parent, and not the child of thought," a premise that has always tended to enhance the status of poetic expression. He judged the media of sculpture, painting, and music to be meager in comparison with the lexical materiality of literature. The music of words, Wilde's mouthpiece Gilbert rhapsodizes in "The Critic as Artist," vies with that of viol or lute, their colors with those of great painting, and their plastic forms with those realized in marble and bronze. Solely because words constitute "the finest and fullest medium" available for artistic exploitation, literature is "the ultimate art," and poetry the highest form of literature. Much of this advantage Wilde ascribed to the aural mode of being which language shares with musical tones, but by no means to that exclusively. In verse the sensuous quality of speech is wondrously wedded to its function as catalyst and instigator of mental activity; and the potential of this double agency he thought was no more fruitfully realized than in rhyme, "the one chord we have added to the Greek lyre." Wilde's tribute to rhyme equals Swinburne's in rapturous eloquence, and exceeds it in the depth and variety of the beneficial effects claimed for it.

> Rhyme, that exquisite echo which in the Muse's hollow hill creates and answers its own voice; rhyme, which in the hands of the real artist becomes not merely a material element of metrical beauty, but a spiritual element of thought and passion also, waking a new mood, it may be, or stirring a fresh train of ideas, or

opening by mere sweetness and suggestion of sound some golden
door at which the Imagination itself had knocked in vain; rhyme,
which can turn man's utterance to the speech of gods.

In the wrong hands, Wilde knew, the device can fail of these glorious effects, can even turn into the downright cacophony he found
in Browning's poetry: "there are moments when he wounds us by
monstrous music." For this reason he denied Browning poetic
greatness, praising him instead as a writer of fiction, memorable
especially for a subtlety of characterization in which his only modern rival was George Meredith. "Meredith," Wilde quips in the
kind of pointed paradox ever so ready to his hand, "is a prose
Browning, and so is Browning. He used poetry as a medium for
writing in prose."[44]

Yet, for all his Pater-inspired recognition of the aesthetic potentials of prose, Wilde seems to have been reluctant to accord it
poetic status. Though in "The Critic as Artist" he quotes at length
Pater's famous meditation on the *Mona Lisa,* it is to hold it up as a
model of creative criticism, not of prose-poetry. Wilde's own prose
poems, such as "The Doer of Good" and "The Master," are at the
furthest remove from lyrical effusion. They are merely secular
parables in which an antinomian "moral" predominates over stylistic attraction.

In his censure of Browning's style, Wilde's wit cannot quite
compensate for a certain narrowness of poetic appreciation fostered by a temperamental bias nurtured by his academic training.
As much as Arnold, and at the same Oxonian source, he had been
schooled in a classical, primarily Hellenic, literary taste, although
Wilde's Hellenism is at times of the more etiolated variety affected
by aesthetes. Not even the sobering experience of Reading prison
could shake his fixed relish for what in the posthumous *De Profundis* he exalted as "the pomp of the Latin line or the richer
music of the vowelled Greek." Any style of poetic utterance closer
than these to natural speech, such as Browning cultivated in his
dramatic monologues, seemed to Wilde a lesser thing.[45]

His ideal of poetic style is best grasped as an aspect of his
deep-seated antirealism, a rejection not only of the positivist nov-
elistic realism advocated by his contemporary Émile Zola, but of
the whole tradition of naively naturalistic imitation which the best
neoclassical critics had sought to qualify and which Coleridge had
excoriated as "idle rivalry" under the rubric *Copy.* Wilde wrote to
the editor of the *Times* that he neither knew nor cared how faith-

fully Kipling's *Plain Tales from the Hills* mirrored Anglo-Indian society, adding in a needless departure from orthodox mimesis that he had never been "much interested in any correspondence between art and nature." As an artistic method Wilde held realism to be a failure. The flawless cosmos envisioned in art cannot be attained by a tame mimicry of real life accurately observed because, "as Aristotle once said"—Vivian in "The Decay of Lying" is glad to remind Cyril—nature cannot carry out her good intentions.[46]

That last clause alludes to Aristotle's statement in the *Physics,* that while art imitates nature it completes ("ἐπιτελει") what nature cannot bring to perfection. Germanely to his antirealist convictions, Wilde was given to sweeping paraphrases of the Greek philosopher's characterization of poetic creation, in chapter 25 of the *Poetics,* in which a representation of the probable impossible is preferable to an improbable possibility. Wilde scorns, for example, "novels so life-like" that no one can credit their probability.[47]

The "doctrine of the new aesthetics" which Vivian propounds to Cyril in their colloquy, while essentially mimetic, reorders the classical relation of nature and art to establish the priority of the second term. The privileged status he claims for art is both historical and creative. Just as art had its origin in abstract and autonomous decoration, admitting thought and external referentiality only with the passage of time, so the genuine artist works not "from feeling to form" but from form to thought and passion.

> He does not first conceive an idea, and then say to himself, "I will put my idea into a complex metre of fourteen lines," but, realizing the beauty of the sonnet-scheme, he conceives certain modes of music and methods of rhyme, and the mere form suggests what is to fill it and make it intellectually and emotionally complete.

Not essentially novel, these remarks carry familiar mimetic principles to arresting extremes. His inversion of nature and art should not be dismissed as a mere shocker of Wilde the poseur, embroidering on his mentor Pater's ideal of "aesthetic" living. His idea is rather the one glimpsed in Hazlitt's suggestion that people acquire a genuine perception of reality only as it is reflected for them in art, which strips the veil from nature itself.[48]

Though Wilde often sounds like a devotee of pure formalism, that was not his considered position. He recognized that a referential function is entailed in the very medium of verbal art. Here again his ardent Hellenism served him well by making mimetic

concepts and terms available to him whenever he turned his attention to literary language. The Greeks, he wrote, aware that literature, the most perfect art,

> most fully mirrors man in all his infinite variety, . . . elaborated
> the criticism of language, considered in the light of the mere ma-
> terial of that art, to a point to which we, with our accentual sys-
> tem of reasonable or emotional emphasis, can barely if at all at-
> tain; studying, for instance, the metrical movements of a prose as
> scientifically as a modern musician studies harmony and counter-
> point, and, I need hardly say, with much keener aesthetic instinct.

Here as elsewhere Wilde's argument is conditioned by his belief that
content was the accession of a later stage of artistic evolution from
pristine beginnings in purely sensuous decoration. Accordingly, any
art could neglect its formal essence only at the cost of decline. The
characters in Renaissance drama speak a language distanced from
daily usage by a "resonant music and sweet rhythm," by "solemn
cadence," "fanciful rhyme," and elevated diction. In depressing
contrast, modern plays, in which the actors mimic in every detail the
vulgarity of common chatter, are downright wearisome; and, paradoxically, for the same reason they fail even to attain that vivid mimicry which is their sole raison d'être. For the resolution of this paradox Wilde calls once more on the Aristotelian principle as Vivian
paraphrases it in his dialogue with Cyril: "Man can believe the impossible, but man can never believe the improbable."[49]

For Wilde true decadence in art occurs only in the final stage
of its development, when "Life gets the upper hand and drives art
into the wilderness." He detected the roots of this baneful naturalistic process in Shakespeare's later plays, where it shows itself in
a more licentious blank verse, an increase of prose, and an undue
concern with verisimilitude, especially in characterization. In many
places he finds the language to be "uncouth, vulgar, exaggerated,
fantastic, obscene even," echoing the voice of "Life."[50]

As theory these observations are less than satisfactory. Wilde
never clarified what he meant by "beautiful style." What can be tentatively inferred from his references to it is not very reassuring. His
emphasis on the decorative suggests that his ideal excluded the category of plain speech, the studied simplicity of Lear's "Pray do not
mock me." The effectiveness of Wilde's campaign against the realist fallacy in verse style was limited by a crippling fastidiousness of
taste most accurately designated by the French term *préciosité*.

On a few basic points relating to poetic language Gerard Manley Hopkins and Wilde nearly agreed. Both held prose style to be something positive, having, as Hopkins put it, "its own technique, its proper rhetoric." Like Stevenson and many others of their time, they agreed that verse was nonetheless the higher form, one differing in kind, not just degree. Both were in essence dictional anti-naturalists, though they defined their positions on the issue differently. In the notebook draft of a remarkable student essay of 1865 entitled "Poetic Diction," Hopkins recorded his dissent from Wordsworth's assertion that the best parts of every good poem would prove to be no different from well written prose. He preferred the sounder majority persuasion that a vital link existed between good verse and current speech. In a letter to Robert Bridges, and again in the unpublished preface to a projected volume of his poems, he justified his use of what he called "sprung rhythm" by its closeness to the natural cadence of oral utterance. He ruled out stereotyped poetic expressions, inversions, the verbal auxiliaries *do* and *did*, and all archaism. "We do not speak that way," he told Bridges. But poetical language as Hopkins conceived it was no simulacrum of daily talk: it was, rather, "the current language heightened." His rejection of such poeticisms as *ere*, *well-nigh*, and *say not* was precisely that they neither belonged to "nor cd. ever arise from" the elevation of contemporary speech.[51]

In a taxonomy too subjective for reliable analytical use, Hopkins discerned three levels of the heightened style needed for poetry. The highest, unlabeled but assigned to "poetry proper," was the language of unalloyed inspiration, coming unbidden only to poets of the rarest genius. On the second level was "Parnassian," an idiom used by poets in less impassioned moments, when they spoke, not when they "sang." Lowest was "Delphic," merely the language of verse as distinct from prose, indulged by poets and poetasters alike. From the evidence of Hopkins's critical thought, anyone can safely conclude that these categories of poetic utterance represented degrees of expressive intensity, not of Wildean ornateness.[52]

In the more fundamental aspects of prosody these two near contemporary Victorian Oxonians were far apart. The relatively vague pan-aesthetic organicism constituting the theoretical ground of Wilde's taste and opinions is replaced in Hopkins by a more specific, empirically deduced concept of poetic structure that actually anticipates a cardinal tenet of twentieth-century structuralist theory. In the draft student essay, he starts from a loosely Coleridgean

set of distinctions between prose and verse, (including a convenient
distortion of STC's aphorism, making poetry the best *thoughts* in
the best words). Prosaic statements are distasteful in metrical
arrangement; meter, rhyme, and other features of verse both entail
and produce "a difference in diction and in thought"; and so forth.
But then, he concludes quite on his own, "what the character of
poetry is will be found best by looking at the structure of verse."[53]

What he discovered by doing so was that all the artificial features of metrical utterance have from the first rested on the principle of parallelism, a concept akin to Poe's sets of equivalences.
Hopkins notes that its manifestations range historically from the
technical parallelisms of Hebrew poetry and the antiphons of
church music to the structural intricacies of both ancient Greek
and modern prosody, foreign and English. He identifies two kinds
of parallelism, one of clearly marked oppositions, the other transitional or "chromatic" (in the musical sense). The lacunae of his
notebook jottings make it impossible to tell whether his second
kind of parallelism is limited to metrical poetry. But the first, op-
positional, does characterize verse structure only, governing virtually every technical feature: recurrences of syllabic and rhythmic
sequences, meter, alliteration, assonance, and rhyme. It operates
with equal effect where likeness is sought, as in metaphor and simile, or unlikeness, as in antithesis. In either case, the parallels of expression induce a parallelism of meaning. Once this principle is
grasped, Hopkins confidently declared, it becomes possible "to
see and account for the peculiarities of poetic diction."[54]

The version of his principle that won enthusiastic commendation from Roman Jakobson occurs in another notebook entry on
the question. "Is all verse poetry or all poetry verse?" Hopkins followed others seeking the answer by distinguishing the two terms.
All poetry is speech calculated to be aurally contemplated "for its
own sake even over and above its interest as meaning," meaning
itself being essential only to support the contemplated "shape"—a
recipe precariously close to severing form from content. But verse
has the additional requirement of being, in the phrase quoted by
Jakobson as crucial, "speech wholly or partially repeating the same
figure of sound." Regrettably, the finality of this arresting formula
is somewhat weakened when Hopkins is forced to admit, like
many other investigators, that all verse is not poetry. He too instances the inevitable mnemonic jingle "Thirty days hath September" cited by Coleridge and Jakobson.[55]

"Accordingly," as he put it in his student essay,

we may modify what Wordsworth says. An emphasis of structure stronger than the common construction of sentences gives asks for [*sic*] an emphasis of expression stronger than that of common speech or writing, and that for an emphasis of thought stronger than that of common thought. And it is commonly supposed that poetry has tasked the highest powers of man's mind. . . . The diction of poetry could not then be the same with that of prose, and again of prose we can see from the other side that its diction ought not to be that of poetry.

As Hopkins sees it, Wordsworth's assertion of parity between the two modes of discourse, taken literally, puts us at a loss to explain why (for one telling example) the sounded final syllable of past participles pleases readers in verse but has the reverse effect in prose. His well chosen illustration comes from Shakespeare's Sonnet 52:

So am I as the rich whose blessèd key
Can bring him to his sweet up-lockèd treasure.

The structure of verse, he explains, makes readers distinctly aware of every syllable of a line. In prose, where the syllables have little or no determinate value, the disproportion between their tenuity and such studied focus of attention would be simply bathetic.[56]

Clearly, his teacher Pater's efforts to blur the difference between verse and aesthetically admirable prose failed to impress the young Hopkins. In another student essay, perhaps written for Pater, "On the Origin of Beauty: A Platonic Dialogue," preserved as a notebook entry for May 1865, the leading speaker concludes that meter is useless "if you are only to say the same thing as you might say without it." Hopkins thus early aligned himself with those who side with Coleridge in regarding verse and prose as mutually exclusive modes of expression.[57]

CHAPTER TWELVE

The Early
Twentieth
Century

A CHRONOLOGICAL AC-
count of twentieth-century English poetics is conveniently divisible
into two phases. The earlier, treated in this chapter, covers roughly
the three decades of work by writers virtually untouched by the
challenges to habitual assumptions mounted by Pound, Yeats, and
Eliot which constitute the second phase. The two phases overlap in
time. While these men and their rebellious allies had begun their attack on the post-Romantic poetic establishment before the out-
break of World War I, some of those who espoused the more familiar notions were still vocal for several years after the Armistice.

Viewed from some historical distance, these two phases, otherwise so divergent in motive and program, agree in one respect.
Both focus on poetic language. By 1900, the traditional cultural
bearings of literature, its moral, intellectual, and recreational functions, were more than ever appropriated to the novel and prose
drama. To what extent the preoccupation with the poetic medium
(still prevalent today) was a symptom of creative crisis will be considered below. Suffice it here to say that the very definition of poetry, derived mainly from lyrical verse, was now framed almost exclusively in verbal terms. In both phases most writers agreed with
T. E. Hulme's view that a poetic work was quite simply "a mosaic
of words."[1]

Not since the Renaissance had serious students of poetry been
so engrossed with its language. An example may epitomize the

change of emphasis. Both Pope in 1715 and A. C. Bradley in 1901 called attention to the aural attractiveness of a line of epic verse. In one from the *Iliad* describing the effect of Agamemnon's harsh rejection of Chryses' plea for his daughter's release, Pope noted how the poignancy of the situation was enhanced by the "melancholy flowing of the Verse." At much greater length Bradley probed the union of sound and sense in the verse from the *Aeneid* (VI, 314) depicting the souls in Hades pleading to be ferried across the river Acheron: "Tendebantque manus ripae ulterioris amore." For Pope, Homer's line merely illustrates one of the graces of poetry, whereas for Bradley Virgil's line epitomizes the art itself, in its distinctive essence.[2]

Within their common stylistic concern the differences between the two phases have for some time now been regarded as marking an epoch. The second phase is the critical accompaniment of the revolution in verse style which Pound and Eliot inaugurated as practitioners and advocates. Iconoclastic in aim and polemical in tone, their earliest critical writing was like Wordsworth's Prefaces: primarily designed not so much to define poetry in general as to inculcate a taste for the kind they themselves felt impelled to write. As Eliot later confessed, the essays which first established his critical repute were largely by-products of his poetic workshop.[3]

Yet in its total fulfillment their campaign was more complicated and far-reaching, especially in the case of Eliot. Despite their irreverent tone, his chief pronouncements are mainly what he professed them to be, reformulations of traditional principles in terms calculated to discredit a poetic taste that had for too long been nourished on a moribund and aberrant Romanticism. The paradox that several readers have pointed out is that Eliot's poetry and poetics alike belie his claim to being a classicist in literature, which they took as a mere slogan of subversive intent. The style of his verse, especially that written before *Murder in the Cathedral,* is far more consonant with Romantic ideals of poetic expression than it is of anything that can be called classical. And the main tenets of his criticism are either rooted in or are rediscoveries of cardinal Romantic principles, especially those propounded by Coleridge on poetic diction. And much the same may be said of his fellow poets and critics.[4]

A further development sets off the second phase of modern poetic speculation from the first: its elaboration into a theory. Drawing mainly on the ideas expressed by Eliot and Pound, and on those more systematically set forth in I. A. Richards's *Principles of Literary Criticism* (1924), *Practical Criticism* (1929), and *Coleridge on Imagination* (1934), and in William Empson's *Seven Types of Ambiguity* (1930), a loosely associated group of critics, mainly American, produced what has ever since been known as the New Criticism. Ultimately Coleridgean in inspiration, the notions about poetry propagated by this group also derived from their independent reading of English verse, especially that of the Metaphysical poets and modern Anglo-American work. The poets among them, chiefly Robert Penn Warren, Allen Tate, and John Crowe Ransom, early attracted academic adherents. The textbook *Understanding Poetry* (1938) by Cleanth Brooks and the poet-novelist Warren took the lead in establishing explicative close reading as the major method of the school. Prominent among their academic associates were René Wellek and Austin Warren, whose *Theory of Literature* (1949) was couched in terms congenial to the New Critical assumptions. The several books by the brilliant scholar-critic W. K. Wimsatt further enriched the New Criticism.

Investigating poetic style, modern critics retained what Doležel has labeled the "contrastive framework," that is, the time-honored strategy of isolating those features of poetic use of language which set it apart from all other uses, whether of common speech or discursive writing. This is the method employed with patient iteration in Saintsbury's volumes on prose style and rhythm, in which he labors to fix the elusive boundary between the regular measures of verse and a prose cadence which constitutes "the harmony of perfectly modulated speech, not of song." To his sense, prose and verse are both scannable, but only on the totally opposed principles of "difference, inequality, and variety" in the one, and "sameness, equivalence, and recurrence" in the other. Critics continued to resort to some version of the old metaphor of prose as "something said" versus poetry as "something sung," as Symons put it. The antithetical concept survives even several protests against its harmful effects on poetic composition. When Symons objected to the effort of some poets to craft a style which should be as far as possible from that of prose or conversation, it was with the reservation that good verse must nonetheless be "dignified speech," not, as too often in Browning, the vulgar idiom of speakers who do not reverence words. The splendid poetry which Shakespeare put into the mouth of Othello is not the words any husband might vent in the throes of marital suspicion. The defining contrast received widely divergent formulation. In 1904 a contributor to *PMLA* reduced Mill's analogy of hearing and overhearing to a rigid formula justifying a clear separation of metered and non-metered composition. Verse is "communication in language for expression's sake, prose is expression in language for communication's sake." A few years earlier, in his *Interpretations of Poetry and Religion* (1900), George Santayana had argued similarly that poetry is speech in which "the instrument counts as well as the meaning," and offered a fresh simile for the contrast. Pure prose and poetry he likened respectively to clear and stained glass. In 1902 Professor Mark Liddell travestied the contrastive method in a vacuous effort to reduce it to laws as "definite and formulable" as those governing economics and ethics. Nonpoetic discourse becomes poetry by adding Human Interest (HI) and Verse Form (VF) to thought. With the confident scientism of the time he supplied the appropriate formulas:

$$X + HI = \text{literature (X being thought)}$$
$$X + HI + VF = \text{poetry.}$$

Non-poetic verse, being without HI, is—sure enough!—"only a versified statement of fact."[5]

Even the docile critics of the first phase occasionally assailed perennial assumptions. Symons argued for a direct reversal of the received opinion that poetry should be ornate and prose plain. Prose he thought needed the "relief" of ornament, whereas poetry flourished in simplicity, "a mere breathing, in which individual words almost disappear into music." Aiming at syntax as well as imagery, he forbade poets even the least obtrusive inversions. In *Studies in Prose and Verse* he quotes a favorite passage from Yeats's *The Shadowy Waters* and challenges readers to find in it a word or cadence that would have been out of place in prose or conversation. Today we may wonder what Symons' notion of prose, or for that matter of simplicity, could have been. The exemplary passage ends

> . . . but love is made
> Imperishable fire under the boughs
> Of chrysoberyl and beryl and chrysolite
> And chrysoprase and ruby and sardonyx.

Surely the polysyndeton alone suffices, without the cascade of exotic gem names, to distance it from prose or talk. And elsewhere

Symons reports without disapproval Ernest Dowson's opinion that the ideal line of verse was Poe's "The viol, the violet, and the vine," the letter *v* being the most beautiful in the alphabet, one impossible to overuse in verse.[6]

As already noted, Symons insisted that both prose and verse, unlike common speech, were products of artifice. In his essay on William Morris's prose, he asserts that in neither form is there such a thing as a "natural" style, Swift's in prose being no more so than Ruskin's. To write so that one's words seem unpremeditated involves a process as artificial and as difficult "as to write picturesquely," a truth he might have learned from Pope among others. Though good composition of any sort, but especially verse, could never survive severance from current speech, Symons knew that the artist's dictional fidelity was less to the common linguistic usages than to the exactions of his message. This is entailed by the organicist aesthetic, which he formulates in terms of the incarnation analogy: true style is "not the dress, but the very flesh, of the informing thought." Symons' aestheticized taste, like Wilde's Paterian in origin and further enforced by the French *Symbolistes* he so much admired, inclined his judgment of poetic style to an excessive antinaturalism. By this norm he convicted Donne of the realist "heresy." Failing to sublimate his emotion in the alembic of Wordsworthian tranquil recollection, "that moment of crystallization in which direct emotion or sensation deviates exquisitely into art," Donne disfigured his poems with words which had had no time "to take colour from men's association of them with beauty."[7]

Symons's founding of effective literary expression in a balance of naturalness and contrivance has behind it centuries of theoretical authority. But certain particulars of his case for it are fairly open to question. Many contemporary critics would have rejected his norm of "beautiful" association in favor of Graves's criterion of currency in literate conversation or good prose. Symons's ban on inversions in verse is countered by their effective application ever since the earliest known poetic texts. There are inversions and inversions, some of them purely manneristic. But many more operate effectively in memorable lines of verse. Would Symons have "corrected," for instance, Wordsworth's "A Pagan suckled in a *creed outworn*"?

While Symons was venting his views, Robert Frost published in England his first book of poems, the best known of which opened with the striking inversion of "Something there is that doesn't love a wall." Syntax in general was for Frost all-important in endowing common words with poetic force. "In poetry and under emotion," he wrote to Sidney Cox, "every word used is 'moved' a little or much—moved from its old place, heightened, made new." He instances Keats's use of *alien* in "Ode to a Nightingale," noting however that its power is released only by placing it next to *corn*. This insight of Frost's deserves more critical recognition than it has received. Its consonance with Horace's advice in the *Ars poetica* (lines 46–48)—that poets write well whenever by skillful juxtaposition they endow a familiar old word with new life ("notum si callida verbum / Reddiderit iunctura novum")—has I think gone unnoticed, though Frost himself, who enjoyed Latin poetry, must have been aware of it.[8]

Regrettably, this trick of semantic enhancement tends to add its onus to that "burden of the past" by which gifted poets have often felt oppressed. When any poet does with a word what Keats did with *alien*, Frost concedes, that word is largely foreclosed for use by other poets. Eliot was later to make the same point, interestingly enough of another word from the same ode, *easeful* ("easeful death"). When his friend John Hayward suggested that he use it in place of another in a draft of "Little Gidding," Eliot objected. "'Easeful' will never be of any use until Keats's trademark has worn off." Frost too rejected his friends' advice to avail himself of the words that "everybody exclaims Poetry! at." Poets must take care not to write

> in a special language that has gradually separated from the spoken language by this 'making' process. His pleasure must always be to make his own words as he goes and never to depend for effect on words already made even if they be his own.[9]

Lascelles Abercrombie's essay *Poetry and Contemporary Speech* (1914), highly commended by Graves, reads in part like a more fully elaborated exposition of Frost's notion of "made" words. To some extent, Abercrombie wrote, all speech may benefit from skillful ordonnance. But in poetry this aspect of style is exploited to "an infinitely greater extent." To characterize the two orders of verbal power, he borrows from Arthur Ransome terms used in mechanics for two kinds of energy, *kinetic* (of motion) and *potential* (of position). In language the kinetic driving force is supplied by logic and grammar, the potential from the way the words are juxtaposed. Their mutual contact and interaction immediately release their latent capacity to "suggest beyond themselves." So "diction is felt to be poetic as it is charged with this potential."[10]

Abercrombie discredits all attempts to ground the essence of poetic diction in "the sensuous qualities of words as apart from their intellectual qualities." At this point he has recourse to a military metaphor. What structural linguists were later to call the poetic "message" is like an artillery shell. Its kinetic power, the projectile impulsion of logical discourse, propels the message to the target where its potential energy triggers the "poetic bang." Abercrombie joins most others in thinking oral speech, not written discourse, to be "the main reservoir of the poetic power of language." To all this little is added in his later *Theory of Poetry* (1924). Like Sapir and other linguists, Abercrombie believed that language itself has an inherent, presumably aesthetic, quality (vaguely styled "an indiscriminate magic") which both the prose artist and the poet can draw on. He insists that the phrase "magic of words," so often applied to poetic language, simply recognizes that poetry "manages to mean more than other language."[11]

In his *Poetic Diction,* Barfield also sought to define the issue in semantic terms, but by a very different method and in more thoroughgoing fashion. He assigns to poets the social burden of responsibility for the intellectual and psychological well-being of civilized humanity. That in itself was nothing new; the difference from past conceptions of it lies in Barfield's thesis that it is fulfilled entirely by the special nature of the poet's language. He demonstrates this by combining introspection with ideas of linguistic evolution and mythology to constitute a kind of neo-primitivism. From personal experience, Barfield found that the main benefit of reading poetry was an expansion of consciousness effected by imagery. The heterogeneous ideas melded in metaphor had been united in primitive speech because uncivilized people experienced them that way in direct perception, a feature of prerational, mythic thinking. This composite apprehension having been fragmented by the self-consciousness resulting from civilized sophistication, it is now "the language of poets, in so far as they create true metaphors, that must *restore* this unity conceptually." This part of his argument, as he admits, is a more systematic version, made possible by modern archaeology, of Shelley's metaphorical language marking "the before unapprehended relation of things." But Barfield differs from the less informed primitivists of earlier periods in his greater awareness that our conscious, rational grasp of the process Shelley envisaged is necessary for appreciating poetry as such. That awareness was necessarily denied to primitive man.[12]

Mythology, Barfield explained, is the "ghost" of "concrete meanings" once immediately perceived as realities. Poets strive to see them again—he does not fully explain how they accomplish this escape from sophistication—and to make others see them. And so a history of language written from a poet's viewpoint rather than a logician's would see in the "concrete vocabulary" of myth "the world's first poetic diction." Barfield thinks the "subtle music which is the very life" of the *Aeneid* was supplied by Virgil's own talent, not by Augustan Latin. In the much older *Iliad*, on the other hand, there is an additional vitality conferred by the Greek itself. Barfield points to the contrast between Homer's epithets and their pale equivalents in Virgil, between πτερόεις (winged) and Virgil's *celer* (swift), for example.[13]

Being gifted at recovering the rich pristine significance of words that have been eroded by the progress of logical thinking, the poet is called upon "to become the true creator, the maker of meaning itself." This is carried out not alone by metaphors, but as well by the mutual positioning of words. In this point Barfield's rationale seems to coincide with Frost's creatively intuited sense of words being "made" in that way. And as Barfield himself notes, it also restates Horace's doctrine of the *callida iunctura*: as a subtle weaver of verbal textures the poet does well to be alert to the revitalizing power of skillful juxtapositions.[14]

To Barfield, rational and intuitive ways of thinking collaborate in the work of poet and scientist alike, to the extent of their cerebrative capacities. To assign them to separate species of intellection, he thinks, leads straight to the "Crocean conception of art as meaningless emotion." Rational thought operating alone can only clear obscurities and enhance the precision of mensuration and enumeration; it cannot expand consciousness. Only poetic vision, by "pouring into language its creative intuitions, can preserve its living meaning, and prevent it from crystallizing into a kind of algebra."[15]

Yet he established no cognitive parity between poetry and prose. He sees no special virtue in meter, asserting, somewhat misleadingly, that very few writers have identified poetry with metrical form. Elsewhere, defining the terms *poetry, prose,* and *verse,* he is less dismissive of meter. Ignoring the feature of lineation (so vital to vers librists in distinguishing their work from prose), Barfield separates "poetic" prose from verse, by ascribing rhythm exclusively to the latter. This unusual position he justifies on the ground that the rhythmic repetitions in verse cadence are regular, or "cyclical," whereas those in good prose are irregular and accidental. Though in metrical compositions the elements of meaning, rhythm, and meter subsist together, verse, "of which the essence is rhythm," is normal to expression in which feeling predominates; prose, "of which the essence is meaning," is normal where "the thinking element" predominates. Since according to Barfield poetry may be written in either form, we are left with the disquieting conclusion that most of the world's most prized poetry, being metrical, is of comparatively thin intellectual quality. But then we have to allow that a few others have reached precisely that conclusion. A few years after Barfield wrote, A. E. Housman, for whom poetry partook more of the physical than of the intellectual, stated flatly: "Meaning is of the intellect, poetry is not."[16]

Though Barfield occasionally invokes Coleridge (on whose thought he was later to write a separate book), he completely leaves out of account the metrical theory propounded in the *Biographia*. He feels no need to deal with "the music of verse" even while admitting that that component may comprise "perhaps as much as half the *meaning* of modern lyric." And inversions are disparaged—despite his having noticed at the outset the semantic efficacy of Milton's "prophets old."[17]

Since the natural progress in languages is from the poetic to the prosaic, the defining phenomena of poetic diction, Barfield believes, "can be grouped under the heading of Archaism," inclusive of much more than obsolescent words. Meter itself is an archaism. So is the poets' preference for concrete over abstract words, their distaste for subordination and corresponding love of main clauses, their recourse to *thee* and *thou* in place of *you*, and so on, to the verb-ending *-eth*, and to such strong aorist tense forms as *clomb* and *drave*. Inversion too is simply grammatical archaism.[18]

Barfield's case for archaism as the essential of poetic utterance is seriously weakened by his assigning inversions to that category. It evades the sticky facts that (1) inversions occur not only in poetic prose but in oratory and, though more rarely, in discursive prose and even common talk ("Insolence I don't take from anybody"); but that (2) they are most frequent in verse. Does this latter fact possibly imply, as other analysts have argued, a beneficial interdependence of syntactic deviations and rhythmic regularity? On this Barfield is silent. He tries to distinguish genuine archaism from the kind of lexical *conservatism* which results from imitating old-fashioned poetic usage and thereby produces mere mannerism.[19] The one is a virtue and the other a vice, even though they may involve identical words. His attempt lacks conviction, in all likelihood because, as other investigators have seen, this paradox, like others that bedevil the subject, cannot—again—be resolved except by taking into account such formal features as meter, rhythm, and rhyme, all of them peripheral in Barfield's book.

Even when he does touch on matters of form and technique his argument seems feeble. Recognizing that in poetry word order is "*an integral part of meaning*" (Barfield's italics), he writes: "The test is, therefore, not simply whether the same words could have been used [in prose], but whether the same words could have been used in the same order." In so closely paraphrasing Coleridge it is strange that Barfield fails to refer to the crucial wording of this point in the *Biographia*. Readily granting a shared vocabulary between the two forms, Coleridge wrote: "The true question must be, whether there are not modes of expression, a *construction*, and an *order* of sentences, which are in their fit and natural place in a serious prose composition, but would be disproportionate and heterogeneous in metrical poetry; and vice versa." Marginalizing meter, Barfield diverges materially from Coleridge's perception of the issue.[20]

Barfield's book deserves better than the casual regard it has received from modern poeticians. Perhaps the best support for this judgment is provided by a confirmation of his governing argument in Ernst Cassirer's *Language and Myth*. "If language is to grow into a vehicle of thought, an expression of concepts and judgments," Cassirer wrote, it can only be by depriving it of the plenitude of immediate experience. But, he adds,

> there is one intellectual realm in which the word not only preserves its original creative power, but is ever renewing it; in which it undergoes a sort of palingenesis, at once a sensuous and a spiritual reincarnation. This regeneration is achieved as language becomes an avenue of artistic expression. Here it recovers the fullness of life; but it is no longer a life mythically bound and fettered, but an aesthetically liberated life.

An ideal, Cassirer thinks, best realized by great lyric poets like Hölderlin and Keats.[21]

Another symptom of modern interest in the verbal medium of poetry was a fellowship dissertation written by George Rylands, later published by the Hogarth Press as *Words and Poetry* (1928), with an introduction by Lytton Strachey. Lacking the systematic grounding of Barfield's book, Rylands's is a mere recital of fashionable truisms. With scant regard for the complexities involved, he adopts Symons's axiom that "the more intense the emotion, the more the poets will abhor ornament." But is this *always* true? Rylands's citations of Wordsworth's "Highland Reaper" and Keats's "Belle Dame" hardly support the contention. Arrayed against it are the countless instances in which powerful emotion can vent itself only in the most daring figuration. The soliloquy in which Macbeth ponders his intent to murder his king begins plainly enough: "Besides, this Duncan / Hath borne his faculties so meek. . . ." But then, appalled by what he aims to do, Macbeth pours out his horror at what will ensue in a parade of similes as ornate as they are powerful: virtues pleading "like angels trumpet-tongued," pity "like a naked new-born babe / Striding the blast," and so on. Equally undiscriminating is Rylands's praise of Shakespeare for having in his mature style "reduced" blank verse to the level of prose. Somewhat lamely, he admits that Cleopatra does indeed speak verse; but the audience hardly notices it, "her dialogue is so natural." One wonders how many people Rylands knew whose conversation reminded him of Cleopatra's. In fairness though, it should be borne in mind that he is not the only critic whose analytical vision has been dazzled by the brilliance of Shakespeare's mimetic genius. Johnson too, it is sobering to recall, had found the speech of Shakespeare's creatures to be "level with life." Rylands even revived the notion that the moon, nightingales, and roses were enduring poetic themes, such words as *moon, rose,* and the like having therefore been endowed with special symbolic appeal. "Poetic diction," he remarked, "is no more than . . . the language of the heart." Rylands's book exemplifies what impelled and justified the modernist revolution in verse practice and theory then well under way.[22]

Late in the first decade of this period the issue of free verse came for the first time into controversial prominence in Britain and America. Though the most concentrated debate was conducted by spokesmen of the radical second phase, more conservative writers also joined in, most often in protest. While Whitman is sometimes regarded as the father of free verse, the main impetus to its widespread adoption by modern Anglophone poets seems to have come from France as part of the *Symboliste* program. Though the abandonment of regular meter was not a central tenet of the *Symboliste* credo, Mallarmé himself having strongly opposed it until his last years, in introducing the movement to English readers Symons could accurately include among its innovations the

breaking of meter, "in order that words may fly, on subtler wings."
Among the earliest vers librists were Arthur Rimbaud, whose *Illuminations* (ca.1873) contains two unmetered poems; and Gustave
Kahn, editor of the review *La Vogue,* who in 1886 published the
two examples from *Illuminations* and shortly thereafter some
specimens of his own. In the judgment of some students of the
movement, however, these two must share credit as "inventors" of
the technique with Jules Laforgue, generally regarded as a more
effective and influential practitioner. Once allowance is made for
the differences between the accentual and non-accentual prosodies
of the two languages, vers libre and free verse are for all practical
purposes interchangeable terms, although rhyme is notably rarer
in English free verse than in its French counterpart.[23]

This virtual terminological equivalence does not hold for the
names (often used indifferently) of the two other forms which
have been adapted as suitable nonmetrical vehicles for poetic expression: *poetic prose* and *prose-poetry.* Though the borderline between them is fuzzy, and samples of each are often indistinguishable, the labels themselves properly applied do not designate the
same thing. Briefly put, poetic prose is *prose,* of the kind written by
Sir Thomas Browne, De Quincey, Ruskin, and Pater among the
best known; prose-poetry is *poetry,* intended as such, but without
meter or lineation, such as we have it in Baudelaire's *Petits poèmes
en prose,* most of the pieces in Rimbaud's *Illuminations,* Eliot's
"Hysteria," or Wilde's so-called prose poems. Unfortunately, confusion is hard to avoid when under this same heading are included
Fénelon's *Télémaque,* which today is taken to be mere prose romance, narrative fiction, and Poe's *Eureka,* a visionary rhapsody
with perhaps the better claim to the poetic status which Baudelaire
was willing to grant it. In any case, free verse—whatever some of
its detractors may say—is *verse* by virtue of lineated arrangement
alone, and its composers poets, even if one sometimes feels the
loss of meter to be too great a sacrifice for rhythmic "freedom."

In this first phase of twentieth-century poetic speculation,
opinions on these three irregular categories of poetic form vary
haphazardly, often unsupported by cohesive argument. Symons,
elated by the poetic prose in Pater's *Renaissance* and glad to call
one of his Imaginary Portraits "really a poem," denigrates De
Quincey's purple passages as "what is frankly called prose poetry, a
lucky bastard glorying in the illegitimacy of its origin." Frost, who
delighted in "all the unversified poetry" of the prose *Walden,*
nonetheless scorned free verse as a simple shirking of the poet's cre-

ative task. Saintsbury, though he identified poetry proper with metrical composition, recognized the legitimacy of a metrically irregular poetry without mentioning the term free verse itself. Robert Bridges accepted the technique but thought that poetry at its best required traditional meter as an important device among several a poet relies upon for mastering the refractory medium of language. His attempt to support this position by breaking up lines of *Paradise Lost* into segments of "free verse," *with no corresponding changes in wording or rhythm,* unfortunately begs the question by failing to distinguish good free verse from bad. John Middleton Murry, in the none too coherent chapter of *The Problem of Style* (1922) in which he tried to explain what separates poetry from prose, undercut his praise of the "superb and majestic" poetic prose of the King James Bible, Milton, and Sir Thomas Browne by complaining that it lacked the "absolute precision of statement" and "flexible, non-insistent rhythm" which belong to good prose.[24]

Whether the boundaries of poetry do or do not exceed those of lineated arrangement, metered or free, came no nearer decision than in the past. The question could hardly be dropped from discussion, because those who felt called upon to consider the nature of poetry—or rather to *re*consider it in the light of changing poetic tastes and fashions—could not long avoid it. The defenders of meter offered the more vigorous arguments, no doubt because its detractors understandably felt that they had only to point to the great volume of stylistically rich prose and to the prestige of those who, from Aristotle to Coleridge and beyond, had given it their blessing. Of course there were those on both sides of the question who, like Coleridge himself, posited a qualitative distinction between poetic prose or prose-poetry on the one hand, and metered poetry on the other. Amy Lowell declared that regular verse was based on "a rhythmic conception quite other than that of prose," whereas vers libre and prose differed only in degree. Yet as an ardent vers-librist she was far from conceding that the peculiar rhythmic type of traditional verse gave it any potential aesthetic superiority. But most writers who considered meter to be a substantive distinction have done so. Santayana, who followed Coleridge in espousing a quasi-Leibnitzian poetic structure in which each part of the organic totality was itself a whole, saw in meter, as a pervasive principle of order, "a condition of perfection." Even if the difference between verse and prose was only a matter of meter, Santayana thought, "that difference would already be analogous to that between jewels and clay."[25]

And of course there were a few, as in every literary age, who at different times (and perhaps prompted by the mood induced by their latest reading) argued on both sides. Though generally an untiring advocate of poetic prose who relished Mallarmé's "beautiful poems, in verse and in prose," Symons on separate occasions identified meter as the one essential difference between poetry and prose and declared that if Dr. Faustus's paeon to Helen of Troy in Marlowe's play were refashioned into even the most poetic prose the result would still not be poetry: "only verse form can make it so."[26]

In the first year of the century came what is perhaps the most enduringly valuable document in the case for meter, and an important forerunner in analytical method of the New Criticism, A. C. Bradley's Oxford Lecture "Poetry for Poetry's Sake"(1901). "We are to consider poetry in its essence," he announces at the outset, including in the idea of poetry metrical form, no "mere accident or . . . mere vehicle." His justification of these assumptions, a model of explicative technique applied to a line in the *Aeneid*, must be displayed in full.

> If I take the famous line which describes how the souls of the dead stood waiting by the river, imploring a passage from Charon: *Tendebantque manus ripae ulterioris amore:* and if I translate it 'and were stretching forth their hands in longing for the further bank,' the charm of the original has fled. Why has it fled? Partly . . . because I have substituted for five words, and those the words of Virgil, twelve words, and those my own. In some measure because I have turned into rhymeless prose a line of verse which, as mere sound, has unusual beauty. But much more because in doing so I have changed the *meaning* of Virgil's line. What that meaning is I cannot say; Virgil has said it. But I can see this much, that the translation conveys a far less vivid picture of the out-stretched hands and of their remaining outstretched, and a far less poignant sense of the distance of the shore and the longing of the souls. And it does so partly because this picture and this sense are conveyed not only by the obvious meaning of the words, but through the long-drawn sound of 'tendebantque,' through the time occupied by the five syllables and therefore by the idea of 'ulterioris,' and through the identity of the long sound 'or' in the penultimate syllables of 'ulterioris amore'—all this, and much more, apprehended not in this analytical fashion, not as *added* to the beauty of mere sound and to the

obvious meaning, but in unity with them and so as expressive of the poetic meaning of the whole.[27]

The superiority of Bradley's conception to most others of the time goes beyond providing for the holistic unity of content and form that constitutes the main virtue of organic theory. He shows that unity manifested on the linguistic level, where the sensuous elements of rhythm and sound fuse with the thought. In this way he avoids the fatal split of matter and form incurred not only by the old decorative conception of poetic diction but by pure formalism as well, especially by the variety entailed in the aesthetic hedonism propounded in Santayana's *The Sense of Beauty* (1896). Here and there in his writings Santayana seems to steer clear of that pitfall. For all his hedonism, he can speak in *Interpretations of Poetry and Religion* of poetry as "metrical and euphuistic discourse, expressing thought which is both sensuous and ideal," a phrasing inoffensive enough to the most uncompromising organicist. But when we find him in this same book proposing as a "tolerable definition of poetry on its formal side," speech in which medium and meaning have equal weight, that is, "speech for its own sake and for its own sweetness," we note the telltale crack in what appeared at first a seamless whole. In contrast, the central tenet of Bradley's theory, as of every truly organic theory of poetic expression, is that the very "sweetness" of diction in metered discourse arises much more from its part in conveying the complex of thought than from any putative aural euphony savored in isolation.[28]

Frost supplied plausible backing for his much-quoted aphorism that writing poetry without meter was like playing tennis without the net, even if his argument is in spots less than clear. In 1913 he told a correspondent that he had rejected the worn-out assumption that poetic music consists in harmonizing vowels and consonants à la Tennyson and Swinburne. In its place he had adopted from live speech the "sounds of sense," which, being "the abstract vitality of our speech," he calls pure form. These constitute the patternless cadence we perceive apart from the meaning of the words which comprise it whenever we overhear people talking at too great a distance to catch what they're saying. Genuine poetic cadence is attained by

> skillfully breaking the sounds of sense with all their irregularity of accent across the regular beat of the metre. Verse in which there

is nothing but the beat of the metre furnished by the accents of the polysyllabic words we call doggerel. Verse is not that. Neither is it the sound of sense alone. It is a resultant from those two.

Since the sound of sense presumably does not convey meaning but only indicates its presence, Frost's description of the process also risks the charge of splitting form and content. But he does join all those who have discerned in Coleridgean tension, the pull and counterpull of structural elements, a condition indispensable to the aesthetic value of metrical communication. Irregularity of speech accent and metrical regularity—Frost was never more pleased, as he told another correspondent, than when he could get these two conditions "into strained relations."[29]

A less known analogy in defense of traditional meter against free verse is George Moore's comparison of the two forms respectively to free steam, powerless, and confined steam, which like verse held "within the limits of ten-syllable lines richly rhymed" generates great power. This observation occurs in his *Anthology of Pure Poetry* (1924). In the theoretically superficial introduction consisting of a trialogue among Walter de la Mare, John Freeman, and Moore himself, pure poetry is uniquely exalted as the genuine article. It is defined simply and vaguely as "something that the poet creates outside his own personality." The implications of this definition, which gradually emerge during the colloquy, are that poetry at its best eschews not only all personal emotive expression and all moralizing, but all intellectual content of any sort. The only lasting poetry is a bare presentation of things, "poetry un-sicklied o'er with the pale cast of thought." Moore thus represents an extreme version of poetic expression more moderately es-poused by Housman. His position goes beyond the formalism of those like Santayana, who while prizing the sensuous qualities of words recognize that the main function of all language, whether prose or verse, is the communication of thought. Moore gladly embraced "art for art's sake," that much misconstrued slogan, here adapted to a poetic "vision" almost devoid of any intrusion of the personal, understood in the most inclusive sense.[30]

In its requirement of ideational vacuity, Moore's position is completely at variance with the notions of objective creativity pro-pounded a few years earlier in Eliot's impersonalist theory. Moore's *Anthology* draws heavily on the songs from Shakespeare's plays because "he never soiled them with thought"; Poe too is dis-proportionately represented because his poems are "almost free from thought"; from Tennyson's far more voluminous output Moore chose only "The Lady of Shalott," because after that the poet merely indulges in "moralities and mumbles them until he was eighty." Moore preferred to rest his case on the verses in his collection rather than on the introduction to it. Ironically, however, no attentive reader can reperuse those familiar lyrics without discovering the fallacy of the norm they are supposed to illustrate. However trivial or trite their thought content, not a one is devoid of meaning. However resistant to adequate paraphrase, they all "say" something, or "sing" it, though their manner of doing so may well weigh more heavily in a reader's consideration than what that something is, e.g., "Full fathom five thy father lies. . . ." Moore's garner of his favorite poems, for all their intellectual tenuity, reminds us in every line of the final nullity of all purist theory in its vain hope of discounting what one scholar aptly dubbed "the incorrigibly referential thrust" of the unique material of the poet's medium: words.[31]

Most critics of this period who bother to discuss poetry at all avoid theorizing about it. Even Saintsbury, who recognized the pertinence of the problem to his comprehensive historical survey of English prosody, disappoints readers of the erudite inquirer who, despite his avowed scorn for literary theory, was willing to devote his salary to furnishing his students with copies of *Biographia Literaria*! Coming in his account to Edmund Spenser, Saintsbury observed that the diction in the *Faerie Queene* had to be made "correlative" with the organic unity of the stanza the poet invented for his poem. To show Spenser's success, he promises to point out how it is suited to the peculiar features of that stanza, to "its prosodic quintessence." But what follows is only the claim that the separate stanzas do not militate against either narrative flow or unity, because the closing alexandrine of each provides the needed transition to the next—without so much as a further reference to diction.[32]

The first phase of twentieth-century Anglophone discussion might well be characterized as one of theoretical rumination. Except for the work of critics like Bradley, Barfield, and Abercrombie, the most satisfactory analyses—to repeat an earlier point—do little more than restate the main principles by which Romantic organicism had sought to amend the deficiencies of neoclassical doctrine. Robert Bridges, for example, rejected the comparison of poetic euphony to musical melody or colors, (e.g., vowels correspond to primary colors), asserting instead, as if it had never been said before, that a "fusion of sound and sense is the magic of the greatest poetry." Granted, such reaffirmations of earlier ideas could be timely. Frank Kermode, observing that all Anglo-American critics since Pater "seem on analysis to be saying the same thing," nonetheless judged Symons's reformulations to be "crucial for the historian." Occasionally, established ideas were graphically encapsulated in one or another arresting figure. These did not always advance argument or clarify conception. F. N. Scott's likening of verse to a cat's purring and prose to its cries is no improvement on Mill's distinction of heard and overheard utterance. Stephen Vincent Benét did better when he considered the "curiously magical effect" of certain words, sounds, and images combined in verse. Although Benét offered no solution of the familiar mystery, his way of asking the question by borrowing a metaphor from Browning's "Abt Vogler" neatly signals the futility of all attempts to do so in the terms used for explaining ordinary verbal communication. "How is poetry written? How 'out of five sounds' does the poet make 'not a sixth sound but a star'?"[33]

CHAPTER THIRTEEN

Aspects of Modernism

THE TWENTIETH-CENTURY change in poetic style was not entirely the work of T. E. Hulme, Pound, Eliot, Wyndham Lewis and a few other rebels. There were also the Georgian poets. As recent specialists have pointed out, the verse of Abercrombie, Rupert Brooke, Gordon Bottomley, W. H. Davies, Walter de la Mare, Wilfred Blunt, and other contributors to the first two volumes of Edward Marsh's *Georgian Poetry* (1912,1915) differed noticeably from what most readers were used to. Nor should we forget that Frost's first two volumes of poems, *A Boy's Will* and *North of Boston*, were published in England in 1910 and 1912, both of them equally departures from the familiar poetic idiom.

In point of style the English Georgians actually made common cause with the Imagists and even with aspects of Hulme's denunciations of the mushy verbiage of decayed Romanticism. "Both Georgian and Imagist," Myron Simon writes, "recoiled from Victorian decorum and solemnity, from turgid and ornate diction, and from enervated sensualism." Both rejected moralizing, and though the Georgians were unaffected by Hulme's preachments (if they had even heard of them), some shared his ideal of "hard, dry" diction, a diction precise, clear, objective, and sparing of abstractions. There was also Yeats's renovation of his early syntax and vocabulary, a "stylistic purgation," in Ellmann's phrase, first apparent in *The Wind among the Reeds* (1899), and thus a decade in advance of the calls for a similar reformation made by Ford Madox Ford, Hulme, and Pound. Yeats's grateful (if sometimes reluctant) submission to Pound's more ruthless further excision of abstractions from his friend's verse was the response of a poet who had already begun the surgical process on his own.[1]

However, the Georgians contributed little in the way of innovative theory, and Yeats's sometimes suggestive observations were largely the random opinions of a mind averse to systematic analysis. As he confessed to Dorothy Wellesley in his old age, "I am unable to define poetry but only to recognize it." Though not all Georgian poets shared Yeats's incapacity, they felt that the needed resuscitation of English poetry would result from the example of their creative performance unsupported by theory. It remains doubtful, however, that the quality of their work could have sufficed for the purpose. Eliot, surveying verse of Davies, Brooke, and other Georgians in a 1917 review of Harold Monro's *Strange Meetings* for the *Egoist,* put his finger on the main deficiency of Marsh's group as a major force for renewal. As one means of ridding their style of rhetorical bombast, moralizing, and abstract language, they had unfortunately concentrated on "trivial, or accidental, or commonplace objects." Their forays into theory, belonging as they did to the first phase of twentieth-century critical thought, were either reaffirmations, extensions, or illustrations of received opinion, not signposts pointing in new directions.[2]

Analysts of literary modernism have underrated the part played in its rise by the post-Victorians' creative distress. Like Dryden and Wordsworth, poets once again faced the impasse inevitably confronting aspirants whose first efforts coincide with the exhaustion of a long honored poetic mode. For reasons as various as the ascendancy of technological positivism and the prestige of artistic prose, this recurrent crisis beset modern poets with unprecedented urgency ("for us," ran Eliot's mot, "anything that can be said as well in prose can be said better in prose"). Poets had besides to contend as never before with the most enervating symptom of the "burden of the past," a persistent tendency to fall into poeticisms whenever they tried to give compelling voice to ideas and affective states prompting them to composition. We recall Coleridge's lament at having finally abandoned poetry because of the fatal ease—"so very difficult, because so very easy"—with which his poetic conceptions took shape in outworn phraseology. Or we think of Keats's struggle, writing *Hyperion,* to exorcize the strains of Milton. But now this creative malady was virtually epidemic among the truly gifted, poets of mediocre talent being rarely discomfited by it.[3]

Recalling in 1937 his first attempts at verse, Yeats reported taking six days to complete six lines because his resolve to use "natural" words and syntax was constantly impeded by an "imagination still full of poetic diction." Pound's famous letter to Harriet Monroe of 1915, containing the aphorism that poetry must be as well written as prose, echoed Coleridge: under the intoxication of metrical composition one fell "into the easy—oh, how easy—speech of books and poems one has read." Pound fully shared with Eliot a conviction of the fecundating power of tradition in the creation of genuinely original verse. Yet ticking off the main architects of that tradition as it stood in the England of 1918, from Chaucer down to Browning and Swinburne, only induced despair. "How the devil a poet writing in English manages to find or make a language for poems is really a mystery."[4]

The chief founders of modernism—each in his own way and after his own literary experience—confirmed the partial truth of Emerson's aphorism that poetry is made only out of poetry. Every work of art is generated out of previous works, Yeats wrote in 1913, a conviction that in one or another aspect remained with him. Near the end of his career he reported in a B.B.C. broadcast talk that his long search for a personal style had convinced him to stick to the metrical forms of the English tradition. "Talk to me of originality and I will turn on you with rage." Yet, as he had known from the outset, originality of some order, or at least change, was a necessity if the tradition was to be kept viable. Modern poets should study the old ballads, he counseled Katherine Tynan in 1888, but only in order to discover "new methods of expressing ourselves."[5]

For new poets seeking an authentic "voice," tradition means first and foremost the various lexical, syntactical, and metrical resources by which successive generations of poets have *energized* (Pound's word for it) the common parlance of their day into an aesthetic medium. But tradition contained no recipe for *how* to do this. Clearly it could not be done by a simple aping of daily speech. Yet what made the difference between such feckless mimicry and the accents of vibrant verse could be fiendishly elusive. Thus Pound's vexation. Eliot too confessed how hard it was to detect, let alone define, the "infinitesimal touch," the "slight transformation," which without diminishing the simplicity of something anyone might say turns it into great verse by effecting "always the

maximal, never the minimal, alteration of ordinary language."
Though Eliot and Pound never tired of insisting that an indispensable condition of personal poetic mastery was patient study of how
this crucial transformation had been accomplished in the past,
they knew the risk and price of the saturation. Only after years of
struggle to rid himself of "Shelley's Italian light" did Yeats attain
his own idiom.[6]

Eliot found the English exemplars too remote and intimidat-
ing for his use, and usually irrelevant to the profoundly altered
conditions of the creative task. Pound warned against the baneful
allure of their language, every bookish word eroding a reader's
"sense of your artistic sincerity." In 1853, Arnold could turn to
the austerity of Sophoclean dramatic verse as an antidote against
being "vanquished and absorbed" by Shakespeare's verve. In the
more straitened creative environment of a half-century later,
Pound and Eliot could find suitable guidance only by abandoning
the all too contagious English models for writers outside the
mainstream of Western tradition. While both men found Dante
congenial to their needs, Pound drew his immediate stylistic aliment from a mixture of Provençal Arnaut Daniel (Dante's "mig-
lior fabbro"), Italian Guido Cavalcanti, the prose of a few select
novelists headed by Flaubert, and Chinese ideogram; from English verse he chose only Browning's unpopular *Sordello*. Eliot's
main recourse, the *vers de société* of Jules Laforgue, was a more
immediately effective catalyst to his own creativity than anything
available to Pound. This is readily apparent when we compare the
French poet's tone and style to those of the poems in *Prufrock
and Other Observations* (1917). To Laforgue Eliot gave credit for
having taught him "the poetic possibilities of my own idiom of
speech."[7]

A striking result of the post-Victorian impasse is that the Romantic faith in inspiration, in which the Horation *provisam rem*
was taken to mean the wondrously impromptu effusions of born
geniuses, was replaced by avowals of the strenuous brainwork
necessary for successful composition. This effort was exerted not
only in the finishing touches of Horace's delicate file ("limae
labor"), but in hard pick-and-shovel work from beginning to
end: like an old pauper breaking stones, as Yeats pictured it in
"Adam's Curse." Pound's prose is studded with similar admonitions to this end, directed to young poets of his acquaintance.
Even the mere avoidance of banality and cliché, he warned, required an unremitting focus of sustained attention till the work

was done, whether the resulting poem was of two lines or two hundred. Eliot agreed, citing as symptomatic of the time Hulme's complaint of how extraordinarily difficult it had become to cut through the barrier of "conventions and communal ideas" inherent in the poet's socially produced medium. Although inspiration remained indispensable, Eliot found a poet's creative experience to be mainly an intellectual, critical effort, a "frightful toil" of "sifting, combining, constructing, expunging, correcting, testing."[8]

The figment of the gifted poet as passive recipient of the muse's unearned endowment had always aroused skepticism. That uneasiness was now superseded by the conviction that the revitalization of modern poetry depended on the poets' taking pains to toughen their cadence and diction with the thews and tendons of live speech. "I believe more strongly every day," Yeats wrote to John Quinn in 1905, "that the element of strength in poetic language is common idiom, just as the element of strength in poetic construction is common passion." But confirmations of this age-old item of compositional wisdom were matched by professions of how hard it had become to honor.[9]

In forging prosodic techniques adequate to the task facing them, English poets were open to hints from the *Symboliste* movement and its immediate aftermath. But their debt to France was minimal, hardly going beyond Laforgue's role in Eliot's early stylistic development. Pound did concede in a 1928 letter in French to René Taupin that his concept of the image owed "quelque chose" to the *Symbolistes,* but only as transmitted to him through conversations with Hulme and from what Yeats had learned from Symons about Mallarmé. He denied ever having read the *Symbolistes* themselves on the subject.[10]

Yeats himself developed a symbolist style quite independently of the French example, one he had mainly propounded around the turn of the century in "The Philosophy of Shelley's Poetry" (1900), "William Blake and His Illustrations to the *Divine Comedy* (1897), "The Symbolism of Poetry" (1900), and "Edmund Spenser" (1902). From these essays we learn that while both images and symbols spring from mysterious, magical sources, symbols—reaching the poet in dream, revery, or trance—are transpersonal and timeless, and as such they are unique expressions of "some invisible essence." What more specifically Yeats meant by "symbolic writing" he found in two lines from Burns's song "Oh, Open the Door, Some Pity to Show":

> The wan moon is setting behind the white wave,
>
> And time is setting with me, Oh!

The sequence of moon, wave, whiteness, setting time, and the final cry of despair release an emotion inaccessible by any other combination of "colours, sounds, and forms." Despite his mention of sounds, Yeats explicitly rejected the *Symbolistes'* assimilation of poetry and music, as Ellmann reminds us. His views do coincide with *Symboliste* doctrine in making the symbol necessary to poetry's lofty function of conveying "some mystery of disembodied life." But this similarity only points to a shared debt to Poe, whom the *Symbolistes* revered, whose criticism Yeats admired, and whose conception of the poet's vision as "an ecstatic prescience of the glories beyond the grave" (in the phrase Yeats recalled from "The Poetic Principle") encouraged his own belief in mystical experience as creative nutrition. There is no reason to question his statement in 1915 that he had never had detailed or accurate knowledge of the *Symbolistes'* work.[11]

The English modernists' respect for the *Symbolistes'* significant advance beyond the restricted mimetic ambience and metrical regularity of the French Parnassians had little impact on their own critical thinking. In his meticulous and largely sympathetic "A Study in French Poetics," Pound could praise Remy de Gourmont's poem "Litanies de la Rose" for embodying the *Symboliste* doctrine that poetry should "suggest," not "present."[12] But in fact *Symboliste* suggestiveness was the very negation of what he thought verse should be and do. He deplored the lack of immediacy in most metrical representation, and demanded direct *presentation* instead of vague description. Nor is it easy to imagine anything more at odds with the Hulme-Pound call for *hardness* and *dryness* in verse language than the nuanced "indefiniteness" which was another bequest in the *Symbolistes'* legacy from Poe. Although Pound's central stress on adapting to verse Flaubert's discipline of the *mot juste* is not of itself incompatible with the *Symbolistes'* preference for suggestion over assertion, a reliance on verbal *justesse* is hard to reconcile with their persuasion that the inadequacy of language as an artistic medium was inherent in the designative imprecision of most words.

Like earlier partisans of meter, Pound and Eliot were convinced that psychic life comprises more than the part communicable by the syntactical structures governing prose. But they and other modernist poets also knew how often their efforts to express exact shades of meaning were defeated by the relative scarcity of *mots justes* in what Hulme decried as "the large clumsy instrument" of language. But he was confident that the clumsiness might nonetheless be overcome in verse by an imaginative inventiveness *facilitated by abandoning the restrictions of regular meter and syntax alike.*[13] To some writers—by no means all—this process produced a kind of symbolization of poetic utterance.

As a term in general aesthetics and poetics (not in linguistics, where it is often a synonym for *sign*), *symbol* is derived from one of the several senses of the Greek *symbolon:* a mark or token implying a thing. Unlike ordinary words, symbols are not mere mediate pointers to entities materially disjunct from themselves. When in the greatest poetry—Attic or Shakespearean drama—words attain symbolic status, Eliot noted, they become a "shorthand" for the whole play, or (we might say) emotion-charged surrogates of the personated "action." Put another way, as Coleridge did in distinguishing the term from *allegory, symbol* "always partakes of the Reality which it renders intelligible; and while it enunciates the whole, abides as a living part in that Unity, of which it is the representative."[14]

A cardinal tenet of the program for revitalizing poetry propounded by Hulme, Pound, Eliot, and their allies urged poets so to dispose common words in verse that their *combination,* though not the words taken separately, functioned symbolically, thereby assuring presentative immediacy. In their poetic practice the *Symbolistes,* for all the obscurity of Rimbaud's "Batteau ivre," Mallarmé's "Après-midi d'un faune," or Valéry's "Cimetière marin," may seem to have adopted a similar procedure. Far from it. Mallarmé's distinction, as Wellek judged it from his richly informed historical perspective, lay in having been "the first poet radically discontent with the ordinary language of communication" who strove to construct as substitute "an entirely separate" poetic language.[15]

Passages in Mallarmé's *Divagations* (1896) lament the frequent failure of individual words to convey simply by their sonority a sensuous surrogate of reality, especially of that supra-mundane and timeless reality that he considered it to be poetry's unique and privileged office to reveal. While the sound of the word *ombre* (shade or darkness) does suggest the opacity of what it designates, he wrote, the aural quality of *ténèbres* is totally inadequate to do so ("à coté d'*ombre,* opaque, *ténèbres* se fonce peu"). The sounds of *jour* (day) and *nuit* (night) run counter to their meanings. Yet from other passages in Mallarmé's book it is apparent that the *Symboliste* strategy for avoiding the deficiency of a verbal medium is to exalt it to a separate realm of autonomous functioning. *Symboliste* poets of Mallarmé's persuasion (they did not all agree in their poetic creeds) aimed ideally at a poetry uncontaminated by discursive logic and devoid of the "rhetoric" of moral suasion and oratorical persuasion. Among English readers, "Take rhetoric and wring its neck" is the best known line of Verlaine's versified "Art poétique." But this purity, Mallarmé argued, entails the "elocutionary disappearance" of the poet, who *yields the initiative to the words themselves*. Verse, which out of several speech sounds forms a new "word," integral, unknown to "language," and, as it were, incantatory, perfects the isolation of the spoken word ("un mot total, neuf, étranger à la langue et comme incantatoire, achève cet isolement de la parole"). And thus at a single stroke, he adds, is abolished the element of chance that is inherent in words despite our best efforts to eliminate it; and thus too some common scrap of elocution is infused with novelty, and the object it designates is bathed in a new atmosphere.[16]

The chief affinity between post-Baudelaire French and modern Anglophone poets is a common Romantic heritage, despite the often strident attacks of the latter on Romanticism and all its works. "Prufrock" and *The Waste Land, Mauberley* and the *Cantos,* no less than the poems of Yeats's final phase, are in their markedly individualized techniques and their modes of predominantly ironic, introspective meditation so many further manifestations of the Romantic *Weltanschauung.* Comparing this with the early modernist attacks on Romanticism by Hulme, Pound, and Eliot prompted some commentators, with Eliot mostly in mind, to complain of a fundamental contradiction between an allegedly anti-Romantic poetics and an ultra-Romantic (even Bolshevist!) poetry. But what Eliot and the rest chiefly deplored in Romanticism was a liberal optimism founded on innate human goodness and a corresponding automatic social amelioration. That aside, their criticism may be called Romantic with even less reservation than their poetry. The reformulations of what are essentially Romantic principles throughout Pound's and Eliot's writings amply support C. K. Stead's conclusion that the modernist poetic is "potential within the poetic theory developed by the Romantic movement."[17]

Yet even Yeats's Romantic predilection, a matter of temperament and youthful inculcation, was restrained by correctives. Early on at the Rhymers' Club he learned to value as prosodic models the poets of the *Greek Anthology* and, with Symons' encouragement, Catullus. Late in life he regretted that his scanty knowledge of Greek had prevented him from realizing a long-cherished wish to emulate Homer and "those that fed at his table." But these attractions no more tempted him to embrace Hulme's nostalgia for classical standards in art and life than Pound's and Eliot's admiration for Homer, Virgil, or Propertius could alone have triggered their gibes at the persistence of a Victorianized Romanticism in poetic taste. Still less did what these three men found valuable in the Ancients prevent their affirming, in their several ways, the dynamic organicism first propounded in English by Coleridge as the governing characteristic of poetic expression.[18]

Since the Renaissance, writers had felt no *fundamental* divergence between the ancient literary achievement and the ideals informing the taste of their day. Though well aware of historic shifts of poetic fashion, and of the gap between perfunctory versifying and the genuine article, they saw in the best contemporary work no basic departure from what good poetry had always been. A change came when Arnold commended Homer and Sophocles as antidotes against tendencies in nineteenth-century poetry he considered detrimental. In the modernist appeal to classical poetry, and to Chaucer, Dante, Villon, and other pre-Romantics, Arnold's strategy is renewed with a focus on language and versification so much more concentrated than his that it occasioned a total reappraisal of the aesthetic function of language.

Pound and Eliot differed considerably in the objects of their "classical" appreciations. The *Aeneid,* which for Eliot embodied quintessential Western classicism, Pound scorned as a "Tennysonized version of Homer." He never shrank from brashly applying to the most revered classics the same merciless standards by which he excoriated the Victorians. Greek tragedy he found cloyingly sententious, and Pindar a "damned rhetorician half the time." But, wherever directed, their praise for what they valued in classical literature was neither perfunctory nor expedient: "3000 years old and still *fresh,*" Pound exclaims of Homer's epics. There is nothing incompatible between these opinions and a validation of Coleridgean poetics. Nor was that poetics at all impugned in Eliot's adverse judgment that the Romantic attitude toward life and letters was fragmentary, immature, and disorderly—a verdict pronounced in whole or part by Goethe, Sainte-Beuve, and Arnold. Much like them, Eliot used *classical* to label both his literary stance and artistic superiority in general. In this inclusive sense, and with no theoretical inconsistency, he could write that Chapman was potentially a greater artist than John Webster, Cyril Tourneur, and Thomas Middleton because his mind was "the most classical," and that Shakespeare's blank verse surpasses Marlowe's by an "almost classical" concision.[19]

The Coleridgean stress on a dynamic poetic structure is reaffirmed in Pound's generalization that the "spirit of all arts is dynamic . . . not passive, not static." Yeats's personal discovery of this principle explains as much as anything else the superiority of his mature work to that written by the poets of the nineties from whom he took his first inspiration. Except for Keats's comparison of poetry to a street brawl, one can hardly find in criticism a more graphic depiction of aesthetic dynamism than how Yeats put it to convince the Abbey Theatre players that verse passion consisted in conflict: "the speakers . . . holding down violence as madness— 'down hysterica passio.'" The source of his own poetry in personal rage or lust, as he told Dorothy Wellesley, was only another form of this same psychic turbulence.[20]

Hulme's points of agreement with Coleridgean organicism, in contrast to those of Yeats, Pound, Eliot, or anyone else, are problematic. Given his sweeping indictment of Romanticism as a pernicious *Weltanschauung* that had vitiated modern European culture, his endorsement of Coleridge's ideal of vital form comes as a surprise, even supposing that Hulme had been made receptive to it by Bergson's instruction. He apparently failed to notice that the otherwise exhausted Romantic dispensation persisted not only in the vague mental attitude he deplored in "Romanticism and Classicism," but as well, and with undiminished vigor, in its distinctive conception of a literary work, one he imperfectly professed himself. There is no necessary incompatibility between his preference for a poetic language that is *hard* and *dry,* and Coleridge's vital structure. Hulme parried in advance any charge of inconsistency in that regard by declaring that Coleridge's term "vital" was itself "dry" and "definite," a term well applied to a unity more complex than a mere aggregate of parts, because in it each constituent partakes of the totality it helps to comprise.[21]

Like Pound and other Imagists, Hulme thought of poetry as essentially visual, pictorial—this in utter contrast to Coleridge's protest against the "tyranny of the eye" so prevalent in neoclassical criticism. But there is nothing classical in Hulme's call to replace Romantic "vagueness" with a verse that is "accurate, precise, and definite," a recipe closer to Pater than to Horace. Paterian too is his stress on artistic sincerity, of which, for Hulme as for Pater, the sole gauge is a poet's success in communicating the *uniqueness* of his experience. As Hulme described it, a "terrific struggle" is needed to extract "the exact curve you want" from a linguistic medium "common to you, me, and everybody." The excellence resulting when some poet does manage it, he adds, has nothing to do with the emotions. On this point Hulme departs from Pater, is in total opposition to Eliot, and could have appealed for support ironically enough only to a predecessor whose talk of the poet's commerce with the "supernal" he would have ridiculed as arch-Romantic—Poe![22]

Hulme was induced to champion free verse more by the ideal of individualized precision than by an unfocused itch to shake off the "shackles" of meter. The point is underlined in his apt likening of free verse to made-to-order clothes as against the ready-made garb of measured lines. Hulme's most significant departure from Pater in theory was his sharp separation of prose from poetry. Like much else in his critical writing, his homely version of the contrastive method is ill-suited to accommodate the subtleties of the issue. Visual "meanings," as he has it, reach us only in "the new bowl of metaphor," prose being a leaky old pot that won't hold them. Surely Pater would have had many allies in objecting to so question-begging a dismissal of the vast territory of poetic prose lying between the highlands of verse and the plains of unadorned exposition. In prose, Hulme argued,

> as in algebra concrete things are embodied in signs or counters which are moved about according to rules, without being at all visualized in the process. . . . Poetry, in one aspect at any rate. . . . is a compromise for a language of intuition which would hand over sensations bodily. It always endeavours to arrest you, and to make you see a physical thing, to prevent you gliding through an abstract process.

Two points follow, one having been glimpsed in the eighteenth century, but both firmly established only in Romantic criticism. In verse, Hulme observes, images are not mere embellishments but "the very essence of an intuitive language." Then, as foreshadowed in the last sentence of the quoted passage, is the figure first used by Coleridge—and occasionally since—to clarify the contrasting procedures of prose and verse. "Verse," Hulme's version of it runs, "is a pedestrian taking you over the ground, prose—a train which delivers you at a destination."[23]

Unlike the treatments of this analogy by Hegel and Coleridge examined earlier, Hulme's insights are unsupported by any unifying dynamic structure. This omission, which flawed the Imagism he and Pound espoused in their first assault on the Victorian establishment, soon led Pound himself to abandon Imagism for Vorticism.

While Pound's leadership in the creation of modernist poetry has long been recognized, his status as a poetician has remained controversial. Even those who—tolerant of his fits of verbal horseplay—have calmly examined the question have disagreed in their assessments. Wellek found no justification for the high estimate of Pound as theorist made by Christopher de Nagy. Eliot, despite avowed personal debt to Pound incurred in their programmatic association, bore inconclusive witness. In 1928, by which time Pound had worked out and thoroughly publicized the fundamentals of his critical credo, Eliot classified him as an extreme Romantic whose literary philosophy was a somewhat antiquated mixture of influences from the nineties, Yeats, and Madox Ford, enriched by his own considerable erudition. The result, as Eliot gauged it, was "a curious syncretism which I do not think he has ever set in order."[24]

In Pound's critical writing there is little of the sustained theoretical argument found in Eliot's. Yet general principles are often alluded to or implied in what he felt impelled to impart by an irrepressibly pedagogical turn of mind. Occasionally his remarks suggest that he may have benefited by Eliot's instruction. Is his observation in *The ABC of Reading* (1934), that an appreciation of new art works entails a constant revaluation of the old, a personal discovery or a recollection of a famous passage in "Tradition and the Individual Talent"? Whichever it be, there are other cases where Pound is clearly seminal. Two years before Eliot elaborated the point, Pound had argued, anent Laforgue, that the most genuine originality "is often in sheer lineage." What in an innovating poet is "most damned for eccentricity, is often most firmly in the track or orbit of tradition." Like "the really new" described by Eliot, Pound's slogan "make it new," first sounded some years earlier, was really a call to *re*novation. In his first book of criticism, *The Spirit of Romance* (1910), Pound had spoken more modestly of great poets setting "their own inimitable light atop the mountain" of all they had begged, borrowed, or stolen from predecessors and contemporaries. This note is heard again in his 1917 review of Eliot's *Prufrock and Other Observations* for the *Egoist,* where he defends him and other innovators against the charge of being drunken helots. Since when, he asks, have helots hit upon "a new method of turning old phrases into new by their aptness?"[25]

The "problem of poetic diction," de Nagy noted, "forms an important centre" of Pound's poetics. That poetics may, as Wellek thought, be minor in terms of the space given it in Pound's quite extensive critical writing, but hardly so in its significance and, frequently, incisive articulation. As F. R. Leavis observed, Pound in all his "romantic excursions" never swerved from a single-minded devotion to the aesthetic, even though his successive skirmishes against the literary establishment left him little leisure for sustained elaboration.[26]

Despite the programmatic "A Few Don'ts," Pound never reduced his generalizations about poetry to an ad hoc manifesto. Already in 1911, to suggestions that he do just that, he replied that he considered the "*corpus poetarum* of more importance than any cell or phalange." No disingenuous rhetorical ploy, this claim is solidly supported in his books, essays, reviews, and even in the intimate exchanges of his correspondence. It jibes with his advice, under the rubric of "Things to Be Done" in *Poetry* (1917), that people intending to write or to criticize poetry should learn languages. "All things are not written in one tongue." Repeatedly finding in Homer the most consummate embodiment of poetic perfection, he ruefully confesses a slim command of Greek.[27]

In a letter to R. P. Blackmur in 1925 Pound wrote of having possibly outlined a new critical system or at least having provided material to that end worth a doctoral thesis. In the letter to Taupin he claimed to have derived from some of Rimbaud's poems and from Catullus "une esthétique plus ou moins systématique." To Herbert Creekmore in 1939 he boasted, with more bravado than substance, that his introduction to Ernest Fenollosa's *The Chinese Written Character as a Medium of Poetry* amounted to an *ars poetica*. None of these claims need be accepted without mental reservation (that made to Blackmur coming closest to unvarnished truth). Nonetheless, several of Pound's statements about verse as a verbal art, though not in every case the novelties he believed them to be, rest on quite valid or at least intellectually respectable foundations in theory.[28]

Not since Aristotle has the definition of poetry as an *art of words* been more exclusively and consistently applied in evaluation than by Ezra Pound—Eliot alone excepted. This preoccupation lent color to the objection that Pound's poetry is at best a brilliant display of verbal technique thin in ideational content. Whatever the justice of that verdict, it is an error to read his conception of poetic language as yet another version of purist theory. Quite to the contrary, his *mot juste* possessed social, moral, and political utility and consequence. A sense of style, he darkly asserted, might have spared America and Europe Woodrow Wilson. He accordingly insisted that good poetry, like good art in any other medium, rendered truthful reports about experience. Scrupulously avoiding any divorce of form and content, he intended no devaluation of moral purpose. When near the outset of his career he discerned in technique the only "gauge and test" of sincerity, he had added that only someone who "cares and believes really in the pint of truth that is in him" will labor for years to attain technical perfection. Honest commitment was prior to formal mastery.[29]

It would not, I think, be fanciful to see in this insight a parallel to Arnold's faith that in poetry man comes closest to uttering truth. "Bad art is inaccurate art," Pound wrote in 1913. "It is art that makes false reports." By bearing true witness, the arts "provide data for ethics." Neither he nor Arnold ever offered any reasoned support for their faith in the interdependence of moral integrity and prosodic prowess. But clearly it assumes a virtual identity of matter and manner, from which not even the minutest constituent of a poem is excluded. Pound's effort in 1917 to define this seamless unity strained his syntax. "The poem is an organism in which each part functionates, gives to sound or to sense something—preferably to sound *and* sense gives something."[30]

Though in *The Spirit of Romance* he preferred to liken verse to the graphic arts and music rather than to "literature" (much in the vein of Verlaine's "Tout le reste est littérature"), Pound soon came to regard the ideational properties of the verbal medium not as regrettable "impurities" but as the indispensable conditions of its aesthetic potence. There is no denying his revulsion from the facile morality and nerveless piety permeating late Victorian verse. But as critic he objected less to what it communicated than to the mode of communication; not that poems should *be and not mean,* but that the style adopted for conveying meaning should make for the highest degree of conceptual and emotive intensity. Like Mill, Pound likened poetry to what anyone might utter in real life "under emotion." His favorite passage in the *Poetics* was Aristotle's dictum that metaphors are the surest marks of poetic genius because (as Pound freely construed it) aptness at figures is clear proof that "the mind is upborne upon the emotional surge." The

Victorians' recourse to such cumbersome machinery as description, predication, and discursive argument made for diffusion and flaccidity, muffling the impact. Moreover, it spawned that "blasphemous" literary libel, Arnold's "criticism of life." Being neither static, passive, nor reflective, the arts' nexus with reality is nondiscursive, something with the vibrancy and immediacy of a symbol. "Poetry," Pound protested, "is about as much a 'criticism' of life' as a red-hot iron is a criticism of fire." Therefore, he preached, do not describe; *present*.[31]

Among the mostly stylistic banalities Pound listed as "Don't's" in *Poetry* in 1913, the definition of an image as an instantaneous presentation of "an intellectual and emotional complex" is exceptional. It provides both for how poetry resembles and how it crucially differs from graphic art. As for the former, C. H. Sisson seems to me quite unjustified in his charge that Pound's concept of an image overlooks the sequential nature of verse. Pound's attribution of instantaneousness aptly describes the tight amalgam of feeling and thought by which the poetic image, as he explained it, effects that sudden liberation from the constrictions of time and space, "that sense of sudden growth, which we experience in the greatest works of art." In suppressing the reader's *perception* of duration, this instantaneousness no doubt approximates verse to painting and sculpture, and so may contribute to what has been called spatial form in literature. But in no literal sense does it deny poetry's temporal mode of existence; an instant, after all, is a segment of time, however infinitesimal. And surely no critic ever assigned greater importance than Pound did to those manifestations of its temporal dimension which verse chiefly exploits for its aesthetic effect, rhythm and sound.[32]

In assigning both intellectual and emotive efficacy to the image Pound centralizes the special—and endlessly enigmatic—distinction of literature among the other mimetic arts. A vocal minority at the time rejoiced that in lyric verse, now the dominant genre, discursive "impurity" had been nearly eliminated. Against this seductive heresy Pound set his face from the very first. He joined Yeats and Eliot in deploring a "lack of intellect" in Swinburne's work owing to his prizing words for their sound alone. He refused to regard even the greatest versificative dexterity as a compensation for poverty of thought. Reviewing Housman's *Name and Nature of Poetry* for the *Criterion* in 1934, he remarked that intellect no more hinders poetry than a railway track hinders the progress of a locomotive.[33]

Pound steadily refused to simplify the problem of verse language. At times he spoke as though it could be "solved" by asserting its kinship to music, painting and the graphic arts. In 1914 he confessed that for him two sorts of poetry were the most "poetic": the aural sort, music on the verge of "just forcing itself into articulate speech"; and the visual, always suggestive of the same metamorphosis from statues or paintings. Yet he was aware that these affinities failed the minimum test of showing how ideas "or fragments of ideas" harmonized with the concomitant emotions of the complex ("for we have come to the intellectual and emotional complex") so as to form an organism, "an oak sprung from an acorn." Nor did they allow for the poet's worst burden, the irreducible dualism of language, at once "the simplest the most arcane" of artistic media. Pound emblematized that dualism in poetry as

> a centaur. The thinking, word-arranging, clarifying faculty must move and leap with the energizing, sentient, musical faculties. It is precisely the difficulty of this ambiguous existence that keeps down the census of good poets.[34]

Pound was intrigued by rhythm and sound, the kinetics of verse in his dynamic conception, never hedonic embellishments but energizing constituents of the emotive-intellectual complex. In the 1915 letter to Monroe he put it *fortissimo:* "Rhythm MUST have meaning." A dozen years later, in the *New York Herald* article "How to Read," he essayed a rough-and-ready taxonomy via the impressive Greek coinages *Melopoeia, Phanopoeia,* and *Logopoeia,* mislabeled *kinds* of poetry. In fact, Pound's discussion suggests that all three categories may exist in a single poem, one of them predominating. A reader unmindful of the referential value Pound always assigns to auditory and visual elements, and aware that the prefixes *melo-* and *phano-* designate song and visual brightness respectively, may assume that Logopoeia alone, "the dance of the intellect among words," bears ideational import. Such is not the case however. In Melopoeia too, he explains, the musical property of words subserves their meaning by directing "the bearing or trend of that meaning." And though Phanopoeia is only "a casting of images upon the visual imagination," it must not be forgotten that by Pound's definition images carry cognitive as well as affective freight.[35]

These reservations duly noted, Logopoeia "holds the aesthetic content which is peculiarly the domain of verbal manifestation, and cannot possibly be contained in plastic or in music." It constitutes the final stage in the evolution of poetry, which for Pound originated with "the yeowl and the bark" and progressed through the stages of dance and music, whence the rhythmic movement which, he warned, it can only abandon at the risk of atrophy.[36]

Onomatopoeia, the device by which sound directly represents ideas, occupied from first to last a privileged place in Pound's poetics. Already in *The Spirit of Romance* he was hailing Dante's mastery in deepening the impression of a speaker's passion and tone of voice by ancillary sonant imagery. In 1922 he told his *ancien maître* Felix Schelling that for fifteen years he had marveled at the deft union of sound and meaning in Dante's "di lontano / Connobi il tremolar della marina" (*Purgatorio*, I, 116–17) [from afar I descried the trembling of the sea]; and that for half that time his imagination had been haunted by the onomatopoeic magic of "παρὰ θινα πολυφλοίσβοιο θαλάσσης" in the line of the *Iliad* that so impressed Pope. For the immediacy of that sensuous presentment of "the rush of the waves on the sea-beach and their recession" Pound tried, in various contexts and confessedly in vain, to find an English equivalent. His best effort, in *Mauberley*,

> . . . imaginary
> Audition of the phantasmal sea-urge,

he thought altogether inferior. Homer's image insinuated itself into "Stele," one of the lyrics in *Personae* (1909), anglicized in cumbersome coinage as "poluphloisboious sea-coast," followed by a line made up of the untranslated Greek. In *Canto* 74, water flows "in diminutive poluphloisboios." All this is perhaps obsession, but obsession from a depth of concentrated prosodic sensitivity that often lends theoretic weight even to Pound's most truculent ejaculations.[37]

In one of his more reasoned anatomies of the centaur-like art, "The Wisdom of Poetry," he argued in thorough-going organic terms that the poetic art consisted in combining "the essentials of thought" with "that melody of words which shall most draw the emotions of the hearer toward accord with their import, and with that 'form' which shall most delight the intellect." Melody he defines here quite simply as qualities of sound mingled with variations of metrical accent. But unless the rhythm and the "vowel and consonantal melody or sequence [seem] truly to bear the trace" of the emotion being communicated, they are at best otiose and at worst offensive. Shelley's "The Sensitive Plant" fails so miserably because it "jingles to the tune" of "A little peach in the orchard grew." Pound never defined what separates the rhythm which beautifies from the rhythm which blemishes. He was content to refer a formal difference (once more) to an ethical genesis: "cadence is not dexterity, it is the emotional man."[38]

Which brings us to Pound's assessment of the prosodic development most controverted in his time, free verse. Perhaps the first thing to notice is that many of his references to it, subliminally at least, are unfavorable. His circumspection may reflect an awareness that his objection to metronomic rhythm in the Imagist "Manifesto" was too readily mistaken (as it still is today) for a rejection of traditional meter *tout court,* instead of an injunction to shape any given metrical pattern into a musical cadence responsive to the writer's governing emotive impulses. The distinctly subordinate place free verse held in Pound's poetics was best revealed when he told John Quinn in 1917 that he had taken "damn small part in the current muck" about that trivial issue. To complaints of the alleged monotony of meter his reply was that overdone anarchy was just as bad; he gladly seconded Eliot's sound maxim that no verse is "free" for the poet who aims at excellence. "To the old school," in Murray Schaefer's just discrimination (and in Pound's) "*vers libre* was an escape from discipline; to the new it was an added discipline for it meant divining the precise meter and shape of each individual poetic thought."[39]

With all attempts to achieve the poetic effect outside the conventions of set meters, stanzaic forms, the refrain, and so on, Pound never felt entirely comfortable. Prose poetry he dubbed "that doubtful connection." Nothing in his favorite verse attracted him more than its formal techniques—Homer's hexameters, the interlaced rhymes of Dante's tercets, the intricately contrived stanzas of Provençal courtly love poems— all so many means for attaining the heightening of common speech that for Pound, as for others, constituted genuine poetry. The structure of his own *Cantos* is another version of the principle, with their repetitions and asymmetrical patternings of sections à la theme-and-variations in music. Free verse he admitted only as one more type of heightening, one well suited to a peculiar cast of the modern poetic temperament but by no means uniquely so. The art of poetry, he wrote in 1912, combines thought with verbal melody and with intellect-delighting form, the latter defined as the arrangement of verse, *sic* into ballades, canzoni, and the like symmetrical forms, or into blank verse or into free verse, where, presumably, the nature of the thing expressed or of the person supposed to be expressing it, is *antagonistic to external symmetry.* (my italics).

Perhaps as obviously in the *Cantos* as anywhere else, Pound's free verse involves not freedom *from* something, but freedom *for* something. In an article written in the same year for Harold Monro's *Poetry Review,* he announced his belief in "an absolute rhythm," guaranteeing on the metrical level, as did *mots justes* on the lexical, that Pater-like stylistic precision and uniqueness to which Pound so ardently subscribed. In poetry, he explained, rhythm is absolute when it corresponds to the exact shade of emotion a particular poet seeks to convey, "uncounterfeiting, uncounterfeitable." Pound valued the concision of *mots justes* equally with their precision. In *Guide to Kultur,* he asserted that with rare exceptions two pages of verse contain more meaning than ten of prose. A few pages later he quotes from Johnson's "Vanity of Human Wishes,"

> See nations slowly wise and meanly just
> To buried merit raise the tardy bust,

observing that "slowly wise" and "meanly just" "summarize long observation." Pound's position in the section of the *Poetry Review* article headed "Re Vers Libre" confirms his belief in rigorously functional form. Free verse is appropriate when it yields a rhythm not only more *beautiful* than any attainable by set meters, but also "more real," meaning "more germane, intimate, interpretative than the measure of regular accentual verse."[40]

Pound's disparagement of prose poetry expressed more than a bias of personal taste. A theoretically significant aspect of the modernist hostility to the Victorians reasserts the distinction between poetry and prose that had been increasingly blurred during the nineteenth century and in Pater had almost disappeared. This reaction, often quite explicit in Eliot and Pound, and implied in Yeats's prose writings as well, is attended by a persistent (if sometimes uneasy) further tendency to confine poetry to verse. For some time Pound seemed inclined to dismiss or evade the thorny issues involved. In *The Spirit of Romance* he had conceded that

Richard of St. Victor had written a prose which rose in intensity to the level of poetry. By 1913 however, though he thought it useless to ask how poetry and prose differed, he tentatively aligned himself with those who distinguished "the two arts" by their relative degrees of intensity. Without denying the intellectual muscularity of Flaubert's prose, he went instead to lines of Dante, "The Seafarer," and current English and French verse for touchstones to convince readers that they are "brought upon the passionate moment" only by the agency of meter.[41]

At times, in detached gnomic pronouncements, he intuited a radical, generic gap between prose and verse, the two forms having been divided by "things born before syntax." More cryptic still was what he admitted, in a 1918 essay on Henry James, to be a "highly untechnical . . . almost theological" way of grasping the distinction. Most prose, he mused, comes from "an instinct of negation," whereas poetry asserts the positive—leaving his readers to divine the evidence for thinking this to be "perhaps the root difference between the two." But his less arcane comparisons between prose and poetry (which almost always means verse in Pound) represent them as linked by a common aesthetic quality, the difference being more one of degree than of kind. "Great literature"—not only great verse—"is simply language charged with meaning to the utmost possible degree," as he put it for the readers of the *New York Herald.* Yet he implied no repudiation of his long-held conviction that verse was the "more highly energized." "The language of prose," he wrote,

> is much less highly charged, that is perhaps the only availing distinction between prose and poesy. Prose permits greater factual presentation, but a much greater amount of language is needed.

With a handful of exceptions such as Flaubert's *Coeur Simple,* not only can verse in two pages convey more meaning than prose can in ten; some things, he agreed with Eliot, can be said only in verse. "You can't translate 'em [into prose]." If poets can learn from good prose, they, in turn, "new-mint" the prose-writers' speech. Tacitus's history, Pound observed, is full of "Vergilian half-lines."[42]

The words *charged* and *energized* in Pound derive their cogency from the aesthetic concept which he and the sculptor Gaudier named Vorticism. Pound substituted that label for Imagism because it more accurately suggested the dynamic quality he had come to see as essential to all art. In poetry this quality required that elevation of the common idiom that Hopkins had made the defining condition of poetic utterance. To Pound, Ford's dictum that poetry should be as well written as prose meant, as he wrote to Miss Monroe, that its diction must depart from the simplicity of quotidian speech only by a greater concentration of thought. This kind of intensity, alias energy, is attained in verse by technical precision operating on both lexical and metrical levels of verse structure, *mots justes* constituting the lexical perfection and "absolute" rhythm the metrical. And the resulting dynamism is further assured on the metrical level, Pound told Mary Barnard in 1934, by making the stress "strain against the duration now and again, to maintain the tension," just as Frost had put it.[43]

These principles fall readily enough under the Vorticist rubric. So too does Pound's conception of the image, for in rejecting Imagism he by no means removed images themselves from a central place in his poetics; imagery remained "the poet's pigment." In Vorticism, however, the image is no longer a static mental picture, but "a radiant node or cluster . . . what I can, and must perforce, call a VORTEX." The Imagist poets' inert copying of light "on a haystack" is thus replaced by the "much more energetic and creative action" generated by formal organization. "Vorticism," Pound wrote,

> is an intensive art. I mean by this that one is concerned with the relative intensity, or relative significance of different sorts of expression. One desires the most intense, for certain forms of expression *are* 'more intense' than others. They are more dynamic.

Also accommodated in this over-arching conception is poetry's heuristic agency. Poets do more than communicate ideas fully conceived prior to composition. They manipulate words in order to probe, discover, or clarify some experience or "truth," poetic language being thus, as Pound has it, "the language of exploration." The dramatic excitement we receive from this momentary suspension of intellectual and emotional certainty, renewed with every rereading of a fine poem, further attests to its vibrancy.[44]

Fittingly to his Vorticist aesthetic, when Pound speaks of poetry being highly *charged* with meaning he employs the adjective in two of its senses at once: both intellectually *laden,* and *imbued with electric potency,* or *galvanic*. Significantly however, his intuition that the latter property inhered exclusively in poetry, especially in verse, actually preceded by over two years, and almost certainly motivated, his choice of a whirlpool to symbolize artistic vitality. It is also important to note that Pound's intuition was no idiosyncrasy of a wayward imagination. Ever since a hitherto dimly understood natural force was clearly identified and the word *electricity* added to the nomenclature of modern physics, a few writers have seized upon it to convey the unique effect of rhythmical utterance. This mysterious natural phenomenon seemed especially apposite to something wondrously present in poetry but never quite accountable in terms of diction, meter, imagery, or any other of its palpable features. Shelley, we recall, had rejoiced in the "electric life which burns within" the poet's words. The metaphor has since undergone considerable attrition in run-of-the-mill descriptions of poetry. Still, Hugh Kenner has spoken of Wordsworth's "great technical discovery or rediscovery . . . of the electric force of startling juxtapositions silhouetted by limped diction," and of Pound's central image of art eliciting from "mute particulars, by their electric juxtaposition," patterns of "an intense, clear, luminous intellective world."[45]

In an ingenious flight of fancy, Pound tried in 1912 to explain how this poetic galvanism worked by inventing what he admitted was an awkward simile—"for I am trying to say something about the masterly use of words, and it is not easy." He compared words to electrically-charged hollow steel cones. From their apexes a force is radiated but with a kinetic activity more complex than the mere negative and positive of electric charges. The force emitted by each "cone" is not merely added to the others' but multiplies them. Three or four words juxtaposed in this precise fashion can radiate "energy at a very high potentiality," latent energy derived from tradition, from "centuries of race consciousness, of agreement, of association." All of this is controlled by the "Technique of Content" (distinguished from the more familiar technique of manner), which, to the slender consolation of puzzled readers, he declared to be comprehensible only to genius.[46]

To some people highly responsive to metered diction, Pound's tortuous figuration may not seem entirely frivolous. But most will find it only a fruitless obfuscation of what writers cited in previous chapters had noted about the importance of adroit verbal juxtapositions, or Horace's *callida iunctura*. Nonetheless, the image of a vortex itself is an apt representation of the forces in play because by the conflict of centrifugal and centripetal tendencies it better mirrors the clash of opposites, the dramatic tension that constitutes the aesthetic dynamism. In contrast to Imagist theory, as R. W. Dasenbrook has recently pointed out, Vorticism recognizes "the play of opposites which alone can assure a coherent aesthetics."[47]

Yet though vortex is a graphic emblem of the polarity of forces which Coleridge was the first to expound in English poetics, his genuine theoretical heir is Eliot, not Pound. For in Eliot's critical essays the intuition of a formal order sustained by opposing impulses is not sporadic, as in Pound, but pervasive, and everywhere crucial in his account of how language is exploited to poetic effect.

⤷

CHAPTER FOURTEEN

Eliot I

The Genesis of
Neo-Coleridgean Poetics

OCCUPYING AS CRITIC IN the twentieth century the places of Dryden, Johnson, and Coleridge in those preceding, T. S. Eliot exceeds all three in his career-long preoccupation with the poet's medium. Whatever the proper definition of poetry—and Eliot always declined to hazard one—he thought a poet's "primary conscious care should be for how he marshals words." The critical enigmas involved intrude even into his verse. Besides the admired passages in *Four Quartets* there is the chorus in *The Rock,* marveling that from "the slime and mud of words" should "spring the perfect order of speech, and the beauty of incantation." Even casual social chit-chat, Eliot sensed, is kin, however humble or removed, that the aristocracy of poetry must acknowledge. He prescribed conversation as the writer's best Gradus, the indispensable scales and exercises of the craft, because "all literary creation certainly springs" from talking to others or to oneself.[1]

Eliot's avowals of an "incapacity for abstruse reasoning" will be quickly discounted by anyone who can grapple with the erudite opacities of his Harvard doctoral thesis, *Knowledge and Experience in the Philosophy of F. H. Bradley* (1964). Yet readers may still be led astray by similar disclaimers prompted mainly by public posturing or the Old Possum streak in Eliot's temperament. The grandiloquence of "What is man to decide what poetry is?" in the essay on Dryden (1921) belongs to a rhetoric of histrionic despair at odds with Eliot's critical composure. The suspicion professed in a 1933 *Criterion* review of Housman's *Name and Nature of Poetry*, that most of the very few things ever said about poetry prove to be either false or nugatory, is itself suspect in the light of his engagement with past critical doctrine and his own unremitting efforts to add to it. He might well have included himself among those disparaged in that same review as indulgers in the "Essence of Poetry fantasy." More accordant with his genuine sense of the matter is the statement, made at Harvard in that same year, that for all the variety of their procedures "there must also be something in common in the poetic process of all poets' minds."[2]

Then there is his declaration that criticism produced by poets aims only to justify their own kind of poetry. But the grain of truth in that assertion counts for little against the fact that the finest poetic theory we have was produced by poet-critics, as Eliot was well aware. He warned against assuming that Dryden's critical analyses applied only to the kind of poetry he wrote himself, credited Coleridge with generalizations about poetry "of the greatest interest," and even admitted that almost everything Keats said about it was true, "and what is more, true for greater and more mature poetry than Keats ever wrote."[3]

Modesty aside, Eliot might have said the same of himself. Granted, his many pronouncements about poetry, its genesis, function, and status as a verbal art, could hardly escape both limitation and enlivenment from personal creative labor. Yet with few (and debatable) exceptions they have fair claim to universal relevance and application because the terms of his argument carry them well beyond introspective musing. The bulk of his exposition is for the most part induction from an incisive scrutiny of literature produced in several ages and languages. And as much as any other critic—perhaps more than most—Eliot sensed the futility of criticizing poems without having a prior "idea of poetry in general." Our inclination to define it, he added, arises "quite naturally from our experience of poems."[4]

Eliot's generalizations about his art constitute the first full reformulation of Coleridgean poetics. He may have intended no personal reference when in 1956 he exalted Coleridge for having inaugurated a transformation of literary criticism and so become the progenitor of its twentieth-century practitioners. But an awareness of his own place among the master's descendants is hinted in his startling avowal five years later that Coleridge was a man much like himself, differing chiefly in his greater erudition and more powerful intellect. In this tribute it is hard to recognize the mildly disreputable exponent of Romantic disorder whom a younger and brasher Eliot had called a corrupter of taste, an inveterate dreamer whose tendency to disappear in "metaphysic clouds" set him below Dryden as a critic of poetry. Eliot for many years felt a distaste for the temperamental ebullience of the man whom Edmond Schérer had aptly dubbed "raisonneur enthousiaste." A grudging estimate in *The Sacred Wood* is matched in the later "Experiment in Criticism" (1929), where the *Biographia* is characterized as "one of the wisest and silliest" of critical books. One reason for the gradual progress in Eliot's references to Coleridge from mild vituperation to unqualified praise was surely an awareness of how closely his own evolving conceptions of poetry had come to coinciding with those of his great predecessor. By 1933 Eliot was confessing that there was a good deal to learn from Coleridge. But the theoretical passages in Eliot's essays suggest that their ultimate agreement was reached as much by Eliot's personal immersion in poetry as from whatever part the *Biographia* may have played in shaping his thought.[5]

The affinity between them consists in Eliot's adherence to the three fundamentals of Coleridge's critical theory: *mimesis, organic unity,* and the *polar dynamism* (far more consistently maintained than in Pound) that characterizes the creative imagination and its products. Of course none of these ideas was Coleridge's exclusive property, but Eliot's conception of them conforms more closely to Coleridge's than to any other on record.[6]

Mimesis: The fundamental principle governing Western art theory since antiquity, mimesis belongs to what Eliot classified as philosophical criticism, a useful but risky type best left to analysts of "a very unusual intelligence." Significantly, he named as exemplars only Aristotle and Coleridge. Nothing is more traditional in Eliot's critical thinking than the idea that all art is representational. Curiously, it was not Coleridge but Wordsworth whom Eliot first commended for reaffirming Aristotelian mimesis, but only for his statement that poetry aims at general, not particular or local, fidelity to reality. Later, however, he came to realize that in Coleridge he had the sounder proponent of mimesis as crucial to his own idea of poetic diction.[7]

In "Tradition and the Individual Talent" (1919), Eliot argued that good poetry is impersonal, not an outpouring of the writer's emotions but an "escape" from them; and he never concealed his contempt for the stream of naked self-portrayals ("personalities") gushing from the modern press. So it is startling to find him objecting, only two years later, to the styles of Milton, Tennyson, and Sir Thomas Browne for failing to incorporate any interesting personality. The inconsistency is more verbal than substantive. All poetry, Eliot maintained, is *primarily* an expression of feeling and emotion. The preeminence of Shakespeare and the other major Elizabethan and Jacobean playwrights is that the oeuvre of each is "united by one significant, consistent, and developing personality." But this is not a subjective state, only an index of creative passion, the artists' "personal drama and struggle," available to us in their plays, not in their biographies. A persistent theme of Eliot's criticism is that a poet's psychic experience is aesthetically nil unless, by an often painful concentration of imaginative effort, it emerges in what he writes in profoundly altered form. Marlowe's and Jonson's comedies achieved their unusual literary value by a "transformation of a personality into a personal work of art." Dante's rage and Shakespeare's disillusionment are "gigantic attempts to metamorphose" bitter frustrations. But no genuine artist produces anything of value by exhibitionist display; he expresses his personality only indirectly, by setting himself a task like that of a skilled artisan who shapes a jug or a table leg. Which is to say, as Eliot does say of the "world" depicted in Swinburne's lyrics: "It is impersonal, and no one else could have made it." The problem was one to which Eliot returned later in "The Three Voices of Poetry" (1953), which argues the obliquity of self-revelation in the finest dramatic poetry. "The world of a great poetic dramatist is a world in which the creator is everywhere present, and everywhere hidden."[8]

Virtually everything he wrote about personality answers to the dialectic nature of the art work expounded in Coleridge's mimetic theory and reaffirmed in Eliot's assertion that actual life and an abstraction, or withdrawal, from actual life coexist in all artistic creation. He seldom let slip an opportunity to enforce the point. In an obituary piece on Sarah Bernhardt he rejected the notion that the cinema was a purely realistic medium. It was Charlie Chaplin's special merit, he pointed out, to have escaped realism by imposing a "rhythm" on the lively antics he displayed on the screen. More venerable examples of the dramatic art were more severely tested by his criterion: no art without conventions. The whole of English drama from Kyd to Galsworthy, he announced a year later, was flawed by an attempt at unrestrained realism, only the earlier morality play *Everyman* being "within the limitations of art."[9]

Poetic style could hardly be exempt from compliance with this universal characteristic of art, manifest in verse as a tensive interplay between approaches to and withdrawals from ordinary speech, as he wrote in "Four Elizabethan Dramatists" (1924). Eliot repeatedly stressed this salutary qualification of the rule affirming a vital bond between good verse and common speech. Reviewing *The New Poetry* (1917), an anthology edited by Harriet Monroe and A. C. Henderson, he warned that a mere mimicry of talk, however faithfully it may echo the real thing (Coleridge's "copy"), doesn't constitute poetry. Nor is it a question of degrees of conversational refinement, as pre-Romantic dictional theory had held. Even *Idylls of the King*, he added, too often sounded like "Tennyson talking to Queen Victoria in Heaven." Poetic imagery too, no less than diction, should eschew a photographic replication of its actual sources. Baudelaire, Eliot wrote in 1930, deserved the gratitude of all poets who came after him for pioneering the poetic exploitation of urban life, but his signal achievement lay in elevating it to "the *first intensity* [Eliot's italics]—presenting it as it is, and yet making it represent something more than itself." Eliot's share of this indebtedness in *The Waste Land* and elsewhere is of course plain to see.[10]

Organicism: When Eliot informed readers of the *Egoist* in 1918 that metaphor is not an externally applied stylistic adornment but the very life of language, he did no more than serve up a reminder of what the more astute among them already knew. Yet even in his earliest speculations on belletristic writing he sensed the error of severing form and content which organic structure most effectively exposes. In "The Borderline of Prose" (1917), an essay which ought to be exhumed from the files of the *New Statesman*, he observed that Rimbaud did well to write his *Illuminations* in prose because they had apparently first entered his consciousness as such. No author, whether of prose or verse, he noted, should even for a moment allow readers to doubt "that his form is the inevitable form for his content." Since this extension of the organic concept into the creative process itself was clearly a discovery made by personal excogitation, Eliot had no call to ascribe it to Coleridge. Within two years he had penetrated, more deeply than in his remark about metaphor, into what organic fusion of theme and form implied for verse. "To create a form," he wrote in *The Sacred Wood*,

> is not merely to invent a shape, a rhyme or rhythm. It is also the realization of the whole content of this rhyme or rhythm. The

sonnet of Shakespeare is not merely such and such a pattern, but a precise way of thinking and feeling.[11]

In applying the principle he went beyond Coleridge, who had commended H. F. Cary's blank verse English version of the *Divine Comedy*. Eliot objected that that meter was a poor choice for the purpose, since "a different metre is a different mode of thought." For the same reason he denied that his own much admired "imitation" of Dante in "Little Gidding" reproduced the quality of the original. Because of the scarcity of rhyming words in English compared to Italian, he was debarred from using Dante's terza rima form. Yet what he adopted in its place for "Little Gidding," the simple alternation of lines of unrhymed masculine and feminine endings, he knew to be at best a compromise, because Dante "*thought* in *terza rima*." By roughly the same rationale, Eliot's all-inclusive organicism, embracing the germination of a poem and each subsequent step of its evolution, underlies his opposition to those who welcomed free verse as a liberation from form. Their error lay in failing to see that a particular metrical pattern "grows out of the attempt of somebody to say something."[12]

Perhaps no piece of theorizing in Eliot's criticism better demonstrates his independent thinking than what he substituted for Coleridge's assertion in the *Biographia* that in a "poem of any length" the unavoidably "unpoetic" parts "must be preserved *in keeping* with the poetry." Alluding to what all readers know, that a protracted narrative or meditation in verse inevitably traverses peaks and valleys of expressive concision, Coleridge thus brought his dynamic organicism to bear on the temporal dimension of the medium. Eliot's version, given in "The Music of Poetry," (1942), has it that

> in a poem of any length, there must be transitions between passages of greater and less intensity, to give a rhythm of fluctuating emotion essential to the musical structure of the whole; and the passages of less intensity will be, in relation to the level in which the whole poem operates, prosaic.[13]

Eliot's way of putting it gives no reason for supposing that Coleridge had influenced him beyond calling attention to the issue, a possibility suggested by his echoing the *Biographia* in the phrase "a poem of any length." In any case, they agree that a long poem should not be everywhere equally "poetic." But in explaining *why* this is necessary Eliot avoided the trap of Coleridge's misleading implication that some parts of a lengthy poem must be prose, albeit prose of his "neutral" variety. For it is clear that Eliot's "prosaic" designates only a lesser degree of poetic quality, since he calls for "transitions between passages of greater and less intensity," not for interweavings of poetry and nonpoetry.

No mere echo of Coleridge's "harmonious whole," Eliot's "musical structure of the whole" is a refined form of poetic organicism. Commending Johnson's *Vanity of Human Wishes*, Eliot nonetheless finds it structurally weaker than Goldsmith's *Deserted Village;* and "structure I hold to be an important element of poetic composition." In Goldsmith's poem he discerns the required "art of transition," the skillful oscillations between degrees of intensity by which a musical structure is achieved. This kind of structure Eliot felt to affect a poet's diction most imperatively in the only genre of long poem still viable in modern times, the verse play. Like all verse, dramatic dialogue must often be a mimetic transfiguration of quotidian conversation. But to make it so, the playwright must find an idiom and a versification that without lapsing into flat prose would permit an "unbroken transition between the most intense speech and the most relaxed dialogue." Without this stylistic gradation, the mimetic illusion of real life would be shattered because the more intense speeches, interspersed in a dialogue otherwise only a mimicry of live talk, would seem intrusive, creating the grotesque impression of actual interlocutors periodically talking poetry—with the attendant destruction of the play's organic integrity.[14]

Neither Coleridge's nor Eliot's way of putting it suggests that the poet's creative effort would diminish with these relaxations of verbal density. In a footnote to the passage quoted above, Eliot was at pains to forestall that inference by offering his account as an alternative to Arnold's touchstone criterion: how a poet handles his "less intense, but structurally vital, matter" tests his greatness. Though the more prosaic parts do not stir our emotions with magical phrases, they are not inert fillers. In fact, whole poems have been written at that stylistic level. As an example Eliot commends George Crabbe's poems of country life, just as Coleridge had instanced those of Herbert and Daniel in making the same point.[15]

What has so far been said by no means exhausts the implications of Eliot's unique conception of musical structure for his theory of verse language. Of that more below.

Polar dynamism: Given a perception of aesthetic structure so radically holistic as Eliot's, it is not surprising to find him at one point glancing at the *incarnation* analogy. In both religion and poetry, he wrote in 1931, language takes on symbolic weight by an "incarnation of meaning in fact." Though that analogy does not occur in Coleridge, it becomes clear as Eliot proceeds that a key passage in the *Biographia* meets his habitual conception of poetic unity. Achieving a union of thought and metrical language so total as to resemble the relation of body and spirit meant, as Pound too was constantly insisting, finding the precise words and by deft arrangements charging them with as much meaning as possible. Doing so, Eliot further explained, required a poet "really to *unite* the disparate and the remote, to give them a fusion and a pattern," and thus to exercise a verbal mastery surpassing that necessary to produce even the finest prose. No informed reader will miss here the silent allusion to the passage in the *Biographia* on how the creative imagination blends and "fuses" the various faculties of the soul, by reconciling such "discordant qualities" as sameness and difference, the general and the concrete, the idea and the image, unruly emotion and unusual order.[16]

That passage (quoted in full in Chapter 7 above) has held almost scriptural authority for Anglo-American proponents of dynamic tension as the cardinal feature that sets poetry apart from other uses of language. Among much else that Eliot must have found appealing in it was Coleridge's support, in the final set of opposed elements, for his own conviction that genuine criticism and appreciation should focus on the poem, not on the poet. But clearly, for Eliot as later for his New Critical disciples, the main significance of the passage was its articulation of the doctrine that the vibrancy of poetry results from the unique power of the creative imagination in "amalgamating disparate experience" into new wholes: falling in love, reading Spinoza, the sound of a typewriter, and the smell of cooking, as Eliot exemplified the range of the possible heterogeneity in "The Metaphysical Poets" (1921). The relevant passage from the critical canon which Eliot mentions in this essay was not that in the *Biographia* but Johnson's complaint in *Lives of the English Poets* that in Donne and his school "the most heterogeneous ideas are yoked by violence together." But Eliot counters that, except in unskilled hands, Johnson's words describe not the blemish of a period style but rather one species of something universal in verse and in itself commendable, since a certain amount of forcibly unified incongruent material is "omnipresent in poetry." In "Andrew Marvell," however, a companion essay of the same year and one of Eliot's finest, Coleridge is enlisted to support the thesis that Marvell's wit is no mere fanciful embellishment but the "structural decoration of a serious idea." The seriousness is intensified, not diluted, by its alliance with the levity. The argument here is in perfect accord with Eliot's dissent from Coleridge's belief that fancy and imagination were distinct and mutually incompatible faculties. Eliot's finding to the contrary is that imagination and wit are rather the upper and lower reaches of the same faculty. Accordingly, the imagery in Marvell's "Coy Mistress" and other poems, he concludes, meets the test of Coleridge's "elucidation of the Imagination," which he then reproduces almost in its entirety, with supportive illustrations from Marvell's verse.[17]

No other theoretical pronouncement in literary criticism figures so prominently in Eliot's prose as that "elucidation." A dozen years later in *The Use of Poetry* he quotes it at length as it had appeared in I. A. Richards's *Principles of Literary Criticism*, with an appended sentence from *Biographia*, chapter 15. There Coleridge delineates the first of what he considered the four "specific symptoms of poetic power" (all of them manifest in Shakespeare's *Venus and Adonis*): "The sense of musical delight" unifying and harmonizing several ideas under one predominant thought or feeling. Eliot could only have welcomed Richards's use of these words to supplement the famous description of the imagination's fusion of opposites, since in his own thinking, even more consistently than in Coleridge, the unifying process is best grasped in terms of a musical structure. But whereas Coleridge focuses mainly on "sweetness" of versification, Eliot's "musical qualities" comprehend much more than the sonant and rhythmic features of verse usually designated by that or some equivalent term. For him they embrace the whole poem, belonging as much to structure as to style, and constituting a major difference of poetry from prose. Arnold, he charged in *The Use of Poetry*, though he knew what poetry was *for*, was prevented by a defective sensitivity to "the musical qualities of verse" from ever discovering what it *was*. Being "musical," these qualities could only be apprehended by a faculty Eliot identified as the "auditory imagination,"

> the feeling for syllable and rhythm, penetrating far below the conscious levels of thought and feeling, invigorating every word; sinking to the most primitive and forgotten, returning to the origin and bringing something back, seeking the beginning and the

end. It works through meanings, certainly, or not without meanings in the ordinary sense, and fuses the old and obliterated and
the trite, the current, and the new and surprising, the most ancient and the most civilized mentality.[18]

Nowhere in Eliot is there a comprehensive exposition of Coleridge's theory that the creative imagination functions dialectically
to produce wholes sustained by the thrust and counterthrust of
a centrifugal content and a centripetal form. Yet almost every
observation Eliot made on verse language and style is implicitly
grounded in a poetics of tension. For him as for Pound, bad verse
was flabby verse. The limpness might be confined to the lexical
surface of a poem, in the form of cliché, facile image-mongering,
or verbosity. More damaging, it could result from a slackening of
the dynamic interplay between technique and message, or even
occur within technique itself. Eliot noted that in the process of lib-
erating blank verse from the stilted rhythms of rhymed couplets,
Marlowe had done more than infuse it with Spenserian melody; he
had also increased its driving power by "reinforcing the sentence
against the line period." The same criterion governs Eliot's attitude toward free verse. It underlies his much-cited aphorism that
no verse is free for anyone who wants to do a good job, and his
impatience with the erroneous notion that free verse meant a total
release from formal exactions. In Pound's practice, Eliot pointed
out, the "freedom" is "rather a state of tension due to a constant
opposition between free and strict." At one point the trope of
Coleridge's theoretic exposition, centripetal and centrifugal forces,
is replaced in Eliot by more graphic figuration. Behind even the
freest verse, as he visualized it, lurks the ghost of some pattern "to
advance menacingly as we doze, and withdraw as we rouse." No
exorcism will avail: "there is only mastery." So the total abolition
of rhythmic pattern from verse lines is an illusion, "for there is
only good verse, bad verse, and chaos."[19]

The word *chaos* here sounds a motif rooted deep in Eliot's
personal *Weltansicht* that surfaces frequently in his writings, usually paired with its opposite, *order*. In any social institution, intellectual persuasion, or partisan opinion that he feared or deplored
he tended to see the disorderly or the chaotic; whatever he hoped
for or favored exemplified one or another form of the orderly. By
no means confined to such cultural polemics as the 1923 essay
"The Function of Criticism"—in which Romanticism is chaotic,
classicism orderly—it is pervasive in his poetics. The word *order*

occurs five times in the single memorable paragraph of "Tradition and the Individual Talent" that describes how new works find their place in the canon.[20]

In the 1917 "Ezra Pound: His Metric and Poetry," after praising his friend's prosody as an exercise in formally controlled "freedom," Eliot quotes a statement by Pound himself that any art work comprises a union of freedom and order, suspended between "chaos" and "mechanics" (i.e., conventions, technique). More deeply pondered in Eliot, the idea is related to the artist's impulse to control a personal psychological turmoil. In some Romantic poets especially, Eliot found a drive toward technical perfection to have been symptomatic of "an effort to support, or to conceal from view, an inner disorder." (From what we now know of his own youthful agonies, *de se fabula!*) In the later criticism the counterpoised forces shape his view of the social function of the arts. In poetry the mastery of unruly thoughts and emotions displayed in effective versification epitomizes the macrocosmic struggle of civilized order against the ever-present menace of barbarism. The function common to all the arts, he wrote in "Poetry and Drama" (1951), is to allow us to see the order in life by imposing order upon it. The messy state of ordinary people's experience—chaotic, irregular, fragmented—is what the poet mimetically subdues to formal control. Seen in a broader social context, the values of tradition must be marshaled against the threat of cultural dissolution, because a society which ignores its literary inheritance becomes gradually more barbaric.[21]

That last observation dates from 1933. By the time of his "Social Function of Poetry" (1945) Eliot had become aware of a complication that placed a special burden of social responsibility on living poets. Owing to constant changes in the language of ordinary communication, people cannot avoid being increasingly alienated from the spiritual nourishment that past poetry might otherwise provide. This occurs because it is not so much as repositories of intellectual and moral edification that older masterpieces are salutary; the benefit lies rather in the capacity of their language to express and, according to Eliot, to enable others to feel "the emotions of civilized beings." The duty to provide for this, to stave off the atrophy of feeling and the cultural degeneracy that would otherwise ensue, devolved upon the contemporary poets, the tiny minority in whom an unusual sensibility is combined with "an exceptional power over words."[22]

Eliot's intuition of an intimate bond between the psychic condition necessary to civilized existence, and the poet's struggle to comprehend multifarious fragments of experience within dynamic verbal constructs, makes plausible two of his assertions that otherwise seem hyperbolic bits of an apologia for a slighted art. The first, dating from 1927, is that the invention of a new verse form is a major event in a nation's history, because it brings about a corresponding transformation of language and sensibility. The second, from the Harvard Norton Lectures of 1932–1933, is to the same effect but with an apparent reversal of the causal direction. "Any radical change in poetic form is likely to be the symptom of some very much deeper change in society and in the individual." These ambitious claims which Eliot makes for poetry's place in the very fabric of culture—deeper than anything of the same general import in Arnold—point to another theoretical accord with Coleridge. Had Eliot collected all his remarks on the poet's social role into a single essay he could have headed it with no more fitting epigraph than an entry of 1804 in Coleridge's *Notebooks:*

> Idly talk they who speak of Poets as mere Indulgers of Fancy, Imagination, Superstition, &c—they are the Bridlers by Delight, the Purifiers, they that combine them with *reason* & order, the true Protoplasts, Gods of Love who tame the Chaos.

Here there is no possibility of Coleridge having fecundated Eliot's thinking. The *Notebooks* were published too late for that to have happened. Nor on the other hand do we have a case of pure coincidence of phraseology. The two men's criticism provides strong evidence of a conceptual congruence brought about by a parallel rationale grounded in prior assumptions and intuitions held in common by Eliot and the poet-critic with whom late in life he was to acknowledge spiritual kinship. The idea of poetry as a civilizing force, glimpsed in Cicero's defense of the poet Archias, can of course be traced back to the Renaissance in modern Western thought. The achievement of both Coleridge and Eliot was to have detected an ultimate source of this beneficial office in how poets employ the verbal medium of their art. But it was Eliot, writing in a time when the more percipient segment of society was alarmed by signs of social decay far more imminent than any felt in Coleridge's day, who more fully explored the ramifications of the idea.[23]

One or two minor points shared by Coleridge and Eliot, less theoretically significant in themselves, are worth noting for their bearing on poetic style. Both men paid discriminating attention to iambic pentameter, as employed in blank verse and rhymed couplets. Both pointed to the generic variety its rhythmic pattern could accommodate. Blank verse alone, Coleridge instructed Southey, uses a technique comprising five or six very different meters. Eliot also noticed the marked contrast "in what is prosodically the same form," one always intimately related to speech, between dramatic blank verse and blank verse used in epic, philosophical, meditative, and idyllic poetry. Coleridge had found the distinction between the first two of these types perfectly exemplified in how the player's recital in *Hamlet* contrasts with the rest of the play's verse dialogue. Even more arresting is their identical diagnosis of the inadequacy of most eighteenth-century blank verse. Without, apparently, having noticed Coleridge's precedence in pointing out that the meter in Thomson's *Seasons* is only "rhyme-craving" five-foot iambics, Eliot echoed even his personification in remarking that in most pre-Romantic blank verse, including Johnson's tragedy *Irene,* "each line cries out for a companion to rhyme with it." To this identity of analytical opinion they were led, one might plausibly surmise, by the more fundamental congruence in mimetic theory that underlay their assessments of verse expression. Almost certainly that congruence, rather than any unacknowledged borrowing from Coleridge, induced Eliot to affirm in "Poetry and Drama" the same "triple distinction" between verse, prose, and conversation laid down in the *Biographia,* and on the identical ground that the two written forms are alike artificial.[24]

Eliot's earliest declared ideal of poetic style was one he shared with, and apparently learned from, his fellow iconoclasts, Pound, Ford, and (minimally) Hulme. This ideal is largely summed up in three tenets of their polemical agenda. The first simply reasserted that poets could best avoid the posturing rhetoric and stultifying grandiloquence of the late Victorian manner by returning to the idiom and movement of live speech. The second, noted above as the core of Eliot's poetics, held that poetry was first and foremost a verbal entity, so pervasively so that all speculation about it was otiose in proportion as it lost sight of that basic datum. The third tenet, the Hulme-Pound doctrine of imagistic "presentation" in place of expository description, was the most original and perhaps the most fruitful to current practice. It conduced to a revitalization of imagery as structural and meaning-freighted rather than decorative, to concision and enhanced emotive power. Eliot declared in *The Sacred Wood* that permanent literature is always a "presentation" of thought or feeling via "events in human action or objects in the external world." In this regard he must be denied much of the credit given him for having discovered the "objective correlative." The famous pronouncement in the 1919 essay on *Hamlet* that the only way of expressing emotion in a work of art was to find "a set of objects, a situation, a chain of events which shall be the formula of that *particular* emotion" does raise Pound's rule of thumb to the status of an aesthetic law. Yet even as such it is only a more impressive rephrasing of a statement by Ford which Eliot had earlier quoted in his essay on Pound: "Poetry consists in so rendering concrete objects that the emotions produced by the objects shall arise in the reader."[25]

For Eliot's generation the premises from which the old comparative inspection of prose and verse had proceeded was notably altered. Until the later 1800s there had been no serious threat to the aesthetic hegemony of verse. Then however came post-Baudelairean prose poetry and vers libre in France, and finally Pater's elevation of prose to virtual parity with verse. So what had long been mainly the relatively limited problem of the metrical-nonmetrical dichotomy had evolved into the more complicated one of the relations among three forms: discursive prose, "poetic" prose, and verse; or, if free verse counted as a category distinct from regular verse, four forms.

As late as 1953 Eliot had ruefully to confess that he had still not seen a full and satisfactory account of the difference between poetry and prose. His earliest attempts to sort it out seem mostly to have been ancillary to solving his creative problems. What forms and techniques of composition would best convey the unruly mix of thought and passion he was trying to reduce to verbal order, without losing touch with spoken English? Even his success in that personal quest, however, did not bring with it an adequate resolution of the theoretical enigma, which had lost none of its urgency for the man who had become more than ever persuaded of the unique and vital importance of his metier. "The task of a poet," he wrote in 1950,

> in making people comprehend the incomprehensible, demands immense resources of language; and in developing the language, enriching the meaning of words and showing how much words can do, he is making possible a much greater range of emotion and perception for other men, because he gives them the speech in which more can be expressed.[26]

For Eliot the one requirement for this exacting assignment was that the poet's words attain symbolic resonance ("showing how much words can do"). And this was something his instincts told him could hardly be compassed without the referential enrichment and emotive intensification that result when the inherent rhythmic potentials of the language are enhanced by meter.

Objecting to the notion that the use of symbols belonged only to a special school of poets, Eliot declared that symbolism was a condition to which words tended both in religious expression and in all poetry, meaning incarnated in fact; "and in poetry it is the tendency of the word to mean as much as possible." The mastery for which the poet strives consists in finding the right word and making it "both exact and comprehensive," a fit instrument for fusing the contrasting elements into a pattern. Nothing in the preface Eliot wrote for Harry Crosby's *Transit of Venus,* where these points are made, expressly confines this symbolizing process to metrical poetry. But it is highly probable that the mastery Eliot speaks of is one of versification, and the other writers whom the master excels are writers of prose. Only three years earlier he had given a clear priority to verse, though he had stopped short of denying poetic merit to all prose. Taken by itself, the generalization made in the "Dialogue on Dramatic Poetry" (1928)—that prose "tends" to treat the ephemeral and superficial, verse the permanent and universal—is untenably exclusive. Eliot's more discriminate position is that all poetic thought, whether it issues in prose or in verse, is thought blended with emotion in a fusion for which he usually reserved the term *feeling;* and when the emotive component reaches a sufficiently high pitch of intensity, "the human soul . . . strives to express itself in verse." For Eliot, the close alliance of poetry and music lay mainly in a shared temporality of their media, a condition of transience which was hard to reconcile with the ideal of permanence. Only through the poet's unremitting struggle for formal control, preferably via meter, could this otherwise insuperable disadvantage be in a sort transcended. In a choice instance of beautifully modulated tension, the process is depicted in "Burnt Norton":

Words move, music moves

Only in time; but that which is only living

Can only die. Words, after speech, reach

Into the silence. Only by the form, the pattern,

Can words or music reach

The stillness, as a Chinese jar still

Moves perpetually in its stillness.[27]

In his edition of Pound's poems published in 1931, Eliot makes caustic reference to such "idols of the prose-poetry romanticists" as Robert Burton, Sir Thomas Browne, and De Quincey, masters of language to whom it probably never occurred that they were writing poetry. Eliot's parenthetical aside, that Pope was poetry and Jeremy Taylor prose, suggests that Coleridge was at this time still in his disfavor among the deplored Romantics, since he had so pointedly lauded Taylor's prose for its "poetic" excellence and depreciated Pope's verse. Eliot's conviction that in his day a taste for Pope, the prince of metrical virtuosi, was a taste for poetry, is underscored by the firm declaration that no one is competent to judge poetry who does not see that it is "nearer to 'verse' than it is to prose poetry." In his late characterization of Joyce's *Finnegans Wake* as "a kind of vast prose poem" one still hears the faintly pejorative tone.[28]

On the other hand, the poet who included the impeccable prose effusion "Hysteria" in his *Collected Poems* could never bring himself to limit poetical expression to verse, or in any way to demean the imaginative resourcefulness displayed in the art of prose. He seconded Pound's advice that poets school themselves in the prose masters, well aware of the reciprocal enhancement. Prose utterly without qualities that are found in good verse, he wrote in 1932, was simply dead; verse without some of those making for good prose was apt to be "artificial, false, diffuse, and syntactically weak."[29]

Two of the four categories routinely invoked in twentieth-century discussion of the relations among literary forms Eliot could easily dispose of. Discursive, expository or "scientific" writing, the commonest kind of prose, was of course not poetry (though he remained uncomfortably aware that no one had yet definitively shown why this must be so). And free verse was verse, not prose. Like Pound, Eliot had no patience with those who had hailed its advent as a radically new departure. By 1928 he thought it clear that the vers librists had constituted no movement, produced no revolution, and evolved no formula. A putative fifth category, verse devoid of poetic quality, could also be set aside, since as with purely expository prose, its poetic nullity had never been disputed. These exclusions once more limited the contrastive method of definition—which Eliot employed with rare discriminative finesse in "The Borderline of Prose"—to a comparative analysis of two categories: genuine verse and prose either designed in advance by a writer to give poetic pleasure or else later admired by qualified readers for doing so whatever the author's intention may have been.[30]

Three pieces of Eliot's, spanning thirteen years and none of them included in the volumes of his selected prose, comprise the bulk of his speculation on this enigmatic aspect of poetic language. All three are in a loose sense occasional, prompted by some recent experience of reading or writing. Besides "The Borderline of Prose" in 1917, there are a letter to the editor of the *Times Literary Supplement* in 1928 and a translation of St. John Perse's French *Anabase* in 1930.

The first, and most extended, was suggested by his reading of the book he judged to have introduced English readers to the prose poem, Stuart Merrill's *Pastels in Prose*, translations of examples by twenty-three nineteenth-century French poets, including Baudelaire, Mallarmé, and Arnold's favorite, Maurice de Guérin. This little volume, published in New York in 1890, contains a brief introduction by William Dean Howells, some of whose opinions Eliot may have been moved to challenge though he does not mention him. Howells's highly commendatory remarks give some indication of the degree of acceptance prose poetry had gained in late nineteenth-century America. He approves of Merrill's title because it suggests the "aerial delicacy" which Howells takes to be the essence of a form adopted by poets who had thrown off "the artificial trammels of verse."[31]

The more immediate motive of "The Borderline" was a current recrudescence of this type of poetry in France and England alike. Eliot begins by asking whether the trend was only symptomatic of a search for novel modes of expression or—the question the rest of his brief essay explores—whether such poems were not also fresh evidence that "poetry and prose form a medium of infinite gradations." Eliot thinks not. As he observes of Rimbaud, no poet can *elect* to use prose or verse, because that choice is predetermined in the originating inspiration. There is a "prose rhythm" and a "verse rhythm," which at this point Eliot thought to be the only tenable distinguishing qualities. This conviction survived even later moments of bafflement by the complexities of the problem. In 1933, in the bewildering variety of what in different times and places had been called poetry, he could find no common item except "the rhythm of verse instead of the rhythm of prose." Although by that time he felt that the rhythmic difference said little about the essential nature of the art, in 1917 he had thought it sufficient to establish that prose-poetry belonged to a mode of poetic expression disparate from the metrical. A prose equivalent of *The Rape of the Lock* was no more possible than a versified *Madame Bovary*.[32]

One device of the contrastive tactic seeks to evaluate the purely external factors of meter and lineation by comparing prose and verse versions of an identical content in substantially identical wordings, as Joseph Warton had done. Both Coleridge and Eliot seized upon the proof case ready to hand in Shakespeare's versified passages of North's translation of Plutarch's *Lives*. Warton had concluded from his near verbatim prose recasting of Pope's couplets that meter conferred at best a nugatory benefit. Coleridge and Eliot both cite the metrical adaptation of North in, respectively, *Antony and Cleopatra* and *Coriolanus* to support conclusions very different from Warton's. Coleridge simply noted without elaboration that what Shakespeare had done with Enobarbus's description of Cleopatra in her barge as it stands in North sufficed to demonstrate once for all the superiority of "poematic" composition over even the finest poetic prose. In 1928, in a letter to the *Times Literary Supplement*, Eliot contested the judgment of a previous correspondent that when Shakespeare's version of Coriolanus's speech offering his services to Aufidius is rearranged as prose it is superior, *as prose*, to North's. Eliot held that great verse becomes bad prose when without any other adjustment its linear structure is dismantled; and, conversely, fine prose segmented into lines of verse with no other change makes bad verse. His opinion of course argues a deep-lying ontic divergence between the two forms of written expression. [33]

It also invites inspection of the skillful incorporation of scraps of Launcelot Andrewes's prose, which Eliot thought very fine indeed, into both "The Journey of the Magi" and "Ash Wednesday." F. O. Matthiessen matched the opening lines of the first poem with its source in Andrewes to show that the engraftment was made with at least no loss of quality. Here is Andrewes:

> It was no summer progress. A cold coming we had of it at this time of the year, just the worst time of the year to take a journey, and specially a long journey in. The ways deep, the weather sharp, the days short, the sun farthest off, *in solstitio brumali*, "the very dead of winter."

And here Eliot:

> 'A cold coming we had of it,
> Just the worst time of the year
> For a journey, and such a long journey:
> The ways deep and the weather sharp,
> The very dead of winter.'

Since most readers seem to agree that Eliot has made a metrically successful adaptation of Andrewes, it is perhaps debatable whether it can be reconciled with the principle of rhythmic disparity posited in his letter to the *Times*. Yet without digressing into a full explication, I would submit that the appeal of Eliot's versification in "The Journey of the Magi" depends on more than the greater concentration achieved by deletion. One might consider that it owes something as well to an inherently poetic cast of Andrewes's style, which Eliot elsewhere praised for "flashing phrases which never desert the memory." But that would introduce an element at best epiphenomenal to a theory which makes crucial a rhythmic difference. (Compare the cadences of Eliot's "such a long journey" with Andrewes's "specially a long journey in.")[34]

In "The Borderline of Prose," Eliot's insistence on the rhythmic dissimilarity of verse and prose benefits from his discerning samplings of poetic prose to show relative degrees of success or deficiency. The first, which he finds defective, is one by Richard Aldington, beginning "For my sake Eos, in a cloudless sky, gliding from the many-isled sea, must be more tender and more thrilling. . . ." Read as prose, Eliot argues, the whole passage is "jerky and fatiguing" because of the intrusive presence of verse rhythms, while prose rhythms defeat any attempt to read it as verse. The first three phrases have a distinctly measured lilt, "but what immediately follows—'must be more tender and more thrilling'—is prose," the more so for including the prosy word "thrilling." Of the three exhibits of good poetic prose, the last is the most telling because taken from so unlikely a source as Bradley's *Principles of Logic*.

> That the glory of this world is appearance leaves the world more glorious if we feel it is a show of some fuller splendour; but the sensuous curtain is a deception and a cheat—if it hides some colourless movement of atoms, some spectral woof of impalpable abstractions, or unearthly ballet of bloodless categories.[35]

Eliot's rejection of the concept of verse and prose forming together a medium of infinite gradations is much relaxed, if not
quite abandoned, by 1930, when in a brief preface to his translation of St. John Perse's prose-poem *Anabasis* he confronted the
issue head-on.

> I refer to this poem as a poem. It would be convenient if poetry
> were always verse—either accented, alliterative, or quantitative;
> but that is not true. Poetry may occur, *within a definite limit on
> one side, at any point along a line of which the formal limits are
> 'verse' and 'prose.'* (italics added)

Regretting, as other critics had done, the difficulty imposed by
lack of a relative term for *good* prose to balance *poetry* in the sense
of good verse, Eliot declined to hazard a general theory. He maintained only that Perse was one of a few poets who have written poetry in "what is called prose," leaving some doubt in a reader's
mind whether he considered *Anabase* to be, in fact, prose at all.
(One's uncertainty here can only be compounded by Valéry Larbaud's reference to its "prosodie" being "basée sur l'alexandrin.")
But Eliot insists that Perse's creation is poetry, because he has used
two "exclusively poetic methods" in composing it. The work's
"logic of imagery," being an imaginative rather than a conceptual
logic, is exclusively poetic; and, largely as a consequence, the "system of stresses and pauses" is also that of poetry alone.[36]

The student of Eliot's poetics is beset at this point by two nag-
ging queries. Is the structural distinction indicated by a "logic of
imagery" to be understood as superseding, or only as supplement-
ing, his doctrine of two rhythms? There is also a broader metrical
question left unresolved in this account. Presumably Eliot's gamut
is said to be "limited" at the prose end in order to exclude discursive writing. Undetermined, however, is whether the progression
from the prose to the verse end is valuatively neutral and generically seamless, or rather a mounting gradation of poetic intensity
culminating in the accretion of meter as a change of expressive
mode. The latter conception is certainly the more consonant with
his later assertions.

In Eliot's estimation, the genre most congenial to venting
powerful emotion was the verse drama, in which during his entire
career he aspired, with indifferent success, to make his mark. In
the title of his essay "Poetry and Drama," *poetry* clearly means
verse, since his stated aim is to show how poetic drama can convey

something "that prose drama cannot." It is here that Eliot posits a "triple distinction" among prose, verse, and ordinary speech. In the English theater, he notes, real-life utterance has been represented on two mimetic levels, both artificial: prose, as in the plays of Congreve and Shaw; and verse, or a mixture of verse and prose, as in Elizabethan drama. Freely conceding the remarkable achievements of Ibsen and Chekhov, Eliot nonetheless believes them to have been "hampered in expression by writing in prose." Only verse permits the "musical design" overarching the dramatic movement and subconsciously checking and accelerating "the pulse of our emotion."[37]

This collaborative blend of action and musical design is possible because verse properly employed, in this genre as in every other, is more than a mere formalizing embellishment; on the stage especially it makes for dramatic intensification. Of course, as in any metrical work "of any length," much of the verse, corresponding to emotive lapses in the dialogue, will be barely poetic. It becomes more fully so as the dramatic situation rises in intensity, because then poetry "is the only language in which the emotions can be expressed at all." The first scene of *Hamlet* shows how in expert hands the transition between emotive levels may occur quite rapidly without incongruous effect. Eliot points out that by Horatio's lyrically figurative exclamation,

> But look, the morn in russet mantle clad
> Walks o'er the dew of yon high eastward hill,

"we are lifted for a moment beyond character, but with no sense of unfitness of the words coming, and at this moment, from the lips of Horatio." Yet they had been immediately preceded by the near-conversational simplicity of

> So have I heard and do in part believe it,

a line almost equally at home in either prose or verse, and immediately followed by a further drop from intensity in the half-line that Eliot considers hardly more than a stage direction: "Break we our watch up."[38]

If in 1930, impressed by Perse's achievement, Eliot had admitted the possibility that the termini of the line along which poetry may occur were of equal value, by 1951 he had reverted to his youthful opinion that only poetry of relatively limited power and restricted range could be realized in prose. "Poetry and Drama," an exercise in retrospective speculation validated by the author's experience as poet and playwright, makes the case for taking the verse pole of his poetic axis to be not alone the high point of an upward progression, but a substantive mutation of aesthetic potential as well. In Coleridge's terms, Eliot's progression of "poetic" intensity culminates in the "poematic."

Before examining Eliot's conception of meaning in poetry, it is well to make a stab at reducing the confusion caused by a terminological puzzle: what he meant by *feeling*, a word ubiquitous in his critical writing, especially in theoretically important passages. For most readers it first comes to unsettling attention in his best known essay, where the terms feeling and emotion are used not as the synonyms or near-synonyms they are usually taken to be, but as terms with mutually exclusive but unspecified referents. Confirming in "Tradition and the Individual Talent" the familiar doctrine that aesthetic experience is generically unique, Eliot argued that a poem may be made of one emotion or of several, to which the poet adds various feelings inhering for him in certain words, phrases, or images. Or sometimes even a great poem may be formed of feelings exclusively. Since, as Northrop Frye observed, he nowhere clarifies by definition this scrupulous "desynonymization," a reader's obvious recourse is to infer their designations from other passages in his writing where the two terms appear. This is not easily done however. According to his account of the objective correlative, it is emotion that requires concrete representation in art; but in the contemporaneous formulation in "The Possibility of Poetic Drama" the elements so represented are thought and feeling. Elsewhere, as in the final two paragraphs of the *Hamlet* essay and years later in "The Social Function of Poetry," emotion and feeling appear as synonyms. Sometimes emotion designates the common passions, love, fear, jealousy, and so on, where feeling stands either for sensation (physical or psychological), sentiment, or—most rarely—opinion. But employed in these familiar senses neither word figures in theoretically relevant contexts, in which *feeling* occurs much more often, and always with quite emphatic critical significance.[39]

Several scholars have maintained with varying degrees of confidence that Eliot's *feeling* derived from F. H. Bradley. Yet Eliot himself complained that Bradley did not satisfactorily elucidate the term, which of course does not preclude his lifting it from Bradley to designate something other than a rough equivalent to *emotion*. It is this designation of *feeling* that requires careful sifting since it is crucial to his view of what confers on poetry, especially metrical poetry, its unique expressive value.[40]

Put most simply, Eliot means by *feeling* what poetry as an art directly communicates, an experience ranging from the amusing to the ecstatic. Often the word appears in tandem with *thought*. The stanzaic form of the Shakespearean sonnet is "a precise way of thinking and feeling." Classical Greek is unrivaled "as a vehicle for the fullest range and the finest shades of thought and feeling." The auditory imagination exclusively empowers a poet to penetrate below "the conscious levels of thought and feeling." And the list goes on.[41]

As Martin Scofield perceived, *emotion* and *feeling* in Eliot seem respectively to name the life and art ends of the mimetic transaction, artistic creation being, centrally, a transformation of personal emotion *into* feeling in the finished product. But the matter is not quite so tidy. The emotions in question may be fictional, forming no part of the author's experience. Sometimes Eliot reverses his terms, feelings being ascribed to the poet's affective state and emotions to the poem. A "new art emotion" is aroused when a speech in Cyril Tourneur's *Revenger's Tragedy* combines certain "floating feelings" with the warring emotions evinced by the speaker. Presumably these elusive feelings are "afloat" not in the speaker's consciousness but in the poet's, which has just been likened to a receptacle where "numberless feelings, phrases, images" are stored against the moment when they all fuse to form a new compound. And—what Eliot never allows us to forget—the density of this compound in the resulting poem is "something quite different" from the intensity of the emotions it embodies, especially when, like those of Dante's Paolo and Francesca, they belong to fictive persons.[42]

Eliot's coupling of feeling *with* thought in verbal art acknowledges the co-presence of the affective and intellective elements in poems. Readers may wonder whether to interpret feeling as only a more refined or sublimated species of emotion, or as a psychic state in which the visceral is so far subordinated to the cerebral in their fusion as to qualify it as a kind of intuiting. While the former option may suffice to justify Eliot's occasional substitution of *sensibility* for *feeling*, the latter is more consistent with his claim that in a work of art feeling is as much an intellectual product as is thought. Since this claim would make the phrase "thought and feeling" tautological, it is understandable that Eliot should often speak of feeling alone in reference to poetic meaning.[43]

Guided by Bradley, Lewis Freed offers a gloss that would assign equal status to Eliot's pair of associated terms. Though distinct, he argues, they are interrelated and mutually transformed. In a poem, thought thus sheds its abstract character and "takes on reality." In the simultaneous transformation of feeling into thought the process is reversed. Poetically verbalized, what was pure feeling loses the immediacy Bradley ascribes to it, to become instead "an object of thought . . . touched with ideality."[44]

But Freed's otherwise lucid exegesis does not adequately distinguish Eliot from the many other critics who, like his friend J. M. Murry, also saw in "a momentary union of thought and feeling" the essence of poetic expression. Freed mistakenly assumes that in the unified sensibility which in both the poet and his society Eliot thinks indispensable for the finest poetry to appear, thought and feeling are of equal weight. Granted, Eliot's habitual coordinate linking of them implies as much. But in his several descriptions of their interaction thought is ancillary to the attainment of the perfected feeling that constitutes the sum total of what a poem conveys. The point is most forcibly put when Eliot considers Dante's struggle to make us "apprehend sensuously" the varieties of heavenly blessedness represented in the *Paradiso*. Beatrice's exposition of the divine will

> is really directed at making us *feel* the reality of the condition of Piccarda; Dante has to educate our senses as he goes along. The insistence throughout is upon states of feeling; the reasoning takes only its proper place as a means of reaching these states.

In like fashion, Eliot sees in the ratiocinative cast of the Metaphysical poets' verse evidence of the direct impact of reading and thought upon their "mode of feeling." Jonson and Chapman incorporated their unusual erudition "into their sensibility," Chapman especially having attained a virtual "recreation of thought into feeling." To Donne a thought was an experience that "modified his sensibility." The gradual dissolution of the unified sensibility began when poets no longer made this inherently hierarchical conception of the cognitive- affective union the ground of their search for "the verbal equivalent for states of mind and feeling."

Thus in Gray's "Country Churchyard" Eliot felt the feeling to be cruder than that displayed in Marvell's "Coy Mistress." The verse of Laforgue and Corbière was propitious to his own poetic development in great part because he saw in it a modern recrudescence of the Metaphysicals' instinct for transmuting an idea or an experience into the "state of mind" he labeled feeling or sensibility.[45]

CHAPTER FIFTEEN

৯.

Eliot II

The Frontiers of
Poetic Cognition

THE DISSIMILAR IDEALS
of the poet's cultural role held by Eliot and Arnold correspond to
differing conceptions of poetic cognition. To both men, intellectual acquirement was part of a poet's equipment, and thinking a
vital part of creative activity. Although their estimates of the English Romantic poets do not otherwise agree, Eliot firmly seconded
Arnold's charge that they "did not know enough." Arnold at times
seemed to have sensed that what society expected from poets—and
what it received from the best of them—was somewhat more than
mere knowledge. Eliot was glad to register his approval of one of
Arnold's "wisest observations about poetry," in his "Memorial
Verses" lamenting the gap left by Wordsworth's death:

Others will strengthen us to bear—
But who, ah who, will make us feel?

But in his criticism Arnold values poetry less for its power to en-
liven sensibility than for its function in conveying great conceptions, the "moral ideas" he constantly stressed as necessary to cultural health, and the source of that consolation which poets were
uniquely qualified to administer to humanity. At this point he and
Eliot part company. Their dissent is portended in differing views
of the critical function. Arnold charged critics with the weighty

task of propagating the ideas by which creative power is nourished—the "best" ideas. Eliot confined them to elucidating literary works and refining the public taste. In poetry too, Arnold proclaimed, "the idea is everything. . . . Poetry attaches its emotion
to the idea." Ideas are the elements the poet works with, and his
service to his culture consists in an undefined application of them
to "life," though of course in conformity to the mysterious laws of
poetic beauty and poetic truth.[1]

Although ideas may not have meant quite the same thing to
Arnold and Eliot, the overlap of meaning between them allows us
to discern a significant disagreement in what each wrote of intellectual activity in the general culture. If Eliot had shared Arnold's
conviction of the primary importance of ideas to poetic creation,
he might well have deplored poetry itself as a corrosive institution,
certain to exacerbate the social malaise he diagnosed in the England of 1918. There at that moment, he observed, as though in
direct refutation of Arnold, "ideas run wild and pasture on the
emotions; instead of thinking with our feelings (a very different
thing) we corrupt our feelings with ideas." Though Eliot conceded that some poems were in fact repositories of ideas, he sided
with those who held that that was not what made them poems,
however sound or salutary the ideas might be. For him a poem resulted only when its creator had employed language to turn ideas
into feelings, a transmutation accomplished by exercising not the
reason but the delicately percipient faculty of human consciousness he called sensibility. As Eliot conceived it, when an idea took
on a life parasitic on a poet's sensibility there ensued a pathology
of the creative imagination that was sooner or later bound to en-
gender a social malaise as well. Health was assured when the opposite relation prevailed: when feelings battened on concepts. The
poetic sensibility he praised in the work of Andrewes, Donne, and
Jeremy Taylor lay in their possessing the tact needed to bring to
bear on theological ideas a host of "floating but universal feelings." This is the psychic condition that makes immediately available to consciousness words that "linger and echo in the mind."
Other writers, by retailing the soundest knowledge old or new revealed by philosophical analysis or scientific investigation, arm the
public against intellectual stagnation. Only poets, Eliot thought,
uniting an exceptional sensibility with verbal skill, could, as noted
earlier, provide against the greater menace of spiritual atrophy.[2]

Recognition of a cognitive quality of any kind in poetry assumes that it shares a communicative function with all other ways

of employing words. That assumption has of course long been challenged by those who wish above all to ensconce poetry in an enclave immune to colonization by the cognitionally sturdier disciplines of philosophy and empirical science. At times these vindicators of the muses have either depreciated the semantic element in poetry as a mere epiphenomenon or else, with the more extreme formalists, decried it as an impurity. But their doctrine has never won general acceptance, mainly because even the kinds of verse that conform most closely to their ideal—such as Shakespeare's songs, the more hermetically obscure modern verse, or "nonsense" poems like Edward Lear's—never completely fail to activate a reader's mental response at some level. Alluding to Poe's poems, which figure so prominently in the pantheon of "poésie pure," Eliot declared that in even the most incantatory of them the "dictionary meaning of words" could never be wholly neglected. The very attempt to do so could only be self-defeating since, as he argued in *Christianity and Culture* (1949), "the arts without intellectual content are vanity."[3]

Yet if for these reasons the most effective retort to Archibald MacLeish's slogan "A poem should not mean / But be" is that no poem can ever "be" *without* meaning, critics have still been increasingly convinced that the meaning we discern and readily respond to in poetry differs from that communicated in ordinary language—in kind, in mode of apprehension, or in both. To isolate and define its peculiar status has long been one of the hardest tasks faced by poeticians. Always at least an undercurrent in Eliot's criticism, the problem of what and how a poem means emerged as a major theme in *The Use of Poetry*, where he admitted that the more one pondered it the more baffling it became. The impasse, as by then he had come to conceive it, lay in the elusive ontology of a poem, irreducible to what the poet aimed to say, to his experience during composition, or to the reader's experience during perusal. It was Eliot's effort to resuscitate poetic drama in viable modern form that finally overcame his reluctance to thread what he had earlier described as "the mazes of intellectual subtlety" barring the way to an elucidation of poetic meaning. What resulted from his exploration of this theoretical labyrinth, though it makes up only a small part of his total criticism, is in many respects the crowning achievement of a career-long reflection on poetic language.[4]

Certain paradoxical statements thrown out at scattered moments in the course of that reflection seem in retrospect to have

been hinting at a conception that sharply differentiated the meaning conveyed by poetry from that conveyed by prose, and in terms
increasingly provocative. He declared that poetic forms are ways of
thinking and feeling (1920), that genuine poetry "can communicate before it is understood" (1929), and that the "philosophy" of
Beethoven's music, though closed to verbal articulation, is more
compatible with that found in Dante than is Shakespeare's philosophy (1930). Addressing a radio audience of school children in
1936, he held it to be common knowledge that some things could
be said in music that could not be said in common speech, and
that other things could be said in poetic drama unsayable in either
music or common speech.[5]

These declarations forecast the idea of poetic meaning Eliot
finally delineated. The notion of poetry communicating things before they are rationally grasped, for instance, is perfectly consistent
with his central thesis that what poetry communicates is feeling.
For in feeling the ideational component has been transmuted in a
way that enables it to short-circuit the sequential process of reasoning to attain immediate apprehension. As a tenet of his whole conception of poetic meaning, Eliot's reversal of the normal order of
the comprehension and conveyance of thought has equally paradoxical corollaries in two other assertions concerning poetic creation. In 1942 he reported that the germ of a poem may be only a
particular rhythm which then engenders both its images and its
ideas. In "Virgil and the Christian World" (1951), he made explicit
what that earlier assertion implies: that all that can be meant by the
worn-out word inspiration is that "a speaker or writer is uttering
something which he does not wholly understand."[6]

No writer was ever firmer than Eliot in believing that poetry
was not a decorous appendage of philosophy, theology, or science,
but an art, defined and appraised by aesthetic criteria. Yet he was
equally sure that those criteria, grounded as they had to be in
human nature, subsumed moral and cognitive components; and
that the utterance of a genuine poet, however metrically alluring,
aimed at something more than refined sensuous titillation. He
could therefore never subscribe to a poetics of formal purity. His
brash dismissal in 1928 of Shelley's "Skylark" as a brainless poem,
in which for the first time in eminent verse "sound exists without
sense," was tantamount to a verdict of poetic nullity. Two decades
later he confronted Valéry's "very neat and persuasive analogy"
that poetry differs from prose as dancing differs from walking. The
French poet had employed it to enforce the conclusion that poetry

conveys no meaning whatsoever, whereas prose does nothing else. In a dichotomy so absolute, Eliot pointed out, both forms are misrepresented. For just as prose may be enhanced by stylistic mastery, poetry is never ideationally void.[7]

Eliot posited two kinds of poetic meaning at different stages of his career. Both are grounded in feeling, envisaged as the state of consciousness in which thought has undergone a transmutation whereby the form of logical articulation is replaced by that of a concrete embodiment. Discursive explanation gives way to imagistic or symbolic presentation. The earlier kind of meaning (alias thought, message, and so forth) is ordinarily amenable to paraphrase—though only with the loss of much of its connotation, most of its cogency, and virtually all of its aesthetic value. The later kind cannot be paraphrased at all or, strictly speaking, even *verbalized* in the poem itself. In all poetry worthy of the name there is meaning of the first kind; in the finest poetry both are present, the non-paraphrasable kind predominating in rare passages of great lyric or dramatic intensity.

The enigma of "how a poem means" is an aspect of the age-old problem of how form and content are joined. For Eliot as for Aristotle the form-content issue posed itself with unusual urgency in the special case of overtly didactic poetry. In the essay on Dante in *The Sacred Wood* he could easily confirm Aristotle's judgment that the versified philosophy of Empedocles was not poetry, since it had long been recognized that metrical form was insufficient by itself to confer poetic value on otherwise prosaic discourse. But Eliot addresses the thornier aspect of the problem raised by verse of obvious poetic merit that aimed among other things to inculcate, or, at the very least, celebrate a particular doctrine. In the *Divine Comedy* and the *De Rerum Natura* Dante and Lucretius were truly poets, and not only because both men had had the good sense to use for poetic purposes philosophical systems ready to hand, thus eschewing what Eliot thought the self-defeating task of combining original thinking with poetic creation. In its original form, he wrote, philosophy cannot be poetic. What we call a philosophic poem is a poem "penetrated by a philosophic idea" which through long and deep-seated conviction has become for the poet "almost a physical manifestation." The form taken by this penetration—and what the poem if successful conveys—is not doctrine itself but its "poetic equivalent . . . its complete equivalent in vision," a conception of the cognitive issue akin to Coleridge's principle of creative imitation. Eliot could later plausibly enough extend his distinction to all intellectually freighted poetry. Pondering the stoical strain in Shakespeare's plays, he generalized that poets who think are poets who "can express the emotional equivalent of thought." He declined to specify exactly what elements of language or structure constituted the "equivalence." But even though to do so is beyond human wit, his term is useful if only because it will always seem an apt label for what readers experience as they follow a versified argument.[8]

Between 1924 and 1929 I. A. Richards published his influential *Principles of Literary Criticism, Science and Poetry,* and *Practical Criticism,* books in which the intellectual status of poetry is a major theme. He raised the vexed problem of "belief," whether a reader's dissent from some doctrine or revulsion from some ethical norm represented in a poem must (or should) inhibit his appreciation of it. Richards cut the Gordian knot by propounding an essentially positivist version of poetic purity. Rightly read, poems can neither offend nor flatter our opinions or convictions because they make no truth claims; only science can do that. Statements embedded in poetry are only "pseudo-statements," calculated not to persuade us of anything but to promote our emotional well-being. Impressed by Richards's analyses, Eliot agreed, in a long note to the second section of his 1929 essay on Dante, that if such a thing as poetry exists, it must be possible to enjoy and fairly judge it without sharing the values the poet advocates. But finding like other readers that the quality of the moral and intellectual content by which a poem is "penetrated" quite properly weighed in his assessment of it, he rejected the notion of pseudo-statements. He could make no sense of Richards's commendation in *Science and Poetry* that *The Waste Land* had been kept free of any beliefs whatsoever.[9]

In the following year, dissatisfied with his earlier remarks, Eliot answered Richards more fully in "Poetry and Propaganda," reaffirming the notion of a "poetic equivalent" but this time melding it with the analogy of incarnation. Granting Richards's point that poetry *asserts* nothing as true, he vindicated its ancient claim to moral and intellectual relevance by defining it as "the creation of a sensuous embodiment" of thought, "making the Word Flesh." The operative difference between forms of cognition in prose and in verse is lucidly stated in the closing words of his essay.

Poetry cannot prove that anything is *true;* it can only create a variety of wholes, composed of intellectual and emotional constituents, justifying the emotion by the thought and the thought by the emotion: it proves successively, or fails to prove, that certain worlds of thought and feeling are *possible*. It provides intellectual sanction for feeling, and esthetic sanction for thought.[10]

Eliot's later contribution to an elucidation of poetic meaning is the more compelling, perhaps because it is drawn from his deepest and most intense creative experience. This is an alternative kind, for the most part conceived after the completion of *Four Quartets* and mainly as an offshoot of the labors on verse drama that occupied his final creative phase. It is resident neither exclusively in the formal elements of a poem nor in what the words "say," but in a play of sonant and rhythmic patterns arising from their arrangement and yet dependent for its efficacy on subtle correspondences with their referential import. These formal features amount to arabesques of the poet's "feeling" which yet mysteriously transcend mere decoration to function as objective correlatives of that feeling. This second of Eliot's two conceptions of poetic cognition presumes the most thorough-going degree of holistic unity ever envisaged for verbal art. It constitutes that "music" of verse, which, he tells us, never exists apart from meaning but eludes paraphrase because it is the fruit of the poet's forays across "frontiers of consciousness beyond which words fail though meanings still exist."[11] This elusive aspect of poetic language is treated in the two most theoretically significant essays in *On Poetry and Poets*, the exposition begun in "The Music of Poetry" being resumed after a nine-year interval in "Poetry and Drama" (1951).

There are, however, fragmentary adumbrations of his theory scattered throughout the earlier criticism from *The Sacred Wood* to the late 1930s. I have already alluded to Eliot's notion that the various stanza forms and meters are essentially different ways of thinking and feeling, which implies by extension that separate rhythms for verse and prose belong to separate orders of cognition. Therefore the only justification for turning a passage of prose into verse would be to articulate feelings (and therefore "meanings") unglimpsed in the prose. By the same token, free verse might never have arisen had poets not felt impelled to vent in novel "interpretations" of life their sense of a profound change in the human condition, which artists, functioning as Pound's "antennae of the race," were the first to detect in the waning 1800s. Of like tendency with Eliot's iterations that some things could be said in verse that could not be said otherwise is his explanation of why Metaphysical verse, unlike the songs of Shakespeare and Campion, would suffer by being set to music. In the work of Donne and his school, "the metrical beauty is so closely associated with the thought" that the verse contains in itself the only possible music.[12]

A more arresting hint of what he was to expound in the essays of 1942 and 1951 was given in Eliot's review of Marianne Moore's poetry for the *Dial* in 1923. The highly idiosyncratic cadences of her poems led him to observe that verse rhythm is "always the real pattern in the carpet, the scheme of organization of thought, feeling, and vocabulary, the way in which everything comes together." Eliot's allusion was to Henry James's tale of an eminent novelist who complains to a young reviewer that no critic had yet detected the central intention running through his fiction. Asked whether it is an element of form or of feeling, the novelist asks in turn whether the heart in the human body is an element of form or of feeling. The reviewer now understands the novelist to be hinting at "the primal plan; something like a complex figure in a Persian carpet." As Eliot construed it, James's ingenious image bespeaks a covert intuition of what he himself would propound only after his views on poetic drama had been "modified and reviewed" by years of personal experimentation with it: that what are lightly referred to as the harmonies of verse are as *thematically* vital as they are aurally attractive. And this holds even when the aural harmony is minimal. For though a musical structure is everywhere felt in a good poem, no poem either need be or should be "wholly melodious."[13]

Ideas in "The Music of Poetry," either stated for the first time or resumed from earlier critical pieces, will function later as subsumptions of the concept of non-paraphrasable meaning described in "Poetry and Drama." In the earlier essay Eliot restates his beliefs that verse may transmit psychic content incommunicable in the rhythm of prose, and that there can be no poetry of notable musical beauty devoid of meaning. This latter point is then elaborated. The music of a poetic word is located at a point of intersection between two orders of contextual relationship. One occurs where a word takes on a coloring from its interaction with other words in the poem where it appears; the other is imparted by the different meanings it has borne in other contexts, "its greater or less wealth of association." The process is an accretion of "secondary" meanings to those which words hold independently of context. This double source of semantic enrichment serves as a gloss to the second of two musical patterns that characterize what people call musical poems, "the pattern of the secondary meanings of the words which compose it"—the first pattern being merely phonic. Eliot's added reminder that the two patterns are "indissoluble and one" is another assumption entailed in his later account of non- paraphrasable meanings. A final reflection in "The Music of Poetry," one obviously relevant to the *Four Quartets,* should also be kept in mind when reading "Poetry and Drama":

> The use of recurrent themes is as natural to poetry as to music. There are possibilities for verse that bear some analogy to the development of a theme by different groups of instruments; there are possibilities of transitions in a poem comparable to the different movements of a symphony or a quartet; there are possibilities of contrapuntal arrangement of subject-matter.[14]

Eliot became increasingly aware that the "profound difference" between the expressive potentials of dramatic and nondramatic verse was that stage poetry bears a relation to the spoken idiom significantly different from what obtains in other poetry. Its mimetic link to real life is complicated by having to provide not only for several speakers individually, in place of a single lyric persona; dramatic verse must at the same time create the simulated "world of persons" they comprise in combination. This complex relation requires the dramatic poet to fashion an idiom operative "at a deeper level" than the idiom that suffices in other genres, one that generates a different order of "music." It is this consideration that mainly motivates Eliot's rule that a playwright is mistaken if he expects audiences to tolerate poetry in his play as a gratuitous embellishment to the action. The only justification for employing it is to intensify the situation by a "kind of musical design . . . which reinforces and is one with the dramatic movement." Only if this condition is met, he argued, will the playgoers, instead of being merely presented with a spectacle of the poet's willful feigning, find the dreary course of their daily lives "suddenly illuminated and transfigured."[15]

It is therefore fitting that Eliot's boldest delineation of the second means whereby metrical language signifies more deeply than prose occurs in an essay devoted to poetic drama. It comes in a closing paragraph which rises at times to visionary fervor as he tries to convey the "unobtainable ideal" he had been striving to fulfill in his own works for the stage.

It seems to me that beyond the nameable, classifiable emotions and motives of our conscious life when directed toward action—the part of life which prose drama is wholly adequate to express—there is a fringe of indefinite extent, of feeling which we can only detect, so to speak, out of the corner of the eye and can never completely focus; of feeling of which we are only aware in a kind of temporary detachment from action. . . . This peculiar range of sensibility can be expressed by dramatic poetry, at its moments of greatest intensity. At such moments, we touch the border of those feelings which only music can express. We can never emulate music, because to arrive at the condition of music would be the annihilation of poetry, and especially of dramatic poetry. Nevertheless, I have before my eyes a kind of mirage of the perfection of verse drama, which would be a design of human action and of words, such as to present at once the two aspects of dramatic and of musical order. It seems to me that Shakespeare achieved this at least in certain scenes—even rather early, for there is the balcony scene of *Romeo and Juliet*—and that this was what he was striving towards in his late plays. To go as far in this direction as it is possible to go, without losing that contact with the ordinary everyday world with which drama must come to terms, seems to me the proper aim of dramatic poetry. For it is ultimately the function of art, in imposing a credible order upon ordinary reality, and thereby eliciting some perception of an order *in* reality, to bring us to a condition of serenity, stillness, and reconciliation; and then leave us, as Virgil left Dante, to proceed toward a region where that guide can avail us no farther.[16]

This remarkable passage, unparalleled anywhere in Eliot's criticism, is itself so nearly a prose poem (Peacock calls it "a poem of theory")[17] that it lends fresh point to Friedrich Schlegel's dictum that poetry can be discussed only in poetry. The elusive nature of the phenomenon he dealt with debarred Eliot from treating it throughout in his usual discursive manner. He could proffer only "a dim outline" of the mirage of dramatic perfection he descried. Since the arcane features of versification that empower poets to voice the ineffable are themselves ineffable, he was reduced to dilating on the spiritually elevating experience afforded readers or auditors by the rare passages of verse where those undefinable qualities are at work.

This is far from suggesting that Eliot's perorational paragraph does not repay rational inspection. Rather it must be classified

among the memorable passages in the literature on aesthetics and
the fine arts which depend for their validation on a collaborative
contribution by readers intimately acquainted with the quality or
effect at which the theorist can only hint. In this instance the
reader's burden is eased when he is told that Shakespeare has come
closest to realizing the "unobtainable ideal." Eliot's words bring
immediately to mind any number of Shakespearean lines that
never fail to stir feelings detectable only "out of the corner of the
eye" and cause a "temporary detachment from action," feelings
more often aroused by exquisitely beautiful music than by poetry.
For the assurance that this sort of experience is by no means idiosyncratic the evidence is incontrovertible, evinced most eloquently
perhaps in the rapt silence that comes over audiences at certain
moments during a Shakespeare performance. One thinks of the
poignantly worded reminiscences of storied nocturnal events exchanged between Jessica and Lorenzo in *The Merchant of Venice;*
Richard II's "For God's sake let us sit upon the ground . . .";
Viola's "A blank, my lord; she never told her love . . ." in *Twelfth
Night;* the exiled duke's "Sweet are the uses of adversity . . ." in *As
You Like It.* Sometimes the momentary entrancement is triggered
by a single line like the blinded Gloucester's "Were all thy letters
suns, I could not see," in *Lear;* or Eliot's own choice from *Othello,*
"Keep up your bright swords, for the dew will rust them."[18] To
demonstrate the expressive intensity uniquely possible in dramatic
verse, Eliot briefly analyzes the balcony scene in *Romeo* and the
first twenty-two lines of *Hamlet.* Yet few readers will fail to notice,
as he was well aware, that these skillful glosses fall short of accounting for the wondrous impressions that inspired his closing
paragraph. It cost him nothing to admit that the extraordinary impact of these scenes is aroused "in some mysterious way," since the
same impasse sooner or later impedes the efforts of every analyst
of the "magic of verse." Not a one but must in most cases confirm
Carl Jung's conclusion that artistic creation can be described in its
manifestations "but never wholly grasped."[19] With this in mind—
and intending no intrusive supplement to Eliot's rationale—I
would call attention to a peculiarity of the "mystery" he confronted. It consists in the fact that the affective impact made by
the passages of dramatic "music" is often out of all proportion to
the relative triviality of the paraphrasable level of their meaning.
To be sure this does not hold true in every memorable Shakespearean passage of extraordinary musical appeal. In Prospero's
moving lines comparing human life to a dream in *The Tempest,* for

instance, which certainly effect the momentary suspension of action Eliot speaks of, the depth of the thought, its challenge to imaginative conception, seem fully commensurate with the incantatory bewitchment of the words. In *A Midsummer Night's Dream*, however, the disproportion between dramatic import and lyrical allure is apparent throughout almost the whole of Oberon's speech to Puck, which is given a kind of framing within the idyllic scene by being set in rhyming couplets:

> I know a bank where the wild thyme blows,
>
> Where oxlips and the nodding violet grows. . . .

The discrepancy is even more pronounced in *Twelfth Night* when, to Olivia's question of what "he" would do to win her love, comes Viola's soaring effusion:

> Make me a willow cabin at your gate,
>
> And call upon my soul within the house;
>
> Write loyal cantons of contemnèd love
>
> And sing them loud even in the dead of night;
>
> Hallo your name to the reverberate hills,
>
> And make the babbling gossip of the air
>
> Cry out "Olivia!"

Whether or not Viola struck Olivia as protesting too much, she has had no such effect on readers, who have always relished her tirade as one of the two or three poetic "high spots" in the play. In the equally memorable passage in *Macbeth* cited above in another connection, "And pity, like a naked newborn babe . . . ," Susanne Langer noticed the gap between the thoughts expressed and what the words manage to convey. As she describes the discrepancy, "the literal sense of these prophecies is negligible, though that of the words is not. . . . Shakespeare's poetry rings with such diction."[20]

Throughout his discussion of cognition Eliot uses *feeling* to designate a state of consciousness imbued with affectively transmuted thought. In the visionary paragraph under discussion the word occurs three times (plus a single substitution of the synonymous *sensibility*). It is this transmutation of their ideational component that makes speeches of the greatest poetical intensity in dramatic verse inaccessible to paraphrase. Eliot characterizes their content as "feelings which only music can convey." As warrant that he intended by this no *ad hoc* acceptance of the pure poetry figment, we have his previous reference to the "philosophy" of Beethoven's music. When he likens the "musical pattern" in the balcony scene to that in early Beethoven, it is after having stressed that the pattern in both cases is one of "unnameable" psychic conditions. If the "philosophy" imparted by a symphony necessarily reaches us by a nonverbal medium, Romeo and Juliet's dialogue similarly emits a plenitude of signification, much of which lies in an ultra-verbal obligato to what is merely predicated. So Eliot's emphasis is on the "*design* of human actions and words," not on what the characters do or say.[21]

Viola's images of "reverberate hills" and "babbling gossip of the air" elicit from enchanted audiences no more apposite characterization than verbal music, but only if it means the kind of music to which people ignorant of English are necessarily deaf. In Eliot's discussion, that proviso comes in his caution that the poetry would be annihilated if it ever attained completely to the "condition" of music. On the other side of the equation his metaphor of Beethoven's philosophy will not seem strained to those who say of some masterpiece of instrumental music, "That speaks to me." Such listeners sense in the admirably "purposive" contrivance of the structural pattern of Bach's monumental C-minor *Passacaglia*, for striking example, a cognitive-moral imperative. Not even the reflection that what so deeply stirs them lies beyond logical scrutiny can ever persuade them to dismiss this imperative as hallucinatory. Why should they, when one of Bach's distinguished interpreters can allude without apology (or much fear of being misunderstood) to "the profounder meaning" of his keyboard *Inventions*? "A splendid melodic phrase," Edmund Gurney wrote in *The Power of Sound* (1880), "seems . . . like an *affirmation;* not so much prompting admiring ejaculation as compelling passionate assent."[22]

A presupposition of aesthetic symbolism is the surmise that all art either presents to consciousness a sensuous surrogate of logically apprehended cognition, or else makes manifest a truth, especially a moral truth, whose "color" lies outside the spectrum of rational comprehension altogether. In the Romantic climate of sensibility, this assumption was exalted to a central tenet of aesthetic faith. It was proclaimed as early as 1789 in Friedrich Schiller's poem on artists, "Die Künstler":

Was wir als Schönheit hier empfunden

wird einst als Wahrheit uns entgegengehn.

[What here we have perceived as beauty will one day confront us
as truth.]

In his *Lectures on Aesthetic Education* (1795), while denying an
immediate didactic role to art, Schiller affirmed that beauty necessarily includes truth in a higher unity of sensuous materiality and
"moral freedom."[23]

It is hard to think of any modern man of letters more hostile
than Eliot, for most of his life at least, to the notion that "what the
imagination seizes as Beauty must be Truth," as Keats put it to
Bailey. The more famous enshrinement of that idea in the "Ode
on a Grecian Urn" Eliot once professed to find incomprehensible.
Yet the Romantic conflation of beauty and truth and the visionary
last words of "Poetry and Drama" are remotely linked by their
common testimony to an ultra-lexical order of aesthetic communication. Eliot's account ends by hinting at a Christian alternative to
Schiller's view that poetry served a wise cosmic design, guiding us
to a blessed future, an "ocean" of universal concord ("Ozeane /
der grossen Harmonie"). In the optimistic ambience of the French
revolution this happy future state could be imagined as secular.
Two of his commentators write of Schiller's "faith in a coming age
in which ideals will prevail against the world's brute resistance."[24]
Eliot believed in no such earthly paradise. For him, the "serenity,
stillness, and reconciliation," which by revealing a hidden order in
reality great dramatic verse can bring us, is not our final destination. It is only a way station where we may be comforted by intimations of the region which in Eliot's eschatology the "Virgil" of
mere art cannot enter. Yet for those who on exposure to great poetry or music are heard to murmur, even in metaphor, "That
speaks of a better world," the intimations themselves seem real
enough.

What degree of certitude they had for Eliot is beyond knowing. Yet here, as everywhere else, he must be taken at his word. If
we attend properly to the course of his argument in "Poetry and
Drama," we can see him acting still as the analytic explorer of poetic style. What he dimly glimpsed in a perfected conjunction of
"the two aspects of dramatic and musical order," attainable only in
dramatic verse if at all, is a rarefied conception of the revelatory
potential of metrical utterance. The techniques involved in that

conjunction being ultra-lexical, we can speak of it as cognitive only in a special sense. The knowledge it conveys is akin to that conveyed by the kind of poetry Eliot had earlier distinguished as one aiming "to extend the confines of the human consciousness and to report of things unknown, to express the inexpressible."[25]

The vatic final sentence of "Poetry and Drama" is not incongruent with his immediately precedent effort to describe an ideal unobtainable if not illusory, a "mirage" which he thought not even Shakespeare had ever quite reached. The practical value of that ideal to Eliot may best be assessed by students of his plays. Our concern here being theoretical, it is perhaps enough that in the "musical" patterns of Shakespeare's dramatic verse he envisaged one of the most daring conceptions of poetic language ever proposed.

Epilogue
Postmodernist Theories

IF BY AN UNLIKELY CHANCE
Eliot pondered the immediate future of critical theory as he lay dying in 1965, he might well have murmured, "après moi le déluge."
The two-decade reign of a New Criticism largely of his inspiration
had ended on the eve of a disruption of Western literary thought
culminating in a poststructuralist phase of unparalleled innovation.
Novel critical methods were fomented less by looking afresh at the
distinctive properties of literature than by consulting extraliterary
disciplines. The first two—deriving their methods respectively from
Edmund Husserl's phenomenology and linguistic science—were
the Geneva critics, or critics of consciousness, headed by Georges
Poulet, and a group aiming at a poetics grounded in linguistic analytical techniques. These completely contrast. Consciousness criticism, largely neglectful of the formal problems encountered in a literary work's verbal materiality, recommended itself quite simply as
a more spiritually enriching mode of literary appreciation. Linguipoetics, to give it a handy nickname, saw especially in the systematic rigor of Ferdinand de Saussure's *Cours de linguistique
générale* (1916) the means for taking traditional concepts of literary language to greater depths of penetration and refinement. In
this collaboration of critic and linguist some saw the promise of a
solid theoretical advance; to others the interdisciplinary marriage
seemed from the start a barren miscegenation.[1] Virtually no one,
however, saw any reason to accuse either the phenomenologists or

the linguists of endangering the fabric of literary study. Tradition-
alists and innovators aired their differences in an atmosphere of
civility and shared institutional security, much as the New Humanists, neo-Aristotelians, and New Critics had done a generation
earlier.

This happy condition was not long to prevail. In rapid order
the benign initial departures from New Critical orthodoxy, which
among linguists included the structuralist poetics brilliantly cultivated by Jakobson, were superseded by a poststructuralism imported from France. Notably in the work of Roland Barthes and
then of Jacques Derrida, not only recently accredited literary
theories, but the very assumptions to which criticism had made
implicit appeal for validation since ancient times, came under
wholesale and relentless attack. Though linked to its immediate
precursors by a shared adaptation of Saussure, poststructuralism
rests centrally on epistemological and ontological doctrines of
Nietzsche, whom Harold Bloom dubbed "the patron saint of
structuralist deconstruction,"[2] and of Martin Heidegger. Their
thinking supplied the premises of the deconstructionist understanding of language both in its normal function and as a literary
medium. Radically disruptive of hitherto accredited concepts, this
understanding more than anything else initiated the period of
confusion, amounting in literary study to a *bouleversement,* which
only now shows signs of abating.

The current disorder, however, was not set afoot exclusively
by Gallic poststructuralism. Other very different movements and
"methods," highly contentious and mutually disparate, have
spawned what an anthologist of recent criticism characterized as
an unsettling "plethora of competing jargons and systems, to say
nothing of antisystems." Yet the heavy indictment brought against
poststructuralism cannot fairly be dismissed as the mere bias of a
reactionary traditionalism. When concessions to its detractors em-
anate from within the deconstructionist camp itself, as they sometimes have done, we confront something of a cultural puzzle.
Howard Felperin, after a searching survey of the warring critical
schools, claimed that deconstruction was the only one in our uni-
versities still willing to engage great literature as literature. If that
claim is correct, then surely it is primarily in deconstructive writings that we should expect to find, among other benefits, a fresh
look at the problem of poetic expression. But Felperin's declaration of faith seems like grasping at straws in light of his immediately preceding admission that the intellectual atmosphere in

which deconstruction came into vogue contained something that "brought western culture very near to anarchy." The irony here is matched by the *angst* of an ensuing question. How, he asks, can the critical and pedagogical literary enterprises withstand the "pitiless gaze" of a doctrine that by unsettling the hierarchical relations among our sacred texts and authors "demystifies our humanistic vision of high cultural and moral purpose?"[3]

At the very least we confront anomaly. Poetics was soon degraded to a subsidiary branch of linguistics, the very discipline to which it had appealed as a source of its own enrichment. Local in linguipoetics, this reordering of priorities quickly became global in humane studies. In poststructural theory the methodological linchpin is that every discipline, not only Claude Lévi-Strauss's anthropology and Pierre Lacan's psychoanalysis, but all institutions and social formations, from modes of philosophy to modes of dress, take linguistic structure as a common paradigm. From this interdisciplinary ground emerged a fortiori a critical orientation which holds that literature, fictive and nonfictive, including critical writing, conforms to this same linguistic model. In 1976 J. Hillis Miller found the contending sects of post-New Critical theory united only by a common focus on "language as the central problematic of literary study." One critic could even conceive human existence itself to be in accord with an omnideterminate linguistic figuration. "How thoroughly the human condition is a verbal condition!" Geoffrey Hartman exclaimed after explaining poetry's mixed power to unsettle and console. In so language-drenched an intellectual ambience we might reasonably have expected critics to probe, with greater zeal and theoretical sophistication than ever before, the nature of poetic expression. Yet—with exceptions few and feeble—compared with earlier periods that subject has been largely neglected or degraded to an aspect of one or another ideology.[4]

Before examining this anomaly, it may be instructive to glance at a related phenomenon bound to interest future historians: the New Criticism's status under the poststructuralist regime. Those who imagine its role in that hostile context to be quite simply that of bête noire are not far off the mark. At the same time, however, this supposedly defunct critical school has been enjoying a kind of afterlife, as one or another advocate of radical change has felt compelled to refer to the New Criticism, to confront afresh some part of its doctrine or method, usually but not always in disparagement. The potential for elucidation of critical problems inherent in such confrontation has been unfortunately thwarted by the tendency of some writers to vent their disapproval upon one or another caricature of the New Criticism, not its true form.[5]

Whether or not their tactic is an expedient substitute for directly challenging the New Criticism at its strongest point, poetic language, poststructuralists have not cared to second Hartman's candid confession in 1988 that New Criticism remains our only systematically argued poetic theory. So far as I've noticed, only Felperin among adherents of the new dispensation has dared to say that no current theory was likely to supplant either New Criticism or Leavisite "practical criticism," because none confronts "the difficult question of what constitutes 'literary' or 'poetic' language as against 'ordinary' language."[6]

Among contemporary theorists the heartiest champion of the New Critics against poststructuralist detraction has been Murray Krieger. But Krieger's spirited apologetics is flawed by his flat-out rejection of mimesis, including the Coleridgean conception of it so salutary in preventing organicist poetics from severing the indispensable cognitive and moral relevance of poetry to real life and human experience. Weightier support for the post-hegemonic viability of New Criticism has come from such prestigious books as Eric Auerbach's *Mimesis* (trans. 1953), E. H. Gombrich's *Art and Illusion* (1960), Susanne Langer's *Feeling and Form* (1953), Nelson Goodman's *Languages of Art* (1969), and Roger Scruton's *Art and Imagination* (1974). In their various ways, these learned specialist studies provided fresh and sophisticated confirmations of the very aesthetic and mimetic assumptions against which New Criticism's severest opponents directed their attacks.

Admirers of New Critical theory, Wellek among them,[7] had all along admitted its inherent limitations. But its final lapse from dominance was initiated mainly by the impact of Northrop Frye's *Anatomy of Criticism* in 1957. Frye's stress on a limited number of universally operative myths as ultimate sources and interpretative keys for all literature, conceived as a global order of words, suggested that the formalist focus upon the verbal structure of separate poems was insufficient support for a complete theory of fictive writing. Besides, Frye's global order, though a verbal one, actually displaces the poet's creative manipulation of his medium from the central critical emphasis it had enjoyed in the second phase of twentieth-century speculation. The critical appeal of a poem—for Frye gives us scant license to speak of its relative *value*—must depend rather on how deeply it taps the psychic power resident in some mythic archetype which, mediated via one or another literary genre, supplies its vitality.

Also effective in the dethronement of New Criticism was Hartman's penetrating essay "Beyond Formalism" (1966), which argued ably for a more inclusive kind of formalism, one that would take into account historical and social dimensions of literature too easily discounted in the medium-centered organicism of New Critical theory and practice.

The stage was clearly set for the arrival, from Europe as it happened, of modes of literary inquiry sharply divergent in aim and method from all that had gone before.

The Geneva critics, as an early expositor frankly admitted,[8] were poorest in their treatment of poetic language. It could hardly have been otherwise. For Poulet, the school's founder and most compelling practitioner, literature properly understood was not language, not even a product of language. Accordingly, the critic of a fictive work in any genre must effectively close his eyes to style, diction, patterns of structure, the contextual plays of meaning, and every other aspect of its verbal materiality. To the extent that his attention is drawn to these things, Poulet thought, he is deflected from his rightful task of submitting his own totally receptive consciousness to an empathic identification with the self-communings transmitted by an author's voice. Verbal ordonnance, prosody, and so on—these are matters germane to aesthetics, and Poulet openly affirmed the starkly unaesthetic conception of literary works entailed by his methodological restrictions.

Any reader of Poulet must admire his skill in executing this critical program, the nuanced graces of the prose in which he recreates writers' various experiences of time. But on reflection what strikes us most is the irrelevance to his terms and method of whether the work under scrutiny is Rousseau's prose or Alfred de Vigny's verse. The latter's "created flight," Poulet perceives, enables him to grasp "a past apt to be converted into a future, and into poetry." But except to note that that poetry is of a prophetic order, and to refer vaguely to poetic thought, Poulet gives no sign that the Vignian temporal sense might not have been as well expressed in prose. Writing of Baudelaire, he offers a string of quotations revealing the poet's states of mind, but again with no hint that his versification in any way affected their delineation. It is the same when he turns to Alfred de Musset in the later *La distance intérieure,* in which the many citations of verse and prose together might have induced a critic of Poulet's sensitivity to take note of their formal distinctions. He describes how Musset's whole mental life is caught up in a "prise de conscience de soi rapide et préci-pité," on the threshold of a "durée permanente" of realized erotic desire which evaporates at the very moment of its quickening an-ticipation. In the presence of such delicate psychological dissection an appreciative reader may wonder whether Musset's verse style in any respect reflects his idiosyncratic experience of temporal move-ment. Poulet never raises the question. Form counts for nothing. For him, as Sainte-Beuve had long ago said of Joubert, the whole charm of criticism is a knowledge of minds.[9]

In *The Disappearance of God* (1963), Poulet's American disci-ple J. Hillis Miller seconded his depreciation of the verbal medium. We attend to the words in a book, he wrote, only because they

> embody states of mind and make them available to others. . . . Criticism demands above all that gift of participation, that power to put oneself within the life of another person, which Keats called negative capability. If literature is a form of consciousness the task of a critic is to identify himself with the subjectivity ex-pressed in the words, to relive that life from the inside, and to constitute it anew in his criticism.

Not all Genevans were so shy of formal analysis as Poulet. His friend Jean-Pierre Richard combined phenomenological thematics with attention to such details of versification, for example, as Mal-larmé's use of rhyme. Miller could observe that De Quincey's style "mirrored" his mental space, that the dilute substance of Arnold's verse resulted from his insensitivity to the divine immanence in nat-ural scenery, and that in Hopkins's consciousness "the structure of the universe is echoed and imitated" in the structure of "Pied Beauty." As we should expect, this formal accessory is retained when Miller focuses mainly on poetry in *The Poets of Reality* (1965), his study of the existential sensibilities of several modern writers. Yet even in a fine chapter on Eliot the formal aspect re-mains a subordinate theme. Both the predominant concern with a writer's intellectual and affective character, and the secondary role of his art as such, are clearly signaled in Miller's method when he detects in the progress of Eliot's poetry "a recovery . . . of God im-manent in reality and revealed by the musical patterns of poetry."[10]

The stylistic and prosodic issues the Genevans thought mar-ginal were the linguistic critics' main agenda. Their enterprise was in essence a more scientifically systematic substitute for the New Criticism's response to J. C. Ransom's call for critics to discover "the secret of [poetry's] strange yet stubborn existence as a kind of discourse unlike any other." Their method took as premise the now common opinion that poets' extraordinary imaginative power consisted primarily of manipulative verbal skill, something directly amenable to scientific inspection. So the more one learned about language, Tzetvan Todorov argued, the easier it became to understand its creative possibilities. It seemed obvious that the moment had arrived, as Gérard Genette announced in 1966, for linguists and critics to join forces in attacking a problem so suited to their collaboration. In fact, Genette reminded his readers, Russian formalist poetics, quite rightly regarded as a matrix of structural linguistics, had had its inception precisely in a coming together of critics and linguists on the "terrain" of poetic language. In America, Jakobson more imperially proclaimed that poetics was simply a branch of linguistic science.[11]

If there has been any substantial advance in poetic language theory beyond the point reached during Eliot's career, it must be credited to Jakobson. Both friends and foes of the New Criticism have stressed what one foe, Christopher Norris, justly called "the deep affinity" between Jakobson's conservative brand of structuralism and New Critical poetics. The resemblance is immediately apparent in Jakobson's frequent assertion that poetics must primarily address the "literariness" of literature, the quality whose predominance in poetry sets the "abyss between the poetic and prosaic genres." Jakobson met head-on the charge by linguistically uninformed readers that his analytical method could never account for the nameless subtle ingredients that allegedly made poetry poetry. The same *je ne sais quoi*, he pointed out, is an equally elusive element in all scientific investigation—whether of language, society, the "mysteries" of physical matter, or life itself.[12]

No more did he adhere to any purist aesthetic, as de Man wrongly asserted. As early as 1933, in "Qu'est-ce que la Poésie?" he insisted that neither he nor such other Slavic formalists as Tynianov, Mukarovsky, or Shklovsky had ever believed in the self-sufficiency of art, arguing only for "l'autonomie de la fonction esthétique." Always the empirically minded (but imaginatively gifted) linguistic scientist, Jakobson considered literature to be a form of communication, a message. In his view, poems fulfilled neither an exclusively aesthetic function nor, exactly, an aesthetic function in tandem with other functions. A poetic work properly defined was a verbal message in which the "poetic function" was dominant in a hierarchic relation to whatever other functions might accompany it. (Jakobson's schema of verbal communication identifies six functions, including the familiar referential, emotive, and conative.)[13]

Three concepts of Jakobson's poetics, evolved from the rich store of his linguistic erudition, deepen the generic cleavage between prose and verse that is implied in his broad claim that in metrical form "any verbal element is converted into a figure of poetic speech." In the most cited concept he unites Saussure's two axes of verbal relation, the paradigmatic (selective) and syntagmatic (combinative), in the formula Wimsatt praised for its "bold compression": *"the poetic function projects the principle of equivalence from the axis of selection into the axis of combination."* This equivalence, which Jakobson followed Poe and G. M. Hopkins in identifying as poetry's defining structural feature, is applied to metrical utterance with something of the weight of a Kantian law. The second concept, an extension of this formula, posits a *grammar* of poetry. He has in mind the kind of verse which, though devoid of lexical imagery, has a poetic quality constituted of "gorgeous tropes and figures." The list of grammatical categories subject to equivalent arrangement (and contrast) is exhaustive:

> all the parts of speech, both mutable and immutable; numbers, genders, cases, grades, tenses, aspects, moods, voices, classes of abstract and concrete words, animates and inanimates, appellatives, proper names, affirmatives and negatives, finite and infinitive verbal forms, definite and indefinite pronouns or articles, and diverse syntactic elements and constructions.

Jakobson maintained that such "relational structures" function not only as attractive patterns; they also help to "foreground" a poem's diction, enhancing its designative force. How seriously he intended his list to be taken is clear from how thoroughly he and Lévi-Strauss applied it in their exegeses of Baudelaire's "Les Chats."[14]

Jakobson adapted a third linguistic concept to poetics in a chapter of his and Morris Halle's *Fundamentals of Language* (1956), "The Metaphoric and Metonymic Poles." Here the rift between verse, chiefly lyrical, and narrative prose, fictive and nonfictive, was newly defined by the different modes of figuration prevalent in the two forms. In poetry the governing trope is metaphor, stressing similarity; in prose it is metonymy, the figure of contiguity, especially prevalent in realistic fiction. Though in isolation this figural polarity seems tidier than the fluid forms of literature can warrant, Jakobson pointed to its consonance with the schema of his linguistic conception of poetry itself.

> "Since poetry is focused upon sign, and pragmatical prose primarily upon referent, tropes and figures were studied mainly as poetical devices. The principle of similarity underlies poetry. . . . Prose, on the contrary, is forwarded essentially by contiguity. Thus, for poetry, metaphor, and for prose, metonymy is the line of least resistance and, consequently, the study of poetical tropes is directed chiefly toward metaphor.[15]

Two weighty objections to Jakobson's poetics, prompted mainly by the critique of "Les Chats," were voiced by Wellek and Victor Erlich. One was a failure to account for poetry's aesthetic quality. The other was a mistaken assumption that all the prosodic, lexical, and grammatical parallels, oppositions, reciprocities, and symmetries in the network of equivalences structuring a given poem could be perceived (and hence enjoyed) by even the most alert readers. Erlich denied that every linguistically identifiable pattern in a poem is "stylistically, poetically, or aesthetically significant." Though this put him in direct dissent from Jakobson's axiom that in verse everything takes on poetic status, Erlich's point is warranted in the *Biographia*. Jakobson was unperturbed. In reply to the second stricture, like Poe he insisted that a sensitive reader would indeed detect the affect of such intricacies. He could only deplore the critics' deafness to meaning-charged phonic figures ("une surdité pitoyable envers les figures phono-sémantiques."). It might be said in some palliation of the aesthetic inadequacy of his theory that he did recognize the "dynamic" qualities of verse, as when he speaks of the "organized violence" in Czech verse or the various kinds of tension—verbal, conceptual, dramatic—that confer a "richesse poétique" on Poe's "Raven." Yet he seems relatively unimpressed by how aptly these qualities validate an aesthetics of tensive structure. For a linguistically grounded formulation of that neo-Coleridgean concept we must turn to Jakobson's fellow Slavic formalist, Jan Mukarovsky.[16]

Compared to the more eclectic linguistic formalism that culminated in the brilliant work of Mukarovsky and Jakobson, the efforts of Anglophone critics to apply linguistics to the elucidation

of poetry as a verbal art yielded a poor theoretical harvest. Quite
apart from the linguists' greater attention to prose fiction, it is
hard to rate very highly their analyses of verse. This estimate rests
on their positive achievement, not on the occasional allegations
that they are critically uninformed, poetically insensitive, or both.
These cavils are not entirely unwarranted. One Chomskian proclaims that phonological and syntactical equivalences are just those
which occur in normal grammar. How this not very surprising fact
is aesthetically effective he does not say. To this he adds the long
since discarded nonsense that free verse can be a more demanding
and *more expressive* form than metrical verse, and the error that inversion is banned from prose.[17]

On the whole, however, such vocal expositors as Samuel
Levin, Seymour Chatman, Edward Stankiewicz, and Sol Saporta
among others evince an aesthetic responsiveness and a grasp of
the critical doctrines immediately pertinent to their enterprise. Its
slender yield is not a personal failure. It is rooted rather in a restricted stylistic method which hobbles efforts to deal with poetry
as anything more than a kind of verbal message much like others.
Levin describes a technique he calls *coupling,* whereby in verse semantically and/or phonically equivalent elements occur at corresponding linear positions. This device both unifies poems and accounts for the expressive superiority of poetry over prose. His
point seems well founded. But, as Helen Vendler observed, linguistic terms are needlessly invoked to reaffirm the well-known
prosodic efficacy of patterned coincidences of sound and meaning.[18]

To their credit, both Levin and Chatman constantly tried to accommodate poetry's status as an art form. Unfortunately, they
often did so most effectively when they ignored linguistic procedures for traditional modes of analysis. Ingeniously—and with no
visible reliance on linguistics—Chatman scans Milton's line "Who
would not sing for Lycidas? he knew" in ten different ways to show
how "metrical richness and diversity" in English verse are enhanced
by monosyllabic words—as Hazlitt had long ago pointed out. In a
crucial chapter on metrical function in his book on its theory, Chatman is glad to rely on the *Biographia* for virtually every principle he
affirms. It is the same with Levin's objection to the overstress on
deviant usage in poetry. Levin argued that stylistic deviance is con-
textually neutralized because each poem comprises an imaginary
world which in toto effects a "phenomenalist deviance." But this
too is largely to enlist linguistics to establish a point already more

lucidly deduced from the familiar concept of the heterogeneous cosmos posited in most mimetic theory.[19]

Some linguistic critics saw in Chomsky's generative grammar persuasive authority for naming deviance as the prime determinant of poetic language. Unfortunately, as other linguists themselves admitted, this thesis ran afoul of the facts that some memorable passages of verse in no way depart from normal syntactic usage, and that some varieties of deviance, notably inversion, function effectively in even the most pedestrian prose, not to mention conversation. In a perceptive review essay of 1954, Alphonse S. Juilland argued that the proponents of deviance tended to forget the essential difference between stylistics and linguistics, namely that the latter, as a science, "operates with judgments of existence," the former with value judgments.[20]

No opponent of linguipoetics has been more forthright in exposing its limitations than some of its most reputable adherents. Essentially they concede that their method precludes any proper accounting for the dynamic quality felt in reading poetry. In a discerning discussion of that issue, Stankiewicz found even Jakobson's "marvelously compact and compelling formula" at fault. His conception of a text built on combinative equivalences, Stankiewicz objected,

> would remain a static structure without goal or integrating movement, whereas an adequate definition of poetry should capture the dynamic and creative aspects that characterize any work of art.

At a symposium on literary style in 1968, some linguists protested when Levin declared that since rhyme, meter, and the like are purely aesthetic entities they must be "isolated from the general linguistic analysis." Yet Saporta had earlier implied the same concession, frankly asserting that to apply linguistics to poetry assumes an identity between poetry and language and "disregards whatever else poetry may be." In the critically informed essay just mentioned, Stankiewicz reminds readers of what the "whatever else" involves: a semantic weight produced by an "interaction between meaning and form" that converts poetry into a unique "code" of which verse is the "optimal and most condensed form." But that statement is *only* a reminder, not an advance beyond what traditional theorists had long been affirming. Those who glimpsed a way out of the impasse in Chomsky's grammatical system fared no better. By 1967 Chatman and Levin were forced to admit that "analysis of even 'deep' grammatical structure yielded linguistic, not aesthetic, results." Examples are not hard to find: see Michael Halliday on "Leda and the Swan."[21]

The linguistic critics' recourses to nonlinguistic critical procedure are largely mandated by their Saussurean foundations. Unlike those of Sapir or Jespersen (and *like* Bloomfield's),[22] Saussure's system all but avoids mention of language as an artistic medium. In the *Cours* literature is simply identified with other kinds of "cultivated language," and "poetic texts" valued only as keys to how words were pronounced in past ages. Versified expression is irrelevant to a meticulously scientific account of language conceived as a semiological instrument distinguished from other such instruments, and superior to them, by its verbal materiality. Saussure dismisses onomatopoeia as a device too rare and trivial to discredit his doctrine of the arbitrary signifier. In perfect consistency he objects to the use of *symbol* to mean *word* as *signifiant,* the sound-image that is linked only conventionally with a concept in Saussure's *sign.*

> One characteristic of the symbol is that it is never wholly arbitrary; it is not empty, for there is the rudiment of a natural bond between signifier and the signified. The symbol of justice, a pair of scales, could not be replaced by just another symbol, such as a chariot.

In the context of the *Cours* Saussure's denial of symbolic potential to words seems unimpeachable. But it clashes with readers' experience of an accrual of semantic density in poetic expression, especially in metered form, that symbolically enriches their designative function. We have seen how from the Romantics onward recurrent speculation has held that poetic language reaches its greatest compression of meaning when its connection to what it designates seems more than conventional. Coleridge's formula of 1816 that a symbol partakes of the reality it represents has been a commonplace ever since.[23]

Saussure held that meaning is produced exclusively by differential relations among the signifying elements comprising the abstract system of his *langue.* But from the testimony of readers and of much poetic theory it would seem that poetry is a highly individualized mode of speech, and for that reason more apposite to Saussure's *parole.* Compounding the incompatibility between *langue* and poetic expression is the strict synchronism of his system, which bars consideration of two diachronic features of poetic style. One is its tendency to initiate linguistic change by neologic aberration, which prompted Dennis Donoghue to declare that the "ideal poetic language is a systematic deviation from the daily forms . . . carried on with subversive intent." The other is the more familiar opposite, archaism.[24]

Saussure's constraining influence extended beyond lingui-poetics to the poststructuralism which culminated in deconstruc-tion. Astute observers will find unintended irony in de Man's affir-mation that contemporary literary theory "comes into its own in such events as the application of Saussurean linguistics to literary texts." At least, what de Man thought of as literary theory gave small promise of a poetics in which the nature of metrical expres-sion would continue to occupy the prominent place it had held in the past. In traditional literary thought poetic diction was es-sentially an aesthetic issue; for de Man and poststructuralists of his turn of mind it has shrunk to one item in a rhetoric of episte-mology.[25]

Given the contentious intricacy of poststructuralist discussion in English, a sound accounting for the relative poverty of poetic language theory—during a time when language has been the cul-tural arch-determinant—must await the conceptual winnowing of future retrospection. Nonetheless, the roles of three pervasive ideas are immediately apparent: stylistic egalitarianism, the "death of the author," and the demotion of the referential function. These, especially the second, owe less to Saussure than to Nietz-sche, Martin Heidegger, Barthes's French structuralism, and Der-ridean deconstruction. Among poststructuralist critics proper they are most overt in the work of de Man and Miller. They are resisted not only by humanists who dissent *toto caelo* from deconstruction, but as well and most revealingly by its two ablest allies in the dis-mantlement of neo-Coleridgean poetics, Bloom and Hartman.

Not exclusive to poststructuralism, literary egalitarianism nonetheless flourished in the critical climate in which that move-ment emerged, often figuring as a methodological premise. To deny that the quality of poetry was in any way distinct from other forms of expression sufficed of itself to discourage further scrutiny of poetic diction, now sometimes scorned as a delusion of cultural atavism. With its dismissal of course went the whole panoply of such prosodic features as meter, rhyme, stanzaic structures, and so on, all consigned to theoretically negligible status. Egalitarianism was also obviously inconsistent with an aesthetic quality in litera-ture. And this meant the rejection of organic unity, the optimum manifestation of the literary aesthetic in the form of an autonomous structure to which proponents of poetry's unique status had constantly appealed since early Romanticism.

De Man himself was no vulgar egalitarian, prone like Stanley Fish, at one time, to level fine literature with advertising copy or propaganda. But what de Man called *literariness,* unlike Jakobson's prior use of the term, was not a property confined to fictive literature. Though no docile follower of Derrida, de Man was thoroughly deconstructionist in using *literariness* to designate the tropological nature allegedly common to all kinds of writing. For him it cannot be an aesthetic element, since he believes literature "involves the voiding, rather than the affirmation of aesthetic categories." In "Criticism and Crisis," an essay in *Blindness and Insight* pivotal to his thought, de Man welcomed the new Continental critics' "methodologically motivated attack on the notion that a literary or poetic consciousness is in any way a privileged consciousness," linguistically immune to the duplicity, confusion, and deception we encounter in common speech. To the new generation of critics he assigned the important task of showing that the rift between sign and meaning occurs in literature exactly as it does whenever we use words. He rejoices that contemporary French and American critics increasingly promote a "demystification of the belief that literature is a privileged language." In this way they explode the Romanticist fancy that in poems words and meanings can collaborate in "the free and harmonious balance that we call beauty." Like others who impute to Romantic theory the belief in a special status for poetic language, de Man blandly overlooks the fact that pre-Romantic writers had made the same claim, albeit not in organicist terms. Elsewhere in *Blindness and Insight* he hails the recent Franco-American consensus on the aesthetic nullity of literature. He would have welcomed Margaret Waller's partial translation in 1984 of Julia Kristeva's massy *thèse d'État* on poetic diction. Though Kristeva does separate the *genotexte* of poetic language from the *phenotexte* of common discourse, in accordance with her Marxist orientation *genotexte* is no more an art than it is a discursive mode ("loin du 'discours', mais aussi d'art"), a point obscured in Waller's version. Kristeva degrades efforts to assert an aesthetic distinction between the two as "ésotérisme esthétisant."[26]

Krieger wrote of Hayden White's argument for the fictional narrative structure of historiography that "the egalitarian principle works to claim, not that no discourse is art, but that all discourse is art." The deconstructionist view of the matter is similar, but with two salient provisos. The tropology that permeates all writing is made to evacuate it of moral-cognitive relevance and confers no aesthetic value. Miller is perhaps the most uncompromising proponent of generic conflation, arguing for example that in the current critical dispensation, the boundary between criticism and literature disappears. This is not because modern critics ape Oscar Wilde's *aim* to write criticism in a poetical style but because they can't help doing so, all language being a network of tropes or, in Nietzsche's striking image, a moving army of metaphors ("ein bewegliches Heer von Metaphern"). It follows that a work of philosophy or psychology must be "read in the same way as a 'literary' text." Of anyone so persuaded, it is fair to ask how poetic language can be recognized, let alone analyzed. Although he speaks of literature as "a mode of the aesthetic," Miller makes no theoretical provision for that fact.[27]

The phrase "death of the author," with its ominous echo of Nietzsche's proclamation of the simultaneous deaths of God and Man, signals the dismissal of personal creativity as an appreciable factor in composition. This much is implied when *book, poem, play, essay,* and the like are replaced by two overlapping terms which suppress the distinctions so named: the French structuralist *écriture,* and *text,* used in a strictly depersonalized sense. The shift of terms had powerful support in the anthropological thought of Lévi-Strauss and Foucault, with their dehumanizing thesis that the concept of Man is only the construct of an historically determined epistemology. Devaluators of the authorial function often cite Heidegger's aphorism *Die Sprache spricht*—"Language itself is the speaking subject" in Hartman's rendering—much as anti-referential theorists appeal (inaccurately) to Derrida's *"Il n'y a pas de hors-texte"* as their justifying scripture. In fact, however, post-structuralists do better to cite Barthes, whose argument in "The Death of the Author" (1968) jibes perfectly with their refusal to accord special status and value to poetry. Heidegger, on the other hand, though he too subordinates individual expression to a prior ontological function of language, "which grants an abode for the being of mortals," actually glorifies poetry as the only genuine speech.[28]

Nonetheless, the German and French slogans together bespeak a degree of literary dehumanization tending to reduce all speculation about poetic language to a will-o'-the-wisp. Common to most attempts to elucidate the eloquence of fine verse is a conviction that it is, quite literally, *expressive,* something conveyed by a moral agent, one or another variety of Wordsworth's man speaking to men. Even the most soberly rational analyses of poetry's extraordinary power to plumb the moral, emotive, and intuitive depths of consciousness subsume the premise that it emanates from an intentional subject. To replace that subject with the involuntary dynamics of language itself goes far beyond the traditional recognition of how much the poetic art owes to its social medium. It not only effaces the uniqueness of each poem and each poet's *oeuvre;* by marginalizing prosodic skill it seriously restricts the very possibility of discriminating degrees of excellence. Since the epics of both Milton and Richard Blackmore are English "texts," what grounds do we have for preferring one to the other—except by pointing to the disparity of personal talent revealed in how each exploited a shared medium? Because it flies in the face of the moral, intellectual, and emotive excitement poetry engenders in readers, a poetics which depreciates authorial agency as the source of psychic content is irretrievably flawed. Sensing this, some deconstructors have adopted from previous poetics the term *persona,* or the alternative term *voice,* as a means for evading the complete dehumanization of literature without reviving the defunct author. But this tactic is a transparent pretense that a persona is not the creative product of the very author allegedly banished in depersonalized semiotic "texts."

The death of the author has not been without deleterious consequences for interpretation. The recognition that a poem is someone's consciously intended product forms one strand of its total context, a frame of reference which both guides and limits what readers can validly make of it. The pretended absence of that factor has been a major cause of such free-wheeling readings as Miller's explication of Wordsworth's "A Slumber Did My Spirit Seal," in which the poet's diction is subjected to etymological excursions utterly irrelevant to the lyric's theme by any defensible reading. It is instructive to contrast Miller's performance with the equally erudite "intertextual" interpretation of Keats's "To Autumn" by Hartman, who resisted the notion of the author's demise. That notion has also encouraged the rash of irrelevant punning among poststructuralist commentators.[29]

Christopher Norris holds that Derrida rejected the poststructuralist libertarian strain celebrating "'the death of the author,' and all the vertiginous prospects henceforth opened up for inventive reading." But if so, Derrida's hermeneutic practice does not always square with his disapproval. In *Glas* and *La Pharmacie de Platon,*

Hegel, Jean Genet, and Plato are badly battered if not quite killed off. Before exploring the ambiguity of the word *pharmakon* in the *Phaedrus,* Derrida warns readers that in his "stitch by stitch" deconstruction of Plato's dialogue the systematic play of its significations is in no way limited by the intention of anyone's *vouloir-dire,* including those of "an author who goes by the name of Plato."[30]

Perhaps the first thing to say of the attenuation of the referential function in literary theory is that is was no Minerva sprung full-formed from the head of the deconstructive Zeus. It has warrant in both modern linguistics and earlier poetic theory. Whether, or to what extent, language is prior to and constitutive of what we "know" of reality has long been pondered, by Coleridge for one. In current speculation the problem has been lucidly formulated in Shoshana Felman's *The Literary Speech Act* (1983). Language, she writes, is not

> a simple reflection of the referent or its mimetic representation. . . . Referential knowledge is not knowledge *about* reality . . . but knowledge that *has to do with reality,* since it is itself—at least in part—what this reality is made of. The referent is no longer simply a preexisting *substance,* but an *act,* that is, a dynamic movement or modification of reality.

That literary referentiality relates to ordinary referentiality more or less as metaphor relates to literal denotation is dimly foreshadowed in the motif of late organic formalism which defines a literary work as a "world" distinct from the world of our immediate experience, however intimately relevant to it. From that persuasion it was an easy step to posit a fictive world totally disjunct from the real one. In extreme versions this further step endowed the verbal cosmos of poetry with a more assured reality than that associated with experiental existence. What is exclusively invoked when a poet writes "une fleur," Mallarmé asserted, is "l'absente de tous bouquets." Glossing this arresting phrase, Maurice Blanchot added that the reader pictures neither a real flower nor even the image or memory of one, but only "une absence de fleur." By an ontological inversion, in which art is the reality and life the illusion, the referential function of literature collapses for sheer lack of any external referent. The paradoxical inference, glimpsed in Valéry's poetics as well, Blanchot asserts in prose of great subtlety and considerable obscurity: words, poetry's communicative medium, being so palpably of the earth earthy, serve by their presence on the page more to occlude than to "realize" thoughts and images. So the poet does best to fall silent.[31]

Clearly, Blanchot's tortuous evasion of reference is not of the deconstructionist kind, though it may just as thoroughly falsify most readers' experience. The difference owes most to the derivation of the poststructuralist treatment of reference (as of cognitive and aesthetic values) from modern linguistics. "By linguistic terminology," as de Man put it,

> is meant a terminology that designates reference prior to designating the referent and takes into account, in the consideration of the world, the referential function of language and not necessarily as an intuition. *Intuition implies perception, consciousness, experience, and leads at once into the world of logic and of understanding with all its correlations, among which aesthetics occupies a prominent place.* (italics added)

Since, as with Saussure's linguistics, the deconstructive methodology shelves the ontological problem, its adherents follow him in simply "bracketing" the enigma of literature's link with the world. Language refers, right enough—but, in effect, to nothing. The strategy appears in de Man's characterization of the new poetics as "a branch of general semiotics." As opposed to semantics, he explains, semiotics studies signifiers, not their putative referents; "it asks not what words mean but how they mean."[32] Of course the same may be said of neo-Coleridgean poetics, but with the crucial difference that its expositors never doubted that even the most involved detours of the poetic *how*, to which they largely assigned the aesthetic value, finally terminated in a *what*.

In Anglo-American formalism the *what* comprehended every aspect of man's consciousness of his environment, including himself. Miller errs with other decriers of the New Criticism when he writes that a "disinterested contemplation of poetry as an aesthetic object" implies that poetry is "value free," and that the New Critics are therefore in this respect at odds with other humanists who maintain the edifying effects of poetry. Norris is another purveyor of this critical bugbear with his too sweeping indictment that traditional critics have trivialized literature "by treating it in strictly non-cognitive terms, as a discourse to which questions of truth and falsehood, referentiality, and so forth, simply don't apply." As shown above, this is sheer nonsense. Neither Coleridge himself nor his formalist heirs ever failed to acknowledge that poetic utterance was cognitively and morally informed. The error is avoidable by arguing instead that the New Critics paid insufficient attention to the unique mode of poetic cognition.[33]

Enfin vint Derrida! To him the referential *what* was the Western metaphysicians' illusory assumption of an originary presence, the ontological "myth" he called logocentrism. In Derridean poststructuralism, the extra-linguistic world, never quite denied, finally fades to a mirage dimly glimpsed through the thickets of the successive signifiers constituting the imprisoning text, the verbal labyrinth in which readers struggle to no exit. If the mirage be taken as a "trace" of some extra-textual denotation, it is always hastily "bracketed"—hugger-mugger like Polonius's burial—lest on sustained scrutiny it prove embarrassingly substantial. It must be exorcized to keep us steadily aware, as Hartman puts it, that the reality we credit may be only "a metonymic charm, . . . an illusion of depth built up by the mirror-play of . . . intertextuality." (His own professed goal was a "restored theory of representation" to meet the timely but discomfiting "deconstructionist challenge"— but that is another story).[34]

It may be, as Frank Lentricchia maintains, that Derrida's *hors-texte* does not imply ontological nihilism. "Derrida is no ontologist of *le néant*," he urged, "because he is no ontologist." But there is also the ethical or moral nihilism propounded by de Man. This kind of nihilism is an extension of a semantic collapse produced by his Nietzschean conception of rhetorical texts, in which the clash between tropological "exuberance" and "the rigors of grammar" creates an "insurmountable obstacle" to any reading or comprehension of a piece of writing. De Man does not shrink from what this implies: that *ethics,* like *morality, man, love,* and *self,* is not the name of an experiential entity but only "a discursive mode among others."[35]

Ethical nihilism presents a much greater block to a validation of poetic language than ontological. For if the real world is non-existent, or simply uncongenial to contemplation, poets may easily resort to Sidney's imaginary one, content to give a local habitation and name to such airy nothings as, in varying degrees, flesh out the frail actuality of *The Faerie Queen, A Midsummer Night's Dream,* or *The Rape of the Lock.* But if the ethics, moral nature, and passions of the inhabitants of those "worlds" were referentially grounded in nothing more than "discursive modes"—instead of being the real toads in their imaginary gardens—their enduring appeal could never have been felt by generations of readers.

To aggravate the grotesque dehumanization of literature
caused by desubstantializing its moral dimension, de Man also virtually nullifies its cognitive value. The referential function not
being an a priori certainty in the kind of semiotic criticism he favors, he tells us, it "is therefore not *a priori* certain that literature
is a reliable source of information about anything but its own language." Since this alleged cognitional poverty must blight all written expression, de Man can grant "poetic writing" only the dubious distinction of simultaneously asserting and denying its own
rhetoric, and in this way being "the most advanced and refined
mode of deconstruction." In Miller's almost identical view, the
"interference of rhetoric in the grammar and logic" of a text, while
not actually demolishing its referential truth, makes any assurance
about it impossible. "Metaphysical" methods of literary study,
Miller explains, assume that literature is in some sense referential.
Deconstructive theory, on the other hand,

> aims to show that in a given work of literature, in a different way
> in each case, metaphysical assumptions are both present and at
> the same time undermined by the text itself . . . by some figura-
> tive play within the text which forbids it to be read as an "organic
> unity" organized around some version of the *logos.*[36]

Given their celebration of poetic expression, Hartman was
right to style himself and Bloom as "barely deconstructionist" in
contrast to such "boa-deconstructors" as Derrida and Miller.
Bloom and Hartman, each in his own way, were repelled by the
dehumanizing tendencies of poststructuralism. How to reconcile
their acceptance of deconstruction with a dissent from its fundamental positions is beside our present purpose. One can only conjecture from the tone of their allusions to the boa-deconstructors
that the affiliation was more polemical than doctrinal. Certainly
nothing could signal a more defiant rejection of de Man's and
Miller's "demystification" of poetry than Bloom's and Hartman's
veneration of Shelley's *Defence of Poetry.*[37]

Without quite excluding the referential function, Bloom di-
lutes it by adopting the notion of intertextuality. He seconds de
Man's reading of Nietzsche as paradigmatic for "our understanding of intratextual encounters, or, as I would term them, mispri-
sions." A poem's referents are in other texts, not out in "life,"
which means—in Bloom's stricter Saussurean analogy—that there
are *no* texts, "only relationships *between* texts." And so the agoniz-
ingly defensive process of composition which he analyzes involves

each poet in "a dialectical relationship . . . with another poet or poets." But this process, as he conceives it, apparently need not terminate in the outright devitalization of poetic expression imposed by more orthodox versions of intertextuality. For to say that one poem is about another poem, he observes, "is to go out into the world where we live."[38]

There is no need to retrace Bloom's recondite dissections of the post-Enlightenment "strong" poet's struggle against the precursory pressures on his own creative vitality. But one aspect of it is crucially relevant to our topic. For underlying the complicated analogies to Freudian and Kabbalistic concepts and to the six "revisionary ratios" that constitute the successive modalities of each new poet's misprision of his forebears, is a vatic view of the poet. One can hardly imagine anything more antithetical to a denial of authorial agency or less accommodated to the suppression of a referential-cognitional function in poetry. Bloom's vaticism is Viconian and thus profounder than Carlyle's, but no less inspirational in conception. "Poetic wisdom—to Vico—" he writes,

> is founded upon divination, and to sing is . . . to foretell. Poetic thought is proleptic, and the Muse invoked under the name of Memory is being implored to remember the future.[39]

Though Bloom's divinatory orientation, like Carlyle's and Emerson's, militates against theorizing about poetic style, both his dissent from literary egalitarianism and his recognition of an aesthetic component in poetry are plain in his work. He can refer to "the mystery of poetic style, the exuberance that is beauty in every strong poet." He uses the words *aesthetics* and *beauty* repeatedly, and refers to aesthetic language without apologetic quotation marks. Much of Bloom's poetics employs terms of startling novelty in order to revitalize and reinstate principles under current attack, especially by those he has most recently labeled the "School of Resentment."[40]

Bloom's sensitivity to the exceptional quality of great verse is obvious, as when he alludes to Virgil's line on the souls in Hades yearning to cross the Styx as "an unforgettable vision." Yet it is doubtful how much of its appeal he would credit to versification. The "Emersonian heritage" he stresses for American poets consists primarily of three precursor "poems"—all in prose: the *Divinity School Address, The American Scholar,* and *Self-Reliance.* Emerson's inspiration, he observed, issued in "the eloquence of prose." The blurring of genres, however, detracts nothing from his refusal to endorse the deconstructionist notion of semantic nullity. He favors instead "a kind of interpretation that seeks to restore and redress meaning rather than primarily to deconstruct meaning."[41]

Given his strained apologies for even Derrida's wildest hermeneutic excesses,[42] Hartman's many protests against the poststructuralist refusal of special value to poetic language have a certain pathos. This impression is only sharpened by the possibly unintended counterthrust of his repeated calls for a creative criticism that would largely efface the aesthetic disparity between discursive and imaginative composition. In any case, what he says of his *Criticism in the Wilderness* is in varying degrees true of his other work: that it deals with "the issue of language . . . , critical diction as well as poetic diction." Clearly one reason for that preoccupation is Hartman's keen perception of the aesthetic qualities that mark off poetic diction from all other kinds. This is sufficiently attested by his penetrating critiques of Romantic and modern poems, sometimes undertaken to probe a particular issue of poetic language, as when he examines Valéry's sonnet "L'Abeille" for what it reveals of the modern flight from referentiality in verse.[43]

Much more significant, however, have been Hartman's direct protests against the devaluation of poetic expression and his reassertions of such traditional critical principles as mimesis, the "deconstruction" of which facilitated the devaluators' negations. He questions Derrida's thesis that mimesis is exploded by its dependence on an illusory prior faith in an originary presence. Hartman doubted that so perdurable a principle could be so easily dismissed. We may find, he imagined, "that representation is all there is, and that we would never experience a self-presence in which we see—and are seen—not as in a glass darkly but face to face."[44]

The Pauline allusion here is a reminder that a persistent theological strand (different from Bloom's mystical sort) permeates Hartman's critical writings. In his next book he conceded to those alarmed by the pretensions of current criticism that it had indeed become "a contemporary form of theology." Earlier he had called Bloom's *Anxiety of Influence* a "poetico- theological tractate" suggesting that poetry is now most notable for its "enormously creative theology." Something like that appears in Hartman's own conception of poetry. The more we scrutinize language, he declared, and especially poetic language, the

> more evidence of archaic or sacred residues comes to light. We
> may not value them, but they are too prevalent and integu-

mented to be undone. The sacred has so inscribed itself in language that while it must be interpreted, it cannot be removed. One might speculate that what we call sacred is simply that which must be interpreted or reinterpreted, "A Presence which is not to be put by."

After a reference to Satan's denial in *Paradise Lost* of any origin outside himself, Hartman broadens his protest in terms which the staunchest humanist opponents of deconstruction would gladly adopt: "without a greatness prior to our own there may be nothing to respond to. There may be no dialogue, let alone dialectic. Culture and tradition would be vain concepts."[45]

Hartman conceded that modern semiotics, by killing off "the human voice and even the human face," had usefully dispelled simplistic notions of reference and the author's role. Yet he insisted that even in the encoded text that survived the slaughter there was "magic in the web" (echoing *Othello*). He actually revived a motif of the standard etiologies of poetic diction when he added that the "sense of an informing spirit, however limited or conditioned, . . . is what holds us." Nowhere does he more emphatically distance himself from the deadening deconstructionist notion of depersonalized inscription than where he insists that "the great work of art is more than a text." Adding Milton's eloquence to Shakespeare's, he extols great literature as "the lifeblood of a master-spirit." Even if the referent of all the "troping of speech" that goes on in a poem is only some other written word, that in itself is no mean thing. It enshrines the "magical idea of speech, literacy as thaumaturgic, the word able to transform or clarify our lives. 'Let there be light.'" Hartman immediately questions the efficacy of his own rhetoric here. Yet even if the culminating allusion to Holy Writ, engaging the illocutionary power of the Logos, was only an effort to harmonize his vindication of great verse with the theological cast of his critical sensibility, it is one many readers will respect.[46]

Notes

Chapter One

1. "In 1362 English was made the language of the law courts, and the next year, for the first time, the chancellor opened Parliament in English, the city of London issued a proclamation in English in 1384 and the earliest known will in English dates from 1387." A. R. Myers, *England in the Late Middle Ages,* rev. ed. (Baltimore: Penguin Books, 1966), p. 94.

2. *Elizabethan Critical Essays,* ed. G. Gregory Smith, 2 vols. (London: Oxford University Press, 1904), I, 378, hereafter cited as Smith; Daniel, Smith, II, 357; Pater, *Appreciations* (London: Macmillan, 1920), p. 266.

3. *The Works of John Dryden* (Berkeley and Los Angeles: University of California Press), 20 vols. (1956–1994), V, ed. William Frost (1987), 329, 330–31, hereafter cited as *Works of Dryden.*

4. Sidney, "Apologie for Poetry," Smith, I, 205; Hoby is quoted in Richard Foster Jones, *The Triumph of the English Language* (Stanford: Stanford University Press, 1953), p. 18; Chapman, Smith, II, 300; Webbe, Smith, I, 257–61.

5. Ascham, Smith, I, 22. The humanists' exaltation of Greek was more than stylistic or aesthetic. "Throughout the sixteenth century," Thomas J. Reiss notes, "Greek (along with Hebrew, no doubt) was considered by the humanist grammarians, poeticians, and philologists to be the nearest thing to a natural 'unmediated' language known to men. It was supposed to allow so precise an expression of, to be in so perfect correlation with, concepts and things immediately apprehended as to come very close to not being a symbolic system at all." *The Discourse of Modernism* (Ithaca: Cornell University Press, 1980), p. 131. Reiss instances works by Ramus and Henri Estienne as well as Ascham's *The Scholemaster.*

6. Joel Elias Spingarn, *A History of Literary Criticism in the Renaissance*, 2nd ed. (New York: Macmillan, 1908), p. 180.

7. Webbe, Smith, I, 241.

8. *The Triumph of the English Language*, p. 168. More is quoted ibid., p. 56.

9. Matthiessen, *Translation: An Elizabethan Art* (New York: Octagon Books, 1965), p. 3; Harvey, Smith, II, 260, 282. For additional glorifications of English as an artistic medium see the chapter on "The Eloquent Language" in *The Triumph of the English Language*. Jones establishes the significant point that the aesthetic powers of the language preceded its regularization by grammars and dictionaries.

10. Meres, Smith, II, 315. George Chapman vindicated even "Our Monosyllables"; see *Chapman's Homer*, ed. Allardyce Nicoll, 2 vols. (New York: Pantheon Books, 1956), I, 11. Around 1620 Michael Drayton memorialized Sidney for having shown that "*English* hand in hand might go / With *Greek* or *Latin*." *Minor Poems*, ed. Cyril Brett (Oxford: Clarendon Press, 1907), p. 110.

11. *The Seven First Bookes of the Eneidos of Virgill, Converted in English Meter by Thomas Phaer Esquier* [London], 1558, no pag.; Dolet, *La Maniere De Bien Traduire D'une Langue En Aultre*, 1540, in *Critical Prefaces of the French Renaissance*, ed. Bernard Weinberg (Evanston: Northwestern University Press, 1950), p. 78; Jones, *The Triumph of the English Language*, p. 211. For an excellent sampling of the arguments by Renaissance defenders of the vernacular in Italy, France, and England, see Vernon Hall, *Renaissance Literary Criticism* (New York: Columbia University Press, 1945).

12. Alfred Harbage, Introduction to *Love's Labor's Lost* (Baltimore: Penguin Books, 1963), p. 15. Cf. Elizabeth J. Sweeting: "In their intoxication with linguistic power and ingenuity, men of the full Elizabethan period became preoccupied with figures, schemes and tropes," *Early Tudor Criticism: Linguistic and Literary* (Oxford: Blackwell, 1940), p. 114; Lanham, *The Motives of Eloquence: Literary Rhetoric in the Renaissance* (New Haven: Yale University Press, 1976), p. 33.

13. Willcock, "Shakespeare and Elizabethan English," in *A Companion to Shakespeare Studies*, ed. Harley Granville-Barker and G. B. Harrison (New York: Macmillan, 1934), p. 134; King James, Smith, I, 218, 220; Saintsbury, *A History of Criticism and Literary Taste in Europe*, 3 vols. (New York: Humanities Press, 1950), II, 209n., hereafter cited as *History of Criticism;* Lewis, *English Literature in the Sixteenth Century Excluding Drama* (Oxford: Clarendon Press, 1944), p. 348; Mulcaster, Smith, I, lvii.

14. Johnson's censure occurs in the preface to his edition of the plays (1765); *Works of Dryden*, IX, ed. John Loftis (1966), 213.

15. Carew, Smith, II, 293; Sidney, ibid., I, 202. Saintsbury, in *Specimens of English Prose Style* (London, 1886), cites as typical of Elizabethan "jingles" Sidney's sentence in his dedication of the *Arcadia* to his sister: "This I say, because I know thy virtue so, and this say I, because it may be for ever so, or to say better, because it will be ever so" (p. 19).

16. Smith, II, 165.

17. *Il libro del cortegiano* (Milano: Ubrico Hoepli, 1928), p. 80; Hoby, *The Book of the Courtier* (New York: E. P. Dutton, 1928), p. 59. The notion of linguistic abuse in verse is central to the poetics propounded in Jean Cohen's *Structure du language poétique* (Paris: Flammarion, 1966). Verse is "anti-prose," and "anti-grammatical" (pp. 51, 72). Deviant syntax figures prominently in recent linguistic prosodic analysis.

18. Aristotle, *The Poetics,* Loeb Classical Library Edition (Cambridge: Harvard University Press, 1982), pp. 6, 74–90, hereafter cited as *The Poetics.*

19. Horace, *Satires, Epistles and Ars Poetica,* Loeb Classical Library Edition (Cambridge: Harvard University Press, 1970), pp. 454, 456, 459, 474, 476; *Ben Jonson,* ed. C. H. Herford, Percy Simpson, and Evelyn Simpson, 11 vols. (Oxford: Clarendon Press), VIII: *The Poems and the Prose Works* (1947), 615, hereafter cited as *Ben Jonson.*

20. Bernard Weinberg notes that Horace's lines were often construed by Italian commentators in terms of the *res-verba* dichotomy. *Res* referred to philosophy, *verba* (style or diction) to grammar or rhetoric. There was thus no occasion for a poetics. *A History of Literary Criticism in the Italian Renaissance,* 2 vols. (Chicago: University of Chicago Press, 1961), I, 84, hereafter cited as *Italian Renaissance.*

21. Sidney apart, the Elizabethan critics' citation of Aristotle is virtually nil. What knowledge they had of ideas set forth in the *Rhetoric* and the *Poetics*—and it was marginal—they derived mainly from Italian commentary. The newly discovered *Poetics* is not mentioned in England until 1570, by Ascham. In Italy the situation was of course the reverse. By 1549 Bernardo Segni had published a vernacular translation of both treatises in his *Rettorica et poetica d'Aristotile,* arguing an affinity between oratory and poetry which, as Weinberg notes, is hardly warranted by Aristotle himself. *Italian Renaissance,* I, 404.

22. Cicero, *De Oratore,* 2 vols., Loeb Classical Library Edition, (Cambridge: Harvard University Press, 1942) I, 50. Quintilian goes so far as to say that poets, unlike both orators and historians, are freed from the requirements of assertive accuracy (*auctoritas*) by their obligation to write in meter ("nam poetas metri necessitas excusat"). *Institutio Oratoria of Quintilian,* 4 vols. (New York): G. P. Putnam's Sons, 1921–1922), I, 112. The slight tone of condescension toward poets in both of these writers should not be overlooked.

23. Frachetta is quoted in Weinberg, *Italian Renaissance,* I, 214. Cicero, *De Oratore* I, 50, 88–90; II, 120, 139, 146, 156.

24. *Institutio Oratoria,* I, 112, 113, 152, 146.

25. Atanagi and Vettori are cited in Weinberg, *Italian Renaissance,* I, 458, 463.

26. Aristotle, *On Poetry and Style,* trans. G. M. A. Grube (New York: Bobbs-Merrill, 1958), pp. 4, 46–49. For Isocrates see J. W. H. Atkins, *Literary Criticism in Antiquity,* 2 vols. (London: Cambridge University Press, 1934), I, 130.

27. The hedging on the question of nonmetrical poetry which Aristotle foisted on his Italian interpreters is succinctly summarized by Spingarn on

Robortelli. "Robortelli answers this question by pointing out that metre does not constitute the nature, force, or essence of poetry, which depends entirely on the fact of imitation; but at the same time, while one who imitates without verse is a poet, in the best and truest poetry imitation and metre are combined." *Literary Criticism in the Renaissance,* p. 31.

28. Quintilian, *Institutio Oratoria,* III, 184, 188, 218, 220, 221, 222; Virgil, *Georgics,* I, lines 181–82. Quintilian commends Horace for following Virgil's example in his proverbial metaphor of mountains laboring to bring forth a ridiculous mouse. *Ars poetica,* 1,139.

29. *Institutio Oratoria,* III, 224; Du Bellay, *La deffence et illustration de la langue françoyse* (Paris: Bordas, 1972), pp. 86, 88; "E. K.," Smith, I, 129–30; *Ben Jonson,* VIII, 662.

30. *Institutio Oratoria,* III, 252, 310, 314, 324.

31. Sidney, Smith, I, 203; Webbe, ibid., I, 228. Poliziano is quoted in Weinberg, *Italian Renaissance,* I, 4. *Ben Jonson,* VIII, 640.

32. Castor, *Pléiade Poetics: A Study of Sixteenth-Century Thought and Terminology* (Cambridge: Cambridge University Press, 1964), pp. 17–18; Sebillet, *Art poétique françoys* (Paris: Edward Cornely, 1910), pp. 21–22.

Chapter Two

1. Aulo Giano Porrasio, quoted in Weinberg, *Italian Renaissance,* I, 98; Weinberg, ibid. I, 151 and passim. Cinquecento Italians did not originate but only codified a long- honored dichotomy. "Words and things, *res et verba,*" W. K. Wimsatt and Cleanth Brooks observe, "was a theme which had come echoing down rhetorical corridors since the days of the Ciceronian *ratio et oratio* and Quintilian's *Curam ergo verborum rerum volo solicitudinem esse.*" [I therefore wish the care for words to be a concern for things.] *Literary Criticism: A Short History* (New York: Alfred A. Knopf, 1957), p. 228.

2. Gascoigne, Smith, I, 48, 51; Sidney, ibid., I, 154.

3. In *The Language of Renaissance Poetry* (London: Andre Deutsch, 1971), A. C. Partridge finds that a "diction for English poetry, distinct from that of prose, begins with Wyatt; there is a fondness for archaic words, for participial adjectives, for rhetorical figures and cumulative effects (many cited by Puttenham), as well as for syntactical inversion. Vices of Augustan diction, such as periphrasis and excessive antithetical structures, were incipient in Wyatt" (p. 45). The term *diction,* to designate an aspect of the poetic art, used by Sidney, becomes a staple of the English critical vocabulary with Dryden. The term *poetical diction* was introduced by John Dennis in 1696.

4. *Ben Jonson,* VIII, 567; Daniel, Smith, II, 359; Bacon, *The Advancement of Learning and the New Atlantis* (London: Oxford University Press, 1959), p. 96. Drayton wrote of Daniel: "His rimes were smooth, his meeters well did close / But yet his maner better fitted prose." *Minor Poems,* p. 111. Edmund Bolton also thought Daniel's diction "fitter perhaps for Prose than Measure." *Critical Essays of the Seventeenth Century,* ed. J. E. Spingarn, 3 vols. (Bloomington: Indiana University Press, 1957), I, 110; hereafter cited as Spingarn.

5. Daniel is quoted in J. W. H. Atkins, *English Literary Criticism: The Renascence* (London: Methuen, 1947), p. 206; *Delle Osservationi nella volgar lingua*, 2nd ed. (Venice, 1550), p. 185.

6. In the *Abrégé* Ronsard views poetic diction as words well chosen and brightened by pithy bits of wisdom, making lines of verse shine like polished stones ("qui font reluyre les vers comme les pierres bien enchassées"). Weinberg, *Critical Prefaces of the French Renaissance*, p. 201. Hawes and Wilson are cited in Sweeting, *Early Tudor Criticism*, pp. 15, 113.

7. The difference between the two conceptions, and the ontological depths they may involve, are put sharply by a modern Aristotelian's objection to the verbal orientation of the New Criticism's poetics. "Just as we should not define a chair as wood which has such and such characteristics," writes Elder Olson, "— for a chair is not a kind of wood but a kind of furniture—so we ought not to define poetry as a kind of language." *Critics and Criticism: Ancient and Modern,* ed. R. S. Crane (Chicago: University of Chicago Press, 1952), p. 564n. So for Olson too, alluding to Yeats's "Sailing to Byzantium," the medium of the poem is words "embellished by rhythm and rhyme." Ibid.

8. Smith, I, 168, 182, 187, 173, 201. Note that Sidney's early use of the term *diction* is neutral, implying neither approval, as in most neoclassical usage, nor condemnation, as in Wordsworth and a host of writers ever since. As late as 1975, we find poetic *diction* disparaged as "a lesser thing" than poetic *language*. John Ciardi and Miller Williams, *How Does a Poem Mean?* 2nd ed. (Boston: Houghton Mifflin), p. 120.

9. Smith, II, 206–7.

10. Ibid., II, 310, 315–16.

11. English criticism of the time has no parallel to the near approach to a purely lexical aestheticism occasionally voiced in sixteenth-century Italian poetics. Girolamo Fracastoro, in his *Naugerius, sive de poetica dialogus* (1555), substituted the terms *materia* and *forma* for the commoner *res-verba* doublet. Only *forma*, defined as *modus dicendi*, constituted the poetic element, which is "the utmost and most absolute beauty of expression of which a given subject is capable" (Weinberg, *Italian Renaissance*, II, 726–27). Another such was Girolamo Muzio, whose metrical *Arte poetica* of 1551 propounded a theory in which poetry itself, as Professor Weinberg notes with neo-Aristotelian disapproval, "seems to be no more than a kind of diction" (ibid., II, 731). As with others of his day, however, the purity of Muzio's formalism is muddied when he adds that this kind of diction ("questo modo di dire") often shows up in prose too. So does Fracastoro's vaunted *modus dicendi*.

12. Weinberg, *Italian Renaissance,* I, 302, 465. Vettori's *Commentarii in primum librum Aristotelis de arte poetica* appeared in 1560. The view which confined poetry to metrical compositions did not, for most critics, rule out the ornamental conception of diction and meter. Reflecting on "prose-poetry," Lodovico Castelvetro wrote: "Verse does not distinguish poetry, but clothes and adorns it" (quoted in Spingarn, *Literary Criticism in the Renaissance,* p. 44).

13. *Ben Jonson*, VIII, 621.

14. Smith, II, 363, 359, 366, 364, 372.

15. Smith, II, 360. The discovery *seems* at least to have been Daniel's own. Saintsbury, who stressed its significance, found nowhere in his exhaustive reading any "frank recognition of it" by any earlier English critic (*History of Criticism*, II, 190). He apparently overlooked Puttenham's observation that classical feet do not exist in English verse because "the nature of our language and wordes" do not admit them (Smith, II 5–6).

16. Smith, II, 304; I, 308; *Ben Jonson*, VIII, 587; Smith, I, 51.

17. Parthenio is cited in Weinberg, *Italian Renaissance*, I, 147; Ronsard, *Critical Prefaces of the French Renaissance*, pp. 254, 257, 264; Sweeting, *Early Tudor Criticism*, p. 15

18. Smith, II, 5.

19. Ibid., II, 165, 142, 154.

20. Puttenham, Smith, II, 165 (italics mine).

21. Smith, II, 148.

22. Ibid., II, 174.

23. This stress on popular speech as a source of poetic diction, which runs counter to the prevailing aristocratic bias of classical literary doctrine, was an item of the *Pléiade*'s program. Before Ronsard, Du Bellay had urged poets to frequent the resorts of artisans of various trades and crafts in order to pick up a jargon ("les termes usitez en leurs ars & metiers") from which to fashion metaphors. *Deffence et illustration de la langue françoyse*, p. 101. Although Elizabethan verse amply justifies Du Bellay's advice, English Renaissance critics seemed to have been unimpressed by it. In Ronsard there is a vein of linguistic populism. Morphology, he maintained, was fixed by illiterates, not scholars. According to his amusing illustration, learned men would have made *bonior* and *bonissimus* the comparative and superlative of *bonus*. It was, he thinks, the common folk of Rome who established *melior* and *optimus* instead. Weinberg, *Critical Prefaces*, pp. 199, 207.

24. Smith, II, 67, 84, 88–89, 138–39.

25. Saintsbury, *History of Criticism*, II, 157; Ascham, Smith, I, 32–34; *Ben Jonson*, VIII, 501.

26. Ascham, Smith, I, 30; Webbe, ibid., I, 280; Spenser, ibid., I, 99; Campion, ibid., II, 351–52. On Fraunce, see Derek Attridge's fine *Well-weighed Syllables: Elizabethan Verse in Classical Metres* (London: Cambridge University Press, 1974).

27. Smith, I, 140.

28. Ibid., II, 333.

29. Ibid., II, 240, 230, 350.

30. Ibid., II, 360.

Chapter Three

1. *Works of Dryden*, V, 330, 336.

2. Ibid., V, 329; III, ed. Earl Miner (1969), 9; *The Yale Edition of the Works of Samuel Johnson*, (New Haven: Yale University Press), 16 vols.

(1958–1990), IV: *The Rambler,* ed. W. J. Bate and Albrecht B. Strauss (New Haven: Yale University Press, 1969), 100, hereafter cited as *Works of Johnson.*

3. Spingarn, III, 210.

4. *Critical Works of Thomas Rymer,* ed. Curt A. Zimansky (New Haven: Yale University Press, 1956), p. 76; *Works of Dryden,* IV, ed. A. B. Chambers and William Frost (1974), 15; V, 339; Temple, Spingarn, III, 98; Hobbes, Spingarn, II, 57.

5. See Austin Warren's excellent essay "Alexander Pope," in *Rage for Order* (Chicago: University of Chicago Press, 1948), which arrestingly begins: "Neoclassic theory of poetry and neoclassic poetry imperfectly agree."

6. *Ben Jonson,* VIII, 183.

7. *Works of Dryden,* VIII, ed. John Harrington Smith and Dougald MacMillan (1962), 101; XVII, ed. Samuel Holt Monk (1971), 69–78; IX, ed. John Loftis and David Stuart Rodes (1978), 8; V, 324.

8. Ibid., IX, 7; II, ed. H. T. Swedenberg (1972), 172; XI, ed. John Loftis and David Stuart Rodes (1978), 8; V, 324.

9. Chapman, Spingarn, I, 72; Bolton, Spingarn, I, 107; Alexander, Spingarn, I, 182.

10. Granville, Spingarn, III, 292; Dolce, *Delle Osservationi nella volgar lingua,* p. 179; Jean-Baptiste du Bos, *Réflexions critiques sur la Poésie et sur la Peinture* (Paris, 1770); photographic reprint (Paris: Slatkine, 1982), p. 85.

11. Du Fresnoy, *The Art of Painting,* trans. William Mason, 1783 (New York: Arno Press, 1969), p. [50]. The tripartite order of graphic composition was itself derived from the *inventio, dispositio,* and *elocutio* of classical rhetoric, later adopted by Renaissance poetics. For extended discussion see Rensselaer W. Lee, *Ut Pictura Poesis: The Humanistic Theory of Painting* (New York: Norton, 1967), especially pp. 9–32. In his annotations to William Mason's 1783 translation of Du Fresnoy, Joshua Reynolds endorsed both the correspondence of the painter's "tints" to the poet's words and their relative unimportance in graphic creation. *The Art of Painting,* pp. 109, 114.

12. "A Parallel betwixt Painting and Poetry," *Works of Dryden,* XX, ed. A. E. Wallace Maurer (1989), 71–72, 76.

13. Temple, Spingarn, III, 102; *The Correspondence of Alexander Pope,* ed. George Sherburn, 5 vols. (Oxford: Clarendon Press, 1956), I, 110; *The Poems of Alexander Pope,* (New Haven: Yale University Press), 11 vols. (1939–1969), VII: *The Iliad of Homer,* ed. Maynard Mack, 9, hereafter cited as *Poems of Pope; Works of Johnson,* II: *The Idler and the Adventurer,* ed. W. J. Bate, John M. Bullitt, and L. F. Powell (1963), 460.

14. Sprat, Spingarn, II, 128–29; *Works of Dryden,* IV, 15. When Dryden and his contemporaries use the word *significant* in speaking of diction, they mean what we should render as *meaning-packed. Sounding,* so often linked with *significant,* is probably best read as an Englishing of *sonantia verba,* which they found in Quintilian or another Latin author.

15. *Works of Dryden,* XVII, ed. Samuel Holt Monk (1971), 33, 14. In 1693 Dryden referred to Waller and Denham as "those two fathers of our English poetry" (ibid., II, 150). The general estimate of Waller is summed up in a 1690 preface to some of his posthumous writings by Francis Atterbury:

"A Name that carries everything in it that's either Great or Graceful in Poetry. He was indeed the Parent of *English* Verse, and the first that shew'd us that our Tongue had Beauty and Numbers in it." *Eighteenth-Century English Literature,* ed. G. Tillotson, P. Fussell, M. Waingrow (New York: Harcourt, Brace and World, 1969), p. 214.

16. A useful study of this question in its English manifestation is K. G. Hamilton's *The Two Harmonies: Poetry and Prose in the Seventeenth Century* (Oxford: Clarendon, 1963).

17. Hobbes, Spingarn, II, 56; Locke, *An Essay Concerning Human Understanding,* ed. A. S. Pringle-Pattison (Oxford: Clarendon Press, 1924), p. 140.

18. Spingarn, II, 132.

19. Trapp, *Lectures on Poetry,* translated from the Latin by William Bowyer (London, 1742), p. 42; Hobbes, Spingarn, II, 68; *Works of Dryden,* V, 337; Scudéry, *The Continental Model: Selected French Critical Essays of the Seventeenth Century, in English Translation,* ed. Scott Elledge and Donald C. Schier (Minneapolis: University of Minnesota Press, 1960), p. 94; Pope, *Correspondence,* I, 101; Johnson, *Lives of the English Poets,* ed. George Birkbeck Hill, 3 vols. (Oxford: Clarendon Press, 1905), I, 433.

20. Phillips, Spingarn, II, 169; Addison, *The Spectator,* ed, G. Gregory Smith, 4 vols. (New York: Dutton, 1945), II, 389; Pope, *Poems of Pope,* X: *The Odyssey of Homer,* ed. Maynard Mack (1967), 390.

21. *Lives of the English Poets,* I, 440.

22. *Works of Johnson,* V, 126.

23. *Works of Dryden,* XVII, 11; Pope, *Correspondence,* I, 107; *Essay on Criticism,* line 346.

24. Wolseley, Spingarn, III, 27; Shaftesbury, *Characteristics of Men, Manners, Opinions, Times,* ed. John M. Robertson, 2 vols. (New York: Bobbs-Merrill, 1964), II, 322.

25. *The Critical Works of John Dennis,* ed. Edward Niles Hooker, 2 vols. (Johns Hopkins Press, 1939, 1943), I, 14, 24–27, hereafter cited as *Critical Works.*

26. Aristotle, *The Poetics,* p. 85. As neoclassical critics no doubt noticed, the root meaning of Aristotle's ταπεινὴν, here rendered as "mean," is, precisely, "low." Voltaire is cited in René Wellek, *A History of Modern Criticism: 1750–1950,* 8 vols. (New Haven: Yale University Press, 1955–1992), I, 266, hereafter cited as *History.* Wimsatt, *The Verbal Icon* (Lexington: University of Kentucky Press, 1954), p. 231; Swift, *The Poems of Jonathan Swift,* ed. Harold Williams, 3 vols., 2nd ed. (Oxford: Clarendon Press, 1958), II, 555.

27. *Poems,* I: *Pastoral Poetry and An Essay on Criticism,* ed. E. Audra and Aubrey Williams (l961), 274–75.

28. *Works of Dryden,* XIV, ed. Vinton A. Dearing and Alan Roper (1992), 105; XV, 3; *Works of Johnson,* IV, 288.

29. *Critical Works,* I, 114.

30. Pope, *Poems: Epistle to Several Persons,* III, ii, ed. F. W. Bateson (1951), 154; *Works of Dryden,* XII, 96, 97. As with most writers of his time, Dryden's knowledge of the *Peri hypsous* (*On the Sublime*) came through Boileau's French version published in 1674.

31. *Specimens of English Prose Style*, p. xxiii.

32. *Works of Dryden*, I, ed. Edward Niles Hooker and H. T. Swedenberg (1956), 118; XIII, ed. Maximillian E. Novak (1984), 232. Aristotle's relegation of diction to only a minor role in poetry is of course also preserved in René Rapin's *Réflexions sur la Poétique d'Aristote*, a work which Dryden cited with approval even before Rymer's English version of it appeared in 1674; *The Collected Works of Samuel Taylor Coleridge*, ed. Kathleen Coburn, (Princeton: Princeton University Press), 16 vols. to date (1969–), XII: *Marginalia II*, ed. George Whalley (1984), 75; hereafter cited as *Collected Works of Coleridge*.

33. *Works of Dryden*, X, ed. Maximillian E. Novak (1970), 212; I, 54–55; XX, 226–27. The phrase from Ovid occurs in the *Metamorphosis* II, line 5.

34. *Works of Dryden*, IV, 64, 88; XX, 72, 75; V, 334, 335. The translated words (*Aeneid*, VIII, 364–65) are those of the rustic king Evander, who welcomes Aeneas and his companions to his humble dwelling, telling them that the divine Hercules had once deigned to accept his hospitality. The phrase "accept our homely food" is Dryden's inferential interpolation, made perhaps in hope of coming closer to the Virgilian charm.

35. *Works of Dryden*, V, 319; II, 175; "To the Memory of Mr. Oldham," *The Poems of John Dryden*, ed. James Kinsley, 4 vols. (Oxford: Clarendon Press, 1958), I, 389.

36. *Works of Dryden*, V, 321. Samuel Say and John Hughes, as cited by Say, ascribe the attractiveness of Denham's "celebrated Distich" to a perfect adaptation of cadence to syntax and meaning. *Poems on Several Occasions and Two Critical Essays. On the Harmony, Variety, and Power of Numbers, Whether in Prose or Verse. On the Numbers of Paradise Lost* (London, 1745), pp. 151–52. But in his *Life* of Denham, Johnson fixed rather on the lines' conveying "so much meaning . . . in so few words," a "felicity" beyond any conscious effort, which only comes "unexpectedly in some hour propitious to poetry." *Lives of the English Poets*, I, 79.

Chapter Four

1. *Works of Johnson*, II, 198, 196.

2. Ibid., II, 198; *Lives of the English Poets*, I, 11; *Works*, II, 494–95.

3. Hume, *Of the Standard of Taste and Other Essays*, ed. John W. Lenz (New York: Bobbs-Merrill, 1965), p. 3; *Oeuvres philosophiques de Condillac*, ed. Georges le Roy, 3 vols. (Paris: Presses Univérsitaires de France, 1947–1951), I, 601.

4. The unfavorable modern sense is actually traceable to the word's Latin ancestry: *homo elegans* in pre-Augustan usage denoted someone given to luxuriousness or overfastidiousness. But as a possibly collateral form of *eligens* (from *eligo*, to choose, select) it was usually complimentary. Its honorific sense in neoclassical criticism had ample classical backing. The *Ad Herennium* names it first among the three qualities making for stylistic perfection ("elocutio commoda et perfecta"): *elegantiam, conpositionem, dignitatem. Rhetorica ad Herennium*, p. 268.

5. *Lectures on Poetry,* p. 294.

6. Curtius, *European Literature and the Latin Middle Ages,* trans. Willard R. Trask (New York: Pantheon Books, 1953), p. 71; Du Bos, *Réflexions,* p. 64.

7. Trapp, *Lectures on Poetry,* p. 307; Dennis, *Critical Works,* II, 35.

8. *Works of Johnson,* II, 239, 241, 240, 242.

9. *Essays on Poetry and Music* (Edinburgh, 1778), pp. 247, 267.

10. How far does the wisdom of Shakespeare's avoidance of embellishment here lie in a sense of the pregnancy of the dramatic moment? Verbal ornament would perhaps only dilute the "poetry" inherent in the situation, so that Lear's decision "to deal plainly" may reflect his creator's artistic instinct as much as his own plight.

11. *Essays on Poetry and Music,* pp. 263, 259.

12. Le Bossu, *Traité du poème épique* (Paris, 1675), pp. 252–53; Trapp, *Lectures on Poetry,* p. 335; Twining, *Aristotle's Treatise on Poetry* (London, 1815), p. 328; Pope, *Poems,* X, 37; Beattie, *Essays,* p. 256.

13. Geoffrey Tillotson has pointed out that stock phrases like "scaly breed" occur in both the prose and the verse of the period. *Augustan Poetic Diction* (New York: Oxford University Press, 1961). See also John Arthos, *The Language of Natural Description in Eighteenth Century Poetry* (Ann Arbor: University of Michigan Press, 1949).

14. *Gray's Poems, Letters, and Essays,* pp. 136–37; Johnson, *Lives of the English Poets,* I, 420.

15. See Partridge, *The Language of Renaissance Poetry,* p. 45.

16. The anonymous commentary on *Hamlet* is reprinted in *Eighteenth-Century Critical Essays,* ed. Scott Elledge, 2 vols. (Ithaca: Cornell University Press, 1961), I, 448, hereafter cited as Elledge; Johnson, *Lives of the English Poets,* I, 420; *Works of Johnson,* VII: *Johnson on Shakespeare,* ed. Arthur Sherbo (1968), 84.

17. *On English Poetry* (New York: Knopf, 1922), p. 41.

18. Hume, *Of the Standard of Taste and Other Essays,* p. 47; Warton, *An Essay on the Genius and Writings of Pope,* 2 vols., 4th ed. (London, 1782), II, 175; Beattie, *Essays on Poetry and Music,* p. 259.

19. *An Essay on the Application of Natural History to Poetry* (London, 1777), pp. 1, 6.

20. *Essays on Poetry and Music,* pp. 206–7, 220–21.

21. Ibid., pp. 229, 230, 235–43. Some light may be thrown on the interaction of common speech and poetic usage by noting that some items on Beattie's list have since his day entered our common vocabulary, e.g., *appal, to picture, shadowy.* Equally noteworthy is that others, such as *yon* and *viewless*—found for example in Coleridge and Keats respectively—survived neoclassicism in poetic use.

22. *Essays,* pp. 247, 249.

23. *Essays,* p. 255.

24. Reynolds, *Discourses on Art,* ed. Stephen O. Mitchell (New York: Bobbs-Merrill, 1965), p. 197; *The Collected Works of Samuel Taylor Coleridge,* VII: *Biographia Literaria,* ed. James Engell and W. Jackson Bate, 2 vols.

(1983), I, 39, hereafter cited as *Biographia;* Johnson, *Lives of the English Poets,* III, 138, 247.

25. Warton, *Observations on the Fairy Queen of Spenser* (London, 1754), p. 367; Johnson, *Works,* II, 215; *Lives of the English Poets,* III, 239.

26. *Réflexions sur la Poésie en general* (The Hague, 1743), pp. 30, 31, 32, 34.

27. Warton, *Essay on . . . Pope,* II, 165; Pemberton, *Observations on Poetry* (London, 1738), pp. 75, 83; Beattie, *Essays,* p. 260; Darwin, Elledge, II, 1006. Perhaps the most damaging refutation of what he regarded as the "hollowness" of Darwin's notion is Thomas De Quincey's appeal to G. E. Lessing's discrimination of temporal and spatial modes of artistic representation in *Laokoon.* De Quincey expunges Darwin's emendation of Pope's line by extrapolating Lessing's theory to include the flat dictum that "no mere description, however visual and picturesque, is in any instance poetic *per se.*" *The Collected Writings of Thomas De Quincey,* new and enlarged edition, ed. David Masson, 14 vols. (Edinburgh, 1889–1890. Reprint. [New York: AMS Press, 1968]), 11, 206 n.

28. Batteux, *Les beaux Arts réduits à un même principe* (Paris, 1746), pp. 166–67; Newberry, *The Art of Poetry on a New Plan,* 2 vols. (London, 1762), I, 41–42.

29. Lowth, Elledge, II, 695; Blair, Elledge, II, 849; Trapp, *Lectures on Poetry,* pp. 74–75.

30. *Les beaux Arts,* p. 41.

31. Addison, Elledge, I, 5; *Spectator* 285; "On the Use of Metaphor," in *The Works of Oliver Goldsmith,* ed. Peter Cunningham, 12 vols. (New York: Harper, 1900), VI, 77.

32. Beattie, *Essays,* p. 225; Batteux, *Les beaux Arts,* p. 171.

33. Du Bois, *Réflexions,* pp. 88–89; Johnson, *Lives of the English Poets,* I, 59; Dennis, *Critical Works,* II, 123; [Anon.], "On Poetry, as Distinguished from Other Writing," in *The Works of Oliver Goldsmith,* VI, 68, 69, 70.

34. Hurd, Elledge, II, 866, 865; Reynolds, *Discourses,* p. 111; Campbell, Elledge, II, 938; Johnson, *Works,* IV, 89, 99. Obviously the metrical requirement did not hold in the casual use of *poet* to designate a comic dramatist, whose characters typically spoke in prose.

35. *Poems,* VII, 11, 88.

36. *Poems on Several Occasions,* pp. 120, 154, 159, 160; Gross, *Sound and Form in Modern Poetry* (Ann Arbor: University of Michigan Press, 1964), p. 216. Say seems to have borrowed the term "power of numbers" from Pemberton's *Observations on Poetry,* which he quotes with approval (p. 155).

37. Pemberton, *Observations on Poetry,* p. 117; Beattie, *Essays,* pp. 294–96; Dennis, *Critical Works,* II, 215.

38. The twentieth-century purist Henri Bremond calls the prose of Bossuet's sermons and funeral orations poetic, Boileau's verse nonpoetic. *La Poésie pure* (Paris: Grasset, 1926), pp. 74, 24. Those for whom poetic quality is less a function of meter than of a studied and subtly nuanced lexical precision will be most receptive to Warton's judgment. La Bruyère actually anticipates the insistence on *le mot juste* which his nineteenth- century countryman

Flaubert was to carry to near monomaniacal lengths. Among the various expressions by which a single thought may be conveyed, La Bruyère observes in the *Caractères*, only one is really adequate ("il n'y en a qu'une qui soit la bonne"); 2 vols. (Paris: Gallimard,), I, 58.

39. *Essay on . . . Pope*, I, iv–v, viii–x.

40. Fénelon, *Oeuvres choisies*, ed. Albert Chérel, 2nd ed. (Paris: Hatier, 1930), pp. 619–20, 621–22; Lowth, *Lectures on the Sacred Poetry of the Hebrews*, Elledge, II, 689–91; Du Bos, *Réflexions*, pp. 91, 134.

41. Montesquieu, *Lettres persanes*, ed. Antoine Adam (Genève: Librairie Droz, 1954), p. 348; Trublet is cited in Van Tieghem, *Les grandes doctrines littéraires en France* (Paris: Presses Universitaires, 1963), p. 93; La Motte, *Odes, avec un Discours sur la Poésie en général*, 5th ed. (Amsterdam, 1719), I, 42; Van Tieghem, *op. cit.*, p. 95. The attack on meter was challenged, notably by a leading spokesman of the Enlightenment. In a lecture to the Academy in 1757, D'Alembert, though not entirely unsympathetic to La Motte's call for a prose tragedy, remarked that anyone not tone-deaf would notice that by dropping the meter and altering the word order in a poem "he had destroyed the harmony created by the original arrangement." *Encyclopédie: Selections*, trans. Nelly S. Hoyt and Thomas Cassirer (New York: Bobbs-Merrill, 1965), p. 369.

42. Lanson, *Essais de méthode, de critique, et d'histoire littéraire*, ed. Henri Peyre (Paris: Hachette, 1965), p. 240; Rivarol, *Discours sur l'universalité de la Langue française*, ed. Maurice Favergeat (Paris: Librairie Larousse, n.d.), p. 54.

43. Though occasionally advanced earlier, only now did the idea of progress become a key item of the social creed. "We will have to wait till the eighteenth century," J. Huizinga writes of its final advent, "—for even the Renaissance does not truly bring the idea of progress—before men resolutely enter the path of social optimism;—only then the perfectibility of man and society is raised to the rank of a central dogma." *The Waning of the Middle Ages* (London: Edward Arnold, 1927), p. 28.

44. *History of English Poetry*, ed. W. Carew Hazlitt, 4 vols. (London, 1871), I, 3, 5.

45. *An Inquiry into the Life and Writings of Homer*, 2nd ed. (London, 1736), pp. 26, 60. Contrast the earlier Renaissance attitude in Montaigne's essay "Des Cannibales," where a savage love lyric is praised precisely because he found no trace of barbarism ("il n'y a rien de barbare") in the imagination that conceived it. *Essais de Montaigne*, ed. Maurice Rat, 2 vols. (Paris: Garnier Frères, 1962), I, 244.

46. Elledge, II, 711; *Essay on . . . Pope*, II, 68, 408; Duff, *An Essay on Original Genius* (London, 1767), ed. in facsimile reprint of the 4th ed. by John L. Mahoney (Gainesville, Florida, 1964), pp. 260–96.

47. The historical priority of poetic to discursive or "philosophic" language did not always imply a value judgment of either gain or, as in these words from Keats's "Lamia," loss. The motif of cultural loss is stronger in Herder, for example, than in Condillac, though both regarded verse as the primordial form of utterance.

48. Elledge, II, 849.

49. Husbands, Elledge, I, 420–21; Lowth, Elledge, II, 695.

50. Blair, Elledge, II, 850; Blackwell, *An Inquiry into . . . Homer*, p. 39; Hurd, Elledge, II, 864.

51. *Lives of the English Poets*, I, 177.

52. Dennis, *Critical Works*, I, 47, 359; Knox, Elledge, II, 1114, 1116.

53. Elledge, II, 689.

54. Blair, *Lectures on Rhetoric and Belles Lettres*, 2 vols. (London, 1783), I, 59, 75, 76, 77. Boileau, *Oeuvres complètes*, ed. Françoise Escal (Paris: Gallimard, 1966), p. 338. Boileau's opposition of sublimity and the sublime style is no gratuitous misreading. The paradox is latent in the *Peri hypsous* itself, perhaps because of its fragmentary state. The close affinity of English Longinianism with Romantic thinking may be glimpsed by comparing Blair's words with the "axiom" Keats expressed in a letter to John Taylor: "That if Poetry comes not as naturally as the Leaves to a tree it had better not come at all." *The Letters of John Keats*, ed. Hyder Edward Rollins, 2 vols. (Cambridge: Harvard University Press, 1958), I, 238–39, hereafter cited as *Letters of Keats*.

55. *Essay on . . . Pope*, I, x, 43.

56. Ibid., I, 280, 142, 279–80.

57. Ibid., I, 173; II, 411.

58. Elledge, II, 781–82, 1161

Chapter Five

1. Johnson, *Lives of the English Poets*, I, 237; Knight, *An Analytical Inquiry into the Principles of Taste* 3rd ed. (London, 1806) p. 125; *Collected Letters of Samuel Taylor Coleridge*, ed. Earl Leslie Griggs, 6 vols. (New York: Oxford University Press, 1956, 1971), IV, 782.

2. Since Cowper's time critical opinion has generally rated both his and Thomson's blank verse above others' in their century. In *Biographia* Coleridge compared the two. "In chastity of diction . . . and harmony of blank verse, Cowper leaves Thomson immeasurably below him; yet I still feel the latter to have been the *born* poet" (I, 25n). Elsewhere Coleridge finds in Cowper some passages of "colloquial Blank Verse excellent though not perfect." In our time George Whalley has detected a beneficial influence of the "flexible blank verse" of *The Task*, its "divine chit-chat," on Coleridge's Conversation Poems, and directly or through Coleridge's prior example, on Wordsworth's "Tintern Abbey." *Collected Works of Coleridge*, XII: *Marginalia I*, 218. "The conversational idiom of Coleridge and Wordsworth," Harold Bloom finds, "is descended from Cowper's softening of Milton's style in his domestic epic, *The Task*." *The Visionary Company* (London: Faber and Faber, 1961), p. 194. Hunt, *Leigh Hunt's 'Examiner' Examined*, ed. Edmund Blunden (Hamden, Conn.: Archon Books, 1967), p. 130.

3. *The Prose Works of William Wordsworth*, ed. W. J. B. Owen and Jane Worthington Smyser, 3 vols. (Oxford: Clarendon, 1974), I, 116.

4. See Coleridge's friendly censure of Thomas Wedgwood's poetic taste in a letter of 1802: ". . . but in point of poetic Diction I am not so well satisfied that you do not require a certain *Aloofness* from the language of real life,

which I think deadly to Poetry." *Collected Letters*, II, 877. The foggy syntax of this clause, with its twin double negatives, has quite understandably caused at least one commentator to mistake its sense for the opposite of Coleridge's intention. See George Watson's edition of the *Biographia Literaria* (New York: E. P. Dutton, 1960), p. xi. In context it becomes clear that what Coleridge thought deadly was the *Aloofness* (his italics), not the language of real life.

    5. *Prose Works,* pp. 125, 160, 161–62.

    6. In Germany alone between the late 1770s and the mid-1800s some fifteen musicians, including Schubert, Mendelssohn, and Brahms, set Ossianic texts or composed instrumental pieces of Ossianic inspiration. There were paintings and sketches of Macpherson's scenes and characters. See Rudolph Tombs, Jr., *Ossian in Germany* (New York, 1901). Paul van Tieghem devoted two full volumes to the phenomenon in France from the eighteenth to the twentieth century, *Ossian in France* (Paris, 1917). As early as 1763 an Italian verse translation of *Ossian* was published at Padua. Goethe's tribute is most effectively recorded in his *Werther* (1774), in which the hero's reading from his translation of Macpherson's work to his beloved Lotte brings their tragic passion to its crisis.

    7. Herder, *Sämtliche Werke,* ed. Bernhard Suphan, 33 vols. (Berlin: Weidmann, 1877–1913), V, 160; Wordsworth, *Prose Works,* III, 78. "Having had the good fortune to be born and reared in a mountainous country, from my very childhood I have felt the falsehood that pervades the volumes imposed upon the world under the name of Ossian." Ibid., III, 77.

    8. Johann Georg Sulzer, *Allgemeine Theorie der Schönen Künste,* 4 vols. 2nd ed. (Leipzig, 1792–1799), II, 327.

    9. *Lectures on Rhetoric and Belles Lettres,* II. 323.

    10. *The Use of Poetry and the Use of Criticism* (London: Faber and Faber, 1933), p. 74.

    11. *De l'Allemagne,* 3 vols., 2nd ed. (Paris, 1814), I, 163–64. Was de Staël's "homme d'esprit" Rousseau himself or, more probably, a fellow disciple? In either case she would have read in Rousseau's posthumous *Essai sur l'origine des Langues* (1781) that since passion first moved him to speak man's first impressions were metaphors; and that poetry antedated prose for the same reason: "puisque les passions parlent avant la raison." Bibliothèque du Graphe edition, pp. 505, 529.

    12. *An Essay on Original Genius,* p. 294. The argument that Wordsworth was offering his exaltation of rustic speech as valid not for all poetry but only for the kind he was "experimenting" with is hardly tenable. Again and again his remarks about language are posited of poetry in general. True, in the 1800 Preface, after rejecting abstract personifications, he wrote: "not that I mean to censure such abstractions, but in these Poems. . . ." But these words were dropped in 1802. See *Prose Works,* I, 130, 131.

    13. Wordsworth, *Prose Works,* I, 142–43. See Shelley's similar convictions in his "Preface" to *The Cenci* (1819).

    14. Wordsworth, *Prose Works,* I, 123, 124; Abrams, *The Mirror and the Lamp* (New York: Oxford University Press, 1953), p. 110.

    15. W. J. B. Owen, *Wordsworth as Critic* (Toronto: University of Toronto Press, 1969), p. 63.

16. *Lectures on Rhetoric and Belles Lettres,* I, 63, 65, 70, 274.

17. Horace, *Ars poetica,* lines 102–3; Du Bos, *Réflexions,* p. 116.

18. Perkins, *Wordsworth and the Poetry of Sincerity* (Cambridge: Harvard University Press, 1964), p. 2; Byron, *English Bards and Scotch Reviewers,* lines 816–17.

19. *The Complete Works of William Hazlitt,* ed. P. P. Howe, 21 vols. (London: J. M. Dent and Sons, 1930–1934), VI, 251, hereafter cited as *Hazlitt.*

20. *Wordsworth's Literary Criticism,* ed. Nowell C. Smith (London, 1905), p. 243.

21. *Prose Works,* II, 84, 85. Coleridge was similarly convinced of "the high importance of Words," and their incalculable moral and practical effects on individuals and nations. See *Coleridge on Logic and Learning,* ed. Alice B. Snyder (New Haven: Yale University Press, 1924), p. 76.

22. Like religion, Wordsworth maintained, poetry is "incapable to sustain her existence without sensuous incarnation." *Prose Works,* III, 65.

23. *The Mirror and the Lamp,* p. 110.

24. Wordsworth, *Prose Works,* III, 82; Wimsatt and Brooks, *Literary Criticism,* p. 350.

25. *Prose Works,* I, 133–34.

26. Marjorie L. Barstow, *Wordsworth's Theory of Poetic Diction* (New Haven: Yale University Press, 1917), p. 135.

27. *Prose Works,* I, 160.

28. Ibid., I, 162–63.

29. *Poems of Pope,* I, *Pastoral Poetry and an Essay on Criticism,* ed. E. Audra and Aubrey Williams (1961), 103; Wordsworth, *Prose Works,* I, 131.

30. *Prose Works,* I, 163–64; Saintsbury, *A History of Criticism,* III, 204.

31. *Prose Works,* I, 135.

32. Enfield, "Is Verse Essential to Poetry?" *Monthly Magazine and British Register,* II (1796), 454–56; Wordsworth, *Prose Works,* I, 135, 144, 150.

33. *Prose Works,* I, 134.

34. *Prose Works,* I, 132, 164.

35. *Prose Works,* I, 147.

36. Coleridge, *Collected Letters,* II, 830, 812. Wordsworth, *Prose Works,* I, 148, 137, 145, 163, 164, II, 76.

37. *Prose Works,* III, 65, 6.

38. Blackwell, *Enquiry into . . . Homer,* p. 39; Brown, *Rise and Progress of Poetry,* (Newcastle, 1764), pp. 12, 26.

39. *Allgemeine Theorie,* I, 324.

40. Coleridge, *Biographia,* II, 65; Wordsworth, *Prose Works,* I, 161 (italics added).

Chapter Six

1. *Promenades philosophiques,* premier série (Paris: Mercure de France, 1905), p. 35

2. Students of philosophy will hardly require documentation for Kant's achievement. Others may most suitably be referred to the recent testimony of

Roger Scruton, who writes that without the *Critique of Judgment* "it could fairly be said that . . . aesthetics would not exist in its modern form." *Kant* (Oxford: Oxford University Press, 1982), p. 79. Another writer concluded that the *Critique* "remains the decisive event in the history of modern aesthetics." O. B. Hardison, Jr., ed., *The Quest for Imagination* (Cleveland: Case Western Reserve University, 1971), p. vii.

3. *Coleridge on Imagination*, (London: Routledge and Kegan Paul, 1934), pp. 5, 232–33.

4. *Biographia*, II, 10–11.

5. Since I have already sought to do this in *Coleridge on the Language of Verse* (Princeton: Princeton University Press, 1981), much of this and the following chapter will, with modifications and additions, unavoidably restate the central thesis of that book.

6. *Biographia*, I, 5; *Collected Letters*, IV, 620.

7. *Biographia*, II, 43.

8. Samuel Taylor Coleridge, *Shakespearean Criticism*, ed. Thomas Middleton Raysor, 2 vols., 2nd ed. (New York: E. P. Dutton, 1960), I, 181, hereafter cited as *Shakespearean Criticism*. Coleridge's originality lies in the meaning he assigns to an imitation, not in having merely separated it from a copy, as for example Henry Fuseli had done. Fuseli's distinction consists only in assigning imitation the loftier role of judgment exercised in selecting and combining the parts of a painting and raising them and the resulting whole "to the highest degree of unison." The two terms are among seven he feels it necessary to define early in his opening lecture, the others being *nature, beauty, grace, taste,* and *genius.* The definitions have little subsequent theoretical significance. *Lectures on Painting* (London, 1801), p. 6.

9. The widest divergence among modern interpreters of Aristotelian mimesis seems to occur between the so-called Chicago Aristotelians and literary critics and aestheticians like Northrop Frye and Roman Ingarden. Contrast Richard McKeon's "Literary Criticism and the Concept of Imitation in Antiquity," in *Critics and Criticism Ancient and Modern,* ed. R. S. Crane (Chicago: University of Chicago Press, 1952), with Ingarden's two-part essay, "A Marginal Commentary on Aristotle's *Poetics*," *Journal of Aesthetics and Art Criticism,* XX (Winter, 1961), 163–73 and (Spring, 1962), 273–85; or with Harvey D. Goldstein's excellent "Mimesis and Catharsis Reëxamined," *Journal of Aesthetics and Art Criticism,* XXIV (Summer, 1966), 567–77. Coleridge's conception of verse language is consistent with Aristotelian mimesis as understood by Ingarden and Goldstein.

10. The formula itself ("ἡ τέχνη μιμειτφι τὴν φύσιν,") appears not in the *Poetics* but in the *Physics,* where art (τέχνη) means any purposive human skill or endeavor, not exclusively fine art.

11. S. H. Butcher, *Aristotle's Theory of Poetry and Fine Art,* 4th ed. (New York: Dover Publications, 1951), pp. 123, 94.

12. Addison, *Spectator* no. 416. Contrast the positivism of William Jones's total rejection of Aristotelian mimesis because neither words nor musical tones resemble visible objects. "On the Arts, Commonly Called Imitative," in *Poems, Consisting Chiefly of Translations from the Asiatick Languages* (Oxford, 1772), pp. 201, 213–14.

13. *Oeuvres de Boileau* (Paris: Librairie Garnier Frères, 1928), pp. 139, 172.

14. *Les beaux Arts,* pp. viii, 14, 8, 16.

15. "Gedanken über die Nachahmung der Griechischen Werke in der Malerei und Bildhauerkunst," in *Winckelmanns Werke in einem Band* (Berlin: Aufbau Verlag, 1969), p. 11.

16. *Works of Dryden,* IX, 6; XX, 60.

17. Coleridge, *Biographia,* II, 35n.; Reynolds, *Discourses on Art,* pp. 105, 206.

18. *The Enneads,* trans. Stephen MacKenna, 4th ed. rev. by B. S. Page (New York: Random House, 1969), pp. 422–23. For citations of Plotinus as a source for Coleridge see the Bate-Engell *Biographia Literaria,* J. Shawcross' earlier edition, 2 vols. (London: Oxford University Press, 1907), and I. A. Richards, *Coleridge on Imagination,* pp. 26–27. *Winckelmanns Werke,* pp. 3, 11. Philarète Chasles named Winckelmann among German thinkers in whose work Coleridge was "adept" (quoted in *Collected Works of Coleridge,* XIV: *Table Talk* [1990], ed. Carl Woodring, 2 vols., I, liii).

19. See Hume's essay "Of Tragedy," in which he argues the conversion of painful emotions in stage tragedy by the "force of imagination, the energy of expression, the power of numbers, the charms of imitation," all of them naturally in themselves "delightful to the mind." Ernst Cassirer finds eighteenth-century European aesthetics characterized by a gradual abandonment of the classical imitational norm accepted in its earlier stages. "But now this norm begins to change. The stress now falls not on proximity to, but on distance from, the object; not on that in which art resembles nature, but on the specific mode of artistic expression and representation. The logical inadequacy of the media of expression, their indirect and metaphorical character, are expressly admitted; but their value is not affected by this fact." *The Philosophy of the Enlightenment,* trans. Fritz C. A. Koelln and James P. Pettegrove (Princeton: Princeton University Press, 1951) p. 302.

20. *Réflexions critiques sur la Poésie et sur la Peinture,* pp. 14, 15.

21. As in William Hazlitt's "On Imitation" in the collection of his essays called *The Round Table* (1817).

22. For notable example, the critical system of Northrop Frye, rightly praised, because "the humanistic element of his criticism is never merely imposed on literature from without, but is rather discovered within the imaginative dimension of literature itself." Peter Cummings in *The Quest for Imagination,* p. 258.

Chapter Seven

1. See *Biographia,* Chapters 17 and 18 passim.

2. *Biographia,* II, 12.

3. Ibid., II, 12, 14. It should be noted that for Coleridge the category of poetic prose did not primarily include fictional works designed as such. His prime examples are Isaiah, the Platonic dialogues, and the devotional prose of Jeremy Taylor.

4. *The Notebooks of Samuel Taylor Coleridge,* ed. Kathleen Coburn, 4 vols. to date (New York: Pantheon, 1957–), II, entry 2211 and note, entry 2274 and note; *Anima Poetae,* ed. Ernest Hartley Coleridge (Boston: Houghton Mifflin, 1895), p. 75; *Biographia Literaria,* ed. Shawcross, II, 273.

5. Coleridge, *Notebooks,* II, entries 2274, 2211.

6. "Ueber das Verhältniss der bildenen Künste zu der Natur," *Sämmliche Werke,* Erste Abteilung, 10 vols. (Stuttgart und Augsburg, 1860–1861), VII, 301, 302.

7. *Biographia,* II, 45. See Walter Jackson Bate, *Coleridge* (New York: Macmillan, 1968), p. 164.

8. "On Poesy or Art," in Shawcross, *Biographia Literaria,* II, 256.

9. *Discourses on Art,* pp. 232, 234; Mendelssohn, *Gesammelte Schriften. Jubiläums-ausgabe* (Stuttgart: Friedrich Frommann Verlag, 1971–), I, 391–92, 433; Smith, "Of the Nature of That Imitation Which Takes Place in What Are Called the Imitative Arts," in *Early Writings of Adam Smith,* ed. J. Ralph Lindgren (New York: Augustus M. Kelley, 1967), p. 141. I am indebted to the late René Wellek for calling my attention to Mendelssohn.

10. Coleridge, "On Poesy or Art," in Shawcross, *Biographia Literaria,* II, 257; Mendelssohn, *Gesammelte Schriften,* I, 433.

11. *Shakespearean Criticism,* I, 177. Coleridge leaves his readers to infer that though both are only copies, stage scenery is in itself not objectionable, since no beholder ever takes it for the reality it is only designed to *represent* by visual resemblance. Marble fruits, however, offered as visual *substitutes* for the real thing, and not, like stage properties, parts of a fictive setting, do often momentarily delude. Thus they are pointless rivals of nature. His aversion would be to the deceptive intention. But Coleridge's reasoning is less than clear on this point.

12. Smith, *Early Writings,* p. 156. Reviewing my *Coleridge on the Language of Verse,* W. J. B. Owen pointed to Beattie's use of Coleridge's opposed terms in his *Essays on Poetry and Music* (*Review of English Studies,* XXXV [August, 1984], 391). The relevant passage in Beattie runs: "For that which is properly termed *Imitation* has always in it something which is not in the original. If the prototype and transcript be exactly alike; if there be nothing in the one which is not in the other; we may call the latter a representation, a copy, a draught, or a picture, of the former; but we never call it an imitation" (p. 87). But Beattie's argument for preferring an imitation to a copy, draught, or picture merely restates Sidney's "golden" and "brazen" worlds minus Sidney's morality. The simplistic hedonism of this traditional defense of poetry is precisely what Coleridge abandons in his analysis of mimesis. In one philosophically informed discussion of Coleridge's poetics, *imitation* and *copy* are included with the other pairings of antithetical terms—like *reason* versus *understanding,* and *imagination* versus *fancy*— characteristic of the conceptual dynamism which constitutes the foundation of his radical transcendence of neoclassical critical categories. See for example Günter H. Lenz, *Die Dichtungstheorie S. T. Coleridges* (Frankfurt am Main: Athenäum Verlag, 1971), p. 84.

13. G. N. G. Orsini, *Coleridge and German Idealism* (Carbondale: Southern Illinois University Press, 1969), p. 169; *Biographia,* II, 43; J. A.

Appleyard, *Coleridge's Philosophy of Literature* (Cambridge: Harvard University Press, 1964), pp. 109–10.

14. *Biographia*, I, 300. Coleridge's *tertium aliquid* prefigures later notions of aesthetic quality as an emergent, e.g., the "third something" that D. H. Lawrence saw resulting from a collaboration between nature and artistic prowess in Van Gogh's paintings of sunflowers. See D. H. Lawrence, *Selected Literary Criticism*, ed. Anthony Beal (New York: Viking Press, 1967), p. 108. German Romantic philosophers had also referred to the *tertium aliquid*, notably J. G. Fichte. See *Biographia*, I, 300, n.2.

15. *Table Talk*, I, 408. Citing Coleridge's use of the term and labeling it rare, the *OED* defines *methosesis* as "something interposed, seeming to correct or reconcile antagonistic agencies or principles." *Shakespearean Criticism*, I, 181. Raysor notes the conceptual parallel with Kant here. Schelling thought painting differed from sculpture in that the former offers its images not as realities ("die Gegenstände selbst") but expressly as images (*Sämmtliche Werke*, VII, 317).

16. *Coleridge's Miscellaneous Criticism*, ed. Thomas Middleton Raysor (Cambridge: Harvard University Press, 1936), p. 49.

17. *Biographia* II, 60–61; Lukacs, *Studies in European Realism* (New York: Grosset and Dunlap, 1964), p. 133.

18. *Collected Letters*, III, 501; IV, 599. These citations from Coleridge's correspondence remove all possibility of misconstruing his imitation as a denaturalized formalism. In poetic recitation as in every other mimetic art, it is clearly a happy medium between formal devitalization and a dead conflation of art and life. The opposed failures of much Shakespeare performance perfectly demonstrate its importance. W. H. Auden made the same point in his own terms. "A good actor," he wrote, "must—alas, today he too seldom does—make the audience hear Shakespeare's lines as verse, not prose, but if he tries to make the verse sound like a different language, he will make himself sound ridiculous." *The Dyer's Hand* (New York: Random House, 1962), pp. 24–25.

19. Appleyard, *Coleridge's Philosophy of Literature*, p. 107; Bate, *Coleridge*, p. 164; Coleridge, *Collected Works*, VI, *Lay Sermons*, ed. R. J. White, (1972), 32; *Shakespearean Criticism*, I, 185; II, 258; *Biographia*, II, 126, 134.

20. *Notebooks*, III, entry 4397; *Biographia*, II, 72. Coleridge's requirement of meter for poetic perfection clashes irreconcilably with his assertion that the finest prose may be poetry "of the highest kind."

21. *Biographia*, II, 64, 17. Here is another Coleridgean discovery since become a theoretical commonplace. In a chapter of *The Poetic Mind* (New York: Macmillan, 1922), significantly entitled "The Impulse and the Control," F. C. Prescott founded verse rhythm and meter in a conflict between passionate impulse and its restraint, and somewhat patronizingly declared Coleridge to have been "on the right track when he finds the origin of metre in 'the balance in the mind effected by that spontaneous effort which strives to hold in check the workings of passion'" (p. 24). In one respect Coleridge's account is a psychological counterpart, applied to the individual creative process, of a motif of Romantic aesthetic primitivism. In his four *Briefe über*

Poesie, Silbenmass und Sprache (1795), A. W. Schlegel pictures savage man as instinctively discovering in the measured beat of song and dance an ordered, controlled expression of his unruly emotions. Schlegel's envisioning of the civilizing effect of measure ("Zeitmass") anticipates Coleridge's notions of the salutary reciprocity of order and emotion in the poet's verse-making. As emotion determined primitive expression, the latter reacted to alter the feeling itself. "In this fashion, as their powerful eruptions were transformed by the introduction of an ordering measure in song and dance, the passions themselves were inevitably softened." *Kritische Schriften und Briefe,* ed. Edgar Lohner, 7 vols. (Stuttgart: W. Kohlhammer Verlag, 1962), I: *Sprache und Poetik,* 174.

22. *Biographia,* II, 67, 69.

23. *Collected Letters,* II, 812. Coleridge's own rare use of the word *superaddition,* whether in careless echo of Wordsworth or, more likely, with gently ironic intent, should not be allowed to obscure their divergence in theory. Coleridge's context always shows that he did not intend it to designate a decorative increment, as it does in Wordsworth's usage. Coleridge's whole metrical theory is a reasoned contradiction of Wordsworth's assertion that meter is "but adventitious to composition." Jakobson, "Linguistics and Poetics," in *Essays on the Language of Literature,* ed. Seymour Chatman and Samuel R. Levin (Boston: Houghton-Mifflin, 1967), p. 321; *Biographia,* II, 12–13.

24. *Biographia,* II, 121, 15; *Miscellaneous Criticism,* pp. 219–20; *Biographia,* II, 92, 78.

25. Shawcross, *Biographia Literaria,* II, 268; Murray Krieger, *Theory of Criticism: A Tradition and Its System* (Baltimore: Johns Hopkins University Press, 1976), p. 122.

26. *Biographia,* II, 64, 71, 60–61. When it first appeared, Coleridge thought, "prose must have struck men with greater *admiration* than poetry. In the latter it was the language of passion and emotion; it was what they themselves spoke and heard in moments of exultation, indignation, etc. But to have an evolving roll, or succession of leaves talk continuously the language of deliberate reason in the form of a continued preconception, of a Z already possessed when A is being uttered,—this must have appeared Godlike." (*Miscellaneous Criticism,* p. 277). The acuity of this bit of imaginative inference loses nothing by the reflection that its primary impulse is the primitivist view of poetry's origin which Coleridge and other English and Continental Romantics inherited from the eighteenth century. Eliot was also to separate conversation from verse and prose alike in *On Poetry and Poets,* p. 76. On at least one occasion traditional poetics had done the same. See Buffon's *Discours sur le style* (1753). Yet conflation of prose and conversation persists, as in Cohen's *Structure du langage poétique,* p. 48.

27. Tate, *Essays of Four Decades* (Chicago: Swallow Press, 1968), p. 94; *Biographia,* II, 14, 15.

28. *Biographia,* II, 13, 16–17.

29. Though this word has a formal etymology in the Greek ποιηματικός, meaning poetical, as desynonymized from *poetic* it is apparently one of Coleridge's many coinages. The *OED,* calling it a nonce-word, cites only a single occurrence— from Coleridge. Its universal adoption would fill a vexing terminological gap in poetic theory.

30. *Collected Letters,* V, 287.

31. Coleridge, *Biographia,* II, 71.

32. *Collected Letters,* II, 955; *Shakespearean Criticism,* II, 34; *Miscellaneous Criticism,* p. 181.

33. *Biographia,* II, 64–65. Cf. *Notebooks,* III, entry 4397: "N.b. how by excitement of the Associate Power Passion itself imitates Order, and the *order* resulting produces a pleasurable *Passion* (whence Metre) and elevates the Mind by making its feelings the Objects of its reflection and how recalling the Sights and Sounds that had accompanied the occasions of the original passion it impregnates them with an interest not their own by means of the Passions, and yet tempers the passion by the calming power which all *distinct* images exert on the human soul." Miss Coburn's note on this entry properly calls attention to its "Schillerian overtones." But the general influence of Schiller on Coleridge's aesthetics does not preclude an even greater, and possibly prior, role played by personal creative effort in his understanding of how the poet shapes his emotions into art.

34. *Biographia,* II, 68–69.

35. *Notebooks,* III, entry 3970; *Shakespearean Criticism,* I, 15; II, 42; *Miscellaneous Criticism,* pp. 163–64; Sapir, *Language* (New York: Harcourt Brace, and World, 1949), p. 161. Elsewhere Coleridge illustrated the distinction between the "logics" of grammar and of passion, stressing the importance of stylistic deviation to the aesthetic quality of the latter. He quoted a line from Wordsworth's "exquisite sonnet" entitled "Upon Westminster Bridge": "The river windeth [glideth] at his own sweet will." He freely concedes that one can call a stream's shifting current its "will" only in a figurative sense. "But who does not see that here the poetic charm arises from the known and felt *impropriety* of the expression, in the technical sense of the word *impropriety,* among grammarians." *Aids to Reflection* (London: George Bell and Sons, 1904), p. 44.

36. Coleridge, *Shakespearean Criticism,* II, 52–53; I, 147. Though generally slighted in modern poetics, Coleridge's insight confirms a motif in the lore of creative psychology in Western thought. "It is the fervor of poesy," Boccaccio wrote, that impels a soul to a longing for utterance. *Boccaccio on Poetry,* trans. from *Geologia Deorum Gentilium* by Charles G. Osgood (New York: Bobbs-Merrill, 1956), p. 39. And Spenser opened his *Hymn of Heavenly Beauty,* "Rapt in the rage of my own ravished thought."

37. Cohen, *Structure du langage poétique,* pp. 76–77; Coleridge, *Miscellaneous Criticism,* p. 183; *Notebooks,* III, entry 3611.

38. *Biographia,* II, 13, 14.

39. Georg Wilhelm Friedrich Hegel, *Werke,* 20 vols. (Frankfurt am Main: Suhrkamp Verlag, 1970), XV: *Vorlesungen über die Ästhetik,* 250–51.

40. Henri Bremond, *La Poésie pure,* p. 17; Valéry, *Oeuvres,* I, 1330; Nemerov, "On the Measure of Poetry," *Critical Inquiry,* VI (1979), 338. Since Valéry's poetry-dance is often regarded as a theoretical *trouvaille,* it may be of interest to mention an eighteenth-century near adumbration of it by Condillac, though he used it to contrast the ratios between "art" and "nature" in the two literary forms. In poetry and the dance acquired skill becomes a habit; "et le poëte est, en quelque sorte, au prosateur, ce qu'est le danseur à

l'homme qui marche" [and the poet is, in a sense, to the prose writer what the dancer is to a man walking]. *Oeuvres philosophiques,* I, 603.

41. *Vorlesungen über die Ästhetik,* pp. 252–53.

42. Ibid., pp. 283, 244, 229.

43. *Shakespearean Criticism,* I, 197. Coleridge's notion of the terminal and instrumental reciprocity at work in organic poetic structure may have been suggested, or at least encouraged, by Kant's statement in the *Critique of Judgment:* "*An organized product of nature is one in which every part is reciprocally purpose [end] and means.*" Trans. J. H. Bernard (New York: Hafner, 1951), p. 222. Cf. W. K. Wimsatt's identical view that in organic structure "all parts and the whole are reciprocally ends and means." *The Verbal Icon* (Lexington: University of Kentucky Press, 1954), p. 243.

44. *Literary Criticism,* pp. 610–34. Wimsatt's and Brooks's "Epilogue" to their book is largely a cogent defense of irony "as a cognitive principle which shades off through paradox into the general principle of metaphor and metaphoric structure—the tension which is always present when words are used in vitally new ways" (p. 747).

45. *The Unanswered Question: Six Talks at Harvard* (Cambridge: Harvard University Press, 1976), p. 39. For Bernstein, ambiguity, or tension, is "the magic secret" in musical syntax.

46. Schiller, *On the Aesthetic Education of Man,* trans. Reginald Snell (New Haven: Yale University Press, 1954), p. 76. Schopenhauer and Nietzsche are cited in Wimsatt and Brooks, *Literary Criticism,* pp. 565, 567. Bosanquet, *Three Lectures on Aesthetic* (London: Macmillan, 1915), passim. For a penetrating exposition of Coleridge's conception of how pleasurable excitement is aroused in readers by "the fruitful tension of poetic form" ("die fruchtbare Spannung der dicterischen Form"), see Lenz's *Dichtungstheorie S. T. Coleridge,* pp. 236 ff. For the German-reading non-specialists, Jochen Schulte-Sasse's *Literarische Wertung* (Stuttgart: J. B. Metzlersche Verlags-Buchhandlung, 1971) provides an excellent brief account of the international status of the idea of "ästhetische Spannungen" (aesthetic tensions) in modern speculation.

47. Brooks, *The Well Wrought Urn* (New York: Harcourt, Brace, 1947), p. 3; Wheelwright, *The Burning Fountain: A Study in the Language of Symbolism,* new and rev. ed. (Bloomington: Indiana University Press, 1968), p. 102; Goodman, *Languages of Art* (London: Oxford University Press, 1969), p. 69.

48. "The Metaphoric Process as Cognition, Imagination, and Feeling," *Critical Inquiry,* V (1978), 148.

49. *What Coleridge Thought* (Middletown, Conn.: Wesleyan University Press, 1971), pp. 36, 112.

Chapter Eight

1. *Hazlitt,* 11, 162.

2. *Hazlitt,* XVI, 134–35. What Hazlitt thought of Wordsworth's exaltation of rustic feelings and the superior language they allegedly produce, the reader may gather from a paragraph in his "Observations" on Wordsworth's

The Excursion that opens: "All country people hate each other." *Hazlitt,*
IV, 122.

3. *Shelley's Critical Prose,* ed. Bruce R. McEldery, Jr. (Lincoln: University
of Nebraska Press, 1967), pp. 61, 65; *Mary Shelley's Journal,* ed. Frederick L.
Jones (Norman: University of Oklahoma Press, 1947), p. 87; *Biographia,* II,
54. Note too the loosely Coleridgean cast of the further observation in Shelley's preface: "As to imitation, poetry is a mimetic art. It creates, but it creates
by combination and representation." *Shelley's Critical Prose,* pp. 66, 77.

4. Schlegel, *Gespräch über die Poesie* (Stuttgart: J. B. Metzlerisch Verlags-
buchhandlung, 1968), p. 285; *Hazlitt,* V, 1, 2; Baker, *William Hazlitt* (Cambridge: Harvard University Press, 1962), p. 314. In 1927 Valéry alerted a lecture audience to the obfuscating double sense of *poetry,* used sometimes to
designate the art properly so called and sometimes its source in emotive experience. He complained that many poetic theories were radically flawed ("vicié
dans leur principe") by the use of a single word for two related but quite different things. *Oeuvres,* I, 1362.

5. *Hazlitt,* XII, 6, 8, 11, 17; V, 104, 146; IV, 72. Not that Hazlitt's
opinion is universally groundless. Pope confessed to being more at ease writing verse than prose. Robert Frost admitted to a correspondent: "If I wrote
myself it would have to be in verse since I write no prose and am scared blue
at any demand on me for prose." Elaine Barry, *Robert Frost on Writing* (New
Brunswick, N.J.: Rutgers University Press, 1973), p. 79.

6. *Hazlitt,* IV, 214; VIII, 243; VI, 208–9. William Gifford charged in
the *Quarterly Review* that Hazlitt's opinions on the antidemocratic nature of
poetry slandered Shakespeare. Regrettably, Hazlitt's rejoinder, a vituperative
pamphlet entitled "A Letter to William Gifford, Esq." (1819), adds little to
his thesis beyond the assertion that Shakespeare's verse "makes us read with
admiration and reconciles us in fact to the triumphant progress of the con-
querors and mighty hunters of mankind." *Hazlitt,* IX, 37.

7. *Peacock's Four Ages of Poetry, Shelley's Defence of Poetry, Browning's Essay
on Shelley,* ed. H. F. B. Brett-Smith (Boston: Houghton Mifflin, 1921), p. 9.

8. *Shelley's Critical Prose,* pp. 6, 26.

9. *The Complete Works of Percy Bysshe Shelley,* ed. Roger Ingpen and Walter E. Peck, 10 vols. (New York: Charles Scribner's Sons, 1930), IX, 231;
Shelley's Critical Prose, pp. 10–11.

10. *Shelley's Critical Prose,* pp. 78, 8.

11. Ibid., p. 13.

12. Emerson, *The Complete Works of Ralph Waldo Emerson,* 12 vols.
(New York: Houghton, Mifflin, 1904), II, 363; *Shelley's Critical Prose,* p. 30.

13. *Letters of Keats,* I, 188; II, 139, 172, 97; *The Poetical Works and
Other Writings of John Keats,* ed. H. Buxton Forman, 4 vols. (London:
Reeves and Turner, 1889), III, 4.

14. Ibid., I, 155; II, 212, 167. Keats, who dedicated *Endymion* to Chatterton's memory and loved to recite his poems, outdid even other Romantics
in adulation of "Rowley."

15. *Letters of Keats,* II, 108; *The Poetical Works of John Keats,* ed. H. W.
Garrod, 2nd ed. (Oxford: Clarendon Press, 1958), p. 472. Keats's dissatisfaction with the sonnet recalls Johnson's time-biased judgment. "The fabrick of

a sonnet, however adapted to the Italian language, has never succeeded in ours, which, having greater variety of termination, requires the rhymes to be often changed." *Lives of the English Poets*, I, 169–70.

16. Winifred Nowottny, *The Language Poets Use* (New York: Oxford University Press, 1962), pp. 97, 85; *Letters of Keats*, II, 323; *Poems of Pope*, IV, 177.

17. *Letters of Keats*, I, 192. W. J. Bate has suggested that Keats's *intensity* is a near synonym for Hazlitt's *gusto*. *Criticism: The Major Texts* (New York: Harcourt Brace Jovanovich, 1970), p. 349. Though Hazlitt never supplied a satisfactory definition of *gusto* his description of it as "power or passion defining any object" does seem close to what Keats meant by intensity. His admiration for Hazlitt as critic is well known.

18. *Letters of Keats*, II, 80–81. Lionel Trilling thought this passage "an awesome utterance" only because like others in Keats's letters it shows his belief "that there is something more important than poetry." *Beyond Culture* (New York: Viking Press, 1965), p. 233. True enough. Yet Trilling curiously overlooks the arresting use of an eagle as a symbol for poetry. Eileen Ward's comment seems more faithful to Keats's main point. Though not so fine a thing as truth, the eagle, she argues, "had the beauty of intensity to the mind that could see it, and this was the wellspring of poetry." *John Keats: The Making of a Poet* (New York: Viking Press, 1967), p. 263.

19. *The Poetical Works and Other Writings of John Keats*, III, 5.

20. The experience suggested by Hazlitt's figure, of memorable lines of verse generating a double effect—a temporal extension of impact, like that of a visual image lingering on the retina after its source has disappeared—is, I think, not especially common. So it is interesting to notice I. A. Richards's adoption of the identical notion and figure, suggested by the couplet from *Venus and Adonis* admired by Coleridge:

Look! how bright a star shooteth from the sky!
So glides he in the night from Venus' eye.

"As Adonis to Venus," Richards remarked, "so these lines to the reader seem to linger in the eye like the after-images that make the trail of the meteor." *Coleridge on Imagination*, p. 83.

21. Cooper, *Letters Concerning Taste* (London, 1755), p. 46; *Hazlitt*, III, 320; *Jeffrey's Literary Criticism*, ed. D. Nichol Smith (London: Henry Froude, 1910), pp. 14–15; Hunt, *Imagination and Fancy* (New York, 1845), p. 133. The misquotations of Shakespeare's line, obviously owing to its being quoted from memory, attest to its fame. That Keats also admired it we may surmise from his having underlined it in a copy of the play. See Caroline F. E. Spurgeon, *Keats's Shakespeare*, 2nd ed. (London: Humphrey Milford, 1929), p. 27.

22. *Shelley: His Life and Work*, 2 vols. (New York: Houghton Mifflin, 1927), II, 424–25. Whether in fact this explication is not by Shelley but by a contemporary, is of little moment here. But Earl R. Wassermann has argued convincingly for Shelley's authorship. See his penetrating essay, "Shelley's Last Poetics: A Reconsideration," in *From Sensibility to Romanticism*, ed. F. W. Hilles and Harold Bloom (New York: Oxford University Press, 1965), pp. 487–511.

Chapter Nine

1. Lord Macaulay, *Critical and Historical Essays*, 3 vols. (New York, 1900), I, 87, 89; John Henry Cardinal Newman, *The Idea of a University*, ed. Charles Frederick Harrold (New York: Longmans, Green, 1947), p. 247.

2. Alba H. Warren, *English Poetic Theory, 1825–1865* (Princeton University Press, 1950), p. 6; Newman, *The Idea of a University*, p. 240; *Essays and Sketches*, I, (New York: Longmans, Green, 1948), p. 65; Mill, *Dissertations and Discussions, Political, Philosophical, and Historical*, 2 vols. (London, 1859), I 90; Pater, *Essays from "the Guardian"* (London: Macmillan, 1914), pp. 4–5.

3. *The Complete Prose Works of Matthew Arnold*, ed. R. H. Super, 11 vols. (Ann Arbor: University of Michigan Press, 1960–1977), IX, 39 (hereafter cited as *Prose Works*); Gautier, *Mademoiselle de Maupin* (Paris: Editions Frères, 1966), p. 20.

4. Whitman, *Complete Prose Works* (Boston, 1898), p. 264; *Letters of Keats*, II, 384.

5. Pater, *The Renaissance* (London: Macmillan, 1910), pp. 271–72, ix; Stephen, *Hours in a Library*, 3 vols. (New York: G. P. Putnam's Sons, 1894); Cassirer, *Philosophy of the Enlightenment*, p. 349.

6. Schlegel, *Gespräch über die Poesie*, p. 285; Carlyle, *Critical and Miscellaneous Essays*, 5 vols. (London, 1899), II, 204, 213; Arnold, *Prose Works*, VI, 403, 362.

7. Carlyle, *Critical and Miscellaneous Essays*, II, 302, 360; Fred Kaplan, *Thomas Carlyle: A Biography* (Ithaca: Cornell University Press, 1983), p. 245; Pater, *Appreciations* (London, Macmillan, 1920), pp. 6, 11.

8. Warren, *English Poetic Theory*, p. 110; Hunt, *Imagination and Fancy*, p. x

9. Ibid., pp. 25–26, 42. Clarence de Witt Thorpe, exceptional in his high estimate of Hunt as critic, thinks he made the best case for what all teachers of poetry "should have deeply impressed on their minds . . . that verse is not an ornamental garment with which the substance of poetry is clothed, but . . . integral to the subject." "Leigh Hunt as Man of Letters," in *Leigh Hunt's Literary Criticism*, ed. Lawrence Huston Houtchens and Carolyn Washburn Houtchens (New York: Columbia University Press, 1966), p. 51.

10. *Biographia*, II, 11.

11. *Imagination and Fancy*, p. 41

12. Edmund Bluden, *Leigh Hunt's 'Examiner' Examined*, p. 205.

13. *Foliage: or Poems Original and Translated* (London, 1818), pp. 32–33; *Imagination and Fancy*, p. 100; *Leigh Hunt's 'Examiner' Examined*, p. 207.

14. *Imagination and Fancy*, p. 246.

15. Ibid., pp. 33–34, 222.

16. *The Collected Writings of Thomas De Quincey*, ed. David Masson, 14 vols. (Edinburgh, 1889–1890), XI, 456, 471; hereafter cited as *De Quincey*.

17. *The Complete Works of Edgar Allan Poe*, ed. James A. Harrison, 17 vols. (New York: AMS Press, 1965), XIV, 225–26.

18. Ibid., XIV, 78–79.

19. "Longinus and the New Criticism," in *Essays of Four Decades*, p. 482.

20. *New Essays by De Quincey*, ed. Stuart M. Tave (Princeton: Princeton University Press, 1966), p. 139; *De Quincey as Critic*, ed. John E. Jordan (London and Boston: Routledge & Kegan Paul, 1973), p. 427; *De Quincey*, X, 131; XI, 299.

21. *De Quincey*, XI, 324.

22. Ibid.

23. Mill's letter to Sterling is quoted in Wellek, *History*, III, 134. Mill, *Dissertations and Discussions Political, Philosophical, and Historical.*, I, 72, 90.

24. *Dissertations and Discussions*, I, 90–91.

25. Ibid., I, 64, 63.

26. Ibid., I, 71; *Keble's Lectures on Poetry 1832–1841*, trans. Edward Kershaw Francis, 2 vols. (London, 1912), I, 30; II, 217–18.

27. *Dissertations and Discussions*, I, 76, 77, 73.

28. Ibid., I, 67; *Autobiography of John Stuart Mill* (New York: Columbia University Press, 1924), p. 123.

29. *Early Essays by John Stuart Mill*, ed. J. W. M. Gibbs (London, 1897), p. 267; *Autobiography*, pp. 7, 10; *Dissertations and Discussions*, I, 325–26.

30. *Dissertations and Discussions*, I, 326–27, 328.

31. *Kritische Schriften und Briefe*, I, 143, 144–45. Despite Schlegel's (and Coleridge's) assurance that meter was no mere inherited discovery ("keine überlieferte Erfindung"), English Romantic critics shared Hazlitt's inconsistency on the point. In one lecture of his 1818 series Hazlitt told his hearers that meter was only a mechanical device, in another that it was poetry's "most obvious distinction," and in a third that the best English pastoral was "that prose-poem, Walton's *Complete Angler.*" *Hazlitt*, V, 13, 33, 69, 98. A common view is that meter is a dispensable convention. See Karl D. Uitti, quoted in *Versification: Major Language Types*, ed. W. K. Wimsatt (New York: New York University Press, 1972), p. 19. But see also the recent case for meter made in Timothy Steele's *Missing Meters: Modern Poetry and the Revolt against Meter* (Fayetteville: University of Arkansas Press, 1990).

32. Mill, *Dissertations and Discussions*, I, 79; *De Quincey*, X, 131 n., 169–73, 101, 102.

33. *De Quincey*, X, 47–49.

34. *De Quincey*, XI, 54–57, 89, 220, 88.

35. Ibid., XI, 320.

36. Ibid., XI, 88–89; X, 293, 230, 262; XI, 203.

37. *Literary Criticism of George Henry Lewes*, ed. Alice R. Kaminsky (Lincoln: University of Nebraska Press, 1964), pp. 52, 63. Regrettably, in a later prolix treatise with the self-assured title of *The Principles of Success in Literature*, Lewes abandoned his distinctive grasp of meter to conflate all good writing within the all-inclusive criterion of *sincerity*. (Hants, England: Gregg International Publishers, 1969), pp. 17–18, 60, 82–83.

38. *Literary Criticism of . . . Lewes*, p. 54.

39. Arnold, *Prose Works*, III, 173. Lowell, *Lectures on the English Poets* (Cleveland: The Rowfant Club, 1897), p. 175. Wondering at "the downward trend in the overtones of common surnames," C. S. Lewis noted that whereas a sixteenth-century tragic poet named Higgins inserted that name

into a serious line of verse, today we balk at Wordsworth's starting a sonnet with the name of Jones. *English Literature in the Sixteenth Century Excluding Drama* (Oxford: at the Clarendon Press, 1944), p. 245.

40. *The Complete Works of Ralph Waldo Emerson*, III, 9; IV, 195; Carlyle, *On Heroes, Hero Worship, and the Heroic in History* (New York: Ginn and Company, 1901) pp. 95–96.

41. *On Heroes, Hero Worship*, p. 103; *Critical and Miscellaneous Essays*, 3 vols. (London, 1887–1888), II, 237.

42. *On Heroes, Hero Worship*, pp. 35, 251, 124; *Critical and Miscellaneous Essays*, II, 3.

43. *Critical and Miscellaneous Essays*, II, 369, 4.

44. Ibid., I, 513, 563; Emerson, *Complete Works*, II, 363.

45. Here Emerson's transcendental idealism and Renaissance Christian Neoplatonism imperfectly correspond. For a lucid exposition of the version prevalent in sixteenth-century Italy, see Robert L. Montgomery, *The Reader's Eye: Studies in Didactic Theory from Dante to Tasso* (Berkeley: University of California Press, 1979), pp. 94–107.

46. *Complete Works*, II, 363; VII, 43. The idealist philosopher Victor Cousin, one of Emerson's mentors, is a faithful witness to the limitations of aesthetic representation of beauty in the idealist conception: "in a world of forms, beauty can exhibit itself only in a manner, which, while it reveals, veils and obscures it." *Introduction to the History of Philosophy*, trans. Henning Gottfried Linberg (Boston, 1832), p. 13. This volume comprises the highly popular Sorbonne lectures of 1828. Emerson was acquainted with both the original French edition of 1829 and Linberg's translation.

47. Read, *The Nature of Literature* (New York: Grove Press, n.d.), p. 348; Emerson, *Complete Works*, III, 9–10, 8.

48. *Complete Works of Poe*, XIV, 274–75.

49. Ibid., XII, 15, 24; XI, 76. Wellek calls attention to Poe's statement that poetry "is not forbidden to depict—but to reason and preach, of virtue." *History*, III, 155.

50. Poe, *Complete Works*, XVI, [183], 202; Auden, "Introduction" to Poe's *Selected Prose and Poetry* (New York: Rinehart, 1950), pp. x–xi.

Chapter Ten

1. Arnold, *Prose Works*, IX, 224; III, 234; John Shepard Eels, Jr., *The Touchstones of Matthew Arnold* (New York: Bookman Associates, 1955), pp. 25–26.

2. *Prose Works*, I, 211, 168.

3. Ibid., XI, 331; VIII, 314, 315, 316; III, 362, 363.

4. Ibid., III, 35, 14.

5. Arnold, *Prose Works*, III, 251; I, 180; Barfield, *Poetic Diction* (Middletown, Conn.: Wesleyan University Press, 1973), pp. 152–67.

6. *Prose Works*, IX, 39.

7. Ibid., I, 136–37, 175. Arnold had earlier used the term *grand style* (thus italicized) in the preface to his *Poems* (1853), where he exalts the Greeks as its "unapproachable masters." *Prose Works*, I, 5.

8. Ibid., I, 116–17, 156, 186–87.

9. Ibid., I, 188–90. *On Translating Homer,* ed. W. H. D. Rouse (New York: AMS Press, 1971), p. 197.

10. *Prose Works,* I, 139, 145–46, 155, 129–30, 213.

11. Eliot, *The Use of Poetry,* p. 146; Wellek, *History,* pp. 171, 172.

12. Arnold, *Prose Works,* IX, 163–69; Symons, *Studies in Prose and Verse* (New York: E. P. Dutton, 1922. Reprint. New York: AMS Press), p. 195.

13. Eels, *Touchstones of Arnold,* pp. 171, 205; Arnold, *Prose Works,* IX, 162; Eliot, *The Use of Poetry,* p. 118.

14. Arnold, *Poetical Works,* ed. C. B. Tinker and H. F. Lowry (London: Oxford University Press, 1950), p. 195.

15. *The Letters of Matthew Arnold to Arthur Hugh Clough,* ed. Howard Foster Lowry (New York: Oxford University Press, 1932), p. 195; *Prose Works,* IX, 52.

16. *Prose Works,* I, 8–12, 112, 204; IX, 178, 39–40.

17. Ibid., IX, 185; I, 120, 166.

18. Ibid., I, 204, 205.

19. Arnold, *Letters to Arthur Hugh Clough,* pp. 65, 124; Trilling, ed., *The Portable Matthew Arnold* (New York: Viking Press, 1949), p. 39.

20. *Prose Works,* I, 7, 4–11.

21. Ibid., I, 7. Arnold had a very clear idea, quite possibly suggested by Coleridge, of the special quality of symbolic communication. Contrasting the styles of Maurice de Guérin and his sister Eugénie, he wrote that "her words . . . are in general but intellectual signs; they are not like her brother's—symbols equivalent with the thing symbolized. They bring the notion of the thing described to the mind, they do not bring the feeling of it to the imagination." Ibid., III, 86.

22. Ibid., IX, 171, 172.

23. Ibid., III, 33.

24. Ibid., IX, 214, 215, 45.

25. Ibid., III, 34n.

26. Ibid., III, 33.

27. Ibid., IX, 227; III, 378–80. We need not pause over Arnold's persuasion that English poets owe their stylistic natural magic to the Celtic ancestral strain. The overkill of Saintsbury's verdict suffices: "With the bricks of ignorance and the mortar of assumption you can build no critical house." *History of Criticism,* III, 527.

28. *Prose Works,* I, 174; III, 377–79.

29. Ibid., VI, 187–90.

30. Richards, *Science and Poetry* (New York: Haskell House, 1974), p. 24; *Essays, Letters, and Reviews by Matthew Arnold* (Cambridge: Harvard University Press, 1960), p. 238.

31. *Prose Works,* IX, 228, 49.

Chapter Eleven

1. More, *The Drift of Romanticism: Shelburne Essays,* Eighth Series (New York: Houghton Mifflin, 1913), p. 99; Buckler, *Walter Pater: The Critic as*

Artist of Ideas (New York: New York University Press, 1987), p. 5. Yeats, *The Oxford Book of Modern Verse: 1892–1935* (New York: Oxford University Press, 1936), p. ix; Pater, *Appreciations*, p. 261.

2. *The Artist as Critic: The Critical Writings of Oscar Wilde*, ed. Richard Ellmann (New York: Random House, 1968), p. 229; Yeats, *Oxford Book of Modern Verse*, p. viii.

3. Symons, Introduction to Pater's *The Renaissance* (New York: Random House, n.d.), p. xv; Pater, *Essays from 'The Guardian'* (London: Macmillan, 1914), p. 5; *Appreciations*, p. 58.

4. *Appreciations*, pp. 24–25, 57–58.

5. *Appreciations*, pp. 88, 74, 80–81; Buckler, *The Victorian Imagination: Essays in Aesthetic Exploration* (New York: New York University Press, 1980), p. 1.

6. *Appreciations*, pp. 51, 58 (italics added), 7.

7. *The Renaissance*, p. 230; *Appreciations*, p. 8.

8. *Appreciations*, pp. 9–11.

9. Ibid., pp. 34, 15, 35, 27, 29.

10. Dante, *Paradiso*, Canto 33, lines 121–22; Flaubert, *Oeuvres*, 2 vols. (Paris: Gallimard, 1951), I, 500.

11. Warren, "Pondering Pater: Aesthete and Master," in *Literary Theory and Criticism*, ed. P. Strelka, 2 vols. (New York: Peter Lang, 1984), II, 1368; Pater, *The Renaissance*, p. 67.

12. *Appreciations*, pp. 35–37. Pater readily conceded the difficulty of the problem. "Personality *versus* impersonality in art:—how much or how little of one's self may one put into one's work . . . whether one *can* put there anything else: —is clearly a far-reaching and complex question." *Miscellaneous Studies* (London: Macmillan, 1924), pp. 35–36.

13. *Appreciations*, pp. 208, 206, 207, 57–58; *Plato and Platonism* (New York: Macmillan, 1895), p. 120.

14. *The Renaissance*, pp. 135, 138. In *Marius the Epicurean* we encounter a certain reconcilement or combination of the two causes of stylistic excellence. After quoting Horace's "Verbaque provisam rem. . .," Pater has Marius reflect that the "happy phrase or sentence was really modeled upon a clearly finished structure of scrupulous thought." (New York: E. P. Dutton, 1934), p. 89.

15. DeLaura, *Hebrew and Hellene in Victorian England: Newman, Arnold and Pater* (Austin: University of Texas Press, 1969), p. 333; Newman, *Essays and Sketches*, p. 65.

16. Baudelaire, *Oeuvres complètes* (Paris; Gallimard, 1964), p. 229.

17. *The Renaissance*, p. 236; *Miscellaneous Studies*, 1924), pp. 68, 75.

18. *Plato and Platonism*, pp. 249, 60.

19. Ibid., pp. 258, 246; Plato, *The Republic*, ed. Paul Shorey (Cambridge: Harvard University Press, 1942), p. 252.

20. *Marius the Epicurean*, pp. 103, 54, 55.

21. Ibid., pp. 57–58.

22. Bloom, ed., *The Literary Criticism of John Ruskin* (Garden City, N.Y.: Doubleday and Company, 1965), p. xxiii. Cf. George P. Landow's finding Wordsworth to be "probably the most important source" of Ruskin's critical theory, and that even his understanding of Coleridge's distinction of

imagination from fancy "was derived not from Coleridge but from Words-worth's Prefaces and Leigh Hunt's *Imagination and Fancy*." *The Aesthetic and Critical Theories of John Ruskin* (Princeton: Princeton University Press, 1971), pp. 53, 382; Ruskin, *The Literary Criticism*, p. 11.

23. *The Works of John Ruskin*, ed. E. T. Cook and Alexander Wedder-burn, 39 vols. (New York: Longmans, Green, 1903–1912), XX, 76, 77; V, 216, 127, 208.

24. Ibid., XII, 352; XXVII, 628; V, 333, 28–29. Late in life, it should be conceded, Ruskin came to envisage the moral dimensions of great literature in broader and more compelling terms. A spiritual, even divine, gift, an "instinct of moral law," informs artistic creation. "And therefore every great composition in the world, every great piece of painting or literature . . . is an assertion of moral law, as strict, when we examine it, as the *Eumenides* or the *Divina Commedia*." Ibid., XXIX, 265–66. On Ruskin's "theocratic aesthetic," see Landow, *Aesthetic Theories of John Ruskin*.

25. *Works of John Ruskin*, V, 205–8.

26. Ibid., XXXI, 369–70.

27. *The Complete Works of Algernon Charles Swinburne*, ed. Edmund Gosse and Thomas James Wise, 20 vols. (New York: Gabriel Wells, 1925–1927), XV, 146, 154; XIV, 95.

28. Ibid., XV, 98, 346; XIV, 157, 158.

29. Ibid., XV, 89.

30. Ibid., XV, 98–99

31. Ibid., XV, 145, 150; XI, 310; XV, 127.

32. Ibid., XIII, 389.

33. Swinburne, *Complete Works*, XV, 336, 145; XIV, 150; XVI, 345; XV, 96–97. Swinburne's later repudiation of the American poet entitled "Whit-mania" (1887), in *Studies in Prose and Poetry*, has been ascribed to "the dictation" of Theodore Watts-Dunton. See Harold Nicolson, *Swinburne* (Hamden, Conn.: Archon Books, 1969), p. 193. Whatever the influence of the man in whose home he found a refuge from his own disorderly living habits, Watts-Dunton's long essay on poetry, expanded from a shorter entry in the 9th edition of *Encyclopedia Britannica* (1884), does contain several opinions identical with those expressed by Swinburne: the all-importance of meter and rhyme, the perfection of "Kubla Khan," and the musical conception of poetry. And Whitman is the obvious target of Watts-Dunton's reference to "the quaint American heresy which seems to affirm that the great masters of verbal music, from Homer to Tennyson and Swinburne, have been blowing through penny trumpets." His strange disparagement of all Keats's sonnets except "Chapman's Homer" was also echoed by Swinburne. Theodore Watts-Dunton, *The Renascence of Wonder* (London: Herbert Jenkins, 1916), pp. 45, 68, 181.

34. *The Writings of James Russell Lowell*, 10 vols. (New York: Houghton Mifflin, 1890), VI, 74; IV, 382–86: II, 136.

35. *Lectures on English Poets*, pp. 174, 175.

36. *Blank Verse* (London, 1875), pp. 14, 17, 19, 24, 25, 27.

37. *Familiar Studies of Men and Books* (New York: Current Literature, 1912), pp. 86, 84, 104.

38. *Essays and Criticisms* (Boston: Herbert B. Turner, 1903), pp. 180, 211, 184, 185, 190, 192.

39. Ibid., pp. 197–99.

40. *The Artist as Critic: Critical Writings of Oscar Wilde,* ed. Richard Ellmann (New York: Random House, 1968), p. 230.

41. Wellek, *History,* IV, 415; Ellmann, *The Artist as Critic,* p. 93; Wilde, *Intentions,* p. 115.

42. Wilde, *De Profundis,* ed. Vyvyan Holland (New York: Philosophical Library, 1950), pp. 88, 89; *The Artist as Critic,* p. 148; Eliot, *Selected Essays,* pp. 7, 284.

43. *Intentions,* pp. 139, 221–63, 68–69, 175.

44. Ibid., pp. 119, 127, 188, 102–3, 104.

45. Ibid., p. 141; *The Letters of Oscar Wilde,* ed. Rupert Hart-Davis (New York: Harcourt, Brace and World, 1962), p. 425.

46. *Letters of Wilde,* p. 297; *Intentions,* pp. 54, 3–4.

47. See Aristotle, *Physics,* II, 8, 119 a 15. *Intentions,* pp. 168, 117, 10.

48. *Intentions,* pp. 53, 200, 32. See Hazlitt's "On Imitation" in *The Round Table.*

49. *Intentions,* pp. 112, 21–25, 50.

50. Ibid., 22–24.

51. *The Journals and Papers of Gerard Manley Hopkins,* ed. Humphry House (London: Oxford University Press, 1959), pp. 84–85; *The Letters of Gerard Manley Hopkins to Robert Bridges,* ed. Claude Colleer Abbott (London: Oxford University Press, 1935), pp. 46, 89, 211, 218; *Poems of Gerard Manley Hopkins,* 3rd edition, ed. W. H. Gardner (New York: Oxford University Press, 1948), p. 9.

52. *Further Letters of Gerard Manley Hopkins,* ed. Claude Colleer Abbott (New York: Oxford University Press, 1938), pp. 69–73.

53. *Journals and Papers,* p. 84

54. Ibid., pp. 84–85.

55. Ibid., p. 289. In "Closing Statement: Linguistics and Poetics" Jakobson hailed Hopkins as "an outstanding searcher in the science of poetic language," who "defined verse as 'speech wholly or partially repeating the same figure of sound.'" *Style in Language,* ed. Thomas A. Sebeok (Cambridge: MIT Press, 1960), p. 358. In his recent compendious survey of Western poetic theory, Lubomír Doležel names Hopkins and Mallarmé as Jakobson's forerunners in stressing equivalence in poetic structure. *Occidental Poetics: Tradition and Progress* (Lincoln: University of Nebraska Press, 1990), p. 207, n.10.

56. *Journals and Papers,* p. 85.

57. Ibid., p. 109

Chapter Twelve

1. *Further Speculations,* ed. Sam Hynes (Lincoln: University of Nebraska Press, 1962), p. 84.

2. *Poems of Pope*, VII: *The Iliad of Homer*, 88; Bradley, *Oxford Lectures on Poetry* (London: Macmillan, 1920), pp. 20–21.

3. *On Poetry and Poets*, p. 117.

4. Eliot, *For Launcelot Andrewes* (Garden City, N.Y.: 1929), p. vii.

5. Doleźel, *Occidental Poetics*, p. 778; Saintsbury, *Specimens of English Prose Style*, p. xxxix; *A History of English Prose Rhythm* (Bloomington: Indiana University Press, 1965), p. 344; Symons, *Studies in Prose and Verse*, pp. 51, 238; *Figures of Several Centuries* (London: Constable, 1917), p. 190; Fred Newton Scott, "The Most Fundamental Differentia of Poetry and Prose," *PMLA*, XIX (1904), 269; Santayana, *Interpretations of Poetry and Religion* (New York: Charles Scribner's Sons, 1911), pp. 255, 256; Liddell, *An Introduction to the Scientific Study of Poetry* (New York: Doubleday, Page, 1902), pp. vii, 51, 71.

6. *Studies in Prose and Verse*, pp. 234, 237, 274.

7. Ibid., pp. 93, 80; *Figures of Several Centuries*, pp. 190, 105, 104.

8. *Selected Letters of Robert Frost*, ed. Lawrence Thompson (New York: Holt, Rinehart and Winston, 1964), p. 141.

9. Ibid., p. 141; Eliot is cited in Helen Gardner, *The Composition of Four Quartets* (Boston: Faber and Faber, 1978), p. 191.

10. *Poetry and Contemporary Speech*, The English Association Pamphlet No. 127 (February–May, 1914), pp. 4–5.

11. *Poetry and Contemporary Speech*, pp. 5–7; *The Theory of Poetry* (London: Martin Secker, 1924), p. 126.

12. *Poetic Diction*, pp. 42, 52, 55, 67, 86–87. The nexus between mythology and poetry was of course no personal discovery of Barfield's. Eliot took approving note of French theorists who had applied the theories of the archaeologist Lévy-Bruhl to argue that "the pre-logical mentality persists in civilized man, but becomes available only to or through the poet." *The Use of Poetry*, p. 148.

13. *Poetic Diction*, pp. 92–93, 97–98.

14. Ibid., pp. 102–7, 115, 131.

15. Ibid., pp. 138–44.

16. *Poetic Diction*, p. 145; *New Statesman* (October 8, 1962), pp. 793–94; Housman, *The Name and Nature of Poetry* (New York: Macmillan, 1933), p. 37.

17. *Poetic Diction*, pp. 41, 150, 157.

18. Ibid., pp. 152–56.

19. Ibid., p. 158.

20. *Poetic Diction*, p. 162; *Biographia*, II, 64.

21. *Language and Myth*, trans. Susanne K. Langer (New York: Dover Publications, 1946), pp. 98–99. Professor Langer noted the "striking" parallels between Cassirer and Barfield in *Feeling and Form* (New York: Charles Scribner's Sons, 1953), p. 238.

22. Rylands, *Words and Poetry* (London: Hogarth Press, 1928), pp. 14, 23, 50–89, 154, 182; *Works of Johnson*, VII, 64.

23. Stéphane Mallarmé, *Divagations* (Paris: Bibliothèque-Charpentier, 1922), p. 243; Symons, *The Symbolist Movement in Literature* (New York: E. P. Dutton, 1919), p. 8. For a succinct overview of the sources and nature

of vers libre, see the entry in *Princeton Encyclopedia of Poetry and Poetics,* Enlarged Edition (Princeton: Princeton University Press, 1974), pp. 884–85.

24. Symons, *Studies in Prose and Verse,* pp. 68, 50–51; Frost, *Selected Letters,* p. 182; Bridges, "Humdrum and Harum- Scarum: A Lecture on Free Verse," *North American Review* (November, 1922), pp. 52–54; Murry, *The Problem of Style* (London: Oxford University Press, 1922), pp. 55–56.

25. Lowell, "The Rhythms of Free Verse," *Dial* (January 17, 1918), p. 52; Santayana, *Interpretations of Poetry and Religion,* p. 252.

26. *The Symbolist Movement,* p. 69; *The Romantic Movement in English Poetry* (London: Constable, 1909), p. 86

27. *Oxford Lectures on Poetry,* pp. 4, 20–21.

28. *Interpretations of Poetry and Religion,* pp. 4, 20–21.

29. *Selected Letters,* pp. 80–81, 128.

30. *Anthology of Pure Poetry,* ed. George Moore (Boni and Liveright, 1924), pp. 50, 34, 18; Santayana, *The Sense of Beauty* (New York: Dover Publications, 1955), p. 167.

31. *Pure Poetry,* pp. 18, 43, 45; Nathan A. Scott, Jr., in *Literature and Belief: English Institute Essays 1957,* ed. M. H. Abrams (New York: Columbia University Press, 1958), p. 112.

32. *History of Criticism,* III, 231; *A History of English Prosody,* 3 vols. (New York: Macmillan, 1906–1908), I, 365–367.

33. Bridges, "The Necessity of Poetry" (1918), in *Collected Essays and Papers* (New York: Olms Verlag, 1972), pp. 224–25n; Kermode, *Romantic Image* (New York: Macmillan, 1957), pp. 3, 6; Scott, *op. cit., PMLA,* XIX, 250; Benét, *The Magic of Poetry and the Poet's Art* (Chicago: F. E. Compton, 1936), p. 9.

Chapter Thirteen

1. Simon, *The Georgian Poetic* (Berkeley: University of California Press, 1975), pp. 37–41, 44; Ellmann, *The Identity of Yeats,* 2nd ed. (New York: Oxford University Press, 1964), p. 130.

2. *Letters on Poetry from W. B. Yeats to Dorothy Wellesley* (New York: Oxford University Press, 1940), p. 7; Eliot, "Reflections on Contemporary Poetry," *Egoist,* IV (September, 1917), 118.

3. Eliot, *The Use of Poetry,* p. 152; Coleridge, *Letters,* III, 469–70.

4. *Uncollected Prose by W. B. Yeats,* ed. John P. Frayne and Colton Johnson, 2 vols. (New York: Columbia University Press, 1976), II, 509; *The Letters of Ezra Pound 1907–1941,* ed. D. D. Paige (New York: Harcourt, Brace, 1950), p. 49; *Literary Essays of Ezra Pound,* ed. T. S. Eliot (Norfolk, Conn.: New Directions, 1954), p. 287.

5. W. B. Yeats, *Essays and Introductions* (London: Macmillan, 1961), pp. 19, 21, 22.

6. Eliot, *On Poetry and Poets,* p. 175; Yeats, *Essays and Introductions,* p. 208.

7. *Letters of Ezra Pound,* pp. 48–49. Pound stuck steadily to the principle which guided his own creative efforts: Much more than an attribute of a

poem, technique, as he put it in 1912, is "the only gauge and test of a man's lasting sincerity." "On Technique," *New Age* (January 25, 1912), p. 298. Fifty years later the point resurfaces in an interview with Donald Hall. *Paris Review*, VII (Summer–Fall, 1962), 25. Eliot, "What Dante Means to Me," in *To Criticize the Critic* (New York: Farrar, Straus & Giroux, 1965), p. 126. The formative impact of the *Divine Comedy* on the two chief architects of poetic modernism can hardly be exaggerated. Contemplating the closing lines of the *Paradiso*, the youthful Pound was moved to the kind of orotund rhetoric the mature Pound found fulsome. "Surely for the great poem that ends herewith our befitting praise were silence." *The Spirit of Romance* (New York: New Directions, 1953) [1910], p. 153. Important to both men, Dante's share in their creative nurture was the greater in Eliot's case. By 1929 he was persuaded that no poet of any language or period could equal Dante as a model for poets, one "safer to follow, even for us, than any English poet, including Shakespeare." *Selected Essays*, p. 229.

8. *Letters of Pound*, pp. 48–49; Eliot, *The Use of Poetry*, p. 149; *Selected Essays*, p. 18.

9. *The Letters of W. B. Yeats*, ed. Allan Wade (London: Rupert Hart-Davis, 1954), p. 462.

10. *The Letters of Ezra Pound*, pp. 216–18.

11. Yeats, *Essays and Introductions*, pp. 116, 155–56, 382; *Uncollected Prose*, p. 131; *Letters*, p. 592; Ellmann, *The Identity of Yeats*, p. 132.

12. *Instigations* (New York: Boni and Liveright, 1920), p. 35.

13. T. E. Hulme, *Further Speculations*, pp. 83, 84.

14. Eliot, *Selected Essays*, pp. 53–54; Coleridge, *Lay Sermons*, p. 30.

15. *Discriminations* (New Haven: Yale University Press, 1970), p. 114.

16. *Divagations*, pp. 242, 246, 251.

17. Stead, "Eliot, Arnold, and the English Poetic Tradition," in *The Literary Criticism of T. S. Eliot*, ed. David Newton-de Molina (London: Athlone Press, 1977), p. 200. In the chapter on Eliot in *The New Criticism*, John Crowe Ransom opposed the "Hyde" of Eliot's poetry to the "Jekyll" of his criticism ((Norfolk, Conn.: New Directions, 1941).

18. Yeats, *Essays and Introductions*, pp. 495, 511; See A. Norman Jeffares, *W. B. Yeats: A New Biography* (New York: Farrar, Straus, Giroux, 1988), p. 81.

19. *Letters of Pound*, pp. 87, 55, 275; Eliot, *On Poetry and Poets*, p. 138; *Selected Essays*, pp. 15, 98, 106.

20. Pound, *The Spirit of Romance* (New York: New Directions, 1953) [1901], p. 222; Yeats, *Letters to Dorothy Wellesley*, pp. 94, 120.

21. T. E. Hulme, *Speculations*, ed. Herbert Read (London: Routledge and Kegan Paul, 1924), pp. 132, 138.

22. Ibid., pp. 132, 137.

23. *Further Speculations*, p. 70; *Speculations*, pp. 134–35.

24. Wellek, *History*, V, 154–55; Eliot, "Isolated Superiority," *Dial* LXXXIV (1928), 67.

25. *The A B C of Reading* (New York: New Directions, 1960), p. 77; *Literary Essays*, p. 280; *The Spirit of Romance*, p. 162; *Egoist*, IV (1917), 73.

26. N. Christopher de Nagy, *Ezra Pound's Poetics and Literary Tradition: The Critical Decade* (Bern: A. Francke Verlag, 1966), p. 62; Wellek, *History*, V, 154; Leavis, *New Bearings in English Poetry* (Ann Arbor: University of Michigan Press, 1960), p. 142.

27. *New Age*, X (1911), 131; *Poetry: A Magazine of Verse*, IX (1917), 312; *Letters of Pound*, p. 274.

28. *Letters of Pound*, pp. 198–99, 217, 322.

29. *Literary Essays*, p. 409; "On Technique," *New Age* IX (1912), 298. George P. Elliott found that reading Pound's verse gave him the impression that "meaning doesn't matter much in poetry, lovely sound is enough." "Poet of Many Voices," in *Ezra Pound: A Collection of Critical Essays*, ed. Walter Sutton (Englewood Cliffs, N.J.: Prentice-Hall, 1956), p. 154. For an able counterargument see Hugh Kenner, *The Poetry of Ezra Pound* (Norfolk, Conn.: New Directions, 1951).

30. *Literary Essays*, pp. 43–46; *The New Age*, X (1911), 179.

31. *The Spirit of Romance*, p. 222; *Literary Essays*, pp. 362, 52, 222, 6.

32. *Literary Essays*, pp. 4–5; Sisson, *English Poetry 1900–1950: An Assessment* (New York: Methuen, 1981), [1971], p. 55.

33. *Literary Essays*, pp. 292–93, 71; Cf. Eliot: "Swinburne's words are all suggestions and no denotation." *Selected Essays*, p. 273.

34. *Literary Essays*, pp. 380, 51–52.

35. *Letters of Pound*, pp. 48–49; *Literary Essays*, p. 25.

36. *Literary Essays*, pp. 25, 51, 437.

37. *The Spirit of Romance*, p. 160; *Letters of Pound*, pp. 181, 274–275; *Literary Essays*, p. 150; *Personae: The Collected Shorter Poems of Ezra Pound* (New York: New Directions, 1971), p. 181. Homer was Pound's favorite Greek author. His own "Russonymic," he told Iris Barry, would be "Homerovitch" (his father having been christened Homer). In Greek he found a fund of "wonderful but impractical rhythms." *Letters of Pound*, pp. 87, 92.

38. *Forum*, XLVII (1912), 498–99; *Literary Essays*, p. 51; "Arthur Symons," *Athenaeum*, (May 21, 1920), p. 664.

39. *Letters of Ezra Pound*, p. 110; *Literary Essays*, p. 241; Schaefer, "Ezra Pound and Music," in *Ezra Pound: A Collection of Critical Essays*, p. 135. Citing Pound's injunction to compose in musical, not metronomic, sequence, Charles O. Hartman concludes that "in the context of the time, Pound was coming down for *vers libre.*" *Free Verse: An Essay on Prosody* (Princeton: Princeton University Press, 1980), p. 5. It is more accurate, on the evidence, to say that Pound's reservations about the *theoretical claims* for free verse, despite his own use of it, were protests against its inflated current vogue.

40. *Instigations*, p. 105; *Forum*, XLVII (1912), pp. 498–99; *Literary Essays*, pp. 9, 11; *Guide to Kultur* (Norfolk, Conn.: New Directions, 1952 [1938]), pp. 121, 179.

41. *The Spirit of Romance*, p. 116; *Literary Essays*, pp. 49, 53.

42. "On Technique," p. 298; *Literary Essays*, pp. 324, 24, 49, 26; *Guide to Kultur*, p. 121; *Forum*, XLVII (1912), 499.

43. *Letters of Pound*, pp. 48, 262.

44. *Gaudier-Brzeska: A Memoir* (New York: New Directions, 1974), pp. 86, 92, 90, 88.

45. *The Poetry of Ezra Pound*, pp. 194, 236.

46. "On Technique," p. 298.

47. Reed Way Dasenbrook, *The Literary Vorticism of Ezra Pound and Wyndham Lewis* (Baltimore: Johns Hopkins University Press, 1985), p. 92.

Chapter Fourteen

1. "A Commentary: that Poetry is Made with Words," *New English Weekly*, XV, 2 (April 17, 1939), 27; *The Complete Poems and Plays* (New York: Harcourt, Brace, 1952), p. 111; *Selected Essays*, p. 447.

2. *The Use of Poetry*, pp. 143, 83; *Criterion*, XIII (October, 1933), p. 153.

3. *The Use of Poetry*, pp. 29, 57, 16–17, 101; *On Poetry and Poets*, p. 117. Of those unduly influenced by Eliot's disclaimers, J. C. Ransom is an egregious example. He wrote that Eliot's expert and infallible critical sense "consists with a theoretical innocence. Behind it is no great philosophical habit, nor philosophical will, to push through it to definition." *The New Criticism*, p. 145. Since Ransom was writing in 1941, we should concede that his further observation that Eliot rarely theorized about poetry "in set passages" was less wide of the mark than if it had been made after the later, more overtly theoretical pieces in *On Poetry and Poets*.

4. *The Use of Poetry*, p. 19.

5. *On Poetry and Poets*, pp. 127, 115; *To Criticize the Critic*, p. 138; *Selected Essays*, p. 21; *John Dryden: The Poet, the Dramatist, the Critic* (New York: Terence and Elsa Holliday, 1932), p. 23; *The Sacred Wood* (New York: Alfred A. Knopf, 1921), p. 1; "Experiment in Criticism," *Literary Opinion in America*, ed. M. D. Zabel (New York: Harper and Brothers, 1951), p. 609; *The Use of Poetry*, p. 79; Schérer, *Etudes critiques de littérature* (Paris, 1876), p. 127.

6. Noting that Eliot used a critical idiom "always on the edge of aesthetics," Ronald Peacock sees its origins in the aesthetics of his day. "Croce, Richards, and Collingwood are all in the wings." "Eliot's Criticism of the Drama," in *The Literary Criticism of T. S. Eliot*, p. 99. If they were in the wings, Coleridge was on stage! Still, Peacock's treatment of Eliot's ideas of poetic drama is the most penetrating I know.

7. *Egoist*, V, 10 (December, 1918), p. 132; *The Use of Poetry*, pp. 74–75.

8. *Selected Essays*, pp. 10, 96, 117, 179–80, 192, 284; *On Poetry and Poets*, pp. 8, 112; "Prose and Verse," *Chapbook* (April, 1921), p. 7.

9. *Criterion*, I, 3 (April, 1923), 306; *Selected Essays*, p. 93.

10. *Selected Essays*, pp. 93, 377; *Egoist*, IV, 10 (November, 1917), 151. Peacock points out that Eliot's essays on dramatic poetry "focus on what became for him a central issue, that of realism versus convention, and the relationship of these two in all poetry, which is both a concern of Eliot and beyond that a perennially interesting problem of aesthetics." *The Literary Criticism of T. S. Eliot*, p. 90.

11. *Egoist,* V, 9 (October, 1918), 114; *New Statesman* (May 19, 1917), pp. 158–59; *The Sacred Wood,* p. 57.

12. *To Criticize the Critic,* pp. 128–29; Coleridge, *Letters,* IV, 779; *On Poetry and Poets,* p. 31.

13. Coleridge, *Biographia,* II, 15; Eliot, *On Poetry and Poets,* pp. 24–25.

14. *On Poetry and Poets,* pp. 207–8, 91. "A verse play," Eliot explained to his fellow-workers in the theater, "must probably have prosaic passages; but I think that the verse ought to be a verse capable of both the poetic and the prosaic, so that the transition between one and the other should be imperceptible." In the relaxed passages the auditors should be unconscious of the verse, and only "think and feel" in the poet's rhythms. But these rhythms also prepare the auditor's ear for the passages of poetic intensity. *The Aims of Poetic Drama* (London: Poets' Theatre Guild, 1949), p. 6.

15. Eliot, *On Poetry and Poets,* pp. 25, 47; Coleridge, *Biographia,* II, 78, 93–97.

16. Eliot, Preface to Harry Crosby's *The Transit of Venus: Poems* (Paris: Black Sun Press, 1931), pp. viii–ix; Coleridge, *Biographia,* II, 15–16.

17. Eliot, *Selected Essays,* pp. 7, 243, 247, 255–57; *The Use of Poetry,* p. 58; Coleridge, *Biographia,* I, 82–85.

18. *The Use of Poetry,* pp. 79–81, 118–19; *Biographia,* II, 19–20.

19. *Selected Essays,* p. 104; *To Criticize the Critic,* pp. 172, 187–89.

20. *Selected Essays,* pp. 4–5, 15.

21. *To Criticize the Critic,* p. 171; *On Poetry and Poets,* p. 93; *The Use of Poetry,* p. 15.

22. *On Poetry and Poets,* pp. 15, 10.

23. *Selected Essays,* p. 84; *The Use of Poetry,* p. 75; Coleridge, *Notebooks,* II, entry 2355. Miss Coburn considered this entry to "embody the very core of Coleridge's view of poetry and art as a way of ordering the chaos." Ibid., II (Notes).

24. Coleridge, *Letters,* III, 434; IV, 782, 687; *Biographia,* II, 60–61; Eliot, *On Poetry and Poets,* pp. 16, 76, 180, 264; *Selected Essays,* p. 205.

25. *The Sacred Wood,* p. 58; *Selected Essays,* pp. 124–25; *To Criticize the Critic,* p. 181.

26. Introduction to Paul Valéry, *The Art of Poetry,* trans. Denise Folliot (New York: Pantheon Books, 1958), p. xvi; *To Criticize the Critic,* p. 134.

27. Preface to *The Transit of Venus: Poems,* p. viii; *Selected Essays,* p. 134; "The Borderline of Prose," *The New Statesman,* May 19, 1917, p. 158; *Complete Poems and Plays,* p. 121.

28. Introduction to *Ezra Pound: Selected Poems* (London: Faber and Gwyer, 1928), pp. 16–18; *On Poetry and Poets,* p. 120.

29. *John Dryden: The Poet, The Dramatist, The Critic,* pp. 43–44.

30. *Dial,* LXXXIV (January, 1928), 5; "The Borderline of Prose," pp. 158–59.

31. *Pastels in Prose,* trans. Stuart Merrill (New York: Harper and Brothers, 1890), pp. vi–viii.

32. "The Borderline of Prose," pp. 158–59; *The Use of Poetry* p. 155. Unlike Saintsbury, who had also posited a rhythmic difference between the two verbal arts, Eliot never gave it extensive illustration. He did, however,

point to verse lineation as one factor involved. Justifying his omission of commas at line ends, he told John Quinn that he thought each line itself made for a sufficient pause in reading, an added comma often tending "to overemphasize the arrest." *The Letters of T. S. Eliot*, ed Valerie Eliot, 2 vols. (projected) (New York: Harcourt, Brace, Jovanovich, 1988), I, 451.

33. *Times Literary Supplement*, (September 27, 1928), p. 687.

34. Matthiessen, *The Achievement of T. S. Eliot*, 3rd ed. (New York: Oxford University Press, 1959), p. 197; Eliot, *Selected Essays*, p. 307.

35. "The Borderline of Prose," p. 158.

36. Eliot, Preface to St. John Perse, *Anabasis* (London: Faber and Faber, 1930), pp. 8–9; Larbaud is quoted from a 1926 preface reprinted as an unpaginated appendix to *Anabase* (New York: Brentano's, 1945).

37. *On Poetry and Poets*, pp. 75, 76, 93, 80–81.

38. Ibid., pp. 78, 81. As Eliot may well have known, his judgment of the superior potential of poetic over prose drama was not novel. The enhancement of the dialogue by meter, and the incapacity of poeticized prose to supply the same advantage, figure in August Schlegel's general defense of meter in fictive representation. The playwright who abandons it, he wrote, abandons all claim to the peculiarly poetic beauties of his dialogue. The tragic dramatist who does so would do better to stick to comedy instead. Schlegel therefore saw in this formal relaxation not an enlargement of poetry's domain, as champions of so-called poetic prose ("so-genannten poetischen Prosa") seemed to think, but a narrowing of it. *Kritische Schriften und Briefe*, pp. 143–44. But Eliot's rationale is his own.

39. *Selected Essays*, pp. 8, 124–26; *The Sacred Wood*, p. 58; *On Poetry and Poets*, p. 15; Frye, *T. S. Eliot* (New York: Capricorn Books, 1963), p. 29.

40. See especially Lewis Freed, *T. S. Eliot: Aesthetics and History* (La Salle, Ill.: Open Court, 1962), p. 150; Wellek, *History*, V, 41; Richard Wollheim's chapter "Eliot and F. H. Bradley" in his *On Art and the Mind* (London: Allen Lane, 1973); Eliot, *Knowledge and Experience in the Philosophy of F. H. Bradley* (New York: Farrar and Straus, 1964) p. 202.

41. "A Brief Treatise on the Criticism of Poetry," *Chapbook*, II, 9 (March, 1920), 4; *The Sacred Wood*, p. 57; *On Poetry and Poets*, p. 138; *The Use of Poetry*, pp. 118–19. Eliot apparently did not consistently confine the union of thought and feeling to metrical composition. In one place he assigns it to verse and prose alike. See *John Dryden*, p. 50.

42. Scofield, *T. S. Eliot: The Poems* (New York: Cambridge University Press, 1983), p. 74; Eliot, *Selected Essays*, pp. 124–25, 8–10.

43. *On Poetry and Poets*, p. 8; "Prose and Verse," p. 9.

44. *T. S. Eliot: Aesthetics and History*, pp. 85–86.

45. J. M. Murry is cited in Wellek, *History*, V, 95; Eliot, *Selected Essays*, pp. 226, 246–49.

Chapter Fifteen

1. Eliot, *The Use of Poetry*, pp. 104, 106–7; *Selected Essays*, p. 13; Arnold, *Prose Works*, IX, 161, 163.

2. "Henry James," reprinted from the *Little Review* of August 1918 in Philip Rahv, *Literature in America* (New York: Meridian Books, 1957), p. 223; *Selected Essays*, p. 318; *On Poetry and Poets*, p. 10.

3. *To Criticize the Critic*, p. 32; *Christianity and Culture* (New York: Harcourt, Brace, 1949), p. 95.

4. *The Use of Poetry*, p. 30; *Criterion*, XIII (October, 1933), p. 154. Eliot's essay of 1928 on Pound's verse showed an unwillingness to broach a vexing problem. He professed indifference to the recondite meaning of the *Cantos*, "being seldom interested in what [Pound] was saying, but only in the way he says it." *Dial* (January, 1928), p. 6. He could hardly have been betrayed into writing anything more alarmingly at odds with his firm insistence on the inseparability of matter and manner in verse.

5. *The Sacred Wood*, p. 57; *Selected Essays*, p. 200; "Poetry and Propaganda," in *Literary Opinion in America*, p. 105; *Listener*, XVI (November, 1936), 994.

6. *On Poetry and Poets*, pp. 32, 137.

7. *Dial*, LXXXIV (March, 1928), 249; "Introduction" to Valéry, *The Art of Poetry*, pp. xv–xvi.

8. *The Sacred Wood*, pp. 146–47; *Selected Essays*, p. 115.

9. *Selected Essays*, pp. 229–31. In his Norton Lectures of 1932–1933, Eliot offered an escape from the poetry-and-beliefs imbroglio involved in his personal aversion to the ideas in Shelley's poetry. "When the doctrine, theory, belief, or 'view of life' is one which the mind of the reader can accept as coherent, mature, and founded on the facts of experience, it interposes no obstacle to the reader's enjoyment, whether it be one that he accept or deny, approve or deprecate. When it is one which the reader rejects as childish or feeble, it may, for a reader of well-developed mind, set up an almost complete check." *The Use of Poetry*, p. 96. Unfortunately, this formula more nearly begs than resolves the question, since it sometimes happens that what one reader accepts as wisdom strikes another as childishness, with no objective means of determining which reader possesses the better mental development.

10. "Poetry and Propaganda" (1930), in *Literary Opinion in America*, pp. 106–7.

11. *On Poetry and Poets*, pp. 21, 22–23.

12. Pound, *Instigations*, p. 109; Eliot, "Thinking in Verse," *Listener*, III, 61 (March 12, l930), 441–42.

13. *Dial*, LXXV (December, 1923), 595; *The Novels and Tales of Henry James* (New York: Scribner's Sons, 1909), XV, 233–34; *On Poetry and Poets*, pp. 75, 25.

14. *On Poetry and Poets*, pp. 21, 23, 25, 26, 32.

15. Ibid., pp. 26, 28, 75, 80–81, 87. A verse play, Eliot wrote, is "more realistic than 'naturalistic drama' because . . . it should expose the underneath, or the inside, of the natural surface appearance." Introduction to S. L. Bethel, *Shakespeare and the Popular Dramatic Tradition* (Durham: Duke University Press, 1944), pp. ix–x.

16. *On Poetry and Poets*, pp. 93–94.

17. "The Literary Criticism of T. S. Eliot," p. 107.

18. *On Poetry and Poets*, p. 89.

19. Ibid., p. 89.; Jung, *Modern Man in Search of a Soul* (New York: Harcourt, Brace, n.d.), p. 177.

20. *Feeling and Form*, p. 244.

21. *On Poetry and Poets*, pp. 93, 94.

22. Ferruccio Busoni, unpaginated Preface to Johan Sebastian Bach, *Fifteen Two-Part Inventions* (New York: G. Schirmer, 1927); Gurney is cited in Richards, *Principles of Literary Criticism*, p. 285, n.1. Cf. Kendall L. Walton, "What Is Abstract about the Art of Music?" *Journal of Aesthetics and Art Criticism*, XLVI (Spring, 1988): "Music may be a vehicle of thought . . . but one which encourages a very different mode of thinking" (p. 362).

23. *On the Aesthetic Education of Man*, trans. Reginald Snell (New Haven: Yale University Press, 1954), p. 123.

24. W. Grabert and A. Mulot, *Geschichte der Deutschen Literatur* (München: Bayerischen Schulbuch Verlag, 1971), p. 210.

25. *On Poetry and Poets*, p. 193.

Epilogue

1. Outstanding among other opponents are F. W. Bateson, "Linguistics and Literary Criticism," in *The Disciplines of Criticism*, ed. Peter Demetz, Thomas Greene, and Lowry Nelson (New Haven: Yale University Press, 1968), pp. 3–16; and René Wellek, "Stylistics, Poetics, and Criticism," in *Discriminations* (New Haven: Yale University Press, 1970), pp. 327–43.

2. *A Map of Misreading* (New York: Oxford University Press, 1975), p. 59.

3. Hazard Adams, in *Critical Theory Since 1965*, ed. Hazard Adams and Leroy Searle (Tallahassee: Florida State University Press, 1985), p. 1; Felperin, *Beyond Deconstruction: The Uses and Abuses of Literary Theory* (Oxford: Clarendon Press, 1985), pp. 220, 215, 216–17.

4. Miller, *Theory Now and Then* (Durham: Duke University Press, 1991), p. 119; Hartman, *Saving the Text / Literature / Derrida / Philosophy* (Baltimore: Johns Hopkins University Press, 1981), p. 133.

5. Paul A. Bové lamented that the New Criticism, "declared dead and buried many times," still affects literary study, and so devoted a separate chapter to its "destruction" in *Destructive Poetics: Heidegger and Modern American Poetry*. Some recent distortions of American formalist poetics are grotesque, as when abusive rhetoric takes the place of reasoned refutation. One Derridean speaks of the New Critics "indulging" in an "adulation of the author," as though to regard a poem worth critical scrutiny as the creative achievement of a gifted human being were an aberrant illusion and not the normal attitude of appreciative readers. Another represents them *gesturing* "forth their theories of paradoxical aesthetic resolutions," apparently ignorant of the source in Coleridge for those resolutions, and as though the late Cleanth Brooks and his fellows had not always taken special care to support them with cogent argument. See Gayatri Spivak's Preface to her translation of Derrida's *Of Grammatology*, and Daniel O'Hara's "Yeats in Theory," in *Post-Structuralist Readings of English Poetry*, ed. Richard Machin and Christopher Norris (New York: Cambridge University Press, 1987).

6. Hartman, *Criticism in the Wilderness: The Study of Literature Today* (New Haven: Yale University Press, 1980), p. 174; Felperin, *Beyond Deconstruction*, p. 16. For other aspects of the deconstructors' "oddly anachronistic preoccupation with the New Criticism" see Robert Alter's "Deconstruction in America," *New Republic* (April 25, 1983), p. 30.

7. See Wellek's "The New Criticism: Pro and Contra," *Critical Inquiry* IV (Summer, 1978), 611–24, and *History*, VI, 157.

8. Sarah Lawall, *Critics of Consciousness* (Cambridge: Harvard University Press, 1968), p. 17. Paul de Man noted of Poulet's neglect of the literary medium in its formal attributes that he was "as remote from an impressionistic aestheticism that uses language as an object of sensation and pleasure, as from a formalism that would give it an autonomous and objective status." *Blindness and Insight: Essays in the Rhetoric of Contemporary Criticism*, 2nd. ed. rev. (Minneapolis: University of Minnesota Press, 1983), pp. 99–100.

9. *Studies in Human Time*, trans. Eliot Coleman (Baltimore: Johns Hopkins University Press, 1956), pp. 231, 234; *La Distance intérieure* (*Etudes sur le temps humain*, II) (Paris: Librairie Plon, 1952) p. 233. Sainte-Beuve is cited from my *Literary Criticism of Sainte-Beuve* (Lincoln: University of Nebraska Press, 1971), p. 8.

10. Miller, *The Disappearance of God* (Cambridge: Harvard University Press, 1963), pp. vii, 48, 234–35, 259, 301–2; *The Poets of Reality* (Cambridge: Harvard University Press, 1965) pp. 130–89; Richard, *L'Univers imaginaire de Mallarmé* (Paris: Editions du Seuil, 1961), pp. 542ff. Richard devotes a whole chapter to "Formes et moyens de la littérature."

11. Ransom, *The New Criticism*, p. 302; Todorov, *Poétique* (Paris: Editions du Seuil, 1963), p. 26; Genette, "Le langage poétique," in *Figures* (Paris: Editions du Seuil, 1966), p. 69; Jakobson, "Closing Statement: Linguistics and Poetics," p. 350.

12. Norris, *Deconstruction: Theory and Practice* (New York: Methuen, 1982), p. 97; Jakobson, "Afterword—Yuri Tynianov in Prague," in Tynianov, *The Problem of Verse Language*, ed. and trans. Michael Sosa and Brent Harvey (Ann Arbor: Ardis, 1981), p. 131; *Questions de Poétique*, 2nd ed. (Paris: Editions du Seuil, 1973), p. 487.

13. *Questions de Poétique*, pp. 123, 147–48; de Man, *Allegories of Reading* (New Haven: Yale University Press, 1979), p. 5.

14. Jakobson, "Closing Statement: Linguistics and Poetics," pp. 377, 358, 375; *Selected Writings*, ed. Stephen Rudy, 6 vols., III: *Poetry of Grammar and Grammar of Poetry* (New York: Mouton, 1981), p. 93.

15. "The Metaphoric and Metonymic Poles," in *Critical Theory Since Plato*, ed. Hazard Adams (New York: Harcourt Brace Jovanovich, 1971) p. 1116. Metaphoric predominance is not unaided as a determinant of poetic style. Jakobson notes that semantically functioning phonemic equivalents and puns also make poetry "by definition . . . untranslatable." "On Linguistic Aspects of Translation," *Selected Writings*, II, 266.

16. Erlich, "Roman Jakobson: Grammar of Poetry and Poetry of Grammar," in *Approaches to Poetics*, ed. Seymour Chatman (New York: Columbia University Press, 1973), p. 25. Wellek argued that neither dense sound structure nor intricate grammatical organization "establish a high poetic quality"

(cited by Erlich, ibid., p. 22); Jakobson, *Questions de Poétique*, pp. 487, 491, 209. Jakobson's reference to "organized violence" is cited with approval by Stephen Rudy in "Jakobson's Inquiry into Verse and the Emergence of Structural Poetics," in *Sound, Sign and Meaning*, ed. Ladislav Matejka (Ann Arbor: University of Michigan Press, 1978) p. 490. See Jan Mukarovsky, *The Word and Verbal Art: Selected Essays*, trans. and ed. John Burbank and Peter Steiner (New Haven: Yale University Press, 1977).

17. Paul Kiparsky, "The Role of Linguistics in a Theory of Poetry," *Daedalus* CII (1973), 235, 232, 238.

18. Levin, *Linguistic Structures in Poetry* (The Hague: Mouton, 1962), pp. 34–39; Vendler, review of Roger Fowler, ed. *Essays on Style and Language* in *Essays in Criticism*, XVI (1966), 458.

19. Chatman, *A Theory of Meter* (The Hague: Mouton, 1965), p. 152; Levin, *The Semantics of Metaphor* (Baltimore: Johns Hopkins University Press, 1977), pp. 131–32.

20. See, for example, Nils Erik Enquist, "On the Place of Style in Some Linguistic Theories," in Chatman, ed. *Literary Style: A Symposium* (New York: Oxford University Press, 1971), p. 55. Juilland, review of Charles Bruneau's *L'Epoche réaliste*, in Chatman and Levin, *Essays on the Language of Literature*, p. 380. Juilland's distinction is similar to Leo Spitzer's in his essay "The Language of Poetry": that in poetry the "material-immaterial activity" of practical verbal communication can "transform itself into the rainbow bridge which leads mankind toward other worlds where meaning rules absolute." *Language: An Enquiry into Its Meaning and Function*, ed. Ruth Nanda Anshen (New York: Harper and Brothers, 1957), p. 231.

21. Stankiewicz, "Poetics and Verbal Art," in *A Perfusion of Signs*, ed. Thomas A. Sebeok (Bloomington: Indiana University Press, 1977), pp. 69, 65; Levin, "The Conventions of Poetry," in *Literary Style: A Symposium*, p. 178; Saporta, "The Application of Linguistics to the Study of Poetic Language," in *Style in Language*, p. 93; Chatman and Levin, *Essays on the Language of Literature*, p. 171; Halliday, "The Linguistic Study of Literary Texts," ibid., pp. 221–23.

22. Besides his chapter on "Language and Literature" in *Language* (1921), see Sapir's "The Heuristic Value of Rhyme," confirming without allusion Dryden's experience of having, as Sapir puts it, come upon "many a felicitous fancy, many a gorgeous bit of imagery," in searching for a rhyme. *Selected Writings of Edward Sapir*, ed. David S. Mandelbaum (Berkeley: University of California Press, 1949), p. 497. Wellek recalls Bloomfield "bluntly" telling him that "he had no interest in stylistics or the study of poetic language." *Discriminations* (New Haven: Yale University Press, 1970), p. 329.

23. Ferdinand de Saussure, *Course in General Linguistics*, ed. Charles Bally and Albert Sechehaye, trans. Wade Baskin (New York: McGraw-Hill, 1966), pp. 195, 35, 70, 68. Saussure's neglect of poetic expression in his linguistics certainly did not stem from total disregard of artistic language. From 1906 to 1909, during which he began work on the *Cours*, he recorded in several notebooks the results of a meticulous study of anagrammatic permutations in verse, especially in Saturnian and classical Latin (with a glance at the

device in Livy's prose). See Jean Starobinski, *Les mots sur les mots* (Paris: Gallimard, 1971); English translation by Olivia Emmet, *Words upon Words* (New Haven: Yale University Press, 1979).

24. *Course in General Linguistics,* p. 117; Donoghue, "Yeats and the Living Voice," in *Issues in Contemporary Criticism,* ed. Gregory T. Polletta (Boston: Little, Brown and Company, 1973), p. 446. For analyzing poetry, Jakobson preferred to Saussure's concept of synchronism one which allowed for the diachronic. It could thus provide for poets' penchant for both archaism and stylistic innovation ("les tendances novatrices. . . senties comme une innovation du système"). *Questions de Poétique,* p. 57.

25. De Man, *The Resistance to Theory* (Minneapolis: University of Minnesota Press, 1986) p. 8. According to Doležel, structural poetics emerged from a "major epistemological shift" consequent to the displacement of the organic "model" by the semiotic. (*Occidental Poetics,* p. 99). For a fair assenting description of the philosophical cast of de Man's deconstruction, see Christopher Norris, *Paul de Man: Deconstruction and the Critique of Aesthetic Ideology* (New York: Routledge, 1988), especially Chapter 3: "Deconstruction and Philosophy."

26. Fish, *Self-Consuming Artifacts* (Berkeley: University of California Press, 1979), p. 408. Fish's egalitarian stance is not enforced by his "reader-response" position, in contrast to Wolfgang Iser's critically sensitive *The Act of Reading,* which isolates the conventions and procedures attending *the uniqueness of literary language.* De Man, *The Resistance to Theory,* p. 10; *Blindness and Insight,* pp. 9, 12, 21; Kristeva, *La révolution du langage poétique* (Paris: Editions du Seuil, 1974), p. 14; Waller, *Revolution in Poetic Language* (New York: Columbia University Press, 1984), pp. 5, 7. In his Introduction to this translation, Léon S. Roudiez points out that Kristeva's treatment of poetic diction "relegates aesthetic and formalist considerations to the background." Ibid., p. 5.

27. Krieger, *Poetic Presence and Illusion* (Baltimore: Johns Hopkins University Press, 1979), p. 182; White, "The Historical Text as Literary Artifact," in *Critical Theory Since 1965,* p. 407. It should be stressed that the convincing thesis White sets forth in *Metahistory* (1973) and *Tropics of Discourse* (1978) differs notably from the tropological conflation of the fictive and nonfictive asserted by de Man and Miller. White's assimilation of the fictional and historiographical modes does not terminate in an *aporia* of a radical and stultifying indeterminateness of all texts effected by an alleged semantic clash of their grammatical and figurative constituents. Miller, *Theory Now and Then,* pp. 119–20, 200; Nietzsche, *Werke,* Third Section, Vol.2, ed. Giorgio Colli and Mazzino Montinari (New York: Walter de Gruyter, 1973), 374. In this much cited posthumous fragment, "Truth and Lies in an Extramoral Sense," Nietzsche questions referentiality as much as he encourages literary egalitarianism. He asks whether language can properly designate objects: "Ist die Sprache der adäquate Ausdruck aller Realitäten?" (p. 372).

28. Hartman, *Saving the Text,* p. 5; Derrida, *Of Grammatology,* trans. Gayatri Chakravorty Spivak (Baltimore: Johns Hopkins University Press, 1974): "There is nothing outside the text" (p. 158). See Lévi-Strauss, *La Pensée sauvage* (Paris: Plon, 1962) and Foucault, *Les mots et les choses* (Paris:

Gallimard, 1966). Barthes, *Image, Music, Text,* trans. Stephen Heath (New York: Hill and Wang, 1977); Heidegger, *Poetry, Language, Thought,* trans. Albert Hofstadter (New York: Harper and Row, 1971), p. 192. For Heidegger's virtual apotheosis of poetic discourse see his *Introduction to Metaphysics* (New Haven: Yale University Press, 1959) and especially his *Erläuterungen zu Hölderlins Dichtung* (Frankfurt am Main: Vittorio Klostermann, 1971). "Dichtung is die Ursprache eines geschichtlichen Volkes. Also muss . . . das Wesen der Sprache aus dem Wesen der Dichtung verstanden werden" [Poetry is the primal language of an historical people. Therefore . . . the essence of language must be derived from the essence of poetry] (p. 43).

29. Miller, *Theory Now and Then,* pp. 176–85; Hartman, *The Fate of Reading* (Chicago: University of Chicago Press, 1975), pp. 124–26. Unrestricted intertextuality, Vincent Leitch points out, "subverts context." It "depends upon and involves a panoply of other formulations, especially the idea, taken over from structuralism, of the death of the subject. This strikes at the heart of all varieties of humanism." *Deconstructive Criticism: an Advanced Introduction* (New York: Columbia University Press, 1983), pp. 161–62. Thomas Docherty displays his paronomastic dexterity in detecting a pun on *penis* in Donne's use of *pinnace* (a small boat) in "Air and Angels." He declares it to be otherwise at odds with the poem's context—despite the obvious congruity of *pinnace* with an extended nautical metaphor made up of *ballast, steadily, wares, sink,* and so forth. "Donne's Praise of Folly," in *Poststructuralist Readings of English Poetry,* p. 93.

See Leonard Jackson on American poststructuralist "practice of obviously wild interpretations and random wordplay" in *The Poverty of Structuralism: Literature and Structuralist Theory* (London and New York: Longman, 1991), p. 197.

30. Norris, *Derrida* (Cambridge: Harvard University Press, 1987), p. 113; Derrida, *Dissémination,* trans. Barbara Johnson (Chicago: University of Chicago Press, 1981), pp. 95, 108.

31. Felman is quoted by Ronald Schleifer, "The Anxiety of Allegory: De Man, Greimas, and the Problem of Referentialty," in *Rhetoric and Form: Deconstruction at Yale,* ed. Robert Con Davis and Ronald Schleifer (Norman: University of Oklahoma Press, 1985), p. 226. Mallarmé, *Oeuvres complètes,* ed. Henri Mondor and G. Jean-Aubry (Paris: Gallimard, 1945), p. 857; Blanchot, *La part du feu* (Paris: Gallimard, 1949), pp. 38–42. In noting Blanchot's agreement with deconstruction on the issue of referentiality we should overlook neither his quite different rationale for it nor his firm rejection of the egalitarian equivalence of literature with other writing. Speaking of fiction Blanchot declares that even in the most prosaic realistic tale language is utterly transformed ("le langage y subit une transformation radicale"). As Blanchot interprets Mallarmé, in the "langage authentique" which is poetry speech functions less to represent than to disperse reality. It annihilates the object ("Elle fait disparaître, elle rend l'objet absent, elle l'annihile"). It is this "absenting power of language" that by Blanchot's antinomial logic entails silence as the final possibility of speech ("le silence comme la possibilité ultime de la parole"). Ibid., pp. 37, 41. Writing of Blanchot's earlier *Faux pas* (1943), Wellek declared that the "angoisse au langage" expressed there later led to "the deconstructionist nihilism

that texts and reality were totally dissevered." *History,* III, 102. But in Derrida's argument there is no certain sign of dependence on Blanchot.

32. *The Resistance to Theory,* p. 8; *Allegories of Reading* (New Haven: Yale University Press, 1979), p. 5.

33. Miller, *Theory Now and Then,* p. 263; Norris, *Paul de Man,* p. 71.

34. See Derrida, *Of Grammatology,* passim, especially pp. lxxvii, 12, 158–59, 208–10; *Writing and Difference,* trans. Alan Bass (Chicago: University of Chicago Press, 1978), p. 211–12, 200. Readers baffled by Derrida's terms *trace* and *différance,* so variously defined (or *not* defined) by his interpreters, may take some comfort in Newton Garner's excellent Preface to Derrida, *Speech and Phenomena,* trans. David B. Allison (Evanston: Northwestern University Press, 1973). See also, for further clarification, M. H. Abrams, "The Deconstructive Angel," *Critical Inquiry* III (Spring, 1977), 430–31. Roland Barthes confirmed Derrida's denial of any referential signified when he compared a written text to an onion, "a construction of layers . . . whose body contains, finally, no heart, no secret, no irreducible principle, nothing except the infinity of its own envelopes." "Style and Its Image," in *Literary Style: A Symposium,* p. 10. Hartman, *Saving the Text,* p. 121.

35. Lentricchia, *After the New Criticism,* p. 171; de Man, *Allegories of Reading,* pp. 17, 105–6, 131, 206.

36. *Resistance to Theory,* p. 11; *Allegories of Reading,* p. 17; Miller, *Theory Now and Then,* pp. 307, 175.

37. Hartman, Preface to *Deconstruction and Criticism* (New York: Continuum, 1992). p. ix. Bloom endorsed Yeats's opinion that Shelley's *Defence* is "the most profound discourse upon poetry in the language." *The Anxiety of Influence,* p. 39. Hartman observed that Shelley ascribed the unacknowledged power of poetry to the "language within language" that constitutes its effective part. *Criticism in the Wilderness,* p. 101.

38. *The Anxiety of Influence,* p. 91; *A Map of Misreading,* pp. 70, 3, 198.

39. *The Anxiety of Influence,* pp. 59–60. "In Bloom's account," Vincent B. Leitch writes, "the successful strong poet possessed a degree of autonomy and freedom—Emersonian self-reliance—out of keeping with the 'death of the subject' proclaimed by structuralism, poststructuralism, and deconstruction." *American Literary Criticism from the Thirties to the Eighties* (New York: Columbia University Press, 1988), p. 296. In *apophrades,* the final stage of Bloom's strong poet's struggle with the burden of the past, it seems that the ephebe "had written his precursor's characteristic works" (*The Anxiety of Influence,* p. 16). Surely nothing but Bloom's contempt for Eliot can explain his failure to acknowledge the adumbration of this idea in "Tradition and the Individual Talent," where a proper grasp of tradition includes the anomaly "that the past should be altered by the present as much as the present is directed by the past." *Selected Essays,* p. 5.

40. *The Anxiety of Influence,* p. 139; *A Map of Misreading,* pp. 38, 104; *The Western Canon: the Books and Schools of the Ages* (New York: Harcourt Brace, 1994), p. 53.

41. *A Map of Misreading,* pp. 136, 162, 173, 175.

42. Perhaps the most egregious examples occur in *Saving the Text.* Undeterred by its mish-mash of "aleatory and overburdening" content (p. 22),

Hartman attempts to vindicate the "high unseriousness" (p. 24) of *Glas*, of which even so devoted a Derridean as Christopher Norris concedes that "it defeats the best efforts of descriptive analysis or summary." *Derrida*, p. 46.

43. *Criticism in the Wilderness*, p. 8; *The Fate of Reading*, pp. 227–42.

44. *The Fate of Reading*, p. 97. In a book published a year before Hartman's, Joseph N. Riddel tried to combine the dynamic version of mimesis with the Derridean explosion of logocentric metaphysics. In the chapter "The Poetics of Failure" this is repeatedly asserted, once with an unacknowledged echo of Coleridge: "The poem is an imitation, not a copy, of nature, because it is the myth which reveals that being and becoming are the same thing and involve an initial and mysterious violation. That is, the poem is an imitation of the dynamic of nature [cf. Coleridge's *natura naturans*], of its seminal adventure, its freeplay." *The Inverted Bell* (Baton Rouge: Louisiana State University Press, 1974), p. 300. Cf. also pp. 273, 274, 299.

45. *Criticism in the Wilderness*, pp. 54, 248; *The Fate of Reading*, pp. 44, 123.

46. *The Fate of Reading*, pp. 254, 255, 262.

Index